WILD DFW

WILD DFW

EXPLORE THE AMAZING NATURE

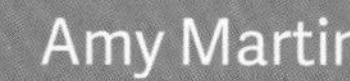

Amy Martin

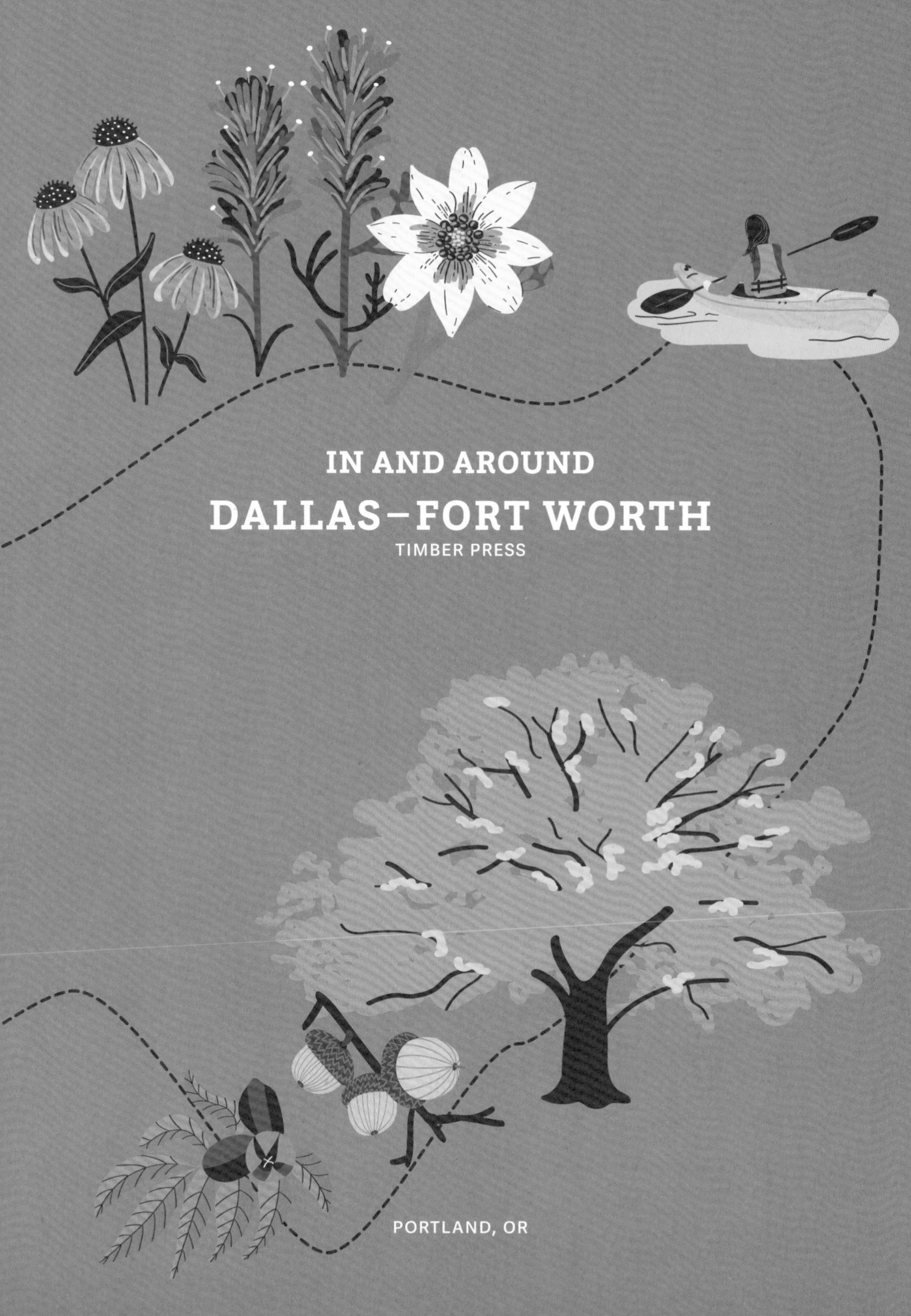

IN AND AROUND

DALLAS–FORT WORTH

TIMBER PRESS

PORTLAND, OR

Dedicated with love to my husband, Scooter Smith, whose support and encouragement made this book possible.

Photo and illustration credits appear on page 363.

Published in 2023 by Timber Press, Inc.
a subsidiary of Workman Publishing Co., Inc.,
a subsidiary of Hachette Book Group, Inc.
1290 Avenue of the Americas
New York, NY 10104

timberpress.com

Printed in China on responsibly sourced paper
Text design by Sarah Crumb,
based on a series design by Anna Eshelman
Cover illustration by Mariell Guzman

ISBN 978-1-64326-084-6
Catalog records for this book are available from the Library of Congress and the British Library.

Black-chinned hummingbird feeds on red yucca flowers.

TABLE OF CONTENTS

FOREWORD

Think about your earliest experiences with nature. For many of us, our first encounters happened in city parks, backyards, or local creeks. Children happily spend hours chasing butterflies, watching bugs crawl in dirt, or collecting treasures like rocks. Kids are experts at finding wonder in everyday experiences. As adults, we tend to start associating wilderness with faraway places. You only need to step outside and see that our cities resound with nature.

Dallas–Fort Worth lies at the junction of ecoregions, where the gnarled and stunted, yet hardy and beautiful, oaks of the Cross Timbers meet with one of the nation's most endangered habitats—the Blackland Prairie. The multiple forks of the Trinity River provide riparian woodlands and a critical source of water. These diverse habitats help make this area a hotspot for biodiversity.

As a child who grew up in this urban expanse, my first experiences with nature included chasing green anoles around my backyard and exploring the nearby creek. Now, as an urban wildlife biologist, it is my job to study and protect the same areas I enjoyed decades ago.

Alongside all the buildings and roads of Dallas–Fort Worth, there is a vast, interconnected network of green space where wildlife roams. This habitat patchwork supports painted buntings, river otters, alligator snapping turtles, bobcats, luna moths, and rare orchids of the genus *Hexalectris*.

Urban green space has significant benefits for people, too. The outdoor recreation industry supports over 400,000 jobs in Texas and generates over $50 billion in consumer spending annually. Homes within walking distance to green space can sell for 20 percent more than those farther away.

Natural areas also provide critical ecosystem services like improving air and water quality, preventing erosion, and reducing air temperatures. People who spend more time outside experience reduced depression, anxiety, and stress; less obesity; and improved brain function and mood. Children who play outside have better concentration and impulse inhibition. All these benefits are excellent reasons to promote the conservation of green space in our communities.

This book is a celebration of the natural things that make the Metroplex great. Amy Martin combines her own experience as an avid naturalist with the knowledge of some of the region's most prominent experts. This book will educate and inspire, whether you are new to the area or a lifelong resident, a seasoned naturalist or just stepping on the trail. Breathtaking natural regions and captivating critters are available to you right now! Just grab this guide, get outside and start exploring!

—Rachel Richter, Urban Wildlife Biologist, Texas Parks and Wildlife Department

▲ The Scyene Overlook in Dallas is a great place to introduce the next generation to the wonders of nature.

PREFACE

North Texas isn't widely known for nature. This book aims to change that. Our nature is not "over there" in remote wilderness. It's here, hidden along rivers and creeks, tucked away on the fringes of reservoirs, on rocky hilltops or floodplains—wherever development was unfeasible. But also in your yard—if you invite it in.

This book will carry you on a rollicking journey through North Texas natural history and ecology, introduce you to the top fauna and flora, and lead you on twenty-five nature adventures guided by the people who know the areas best.

First, some orientation to ease reading and navigating. This book defines North Texas as four counties: Collin County (cities of Plano and McKinney); Tarrant County (cities of Fort Worth and Arlington); Dallas County (city of Dallas and suburbs); and Denton County (cities of Denton and Lewisville). If you read, for instance, that the only river in North Texas is the Trinity, I'm referring only to these four counties.

When it comes to the common names of plants and animals, I've followed *Merriam-Webster*'s online dictionary and Timber Press's house style, which do not capitalize common names except where one is derived from a proper noun. Scientific names generally adhere to these authorities: Cornell Lab of Ornithology for birds; Texas Parks and Wildlife for mammals; Lady Bird Johnson Wildflower Center for plants; Society for the Study of Amphibians and Reptiles for, surprise, amphibians and reptiles; and Texas A & M Forest Service for trees.

▼ Kayaking at Fort Worth Nature Center and Refuge (FWNCR)

NORTH TEXAS

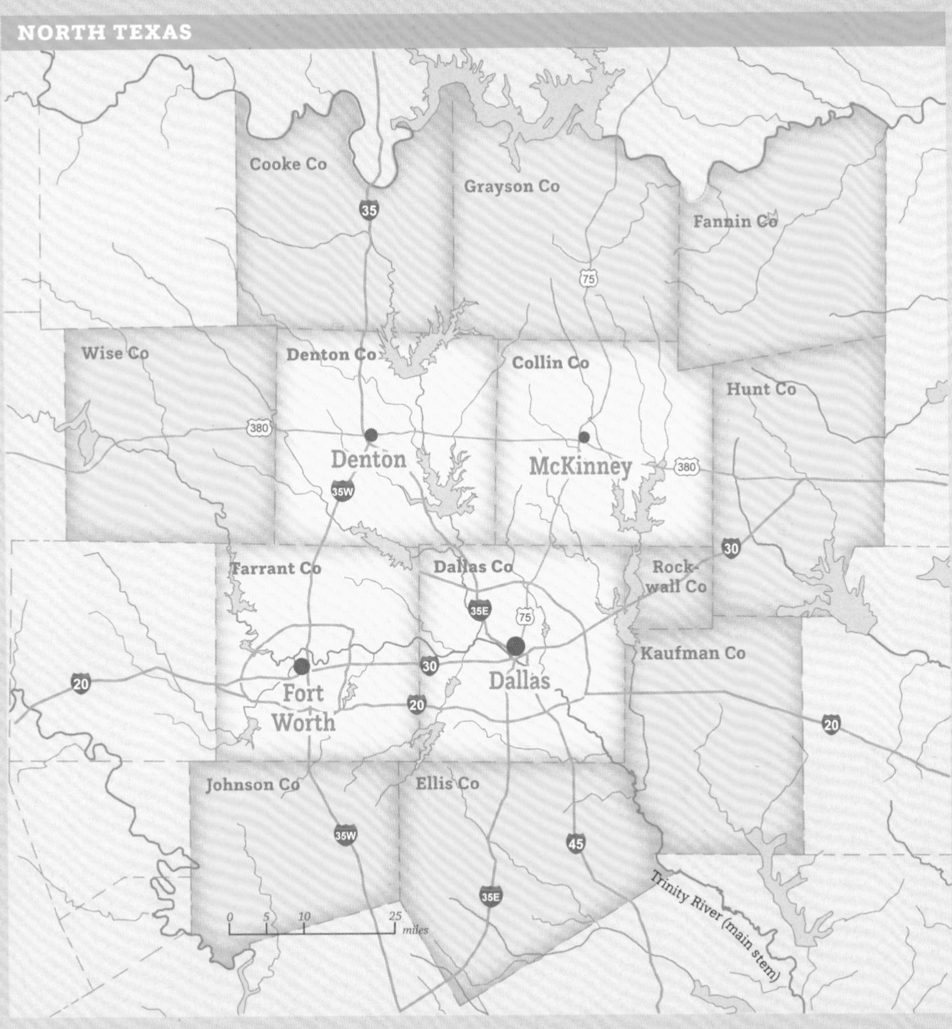

Look for @WildDFW on Facebook, Instagram, and Twitter, tag us in your nature activities, and visit wild-dfw.com.

NATURAL HISTORY AND ECOLOGY

Wild Dallas–Fort Worth

"Around 1962, I was given a gift that lasts a lifetime. I was introduced to a creek in western Tarrant County with clear running water rippling over white limestone," said Michael A. Smith, author of books on Texas herpetology. "At about twelve years old, I would spend entire days there, chasing white earless lizards over jumbled limestone rocks. It's hard to imagine a more carefree existence than a day discovering the life of a creek."

Once enraptured with North Texas nature, his passion turned into an avocation. When he moved back to the area, the creek called once more, but this time he had company.

"I took Elijah exploring at the creek. In many ways, he's a grandson to me. He asked how I knew so much about nature. I explained I'd been doing it a long time, read many books, and hung out with people who knew a lot, just as he was doing today." Elijah replied, 'When I'm older and I can read better, we'll find things and I'll look them up in books.' It was a dream come true."

I'm a creek kid too. Spent my days on a White Rock Creek tributary in North Dallas pretending I was on a tropical island subsisting on elephant ear plants escaped from yards. Now that I've spent decades as an environmental journalist and trained as a Texas Master Naturalist, I'm like Michael and Elijah—more knowledge deepened my understanding and love of nature. Just as I hope this book will do for you.

▲ Bison at Fort Worth Nature Center and Refuge evoke our history.

◄ Many initial nature experiences happen at creeks.

There are so many possibilities for exploring nature around Dallas–Fort Worth. Here are just a few:

- Discover Lewisville Lake Environmental Learning Area. Over 2000 acres of upland Eastern Cross Timbers, Blackland Prairie, and wetlands, where whitetail deer and wild turkeys roam. Hear the whistling call of northern bobwhite quail thanks to a major reintroduction effort.

- Learn how to make your yard wildlife friendly. Add native plants that pollinators adore, along with bee hotels, amphibian abodes, bird feeders, water features, and the right trees.

- Visit Heard Natural Science Museum and Wildlife Sanctuary. Fossil-filled limestone cliffs and a modern educational center overlook a wide valley and wetlands accessible by a long, winding boardwalk.

- Explore nature after dark with ultraviolet lights and silent walks. Tune into the moon, listen to the nocturnal symphony, and watch bats and moths.

- Make a trip to Fort Worth Nature Center and Refuge. More than 3600 acres frame Lake Worth and the West Fork of the Trinity River. Bison roam sprawling savannahs, alligators float in the lake, and roadrunners dart about after snakes.

Decades after my childhood creek explorations, a friend helped me hike deep in the Great Trinity Forest to White Rock Creek's confluence with the Trinity River. It was a pilgrimage, a homecoming. I was ecstatic, like when I was a kid, while being buoyed by knowledge.

Let's explore the wild in North Texas, from our backyard delights to vast natural preserves. In the process, we'll learn to see the land through new eyes. It is indeed a gift to learn about nature. To help preserve it is to create a true legacy.

East–West

As sister cities, Dallas and Fort Worth are wildly different. Dallas has the stock market, while Fort Worth has its stockyards. Dallas boasts modern architecture and a glossy fashion industry. Fort Worth scores for historic preservation and a cultural district that includes the Fort Worth Stock Show and Rodeo.

Their differing ecology captures that dichotomy. In North Texas, the lush deciduous forests of the east give way to the semiarid grasslands of the west. The region is an ecotone, an epic edge where two disparate ecological regions merge. Edges always feature more interaction, more diversity.

> Annual rainfall decreases about one inch approximately every twenty miles westward from Texas's eastern border.

The Trinity River's many forks thread North Texas together. From the rocky, shallow watercourses of the west, to the broad, flood-prone prairie rivers of the east, each features reservoirs and wetlands.

Abandon the idea that prime outdoors means majestic mountains, deep canyons, and ocean views. North Texas nature fosters a profound intimacy best experienced close-up, with unfolding layers that invite lingering exploration. Nature here is not a distant vista that you admire. It's something to immerse yourself in and be a part of while it is a part of you.

▾ Precipitation amounts in North Texas.

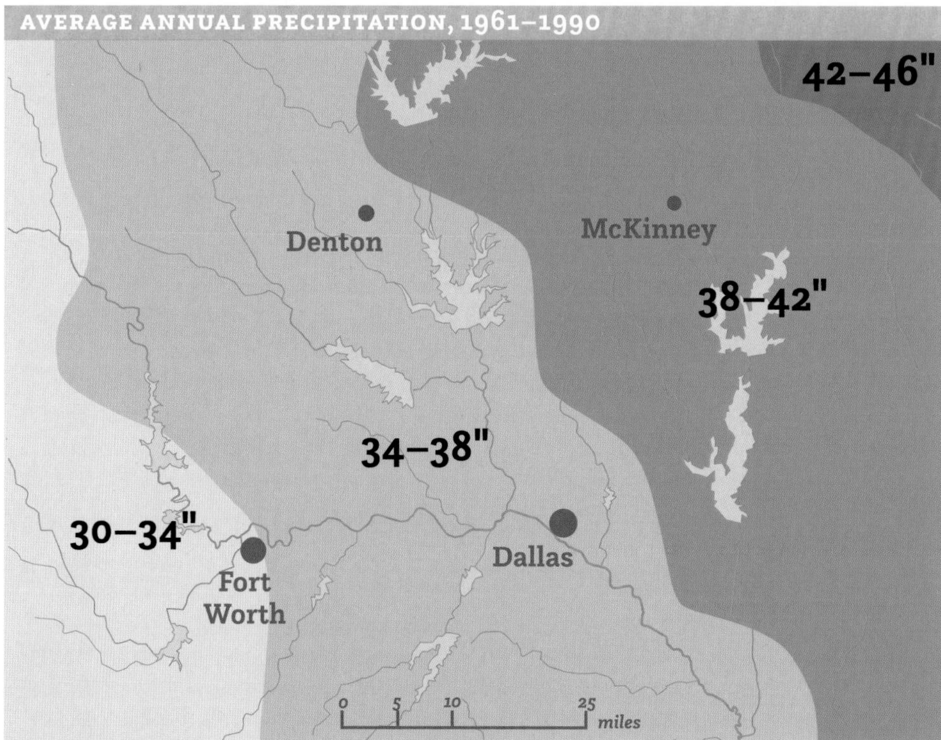

NOAA, USDA-NRCS

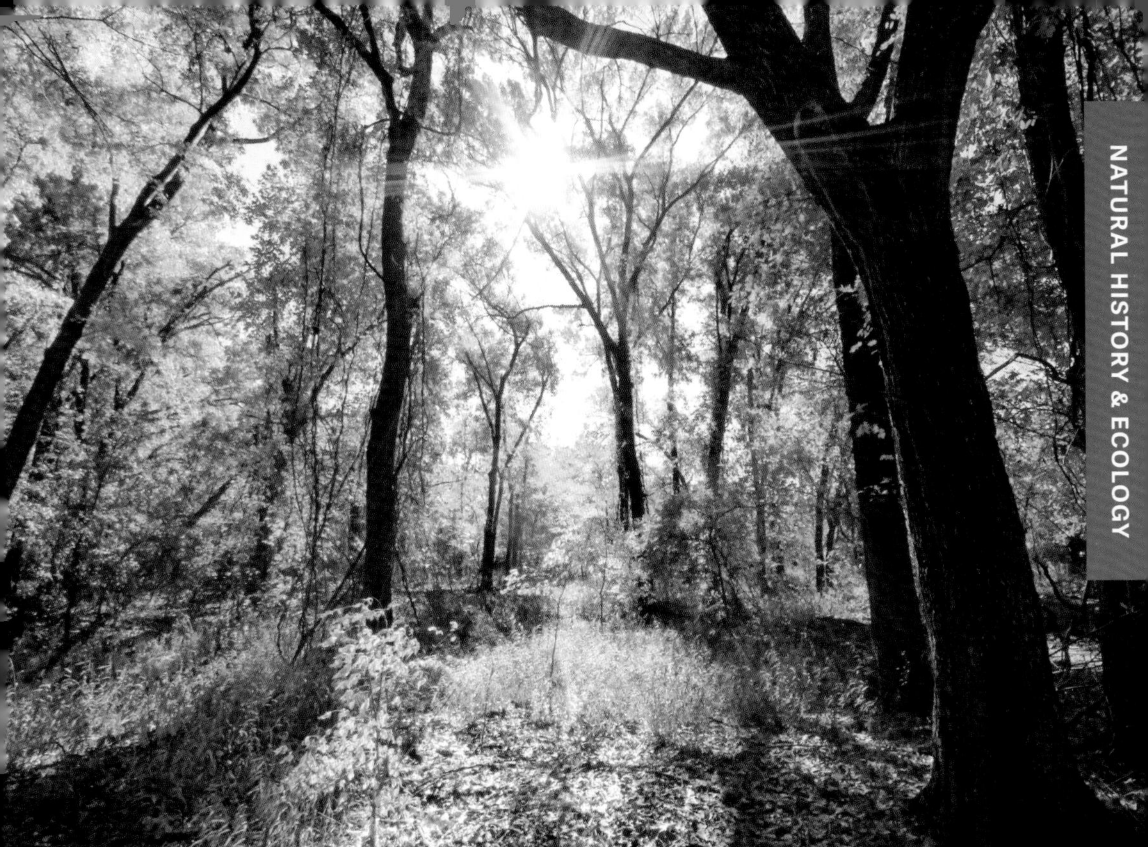

▲ Fall color of Cross Timbers delights at Fort Worth Nature Center.

Natural Dallas

Starting in the east, Dallas County lies upon Austin Chalk laid down in the Early Cretaceous period, 145 to 100 million years ago. The startlingly white rock weathers over centuries into fertile, clay-rich black soil, which gives Blackland Prairie its name. Locals call it "gumbo" for its stickiness when wet. The sandier Eagle Ford Shale arises in the county's western half.

The great eastern deciduous forest once stretched from the Atlantic Ocean to west of the Mississippi River, so dense according to folk tales that a squirrel could cross by leaping from tree to tree, never touching ground.

Less than 1 percent of Blackland Prairie remains—the most endangered ecosystem in the nation. The remnants exist in areas too rocky for row crops or cultivated pasture. These tallgrass prairies feature prolific wildflowers and native grasses reaching over six feet—a pollinators' paradise.

Dallas County is furrowed by major creeks, some with watersheds greater than 140 square miles. Along riparian corridors and floodplains, trees tower sixty feet and more. A mounting chalk escarpment slices across the southwest corner, boasting epic views and intricate topography.

CONVERGENCE OF TRINITY RIVER'S ELM, WEST, AND EAST FORKS

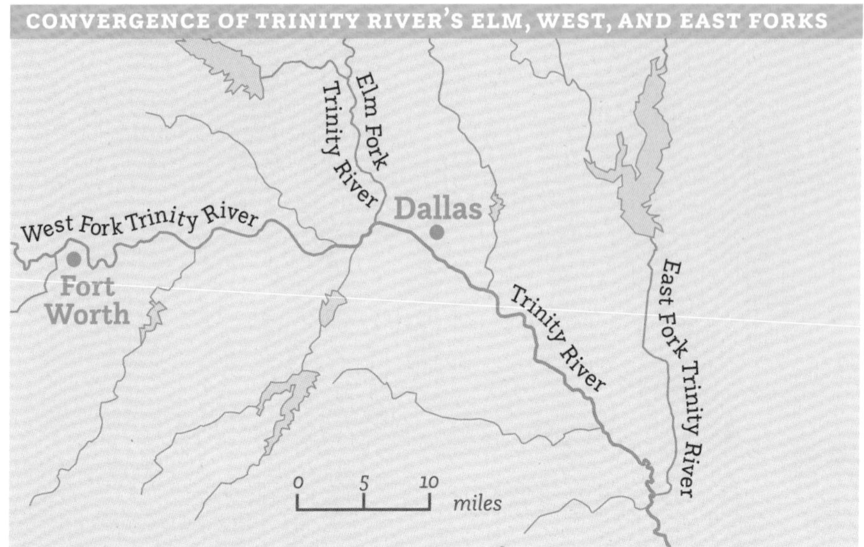

The Elm Fork south of Lake Lewisville and Lake Ray Roberts snakes along the county's west side, nearly hidden by highways. North of downtown, the West Fork joins the Elm Fork to form the much larger Trinity main stem. Downriver of Lavon Lake and Lake Ray Hubbard, the East Fork unites with the Trinity just east of the county line.

Flanking the Trinity main stem is the 6000-acre Great Trinity Forest, a western outpost of the eastern deciduous woods. Located just south of downtown, it is the largest urban bottomland hardwood forest in the United States.

Natural Fort Worth

The 97th parallel roughly separates Dallas County from Tarrant County, home of Fort Worth. Along it runs the Eastern Cross Timbers—a mosaic of woods and grass fostered by tan, sandy soil. With few exceptions, trees top out at thirty feet. Sections with an impenetrable, dense understory gained it the nickname "cast-iron forest."

Elevation rises going westward, from an average of 430 feet in Dallas to 653 feet in Fort Worth. Erosion of Late Cretaceous limestone creates a shallow, rocky soil and carves a dry, angular landscape with an authentic western flavor.

Endemic plant or animal species exist only in one geographic region.

The Trinity River also threads through Tarrant County. While the Clear and West Forks have modest flows, their importance to wildlife in a dry territory cannot be underestimated.

The far-reaching West Fork from the northwest is impounded three times to provide water for a parched territory. The short, rocky Clear

In the mid- to late 1800s, cattle were driven 500 miles along the Chisholm Trail through the Fort Worth area to Kansas railheads.

▲ The slow beauty of the West Fork enchants.

▲ Dallas deemed Fort Worth so sleepy that a panther could nap downtown.

Fork from the southwest hosts the city's cultural core. The Clear Fork meets the West Fork at the popular Panther Island area.

Midway through the county, patches of Eastern Cross Timbers give way to the west's Fort Worth Prairie, with grasses that strive to reach waist high. The city claims its historic moniker as Queen of the Prairie.

Dry prairie barrens on hilltops host drought-tolerant plants such as white rosinweed, endemic only to a small region of North Texas. Yet just yards away, seeps emerge from the stratified limestone, creating microhabitats that nurture delicate wildflowers.

Lingering one day at Benbrook Lake's Sid Richardson Tract, I could imagine cattle herds thundering on the Chisholm Trail that once ran nearby. The sun set on a near-infinite west unfolding into the dimming light. I stood amid memories fading into time.

Where Forest Meets Prairie

The North Texas ecotone features eastern deciduous forest easing into western grasslands, creating a series of ecoregions that run in vertical strips from east to west: Blackland Prairie (tallgrass prairie); Eastern Cross Timbers (woodland and prairie); and Fort Worth Prairie (midgrass prairie). There are also sections of Post Oak Savannah in the southeast and Western Cross Timbers in the northwest.

Each ecoregion features unique soil types. "The soil is going to decide what sort of plants grow there. And the plants determine what kind of animals you're going to see," explains Dan Northcut, director of environmental

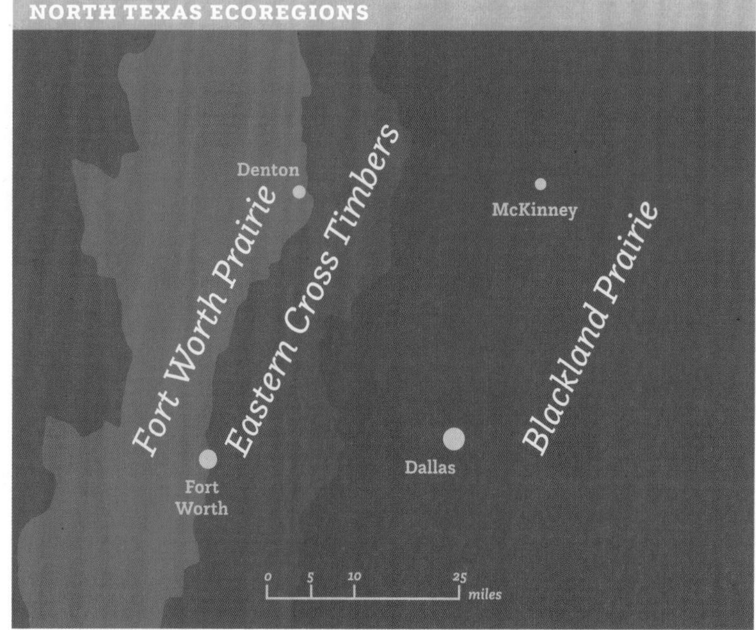

Agrilife Research Texas A & M University

▲ The sky is an overwhelming presence on the prairie.

studies at St. Mark's School of Texas. With North Texas's wide variety of soils, he notes, the result is astounding biodiversity.

Ecoregion edges are not precise. Long extensions, deep insets, isolated outposts, and places that blend with the adjacent ecoregion blur boundaries.

Blackland Prairie

The first time I drove up to Clymer Meadow, a Blackland Prairie owned by The Nature Conservancy (TNC), it seemed like an open field of unmowed grass. Then I walked it with Jim Eidson, TNC's now-retired North Texas preserves manager. Beneath my feet, he said, no plow ever tore the soil asunder, leaving intact its biome of fungi and microorganisms many thousands of years old. I stood on ancient living history.

It's easy to be impressed by towering mountains and redwoods. A prairie is receptive and horizontal—the sky is half the landscape. Yet it begs intimate inspection. Kneel and gaze at the first eighteen inches. The riotous tangle of foliage is as thick and diverse as a rainforest.

The prairie profile is a landscape of leafy mounds. Long, strappy leaves of big bluestem, Indiangrass, and switchgrass extend up five feet or more and then arc to the ground, creating shelter domes for animals. Eidson showed how bunchgrasses form bird-nesting cavities in the center.

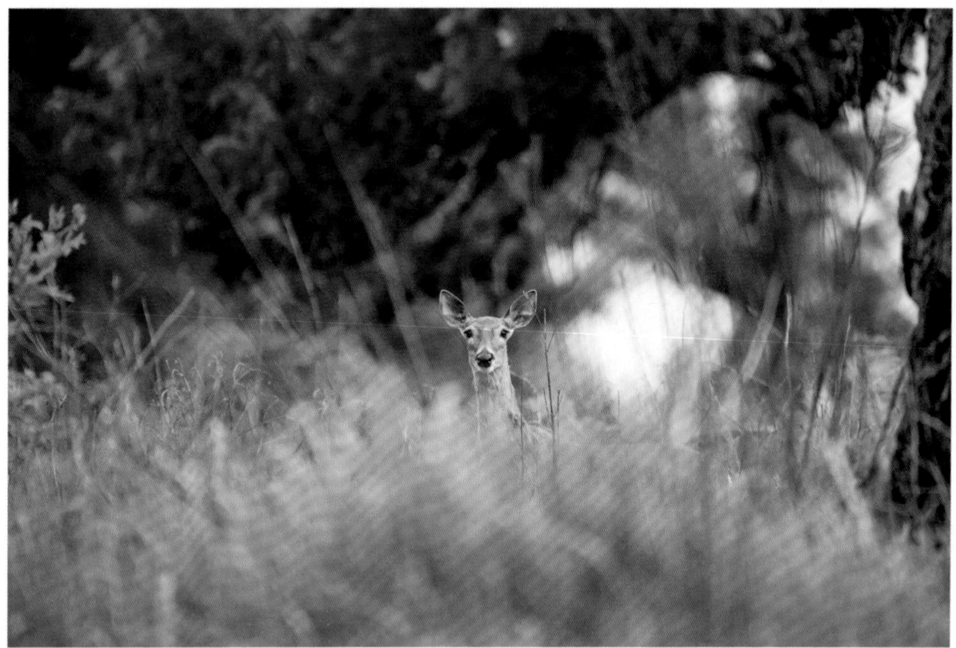

▲ A curious deer feasts on native grasses at Clymer Meadow.

North Texas Blackland Prairies feature a type of soil called vertisol, from *vertere*, Latin for invert. These dark, clay-rich soils shrink during dry periods, forming cracks that fill with debris. Precipitation swells the fissures closed, pushing dirt up. Over centuries, rings or ridges called gilgai form as the soil tills itself.

The tallgrass prairie palette changes weekly. Waves of wildflowers paint it pink, purple, orange, and red. Sunflowers compete to see whose yellow is most beloved by the sun. Fall brings the bronze and gold seedheads of native grasses, undulating in the breeze like ocean waves.

BLACKLAND BIODIVERSITY

Because its soil has never been disturbed, a preserved Blackland Prairie can host over 300 plant species. Now that's diversity! A typical pasture has a handful. The deep, dark, fertile soil manifests an astounding three to five tons of biomass per acre, much of it below ground in extensive root systems.

Untilled grasslands can store up to five tons of carbon per acre in their roots. "Trees store carbon in their leaves and woody biomass. So when trees are burned or mechanically harvested, they release their stored carbon," explained Dan Caudle, resident research associate at Botanical Research Institute of Texas. "That's why grasslands are better carbon sinks than forests."

> "The prairie remnants of north-central Texas are islands in a sea of injured land. Land talks to us. In those places where process and diversity are intact, they emit a sense of health and wholeness. When you step into an old cotton field, you can feel its brokenness."
>
> *—Jim Eidson, retired North Texas preserves manager, The Nature Conservancy*

Plant diversity gives rise to insect diversity. Each tallgrass prairie acre hosts an estimated 3000 species of insects and arthropods. Abundant insects anchor the food chain, feeding rodents, songbirds, and small mammals that in turn sustain larger mammals, snakes, and birds of prey.

Walking through the dense grass at Clymer Meadow, I see critter burrows pitched downward into the soil, woven tunnels of dried grass blades built by Eastern meadowlarks, and, wedged between sturdy stalks, the nests of dickcissels, imperiled grassland birds whose numbers are declining rapidly with their habitat.

PRESERVING THE PRAIRIE

The Blackland Prairie originally covered about twelve million acres. Flat and fertile with a few scattered trees, it was ripe for cultivation and urban development. As the most endangered ecosystem in the nation, some of its most critical parcels are within a two-hour drive northeast of Dallas, including TNC's 1131-acre Clymer Meadow Preserve and the 992-acre Daphne Prairie, protected by a Native Prairies Association of Texas conservation easement.

On that long-ago visit to Clymer Meadow, the peace of the Blackland Prairie swept up from beneath, reminding me, as the poet Mary Oliver wrote, that my sole job in this life is to pay attention. I listened to the melodic whispers of history woven from roots and leaves, minerals and rain, and the brilliant sun. The land holds memory, weeping and laughing as required. The prairie is a song.

> **Blackland Prairie and Eastern Cross Timbers merge at Lewisville Lake Environmental Learning Area.**

▲ A mix of prairie and woods marks the Eastern Cross Timbers.

Eastern Cross Timbers

It was as unmistakable as a mountain range to settlers heading west across the flat prairie: a wall of woods stretching from north to south as far as one could see. Gnarled, tough trees modest in height but dense; only fifteen miles across at the forest's widest, but almost impossible to cross.

The Eastern Cross Timbers, as the woods became known, arise from coarse, sandy soil. Post and blackjack oaks—tough trees capable of surviving severe drought, harsh freezes, and battering west winds—make up three-quarters of the forest.

In its mosaic of grasslands and woods, midheight grasses like little bluestem and sideoats grama flourish in the sunny prairie patches. Delicate wildflowers like prairie acacia, with its feathery mimosa leaves and white poms, grow between grass clumps, along with prickly pear cactus and a variety of yucca.

> "I shall not easily forget the mortal toil, and the vexations of flesh and spirit, that we underwent occasionally in our wanderings through the Cross Timber. It was like struggling through forests of cast iron."
>
> —*Washington Irving*

"People tend to have a European view of what a forest should look like: tall trees in open parkland without a lot of understory," said Nature Center Manager Rob Denkhaus, of the Fort Worth Nature Center and Refuge. "Cross Timbers is not that. It's far more interesting."

With the Fort Worth Prairie to the west and Blackland Prairie to the east, the Eastern Cross Timbers abound in prairie and forest plants. The barrier to pioneers was a boon to Indigenous communities. "Because such edge areas support the largest, often most diverse populations of game animals, they likely attracted Native American hunters," wrote Richard V. Francaviglia in *The Cast Iron Forest*.

TREES THAT WILL NOT BE TAMED

The short stature and low, spreading crowns of post oaks and blackjack oaks result from the shallow soils and bedrock they grow from. Roots grow wide rather than deep, utterly fused with the sandstone bedrock. The trees contort adjusting to winds and slopes, causing the wood to form a spiral grain.

Demanding its freedom as a wild tree, post oak loathes having its roots contained by development. Branches jut out horizontally with weathered boldness. The tree thrives in poor soil. No wonder it's the most prevalent oak in Texas. "A relatively large percentage of Eastern Cross Timbers remain because the trees never had a timber value. They rarely grew tall or straight," noted Denkhaus.

Another band of sandy soil gives rise to the similar Western Cross Timbers, starting on the western side of Tarrant County and sprawling toward Abilene, ranging from twenty-five to 110 miles wide. Clay soil caps many ridgetop glades, fostering unique plant communities.

Like in the prairie, wildfires once raced through the Cross Timbers, not harming older blackjack and post oak with fire-resistant bark. Now with fire suppression, the Timbers struggle with overgrown understory and invasives such as privet.

Because development consumed much of the Fort Worth Prairie, Eastern Cross Timbers, and Blackland Prairie, most natural recreation in North Texas occurs along wooded riparian corridors and around reservoirs.

Fort Worth Prairie

As the Eastern Cross Timbers ebb away, the Fort Worth Prairie comes to the fore, a grassland band just ten to thirty miles wide, part of the greater Grand Prairie that encompasses the Lampasas Cut Plains to the south.

The Fort Worth Prairie is where the west begins. The shallow calcareous soil supports low-density grazing of cattle and other livestock but not much in crops. Natural gas reserves trapped in geologic layers create a hotspot for fracking.

Because the layers of North Texas bedrock are inclined, older rock emerges as you head westward. The Fort Worth Prairie arises from Early Cretaceous limestone laid down 100 to 66 million years ago when this dry land was beneath a shallow inland sea.

▲ The thin Fort Worth Prairie soil produces magnificent wildflower displays.

A HARSH BEAUTY

The area's modest rainfall and shallow soil over limestone hamper the growth of trees except in riparian corridors. Exceptionally rigid limestone caps the cuestas and buttes, while softer marly clays beneath erode faster, creating cantilevered formations with right-angled rims.

Dryland plants fill the prairie barrens on top. Slopes terrace over time, exposing bench seeps where lush herbaceous life flourishes when they flow and disappears when they don't. Soil gathers at the slope base, fostering woody plants. An epic span in a few dozen yards.

Fort Worth Prairie has sections of scarplands, with many cuestas and plateaus separated by lowlands. Due to the inclined bedrock, many North Texas cuestas face west, as if adoring the sunset.

Water remains a linchpin in this semiarid terrain. Flora and fauna adapt to boom or bust cycles of moisture. Rainfall brings a swell of green as perennials seize the opportunity and grow larger. Ephemeral annuals spot the spaces between.

▲ Roadrunners sprint across the prairie after snakes.

LIFE FINDS A NICHE

Do you have prairie on your property or think you might? Texas Parks and Wildlife Department's Private Lands and Habitat Program can help.

In May, the Fort Worth Prairie reaches an apex of beauty as low, soft mounds of purple Engelmann's sage contrast with spiky pale yucca in bloom. Walking the Fort Worth Nature Center and Refuge prairie path, my steps crunched loudly on the gravel of fossilized oysters and sea urchins. A four-foot rat snake crossed my path, intent on prey. A Texas spiny lizard was far more curious, zipping up a post oak trunk to show off its stripes.

It will be a different prairie in two months, hunkered down for the heat, the sun more opponent than ally. Plants will scale back their size and leaf surface. Wildlife will emerge mainly in the crepuscular (twilight) hours when the light is dim and the shadows long. Creeks will disappear. Until the rain comes, as it eventually does, to a landscape ever in flux.

Bound by the Trinity

Caution: Water levels vary and hazards can be unpredictable. Always check gauges at the Trinity River Paddling Trail website first and go with a guide on your first exploration of a river.

Softly illuminated by late-afternoon light, a group of us slide our kayaks down the levee's gentle mowed slope and into the water at Trinity Park in Fort Worth. Trinity Coalition activist Kristi Kerr Leonard and I settle in for a sunset paddle down the Clear Fork. At the West Fork confluence, we'll gaze at the full moon rising over downtown.

Teresa Patterson of Adventures Unlimited Paddling and the Trinity River Paddling Trail zips to the head of the pack in her sporty kayak and the group follows. Tiny splashes of many paddles make an animated chatter. The banks lack the lush grasses and brushy plants of a healthy riparian corridor. On the Trinity Trails atop the levees, a constant flow of people bike, hike, and roller skate.

The group heads up the West Fork. Light ebbs to a whisper, forms lose their shape and divisions blur. Teresa directs us to turn our boats around. The full moon rises over downtown; the water is luminous. We bob in the mild current, attuned with the river's flow, the lunar rhythms, and each other.

► The Trinity River winds through the Great Trinity Forest.

Trinity Matrix

There is only one river in North Texas: the Trinity. The Trinity's four forks and major creek tributaries are home to the largest nature preserves. Its reservoirs provide the region's primary water source.

Once rejected and forgotten, paid attention to only when it flooded, valued solely for its ability to carry toxic trash downstream, the Trinity now is transforming. The rise of river recreation, from shoreline paths to paddlers, is reclaiming the river, changing it from a place of refuse to refuge.

In the late 1600s, the Trinity was termed Riviere des Canoës (River of Canoes) by French explorers. Long before that, the Native American Caddos called the river Arkikosa.

TRINITY RIVER WATERSHED

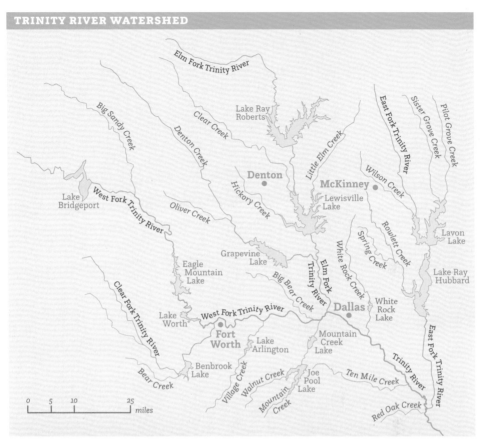

Elm Fork Trinity River
Lake Ray Roberts
Clear Creek
Big Sandy Creek
Denton Creek
Little Elm Creek
East Fork Trinity River
Sister Grove Creek
Pilot Grove Creek
Denton
McKinney
Wilson Creek
Lake Bridgeport
West Fork Trinity River
Oliver Creek
Hickory Creek
Lewisville Lake
Rowlett Creek
Spring Creek
Lavon Lake
Grapevine Lake
Eagle Mountain Lake
White Rock Creek
Elm Fork Trinity River
Big Bear Creek
Lake Ray Hubbard
Clear Fork Trinity River
Lake Worth
West Fork Trinity River
Dallas
White Rock Lake
Fort Worth
Lake Arlington
Mountain Creek Lake
East Fork Trinity River
Benbrook Lake
Bear Creek
Village Creek
Walnut Creek
Joe Pool Lake
Ten Mile Creek
Trinity River
Mountain Creek
Red Oak Creek
0 5 10 25 miles

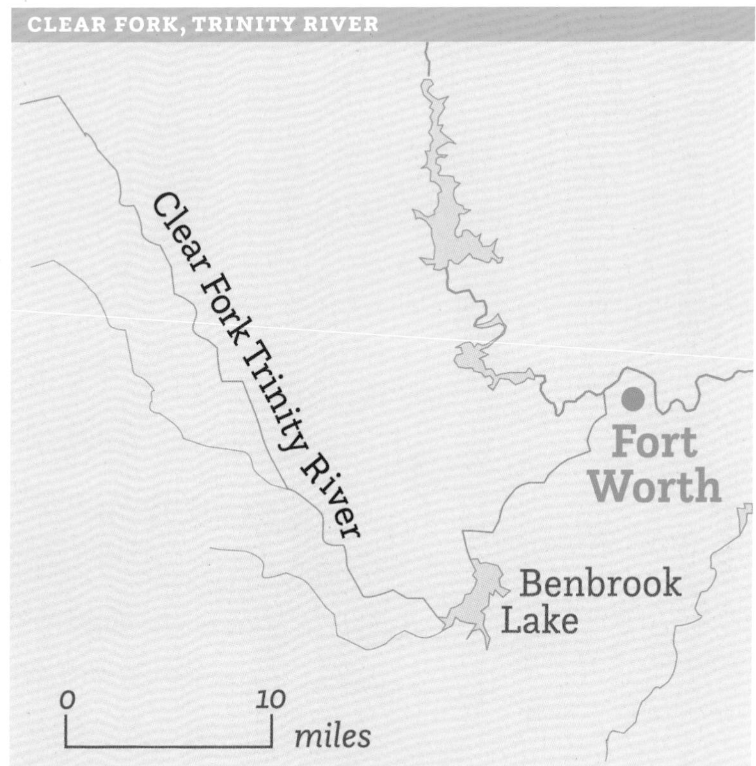

Clear Fork: Bejeweled and Capricious

Arising west of Fort Worth, the Clear Fork dips south, flows into Benbrook Lake, and heads into the city. Its sparkling water runs shallow over the dense, fossiliferous Fort Worth Prairie limestone.

Deceptively meek, the Clear can be dangerous. In 1949, eleven inches of rain fell in its upper watershed. A massive water wave rushed into Fort Worth, killing at least ten people. The Fort Worth Floodway, a twenty-seven-mile system of levees, arose in the following decades.

With its extensive parks and attractions, the Clear anchors much of the city's leisure life, including its sprawling Cultural District, boasting botanical gardens and significant art, history, and science museums.

Look for some of these in "West and Clear Forks of the Trinity" in Adventures.

Nature Jewels (starting upstream): Oakmont Park • Trinity Park • Botanical Research Institute of Texas • Fort Worth Botanic Gardens

Reservoirs: Benbrook Lake • Lake Weatherford

Best Paddling Stretch: Trinity Park to Panther Island Pavilion.

Paschal High School science teacher Andrew Brinker and students conduct the Trinity River Turtle Survey in the Clear Fork. Turtles are trapped, weighed and measured, tagged, and released to see how they're faring amid urban development.

▲ Autumn colors on the Clear Fork.

◄ The Clear Fork can become turbulent after rain storms.

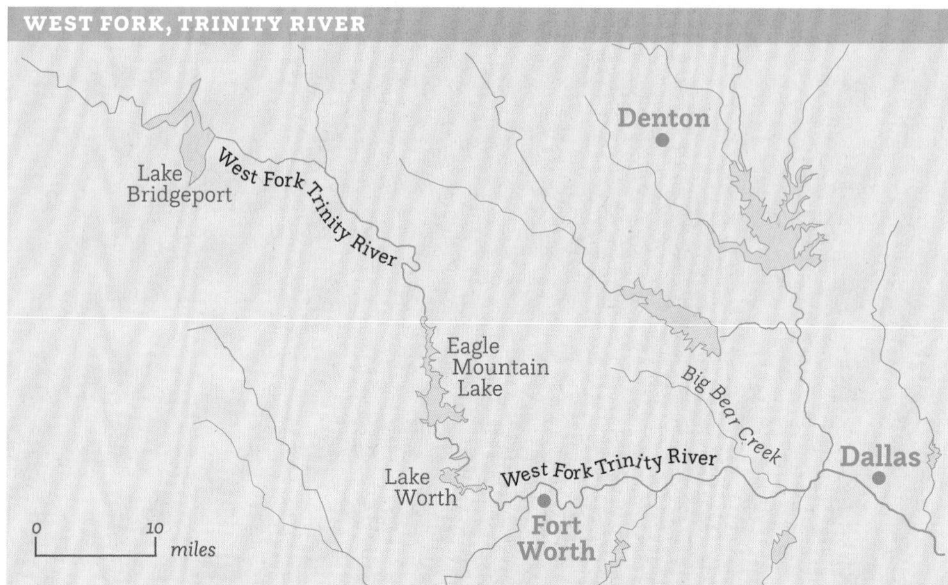

West Fork: The Tie that Binds

The longest fork of the Trinity at 145 miles, the West's headwaters start southeast of Wichita Falls. It's impounded three times: Lake Bridgeport, Eagle Mountain Lake, and Lake Worth, the Trinity River Paddling Trail's beautiful western terminus.

After being joined by the Clear Fork, the manicured and levee-constrained West Fork snakes through downtown Fort Worth past the Stockyards and turns east toward Dallas. Over a hundred miles of paved Trinity Trails trace the river from northwest Fort Worth to mid-Arlington.

Long and lanky, the West Fork spans three North Texas ecoregions. Industrial operations, scattered residences, and recreation fields frame it in the mid-cities. Yet to paddlers, it's wonderfully wild and wooded, boasting sections of the river's original meanders.

► The West Fork passes through the Fort Worth Nature Center and Refuge.

► An American lotus emerges from a marsh at Fort Worth Nature Center and Refuge.

Look for some of these in "West and Clear Forks of the Trinity" in Adventures.

Nature Jewels (starting upstream): Fort Worth Nature Center and Refuge • Marion Sansom Park • River Legacy Nature Center

Reservoirs: Eagle Mountain Lake • Lake Bridgeport • Lake Worth

Best Paddling Stretches (starting upstream): Eagle Mountain Lake to Lake Worth • Handley Ederville Dam to River Legacy Parks

Arlington's River Legacy Nature Center and interpretative nature trails educate about the Trinity River and its ecosystems.

Fort Worth Nature Center and Refuge—one of the nation's largest city-owned nature centers—containins more than 3600 acres of prairies, forests, wetlands with over twenty miles of hiking trails, and ideal habitat for all kinds of wildlife.

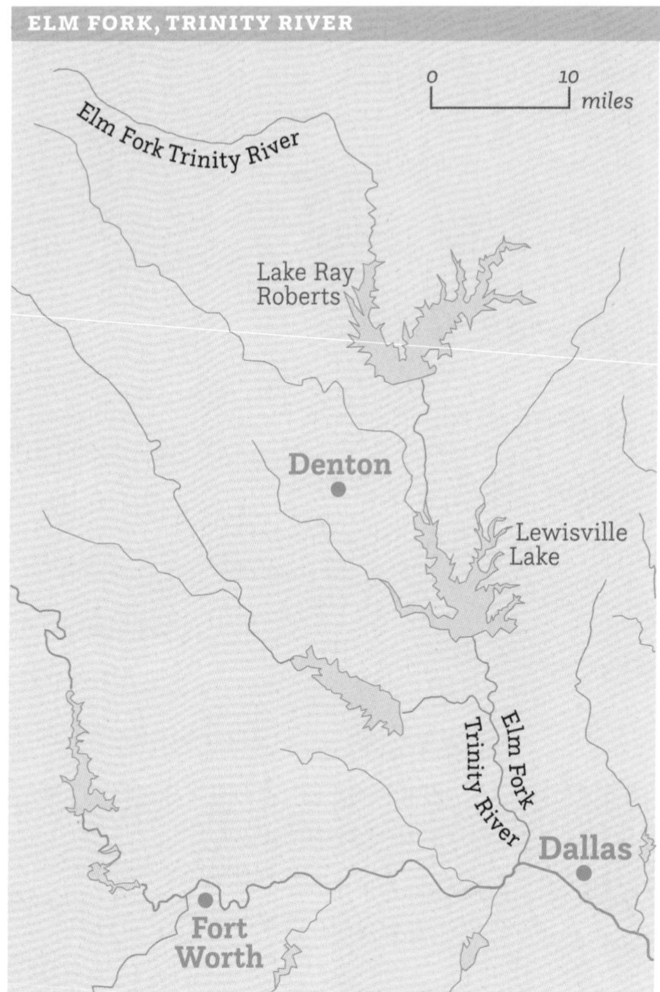

Elm Fork: Core of the Trinity

The Elm Fork of the Trinity's headwaters begins northwest of Dallas within a few miles of the Oklahoma border. It forms in Eastern Cross Timbers' sandy soils and eases into dark Blackland Prairie clay as it courses south.

Collecting a tremendous amount of rain in its watershed, the Elm Fork quickly grows wide with looping meanders. Soaring trees grow along the steep, soft banks, toppling into the river during floods.

Ray Roberts Lake State Park's 3777 acres nestles in the Elm Fork's upper reaches. A ten-mile-long bottomland greenbelt with trails connects it to Lewisville Lake. Clear Creek Natural Heritage Center occupies 2900 acres on the river's west side. Lewisville Lake Environmental Learning Area (LLELA) covers 2600 acres just south of the lake. All feature a mix of Eastern Cross Timbers upland and bottomland woods, prairie, riparian corridors, and wetlands.

Canoeists and kayakers favor the Elm Fork. The Trinity River Paddling Trail's north end begins at Lewisville Lake and runs an epic thirty-seven miles in nine segments to near downtown Dallas, segueing from lush bottomland forest to manicured urban green space.

▲ A fun day for floaters on the Elm Fork.

Once the Elm Fork enters Dallas city limits, it's fully a Blackland Prairie river—the "Little Muddy" as one canoeist calls it. Frequently soggy lowlands are home to heavy industry and recreation, along with some wonderfully wild parks. Greenspace Dallas transformed a debilitated stretch into Frasier Dam Recreation Area.

Look for some of these in "Elm Fork of the Trinity" in Adventures.

Nature Jewels (starting upstream): Ray Roberts Lake State Park • Ray Roberts Lake State Park Greenbelt • Clear Creek Natural Heritage Area • LLELA • McInnish Park • Elm Fork Nature Preserve Trail • Elm Park • Sam Houston Trail Park • John F. Burke Nature Preserve • L. B. Houston Nature Trails • Frasier Dam Recreation Area

Reservoirs: Lake Ray Roberts • Lewisville Lake

Best Paddling Stretches (starting upstream): LLELA to Trinity Fork Park (Hebron Parkway) • Trinity Fork Park (Hebron Parkway) to McInnish Park • Elm Park to California Crossing Park • California Crossing Park to Frasier Dam Recreation Area

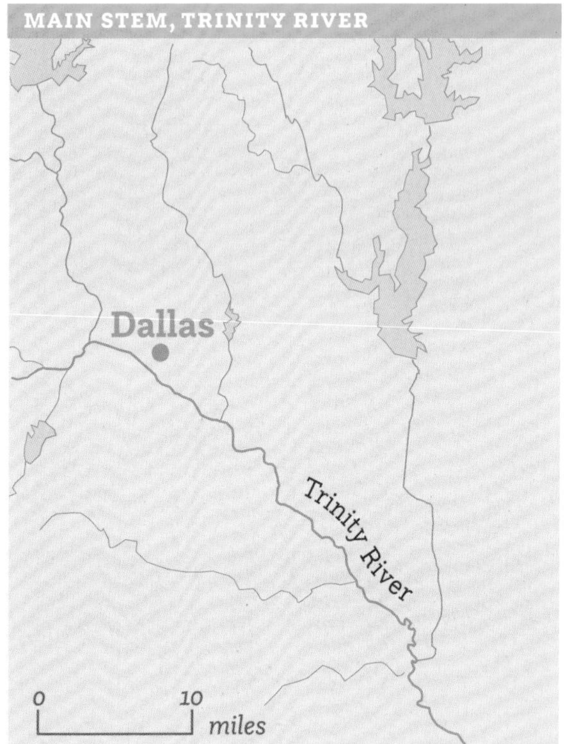

Main Stem: From Urban to Wild

The Elm and West Forks merge northwest of downtown Dallas to form the Trinity. Once a classic prairie river with broad basins, marshes, and sprawling meanders, the 1908 flood changed that. Fifteen inches of rain fell in three days, swelling the river to more than half a mile wide and leaving eleven dead.

Channelization came to the marshy confluence by the early twentieth century, moving the river significantly westward. Immense, tall levees now constrain the river and hide it from awareness, creating a half-mile-wide trough of mowed grass. Several miles of paved trails run on top and in the floodplain.

The Trinity main stem is a river of dreams and schemes. Locks and dams for barge traffic were a failure. Plans for canalization for a Gulf of Mexico connection cratered in the 1970s. Floods in 2015 that filled the levees for weeks helped end a planned tollway in the floodplain. Arguments rage between rewilding proponents and those lobbying for landscaped parks.

Educational displays and trails at Trinity River Audubon Center bring awareness to the river and Great Trinity Forest.

Once freed of its levees, the river sprawls into the 6000-acre Great Trinity Forest south of downtown.

Channelization excavates and straightens a river or creek, usually confining it between levees or embankments. Meant to prevent property damage from flooding, it can negatively impact the river's natural regenerative cycles. Levees can exacerbate flooding and erosion downstream by increasing water velocity.

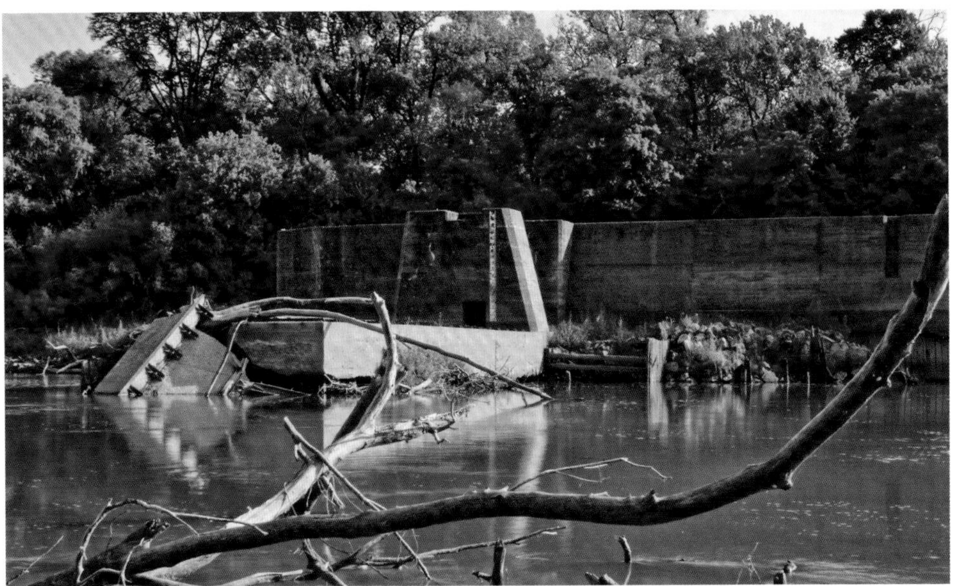

▲ Only ruins remain from attempts to make the river navigable.

This wilderness enraptures with centuries-old trees plus natural and human-made wetlands and ponds.

White Rock Creek joins the Trinity in the Great Trinity Forest's wild heart. River otters, whitetail deer, and even alligator snapping turtles call the Great Trinity Forest home. Avian life is plentiful: shorebirds, waterfowl, birds of prey, and songbirds. It contains wild preserves, including one for alligators and rare plants, and astounding scenic beauty, and is home to the Trinity River Paddling Trail's southern segment.

Look for some of these in "Great Trinity Forest" in Adventures.

Nature Jewels (starting upstream): Santa Fe Trestle Trail • Upper Chain of Wetlands • William Blair Jr. Park (Bonton Woods) • Ned and Genie Fritz Texas Buckeye Trail • Big Spring Preserve • Lower Chain of Wetlands • Trinity Forest Trails • Joppa Preserve • McCommas Bluff Preserve • Trinity River Audubon Center • Goat Island Preserve • Goat Island East Preserve

Best Paddling Stretch: Moore Park/Santa Fe Trestle Trail to Loop 12

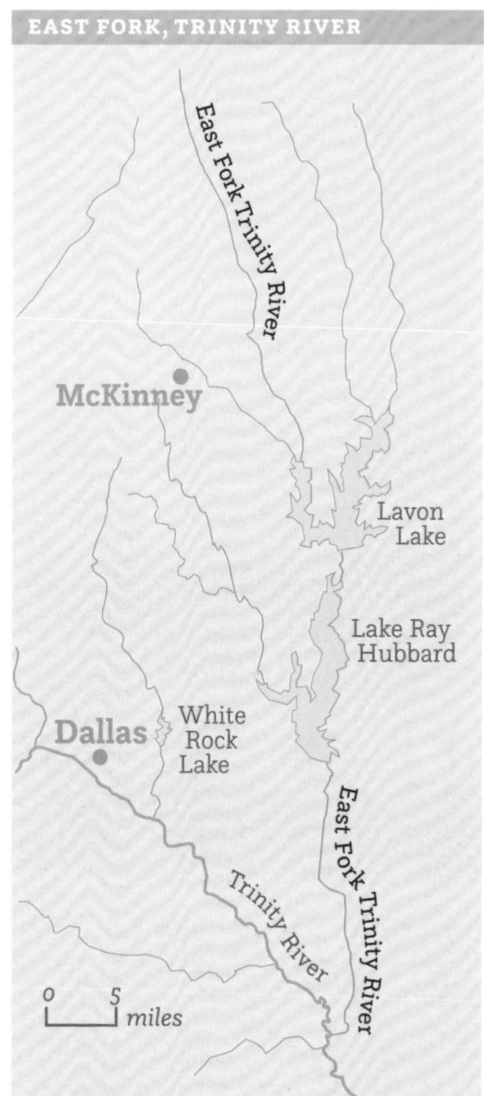

East Fork: The Forgotten Fork

Easing in from rural lands north of Dallas, the Trinity's East Fork flows southeast to Lavon Lake's west arm where it fosters a dense bottomland forest. A scant two-mile stretch of swampy woods separates Lavon Dam from the Lake Ray Hubbard headwaters.

South of the Ray Hubbard reservoir, the East Fork, formerly called the Bois d'Arc River, meanders through dense, boggy bottomland forests. As it approaches the Trinity confluence, channelization ensues with large forest swaths cleared for ranches and industry.

North Texas Municipal Water District diverts East Fork water into an immense constructed wetlands: the East Fork Wetland Project, home to

▲ Aquatic life abounds at John Bunker Sands Wetlands Center.

► Black-crowned night herons thrive in the East Fork's quiet waters.

John Bunker Sands Wetland Center. Pumps then move processed water forty-three miles back north to Lavon Lake, a primary municipal water source.

Look for some of these in "Wild Waters of the East" in Adventures.

Nature Jewels (starting upstream): Sister Grove Park • Trinity Trails • John Bunker Sands Wetlands Center

Reservoirs: Lavon Lake • Lake Ray Hubbard

Shores of an Ancient Ocean

Mick Tune, now a frequent speaker on fossils for Dallas Paleontological Society, relates the curiosity and wonder he felt on his initial exploration many years ago of Ladonia Fossil Park, located in a rural area northeast of Dallas.

"Curiosity and wonder got me into fossils when I was turning fifty. I love hiking and fossil hunting is just hiking with a purpose. The place is out in the country. After parking off a farm-to-market road by a bridge, I figured out how to get down to the river. I had the whole place to myself.

"After about two hours, a couple of miles walking, maybe two-thousand inspected and discarded rocks—plus four snakes, a pack of wild hogs, and a gang of turkey vultures eating something stinky—I noticed an odd and intricately curved rock. No digging or chiseling; this loose piece was just sitting there chilling after rolling around in the river for who knows how long.

"It was a good-sized mosasaur vertebra. Even though I barely knew what I was looking for, the purposeful and exquisitely detailed shape and structure of a well-preserved fossil bone are unmistakable. I was holding a seventy-five-million-year-old bone of a marine reptile that I found by myself by taking a hike just an hour from my house. How utterly amazing is that?

"I had so many questions. What else lived in this ancient ocean? Why was there an ocean here in the first place? I had to find answers. So it began. Now that mosasaur vertebra chills on a shelf in my home office along with hundreds more fossils, and the questions and searching never ends."

Ancient Ocean

Welcome to the Cretaceous Coast and the land of limestone. Cretaceous comes from the Latin word *creta*, meaning chalk, a fine-grained, porous type of limestone. The Cretaceous period 145 to 66 million years ago featured a warm climate and fluctuating sea levels. North Texas was beneath the Western Interior Seaway, also called the Cretaceous Seaway, bisecting North America.

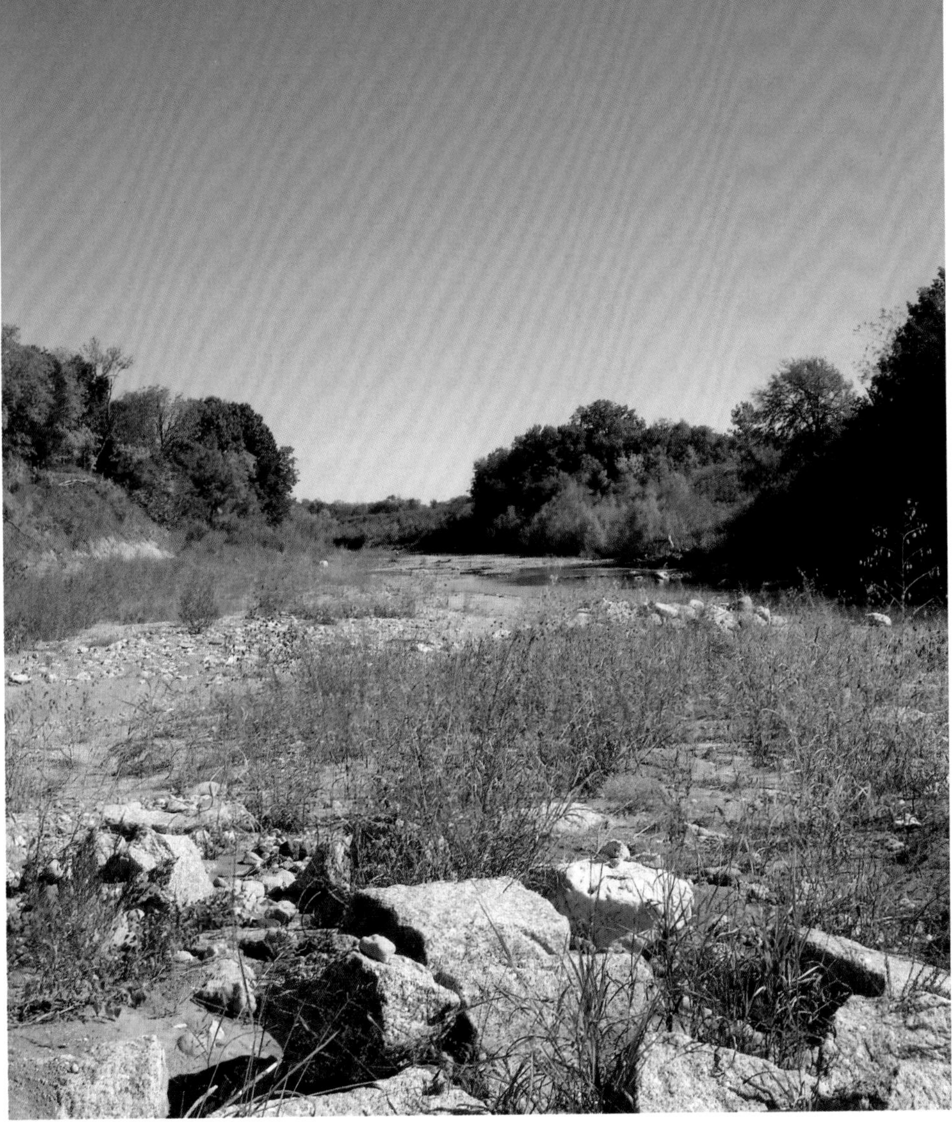

▲ Erosion exacerbated by straightening the river exposes plentiful fossils.

Over epochs, water repeatedly receded and rose with epic climate fluctuations and tectonic events, creating aquatic environments from deeper than skyscrapers, to vast shallow seas and swamps, to sandy shores. Layer upon layer of deceased microscopic calcareous sea creatures turned into Cretaceous limestone.

Learn more in the *Ocean Dallas Field Guide* by Southern Methodist University's Institute for the Study of Earth and Man.

University of Texas at Dallas geosciences professor Robert J. Stern writes in Geology of the Dallas–Fort Worth Metroplex, "Beneath the surface, limestone bedrock holds echoes of an ancient inland ocean in which monstrous sea lizards swam." These aquatic reptiles include mosasaurs—such

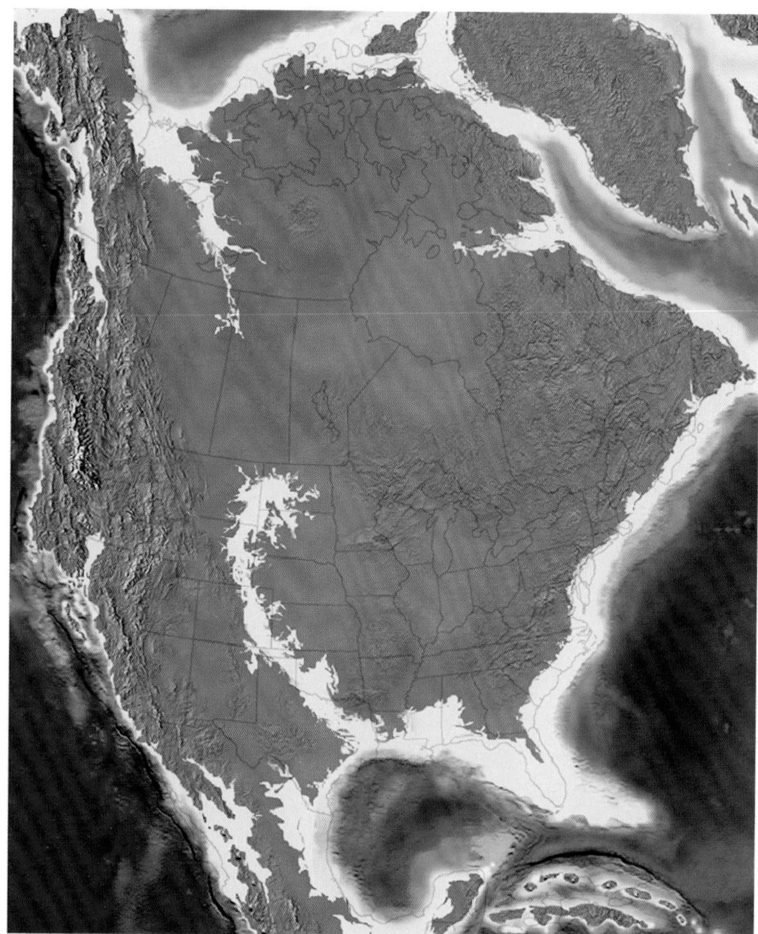

◄ A shallow sea once bisected North America.

Dallas Paleontological Society is a powerhouse of fossil activism, responsible for many specimens at area museums, partly through their Fossil Bureau of Investigation operations.

as *Dallasaurus turneri*, named for the city and Van Turner who discovered the specimen—and plesiosaurs, whose long-necked variety evokes the mythical Loch Ness monster. The continent's oldest mosasaur fossil was found north of I-30 near Chalk Hill Road.

Sedimentary layers of the inland sea ended up slightly inclined, bringing older layers to the surface in the west. On the western edge is 300-million-year-old shale of the Fort Worth Basin and Early Cretaceous limestone from 100 million years ago. Dallas's Austin Chalk from the Late Cretaceous is 85 million years old and the Ozan Formation farther east is 75 million years old.

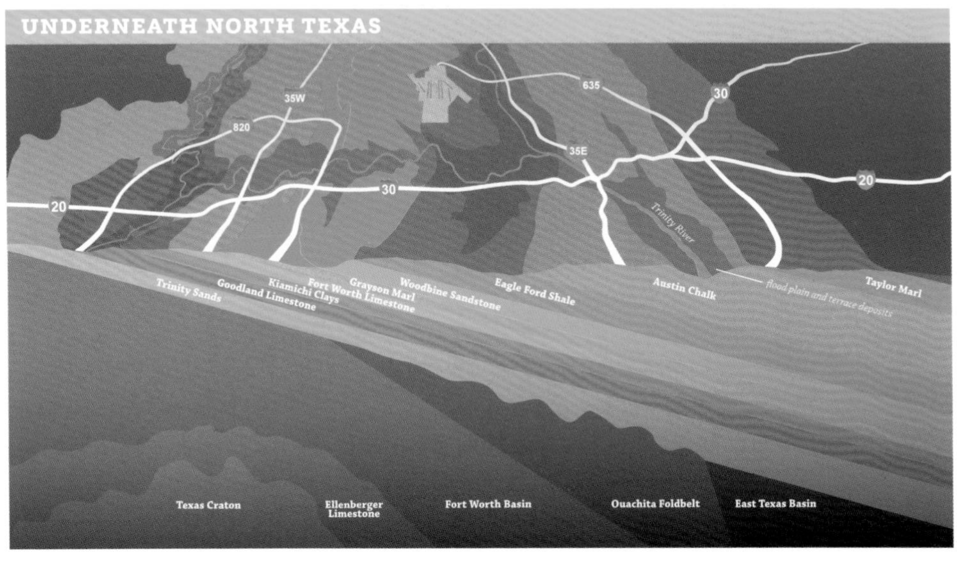

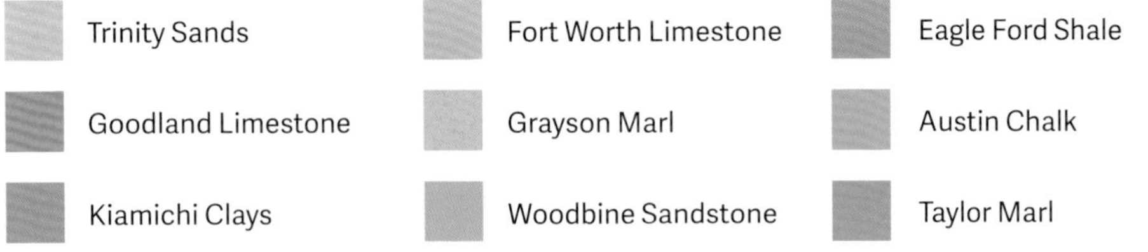

▲ Tilted layers of time underlie North Texas.

These overlay a far more ancient geologic record, including remnants of the Ouachita Mountains, formed during the assembly of the supercontinent Pangaea, and the Texas Craton dating back over one billion years. The past is not behind us; it's below us, and it's full of dramatic storytelling.

Land of Limestone

Everyone in North Texas knows limestone. It's the white dust coating cars after driving rock roads and the chalk rocks kids use to make sidewalk drawings. The bluffs and escarpments so visible on the flat prairie terrain are usually limestone; shale erodes faster. Defined as at least half calcium carbonate, limestone is highly alkaline. Acidic rain associated with pollution hastens its erosion.

If it's a ridge road, chances are it's on limestone. Austin Chalk, which extends northward from that city into North Texas, traces the Balcones Fault Zone and forms the roadbed for I-35 down to Hillsboro, where it shifts to shale. Mammoth and then bison herds, Indigenous people and then settlers traveled the curved diagonal route.

◄ A selection of fossils found by Don Young in Tarrant County limestone.

Austin Chalk in the eastern half of DFW prompts the frequent use of "white rock" in place names, including White Rock Lake. The soft, pale limestone transmutes with weathering and decomposition into deep, black, clay-rich soil. Limestone in western DFW is exceptionally hard. Straddling sea to shore, the strata is flush with fossilized seashells of bivalves and other larger invertebrates.

The disparate personalities of Dallas and Fort Worth arise from bedrock. Soils formed from the soft Taylor Marl and Austin Chalk of the east side fostered a mid-1800s to 1900s agricultural economy of cotton and grain. The thinner, drier soils of the west were primarily suitable for less prosperous cattle ranching. Fort Worth's fortunes changed when petroleum reserves were discovered in regional sandstones and shales.

Shaped by Water

Unimaginably immense cross-continental rivers flowed to the inland sea, sometimes forming massive deltas where land and water blurred. The alluvial detritus spreads for miles. "The youngest rocks in the Metroplex are Ice Age river gravels found along the Trinity River and its tributaries. These loose, unconsolidated Pleistocene rocks are much less than a million years old. They contain the bones of mammoths, ground sloths, sabertoothed tigers, and other Ice Age animals," writes Stern.

Much of the concrete produced here contains alluvial sands. Gravel mining pits dot the broad river floodplains. Once played out, the quarries fill with rain, becoming ponds and wetlands, especially abundant in southeastern Dallas County. As a result, habitat for water-loving birds increases.

Between Eagle Ford Shale and western limestones resides the Woodbine Formation sandstone, forming the sandy soil of the Eastern Cross Timbers. The porous sandstone's ability to trap water in its layers creates water tables accessible through seeps, springs, and shallow wells—crucial to early inhabitants.

Interested in ancient human history? Check out the North Texas Archeological Society meetings with fascinating speakers, as well as fieldtrips and excavations.

Road Trip Through Time

"The mountains were here 300 million years ago, a broad white sand beach was here 110 million years ago, and the great river was here 100 million years ago. These beautiful scenes all existed where we are today; we just arrived too late to enjoy them," writes Stern. "But it's not too late to see evidence that these beautiful scenes once existed where we live today."

Let's car surf the Cretaceous Coast. Many travelers along I-30 on the western edge of Dallas notice a historic building high on a ridge. It once housed the Eagle Ford School, a mid- to late 1800s community founded around a sloping shale crossing of the West Fork.

Navigate to the south side of I-30 and Chalk Hill Road. Head up the hill and pass the old school. The easily accessible limestone and alluvial gravel led to the area's nickname, Cement City.

Continue and wave at the rise where *Dallasaurus turneri* was found. Chalk Hill ends at West Davis and the Mount Carmel monastery. Take a moment to appreciate the more-than-640-foot elevation. Navigate to Loop 12, also called South Walton Walker Blvd. Traveling south and then veering southwest on TX 308, you follow the Austin Chalk ridge along Mountain Creek Lake—the mountain of its name.

South of I-20, navigate to FM 1382, also called Belt Line Road. Heading southeast to US-67, the highway splits around a massive limestone knob in

▲ The Texas Nessie display at Heard Natural Science Museum brings ancient marine life alive for viewers.

a broad, central median. Once past it, Eagle Ford Shale spreads to the right and Austin Chalk to the left.

Find a Fossil

When fossil hunting, Mick Tune recommends, "Explore a little. When you pick up your first fossil and start asking a few questions, you'll be hooked." Here's where to go.

LADONIA FOSSIL PARK

Located north of Greenville near the town of Ladonia, the park consists of a parking area and a path to the North Sulphur River, which takes a steep climb to access. Voluminous rains expose Late Cretaceous and Pleistocene fossils such as the mosasaur vertebrae (which local ranchers call "dinosaur knuckles"), ammonites, bivalves, gastropods, nautilus, and shark teeth. The river's western half will be inundated by 2025 for Lake Ralph Hall, significantly reducing fossil-collecting opportunities.

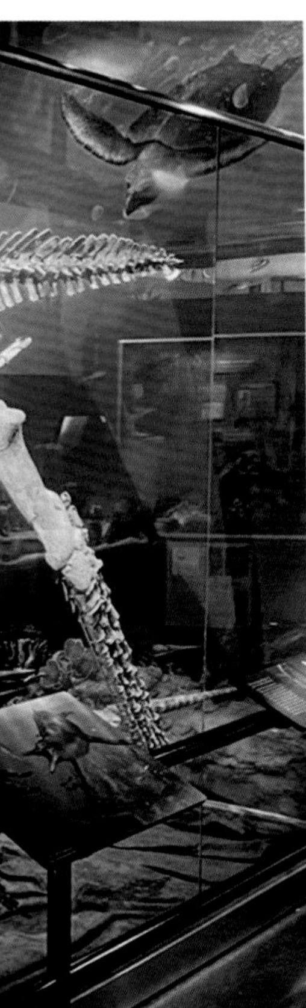

MINERAL WELLS FOSSIL PARK

Excavation exposed a treasure trove of 300-million-year-old Pennsylvanian era marine fossils, including crinoids, urchins, bivalves, corals, trilobites, and sharks. Dallas Paleontological Society lobbied for creation of a public fossil park.

DINOSAUR VALLEY STATE PARK

Once on the edge of the Western Interior Seaway, Cretaceous epoch sauropods left their elephant-like tracks and theropods imprinted their distinct three-toed tracks in what is now the Paluxy River. Experience the fabulous local fossil finds then explore the hilly park, wading in the river or watching for golden-cheeked warblers and black-capped vireos.

HEARD NATURAL SCIENCE MUSEUM

See a mosasaur found in Garland and the partial skeleton of Texas Nessie, a plesiosaur fossil discovered in 1991 in Collin County by Mike Donovan, showcased against a colorful mural of ancient sea life. At Grapevine Lake, nine-year-old Ty Leslie Goble noticed the fossil of an ancient aquatic turtle, *Trinitichelys maini*, a species first discovered in Tarrant County by Dr. Derek Main and exclusive to the Woodbine formation. Now dubbed Ruby, Ty's turtle is on display after being excavated by professionals and prepared by volunteers in the Heard Paleontology Lab.

PEROT MUSEUM OF NATURE AND SCIENCE

Paleontology hall showcases several impressive, locally found fossils, including Ellie May, a Columbian mammoth discovered in an Ellis County gravel pit. *Flexomornis howei*—a pheasant-sized bird and the oldest known bird in North America (about ninety-five million years old)—was found by amateur paleontologist Kris Howe at Grapevine Lake. Plus, there is a tylosaurus skeleton from the shores of Lake Ray Hubbard, and *Dallasaurus turneri* found in West Dallas.

WACO MAMMOTH NATIONAL MONUMENT

Gain insight into the Ice Age with Pleistocene epoch fossils of Columbian mammoths that weighed 20,000 pounds and stood fourteen feet tall. See a paleontological dig site preserved under a shelter and a museum with excavated fossils.

Tip of Tornado Alley

When the north wind comes sweeping down the plains, it crashes into Dallas–Fort Worth. Add warm wet breezes from the Gulf Coast, hot dry winds from the southwest, and weather fronts from the west, and the conflicting forces can result in catastrophic weather. Just as North Texas is an ecotone where biological forces of east and west fuse, it's an even more complex nexus in the sky.

Classified as a humid subtropical climate with hot summers and mild winters, increasingly exceptions are the rule. Such as the Big Freeze of 2021, when it didn't rise above freezing for six days, thousands lost power, and dozens died statewide. Or that time in 2010 when temperatures plummeted

▼ Storm clouds gather northwest of Fort Worth.

National Weather Service temperature, wind, and rain data for North Texas are collected at the Dallas–Fort Worth International Airport.

Satan's Storm: When dry air rapidly descends in a thunderstorm, the compression can create a heat burst. South of DFW on the edge of Lake Whitney in June 1960, a downdraft gusted to over 75 mph. Thermometers able to register up to 140 degrees Fahrenheit cracked. Feeling extreme heat and fearing their houses were on fire, people rushed into the scorching night accompanied by anguished screams of livestock.

▲ Snow and ice cover Goat Island Preserve in 2021's Big Freeze.

to thirteen degrees Fahrenheit with over twelve inches of snow in twenty-four hours—in an area where it rarely snows.

Heat, however, you can count on. Temperatures in the hundreds are typical, often in August but even in June. Few thought 1980 in Dallas could be topped, with forty-two consecutive days over 100 degrees—twenty-eight days above 105 and five over 110—climaxing at 113. Then 2011 came along, with seventy-one days over 100 degrees (forty in succession) and thirty-seven overnight lows in the eighties, for the hottest summer on record. Over 300 million trees perished statewide.

Heat complicates the area's tendency toward drought, with spells over five years occurring in the 1950s, 1960s, and 2010s. One- to two-year droughts are common. Due to most area aquifers' high sodium adsorption ratio, municipal water sources in North Texas are drawn from surface reservoirs and rivers, making drought more than an agricultural crisis.

▲A supercell indicates impending severe weather.

Twister Towns

Tornadoes are North Texas's weather claim to fame. In the astounding swarm of seventy-five tornadoes over the eastern United States in April 1957, twenty-five were in North Texas. An F3 blasted through Dallas, killing ten. Recent deadly tornadoes include 1994 (F4, three dead), 2000 (F3, three dead), 2012 (F3, no fatalities), 2015 (F4, nine dead), and 2019 (F3, no fatalities). April and May are top months for tornadoes, though October, January, and December are contenders, spawning tornadoes on unseasonably warm days.

"We're the most populated target in all of Tornado Alley," says David Finfrock, longtime senior meteorologist for NBC 5. "When you look at the population and the way that DFW is spread out, it's phenomenal luck that we've not had worse disasters. So it's probably just a matter of time before a big F4 or F5 comes through."

Over time, North Texans learned tornado defense. In the 2015 winter tornado, "many hundreds of homes were destroyed," notes Finfrock, "but in the middle was a small room where they managed to survive. People paid attention to weather notices and got to their safe place in time." It was the same with the devastating 2019 tornado, whose wide path plowed over dense residential areas, yet no deaths occurred.

Inside the Storm, a web-series by NBC 5, features explorations of historic weather events, including the 1985 airport crash, 1995 Mayfest storm, and 2011 Super Bowl ice storm.

▲ A trained storm spotter would know if these rising clouds posed a potential storm threat.

Be a Storm Spotter

The font of North Texas weather data is the Fort Worth office of the National Weather Service (NWS). Long before the internet and apps, there was battery-powered weather radio from the National Oceanic and Atmospheric Administration (NOAA) that broadcasts weather reports. Keep a weather radio at home to stay informed during power and internet outages.

You can also become a weather spotter and help everyone stay safe. NWS offers SKYWARN Storm Spotter Training and outreach classes. Learn how to read clouds, wind, and precipitation to detect worsening weather. NWS's website also abounds with helpful information. Suggest that your community join NOAA's Weather-Ready Nation initiative.

A home weather station can help you learn about weather patterns and can also connect you to Weather Underground. Finfrock relates that while temperature and wind are fairly uniform across North Texas, rainfall varies. "You could have three inches of rain in one spot and not a drop five miles away. That's where these home weather stations do help us out considerably."

Human weather skills are still essential. Weather indicators appear in bird and insect behavior, plant responsiveness, smoke and sound changes, and much more. Eric Sloane's *Weather Almanac* and *The Secret World of Weather* by Tristan Gooley can help you become a weather naturalist.

Tornado Alley is a wide swath of the Great Plains and Midwest where tornadoes are most frequent, peaking in Kansas and Oklahoma.

▲ West Fork floods tear through the Fort Worth Nature Center and Refuge.

Freaky Floods

Weather spotting is vital because of flash flooding—the top cause of weather deaths. Most common in May and June, flash floods occur with little or no warning, usually from intense rainfall over a relatively small area that overwhelms storm sewers, creeks, and rivers for a short period. Sometimes areas where no precipitation fell will incur flash floods from rain upstream, catching victims by surprise.

Unlike in other weather disasters, human carelessness causes most flash flood deaths. "Year in and out, we lose more lives to flash flood events than anything," says Finfrock, "because people don't heed the 'Turn around, don't drown' slogan." Six inches of fast-moving water can knock a pedestrian down and stall a vehicle, causing a loss of control. A foot of water can float many cars, even SUVs. A high percentage of victims are under ten years of age, unable to escape vehicles driven into floodwaters. Two-thirds of flash flood deaths are males.

Nine and a quarter inches of rain in a concentrated period equals a hundred-year flood. North Texas has endured several in the last century.

North Texas caps Flash Flood Alley, which follows I-35. Clay soils and chalk bedrocks are poor water absorbers. Impervious surfaces make matters worse by shunting massive quantities of rain into overwhelmed storm sewers and then into creeks at high velocity.

"But floods on rivers," says Finfrock, "may last for days or even weeks before the water gets downstream to the Gulf of Mexico." The driest year on record, 2011, kicked off a severe multi-year drought, only to be broken by rains that wouldn't stop. Over twenty inches fell in May and June 2015 on already saturated soil, making it the wettest year on record.

Reservoirs filled to the maximum that spring, and their necessary releases led to record-setting river crests. Between the gargantuan levees of Trinity's main stem near downtown Dallas, water rose to the brim. River and creek floodplains are home to significant parks and preserves. Many went underwater, at times several feet deep, for months. Rebuilding structures and trails took months of municipal and volunteer effort.

Turbulent Thunderstorms

North Texas's weather nexus of north, south, and west influences can create massive thunderstorms with torrential rain, large hail, and cloud-to-ground lightning. Downbursts can lead to straight-line winds of over 150 miles per hour that level forests and rip roofs from buildings—or worse. Delta Air Lines Flight 191 attempted to land at Dallas–Fort Worth International Airport in 1985 when a microburst-induced wind shear caused the plane to plummet at fifty feet per second, causing a horrific crash that killed 137 people.

Softball-sized hail has pummeled the area at least eight times in the last three decades. The 1992 hail outburst produced grapefruit-sized ice. Hailstorms hit twice in 2012, lasting at least thirty minutes in some places. The 1995 storm that pounded 10,000 attendees with hail at Fort Worth's Mayfest sent over ninety people to the hospital. Flash floods, lightning strikes, and collapsed roofs killed at least twenty people. Now NWS sends out emergency alerts on cellphones about severe thunderstorms, high winds, and more.

Dense cumulonimbus clouds, formed by powerful upward air currents, tower 35,000 feet or more. They often herald severe thunderstorms, particularly if a cloud peaks in a flat, anvil shape.

Human-Influenced Weather

With its dual cities, developed suburbs, and extensive highways, the Metroplex generates a significant urban heat island effect, most noticeable at night, summer and winter, and during periods of stagnant wind. Explains Finfrock, "Concrete and pavement soaks in the sun's energy and then releases the heat at night. It's not at all uncommon to see Dallas and Fort Worth five to eight degrees warmer than outlying areas in northern Denton and Collin

▲ Some researchers see a connection between cloud-to-ground lightning and urban heating.

North Texas has so many reservoirs that evaporating water contributes to higher humidity levels.

counties, but now Plano is just as hot as Dallas."

"Because of that urban heat island and global warming," continues Finfrock, "it's not cooling off as much at night. Much more frequently, we set records for the warmest minimum temperature than we do for hottest afternoon temperatures." The heat island effect increases pollutants such as ozone. Heated water in creeks, rivers, and lakes fosters algal blooms and lowers oxygen, impacting wildlife.

Global warming promises to bring higher humidity levels, because hot air can hold more humidity. In addition, says Finfrock, "Our first freeze is taking place later, and the last freeze is earlier." As a result, plants become out of sync with the pollinators they depend on.

"While the temperature is going to get hotter," says Finfrock, "we can still get into periods of very long, dry spells. As the population continues to grow, water sources are going to become very stressed. But we're running out of places to put new lakes." Every reservoir inundates irreplaceable wildlife habitat in bottomlands and riparian corridors.

"When I started weather forecasting in the '70s," says Finfrock, "our average rain was about thirty-two inches. Now it's over thirty-four inches. And that's probably largely due to climate warming. Warmer air can hold more moisture so that we will get more frequent and heavier rains."

Native Species

"Raccoon Heights—leasing now! Choose your abode from tall trees, accessible crawl spaces, or underneath storage sheds. Ample food: plentiful trash bins (unsecured!) and compost piles, well-irrigated lawns with big grubs, lots of acorns and pecans in fall. Water available 24/7."

That's a wildlife-centric advertisement for my neighborhood. The city can provide a comfortable living. Urban raccoons, opossums, bobcats, and coyotes generally grow larger and produce bigger litters than their country cousins. They live longer, too, though their general health may be less robust.

Minimize nuisance attractions like unsecured trash and feral cat food stations and wildlife can be good neighbors. If you've got too many rats, are occasionally overrun by rabbits, or have squirrels taking over your birdfeeders, then you don't have enough bobcats and coyotes in your neighborhood.

▼ Got large trees? Then you have raccoons.

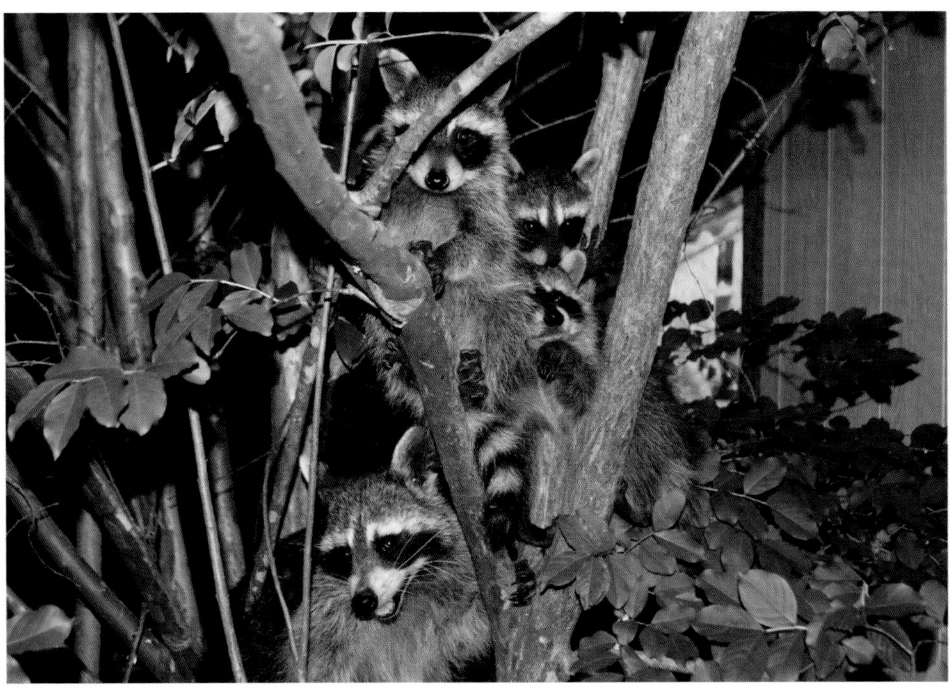

▲ Roofs and fences are bobcat thoroughfares.

Consult the DFW Wildlife Coalition website for education and solutions to urban wildlife issues or call their hotline.

Urban living has its benefits. Many species enjoy prolonged breeding seasons, partly because cities warm up earlier in spring and stay hotter in autumn due to the urban heat island effect. Access to water even in dry times is a huge plus.

Downsides of City Life

A considerable challenge to urban wildlife is habitat fragmentation. Thoroughfares and development separate animals from their food sources and restrict their range too much for survival. Often spared from development, riparian zones along creeks become crucial travel corridors for wildlife. Some animals make use of storm sewers.

As a Texas Parks and Wildlife urban wildlife biologist in North Texas, Rachel Richter has the essential task of identifying weak links and potential connections in this patchwork habitat. City dangers for urban wildlife cited by Richter and other experts include:

- Excess outdoor lighting, which interferes with bird navigation, and collisions with windows in buildings, which lead to high mortality, especially during migration periods.

- Some pest control companies indiscriminately trap and kill rather than removing attractants and eliminating wildlife access into client buildings.
- Excessive pruning leads to a lack of tree cavities, leading to a shortage of nesting sites for arboreal bats as well as owls and other cavity-nesting birds.
- Indiscriminate pesticide and herbicide use leads to developmental impairment and death in amphibians.
- Rodents weakened by rodenticide make easy pickings for coyotes, bobcats, and birds of prey who then become poisoned themselves.
- Domestic and feral cats exert enormous predation pressure on songbirds.
- Road mortalities are a constant issue.

Urban Improvisers

"Wildlife in the city has three options: move, adapt, or die," says Richter. Adaptation of wildlife to urban environments is called synurbanization, and versatile masters of synurbanization share some essential characteristics, allowing them to ace urban living.

Less territory maintenance. Territories overlap more in the city due to population density. Mammals with high territorial needs find it impossible to keep up constant scent marking and vocal calls.

Acceptance of humans. Urban masters like crows not only don't fear humans, they can recognize individuals' faces and even their cars.

▼ Consuming rodenticide-affected prey leads to sometimes-fatal mange in coyotes.

Trap and release is not an option for relocating wildlife deemed "problematic" for people. A majority of animals perish within a few weeks from stress, lack of food and shelter, conflict with wildlife into whose territories they've been released, and vehicle encounters while trying to return home.

Behavioral flexibility. Adapt to survive. In cities, diurnal species, which usually prefer daytime activity, move about more at night. Arboreal bats find ways to roost in buildings instead of trees.

Generalists excel. Wildlife with specialized food or nesting requirements suffer with the city's limited options.

Bigger brains do better. Corvids—which include crows, ravens, and blue jays—are renowned for their memory and logic-puzzle mastery. Urban living may even increase animal smarts. In one study, urban white-footed mice and meadow voles had larger cranial capacities than rural ones.

AVIAN ADAPTERS

Birds have lost 25 percent of their population in the last fifty years. That's 2.9 billion breeding adult birds! In the past decade, weather radars have detected a 14 percent decrease in nighttime spring migration. Grassland and arboreal birds have suffered the most loss. Yet wetland birds have grown in number, partly due to an increase in constructed wetlands.

"Birds like common nighthawks do well with city lights that attract insects. Most species of waterfowl have no problems on city golf course ponds, streams, or water reservoirs," says Jim Peterson, who maintains records for North-Central Texas Birds.

▼ A Cooper's hawk dines on a white-winged dove.

"Western kingbird is doing really well in urban parking lots because it'll feed well into night under the lights," says David Hurt of Wild Birds Unlimited. "Common nighthawks as well." At a time when insect numbers are declining, lights help concentrate them for birds.

Peterson notices that "Cooper's hawks have begun to thrive in suburban environments and in the last few years, Mississippi kites have decided they can coexist in suburban environments as well, so it's a dynamic process taking place."

White-winged doves, a Texas tree-roosting native, have pushed into North Texas, displacing mourning doves that tend to nest in human structures. Hurt attributes the Cooper's hawk increase to the nimble fliers realizing urban treetops were full of plump dove morsels.

Seed-eating urban birds have benefited from the proliferation of bird feeders. And while pollinator gardens and pocket prairies have created more larval host plants and nectar flowers for pollinators, they have the added benefit of producing more seed for birds.

INVENTIVE BUTTERFLIES AND MOTHS

Butterflies are generalists in the adult pollen- and nectar-eating stage, so they do well with typical landscape plants. But many have particular host plant needs for larvae, making a good pollinator garden very important. Dale Clark of Butterflies Unlimited cites how eufala, fiery, and sachem skippers adapted to ubiquitous Bermuda and St. Augustine grasses as a larval host plant. The clouded skipper now uses Johnsongrass and St. Augustine grass as hosts.

A common host plant is a bonus, like eastern tiger swallowtails and various ash tree species. Gulf fritillary has benefitted from the popularity of blue passionflower, which unlike native species tend not to die back in winter, allowing the butterfly to breed longer.

"Hackberry emperor, tawny emperor, American snout, and question mark butterflies have all done quite well in an urban setting because of the abundance of hackberry," says Clark. "American elm is a favorite of question marks."

Sam Kieschnick, moth enthusiast and urban wildlife biologist for Texas Parks and Wildlife, notes a "tremendous diversity of moths here in DFW. With all the urbanization and loss of habitat, how can there still be a thousand moth species?"

Two reasons, it turns out: moths' broad range of forage plants, including non-natives, and pockets of habitat left in urban parks. The moonseed moth, which Kieschnick calls "super charming," feeds on Carolina snailseed, a red-berried vine that's common in cities.

Moths appear to be evolving. "Those that grow up in high light pollution areas aren't as prone to come to artificial lights," says Kieschnick.

REPTILE WINNERS

North Texas natives include common and alligator snapping turtles, common and razorback musk turtles, eastern river and Texas cooters, pallid spiny and spiny softshells, Mississippi map turtles, and the omnipresent red-eared slider.

Carl Franklin of Texas Turtles notes: "The Trinity River has a thriving turtle diversity throughout its course in Dallas. Urbanization hasn't shown any seemingly deleterious impact. Cities are convenient places to not only find but to learn about our native turtles."

Michael A. Smith, coauthor of *Herping Texas*, is less upbeat about snakes due to ophidiophobia, yet finds hope. "You would think the western rat snake is too big to do well in cities but being an excellent climber, it uses tree canopies to get around. Other nominees might be the DeKay's brown snake, rough earth snake, and little brown skink."

ANXIETY ABOUT AMPHIBIANS

Amphibian populations decline by about 4 percent each year due to disease, habitat loss, and lawn and agricultural chemicals. But the tough-skinned Gulf Coast toad aces the urban environment. They breed later than other amphibians, and the urban heat island effect allows them to keep on breeding.

Blanchard's cricket frogs live most of their lives in trees and breed in lush lawns and standing water (while relatively numerous, they're still in decline). The Rio Grande chirping frog is a rare amphibian that expanded its range, moving north from Mexico. Green tree frogs benefit from urban landscaping irrigation.

▼ Green tree frog song fills the night in certain neighborhoods.

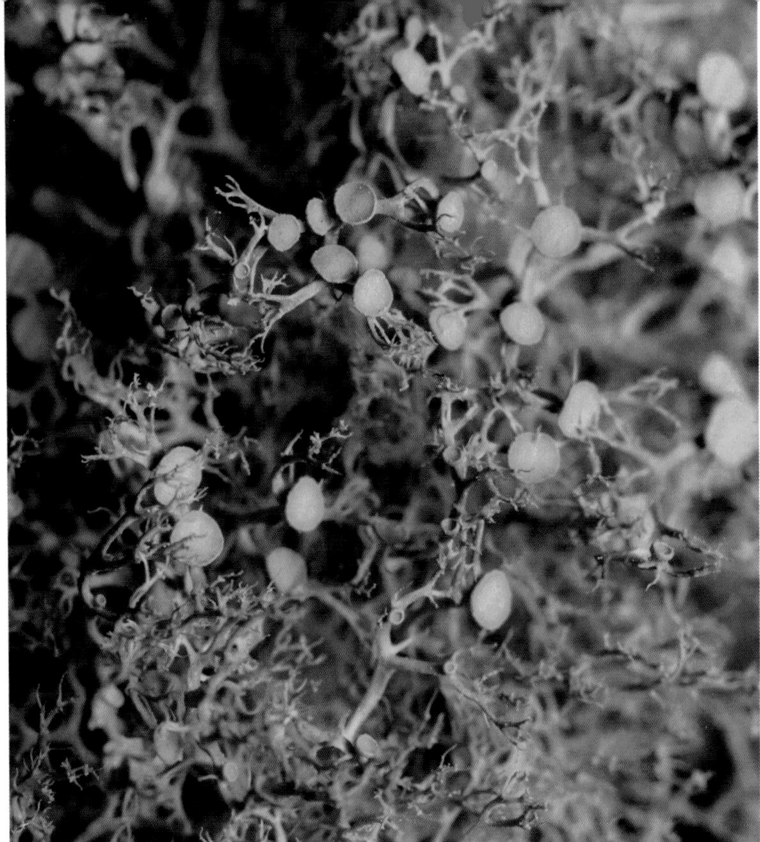

► Fruticose lichens respond negatively to urban pollution.

LICHENS ON THE LINE

Lichens are bioindicators. If the urban air is too warm or polluted, or if the rain is too acidic from excess sulfur dioxide and nitrogen oxide, lichens rapidly respond. They absorb gaseous pollutants through their entire surface and accumulate metals in their tissues, providing a way to gauge pollutants and radiation if not excessive.

The urban heat island effect creates higher temperatures, reducing lichen diversity. Because of lichens' responsiveness, those on tree bark can indicate the effect's strength and gauge tree planting success for heat mitigation.

With its intricate absorptive structure of many fine branches, fruticose lichen struggles in the city. Yet some foliose and crustose lichens, which look like stains or spills, thrive even on pavement.

PERSISTENT PLANTS

Urban land is constantly disturbed by construction. With their prolific seeding, cedar elms are often first to arise on bulldozed land, followed quickly by hackberries. Giant ragweed thrives on disturbed ground, creating bamboo-like thickets that shade out beneficial plants.

Native trees like cedar elm, green ash, pecans, and various oaks dominate as shade trees. Due to the urban heat island effect and more consistent water, urban trees grow faster than rural ones.

To find where native plants are lurking, walk alleys. Carolina snailseed, trumpet vine, and yellow passionflower climb the fences. Dakota mock vervain, inland sea oats, and white avens fill the strip between pavement and back fences. Yaupon holly thrives as an understory shrub. Straggler daisy quickly covers any bare dirt.

▲ Yaupon berries are savored by birds like American robins.

Where Native Plants Are Exalted

Botanical Research Institute of Texas (BRIT) in Fort Worth is where serious botanists work, including a herbarium boasting approximately 1,445,000 plant specimens. The BRIT grounds— with native-plant landscaping, rain and research gardens, and wetlands pond—are open to the public. At the adjacent Fort Worth Botanic Garden, attractions include the Native Texas Boardwalk outdoor classroom.

Texas Discovery Gardens in Dallas features nearly eight acres of native and adapted plants selected to benefit native wildlife, butterflies, bugs, and birds, including extensive pollinator gardens. It is home to the two-story Rosine Smith Sammons Butterfly House and an insectarium.

Also in Dallas, the fifteen-acre Native Texas Park at George W. Bush Presidential Library and Museum is a tribute to former president Bush's beloved Prairie Chapel Ranch. A one-mile network of paved and dirt trails takes visitors through re-creations of Blackland Prairie, Post Oak Savannah, and Eastern Cross Timbers. Free guided tours are offered on many weekends.

Native Plant Society of Texas celebrates the state's more than 5000 species of natives with meetings, workdays, field trips, and socials. Learn directly from other native-plant enthusiasts. Chapters host sales of hand-raised native plants.

Exotic Species

The exotics are everywhere. They're taking over parks and prairies, infiltrating ponds and lakes, leaving devastated ecosystems in their wake. They've killed thousands of trees, led to the near extermination of species, and threatened water supplies. Most likely, they're in your yard or neighborhood park.

As a volunteer steward of the Dixon Branch Greenbelt in East Dallas, I saw the *Scabiosa atropurpurea* flower, native to southern Europe, and pulled and stuffed it in my litterbag. Next year: a half dozen more. They keep appearing in our prairie restoration and volunteers keep pulling. The cost is too great if we don't. A half mile away, scabiosa got into a rare Blackland

▼ *Scabiosa atropurpurea* has a pretty blossom but creates dense mats that prevent native wildflowers and grasses from growing.

"In twenty years, scabiosa has made massive advances. It is decreasing plant diversity at a pace we can observe."

—*Carol Clark, North Texas*

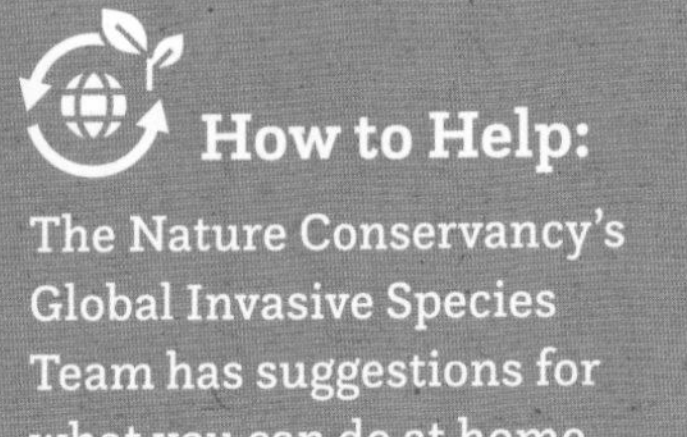

How to Help:

The Nature Conservancy's Global Invasive Species Team has suggestions for what you can do at home.

Prairie remnant. Within a few years, a plethora of unique wildflowers withered under a scabiosa monoculture.

Scabiosa is just one of the greenbelt's exotic foes. Several species of privet and honeysuckle, introduced from Asia in the 1700s and 1800s, clog the riparian forest. Our prairie restoration battles King Ranch (KR) bluestem from Eurasia, commonly planted along highways and utility corridors.

Pushing back on exotics is strenuous work, yet rewarding. Trout lilies appeared where we removed privet. Less amur honeysuckle in riparian woods allowed inland sea oats to take hold. Surging amid the KR bluestem are eastern gamagrass, little bluestem, and prairie wildflowers.

But not all exotics are invasive. Blue Indian peafowl, better known as peacocks, started as an attraction for a horse stable in East Dallas. They spread out in roaming flocks that are treated as neighborhood pets. Mediterranean geckos found an urban niche consuming insects drawn by nighttime lights. Monk parakeets are obviously exotic, but inability to tolerate cold keeps numbers low.

Some bird species are so well established, such as house sparrow, we forget they first came from far away. Rock pigeons found a noncompetitive niche inhabiting tall structures like office towers and bridges evocative of the Mediterranean cliffs back home. More than a parking-lot poop menace, European starlings outcompete native cavity-nesting birds.

▼ Peafowl thoroughly check yards for crickets and other insects.

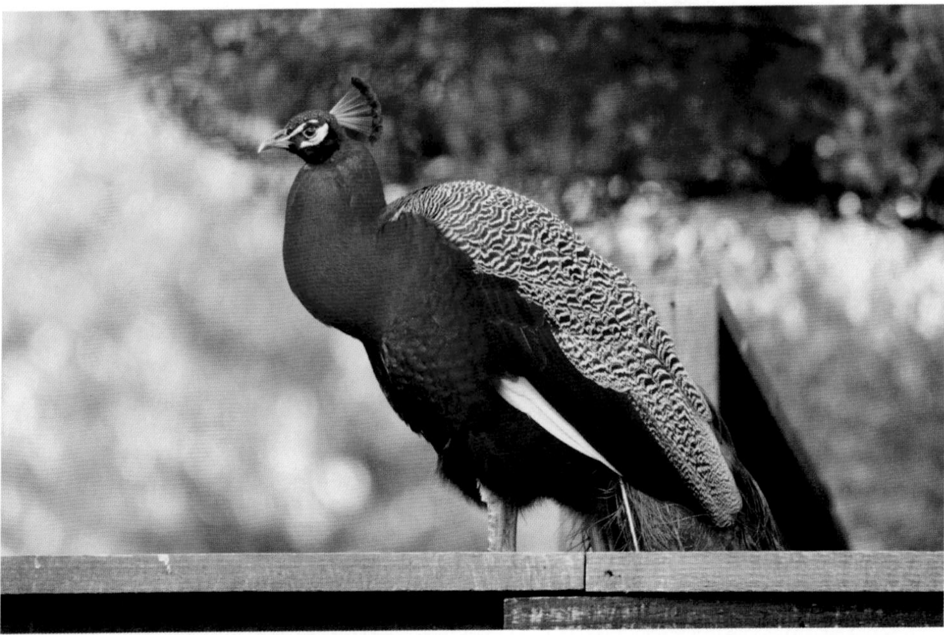

Not the New Normal

Exotic species—plants, insects, and wildlife that are not native to your area—are ubiquitous. Invasive ones tend to grow, mature, and reproduce rapidly. They lack the predators, competitors, and diseases that kept them in check in their homeland, enabling them to outcompete native species.

Nature's ecological systems fine-tuned over many thousands of years can't adapt to this sledgehammer evolution. Texas Invasives states, "As invasive species spread and take over ecosystems, they decrease biodiversity by threatening the survival of native plants and animals."

Costs are financial as well: decimated crops, lost tourism revenue, damaged water systems, and more. "To date, more than 800 aquatic and terrestrial species have invaded Texas," states Texas Invasive Species Institute. "Existing impacts in Texas are in excess of one billion dollars per year."

Exotic and Invasive Mammals

The bane of Texas since the 1680s, wild hogs are domestic swine that escaped or were released, occasionally crossing and creating hybrids with Eurasian boars. Feral hogs can gain up to a hundred pounds a year. Females can breed at six months and produce up to two-dozen piglets annually. A well-fed wild hog population can double in four months.

About half of the nation's feral hogs live in Texas—two million and climbing. They cause over fifty million dollars in agricultural damages. But they are urban as well, digging up golf courses, parks, even corporate campuses, and are a plague in some Trinity River bottomlands.

Wild hogs can be dangerous. When hiking, stay aware from signs like digs

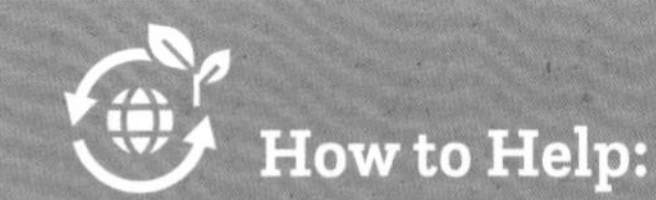

How to Help:

If on rural land, be aware that deer feeders that dispense corn can also attract wild hogs.

▼ Feral hogs rooting for food destroy habitat and damage property.

Smuggler looking content at In-Sync Exotics.

The United States has more tigers in captivity than exist globally in the wild. In-Sync Exotics northeast of Dallas is home to over five dozen tigers, many rescued from abusive situations. Smuggler was discovered by US Customs and Border Protection agents in Laredo who found the Bengal tiger—twenty pounds underweight at four months of age—stuffed into a small wire cage. The alleged smugglers had attempted to declaw the tiger with pliers. In-Sync's team repaired the damage and helped Smuggler become the happy, healthy tiger he is today.

(patches of plowed ground), wallows (large shallow puddles), and rubs (mud smears low on trunks). Since wild hogs are primarily nocturnal animals, you're unlikely to encounter them. But if you do, find safety up a tree.

Another mammal invader that's almost as much trouble as the wild hog is the nutria. Often confused with beavers but lacking the sizable flat tail, nutrias are semiaquatic, twenty-pound rodents introduced from South America for the fur trade. Devastating to wetlands, they consume a quarter of their body weight daily and destroy about ten times more plant matter than they consume.

Insect Invaders: Red and Green

Red imported fire ants can swarm and sting at once, able to cause fatal anaphylactic shock. Built to bite, the tiny red ants possess a dedicated venom-injecting stinger dispensing alkaloid venom that causes necrosis. Fire ants are a severe threat to the young of ground-nesting birds, reptiles, and mammals, including livestock. Fire ants attack nests of harvester ants, a primary food source for Texas horned lizards, the state reptile. Annual damage costs in Texas are around one million dollars.

Green and Texas ash are popular landscape trees threatened by the emerald ash borer (EAB), a metallic-green beetle from China with wood-burrowing larva. It has killed hundreds of millions of ash trees in the United States and Canada, damaged serious acreage in Tarrant County around Eagle Mountain Lake, and is becoming established in Denton.

EAB is bound for Dallas and could be a disaster for its major nature attraction, the 6000-acre Great Trinity Forest. Consulting arborist and tree activist Steve Houser estimates that ash is 40 percent of the canopy. Brett Johnson, senior environmental coordinator and urban biologist with the City of Dallas, is concerned for the dozens of insect and spider species that feed on ash trees.

Other insect invaders include the Asian ladybeetle, which displaces our more beneficial and friendly native ladybug (visit the Lost Ladybug Project for more information); crazy worms, from Japan and Korea, which look and act like earthworms, but damage rather than enhance soil; and hammerhead flatworms—foot-long earthworm predators from Southeast Asia that secrete noxious chemicals and can replicate if smashed or cut in pieces, so they must be chemically killed and safely disposed of.

How to Help:

Learn to identify EAB and their damage. Report all incidents through iNaturalist and Texas Invasives apps.

▼ Emerald ash borers are both beautiful and devastating.

Crustacean Conquerors

A female zebra mussel can birth more than one million offspring a year. No wonder the small bicolored bivalves are taking over area lakes. Eagle Mountain, Worth, Grapevine, Lewisville, and Ray Roberts reservoirs are rated as infested, with populations seen in Lavon and Ray Hubbard. North Texas gets most of its water from reservoirs. Mussel multitudes attach to pipes, pumps, and valves, endangering water supplies.

Native to western Asia, the mussels spread by hitchhiking on watercraft. Voracious filter feeders, zebra mussels deplete water nutrients needed by aquatic plants and wildlife. Their microscopic larvae are almost impossible to detect or filter. When reservoir water levels drop and stranded mussels die off, it causes a horrendous stench.

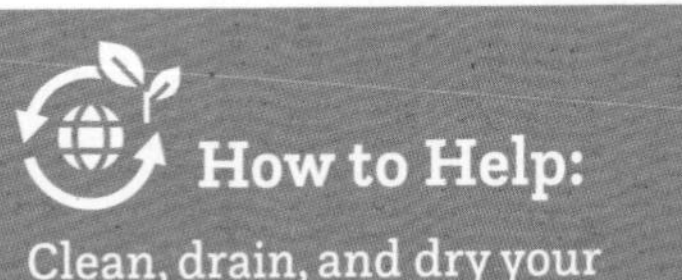

How to Help:

Clean, drain, and dry your watercraft, trailer, and gear following Texas Invasives instructions to avoid spreading zebra mussels.

Privet Peril

"I love cedar waxwings, but I cringe to think how many privet berries they disperse," says David Hurt of Wild Birds Unlimited. The flocks visit each winter and strip berries from ornamental shrubs. USDA rates the privet berries' food value to wildlife as low. It's been called "popcorn for birds."

Species of privet were brought to the United States in the late 1700s as an evergreen landscape shrub and soon spread. Chinese privet is estimated to inhabit two and a half million acres across southern states.

Sam Kieschnick, Texas Parks and Wildlife urban wildlife biologist for DFW, estimates "at least half of forested parkland here contains privet—and the invasion is continually spreading," noting a preponderance of iNaturalist observations. Michelle Villafranca, Fort Worth Park Operations and Natural Resources planner, concurs, adding that "most older parks, especially ones with riparian habitat, have privet in the understory."

Privet in North Texas is a triple threat:

Glossy privet (*Ligustrum lucidum*), with two- to four-inch shiny leaves, adapts to low-light environments by growing tall and branching high. Natives displaced: Carolina buckthorn, cherry laurel, and rusty blackhaw viburnum.

Chinese privet (*Ligustrum sinense*), small-leafed and less bulky, takes the next tier. Its flexible wood reaches twenty feet tall and turns woodland trails into tunnels. Natives displaced: beautyberry, roughleaf dogwood, possumhaw, yaupon holly, and native swamp privet.

How to Help:

Do not plant these species (and discourage others from using as well). Plant natives and volunteer to remove invasive species at your local park or preserve.

▲ Cedar waxwings poop and plant a plethora of privet bushes.

◄ A Georgia study demonstrated that removing privet infestations quadruples bee species.

Quihoui privet (*Ligustrum quihoui*), at three to ten feet tall, is slighter with small narrow leaves. But its lower growth and tangled branching patterns can make passage impossible, even for wildlife.

Ten More Terrible Plant Tyrants

Amur honeysuckle. Almost as bad as privet in urban woods; introduced from Asia in the 1700s.

Bastard cabbage. Over a yard tall and covered in yellow flowers. It is outcompeting beloved bluebonnets along roadsides.

Bradford/callery pear. Bradford pear is a cultivar of callery pear, native to Southeast Asia. Its showy flowers produce berries that revert to the thorny callery when sprouted.

▲ Water hyacinth can grow so thickly that other plants can't receive sunlight.

How to Help:

Do not empty your aquarium or water garden plants or creatures into local waterways.

Chinaberry. One of the top ten invasive species in Texas. Its waxy round fruit can float far. Originally from Australia.

Chinese tallow. As bad as chinaberry, a mature tree can make 100,000 seeds each year.

Johnsongrass. Rated in the ten most noxious weeds worldwide. The six-foot-tall grass from Asia and Africa infests parklands and prairies. One plant can spread two hundred feet by rhizome.

KR bluestem. Popularized for forage by the King Ranch in South Texas, it now grows in over half the state, threatening the minuscule number of prairies remaining.

Tree of heaven. The flowers are pretty, but this plant smells terrible, secretes chemicals toxic to other plants, and releases fumes that can cause human illness.

Rounding out the offenders are two aquatic plants that block sunlight for native plants, reduce water oxygen, foster mosquitoes, and clog waterways. Noted for its attractive flowers, **water hyacinth** escaped from residential water gardens into Mountain Creek Lake. **Hydrilla**, a floating fern that can grow an inch a day, is present in Grapevine, Lewisville, and Ray Roberts reservoirs.

Migration

It's ninety-nine degrees in August and fall bird migration is underway. Nearctic-Neotropical birds that fly to the northern states and Canada to breed have finished raising young. It's time to go home. Bird photographer Nick DiGennaro is sweating in the heat, snapping photos of colorful warblers. Fort Worth Audubon Society member Charley Amos is tracking raptors that follow migrating songbirds.

Birds, along with some insects, are the only great migrations remaining in North Texas. Gone are bison herds that once maintained the prairie with

▼ Sunrise stirs migrating waterfowl at Hagerman National Wildlife Refuge.

The 100th anniversary of the Migratory Bird Treaty Act was 2018.

voracious appetites, trailed by wolf packs, also extirpated. The rhythms of migration tie us to a larger world, to a sense of time not artificially defined. To participate in migration, even as an observer, reunites us with our human core.

The Rhythm of Migration

North Texas sits on the eastern edge of the Central Flyway. In spring migration, a couple billion birds from the tropics funnel through the American heartland. They spread across the continent's northern tier, where fewer predators and more food aid in raising young. Starting in late summer, the course reverses for fall migration.

Two-thirds of the continent's birds migrate, some on facultative journeys in search of resources or warmer weather. Others endure hard-wired obligate pilgrimages of origin—a sense of home so intense they travel long distances to return every year. We do as well—it's called Thanksgiving, and we often fly there, too.

Viewing avian migrators takes planning, patience, and a bit of luck. Timing and locations adjust for weather. The BirdCast website from eBird helps by providing up-to-date predictions of bird migrations in easy-to-read map form. Yet nothing tops years of experience. Local birders and North-Central Texas Birds offer these tips:

▼ Hudsonian godwits visit Hagerman National Wildlife Refuge on their way south.

- Spring migration is very weather driven. Lingering winters and ice storms in the north and tropical storms and heatwaves in the south can cause massive changes in migration.
- Shorebirds are sometimes the first arrivers in March on their way north, but most pass through in April and May. The same goes for songbirds and the raptors that pursue them. Wading birds and waterfowl follow.
- In most years, migration peaks the first week of May. Some birders don't sleep.
- May and June are all about nesting. Scattered bird migration movement begins in July.
- Fall migration keys around when young are fledged, stretching from August to November. Hummingbirds and shorebirds take off first. Then songbirds and birds of prey head south in waves.

▼ A few pairs of bald eagles raise young at Lake Texoma each year.

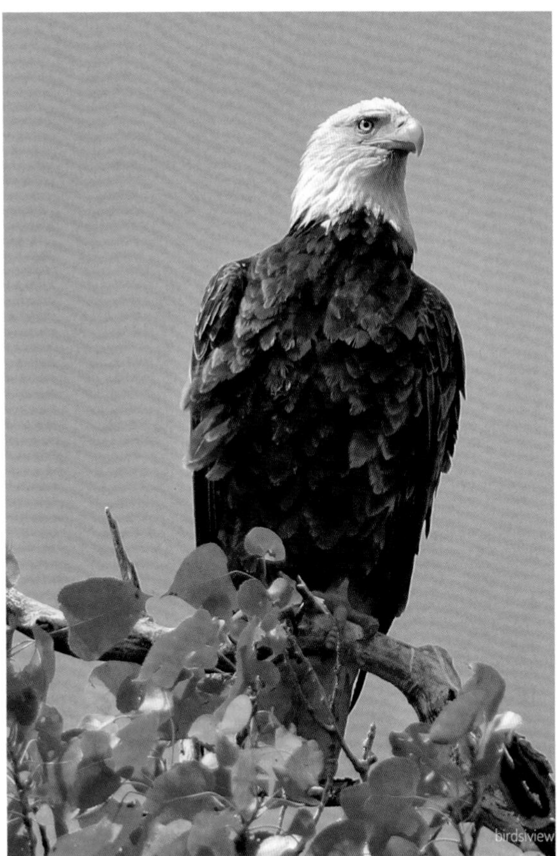

Peak times for watching feeders are April and May and October and November. Take note of how bird species change. Add foods especially suited for your migrators. Participate in Backyard Bird Count and FeederWatch.

Birds pack on fat for energy, adding a third or more to their usual weight. Some diurnal migrators can eat on the wing.

▲ An American robin and cedar waxwing argue over yaupon berries.

Hagerman National Wildlife Refuge is legendary for its winter waterfowl, with geese by the tens of thousands.

- Bald eagles arrive late autumn at reservoirs and wetlands, nest from winter to spring and depart by midsummer.
- "When ducks fly south for the winter, we are the south," reminds Charley. Peak season for viewing geese, cormorants, and other waterfowl is mid-November to January. Some will continue southward as weather worsens.
- Cold weather and reduced insects prompt some local breeding species, such as buntings and flycatchers, to fly farther south for winter.
- Northern cardinals and blue jays from the north swell the local ranks in winter, along with berry-raiding cedar waxwing and robins.
- Drawn by a better supply of prey, new raptors join the usual mix in winter, including ferruginous, sharp-shinned, and rough-legged hawks, northern harriers, and more.

Prairie parks like Parkhill and Connemara are excellent for winter hawk watching.

► A volunteer holds three expired yellow-breasted chats in front of collision-killed birds being counted by Lights Out volunteers.

Reducing Bird Strikes

Migration is a perilous journey. Mortality rates are about six times greater during migration. Topping the list: predators, food scarcity, weather threats, hunters, exhaustion, and building collisions, particularly office towers. Bright lights attract and disorient night-migrating birds, leading to window strikes, killing over 900 million annually nationwide.

The Lights Out Texas campaign urges homes, businesses, and municipal operations to turn off nonessential exterior lights during peak migration periods from eleven at night to six in the morning. Dark terrain below offers birds little incentive to veer off course. Energy and money savings are a good side benefit.

In Dallas, volunteers count collision-killed birds in a defined downtown area on mornings during Lights Out. The data informs scientists which bird species are most susceptible to collisions and how much impact Lights Out efforts make.

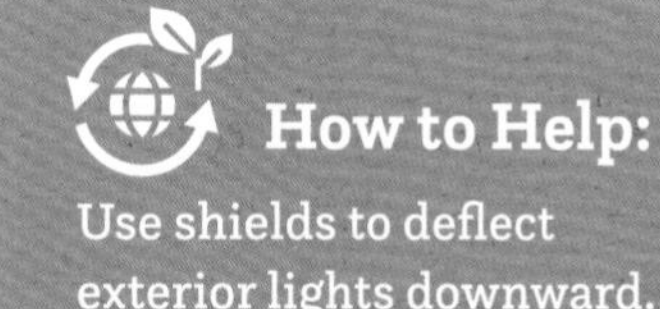

How to Help:

Use shields to deflect exterior lights downward. Install motion sensors to minimize use.

Monarch Flutterby

Flying along with birds on a route similar to the Central Flyway are monarch butterflies. From North America's northern tier, monarchs funnel down to winter homes in Mexico and return in spring. The State Insect of Texas, millions pass through annually. North Texas lies on the main path's eastern edge, making sightings range from scattered to sizable flocks. Monarchs migrate up to a hundred miles a day, flying a quarter mile or higher at speeds up to thirty miles per hour in favorable winds.

◄ North Texas Master Naturalist volunteer delicately places a Monarch Watch tag.

Explore the world of monarchs at Monarch Joint Venture, Monarch Watch, MonarchNet, Pollinator Partnership, and Xerces Society.

When they pass through, monarch enthusiasts are ready. Alarmed by a 90 percent decline in monarchs over the past two decades, volunteers install milkweed, a host and nectar plant for monarchs, in gardens and parks, often working with Monarch Watch's Bring Back the Monarchs Campaign.

Without intense intervention, monarchs may become seldom seen. Loss of milkweed to development, agriculture, and excessive mowing is enormous, and the use of herbicides and pesticides causes further damage. Declining winter habitat in Mexico and climate-change induced severe weather are serious threats. US Fish and Wildlife service is working with volunteers to create Monarch Waystations along I-35, from the Mexico border into the Great Plains. Other ways to help include:

- Lobby your local park department to reduce mowing to allow for more wildflower nectar plants and leave standing foliage for overwintering eggs.
- Urge cities to create pollinator gardens in parks, schools, and municipal operations.
- Start a pollinator garden at your church, business, or other enterprise.
- Get your yard or enterprise registered as a Monarch Waystation.
- Plant more native milkweed (not tropical milkweed).

Creeks and Watersheds

Were you a creek kid? Many naturalists and nature professionals started out as creek kids who whiled away their childhood days exploring their local creek. North Texas Master Naturalist Karen Wiley remembers her creek adventures: "My earliest childhood home was on Waco Creek. Kids built a shelter fort on the bank with sticks for a roof that gave some shelter from the rain. Parts of the drainage were exposed limestone so we could easily find fossils, including a perfectly preserved fern."

And the creatures! Steve Houser, president of Arborilogical Services and fellow creek kid, remembered how "there was always something new to see or learn about at the creek. We would trample through the water in our bare feet and try to net fish and tadpoles and frogs to study. We would tie a piece of bacon to a string and poke it down a crawdad hole, and when they grabbed it, we'd pull them out."

I was a creek kid, too. As I grew older, I followed the tributary downstream, crawling through honeysuckle tangles, sneaking along the edges of lawns, until I reached the towering pale limestone walls of White Rock Creek. Just seven years old and a mile from home, I dared not go farther. I stared and wondered where the creek was bound and if there were kids like me along it, chasing tadpoles.

Creeks as Connectors

Creeks are conduits of a child's imagination. But the creek-kid experience is sadly less common now, too many fears of snakes, poison ivy, and weird stuff in the water. An uncontrolled, unsupervised environment with some risk—no wonder we creek kids adored it!

Creeks connect. Long before roads, creeks were our infrastructure, borders,

Reservoirs exist on some large creeks, including Denton Creek (Grapevine Lake), Mountain Creek (Joe Pool Lake, Mountain Creek Lake), Village Creek (Lake Arlington), and White Rock Creek (White Rock Lake).

Creek kid Dan Northcut, director of environmental studies at Saint Mark's School of Texas:

"I was born and raised in Oak Cliff and spent a lot of my childhood at Coombs Creek. I tell my students all the time, 'Figure out where the nearest creek to your house is and go there.' I can hear the city all around me, but in the creek is another world. Nature is there. All wildlife needs water and vegetation along our creeks is a major food source. One of the highlights of nature in Dallas is always going to be creeks."

and identity. Just as streets move vehicles and connect communities, streams do the same with water while also providing travel corridors and habitat for wildlife.

White Rock Creek's journey starts in Frisco in Collin County and crosses Plano, Richardson, and north Dallas to White Rock Lake near my home in East Dallas. It continues southeast of downtown where it joins the Trinity. The watershed, including over thirty tributaries, covers a hundred square miles (64,000 acres).

Confluence

Nearly sixty years ago, I gazed down White Rock Creek and wondered where it went. On this day, I stand at its confluence with the Trinity. Scott Hudson, president of the North Texas Master Naturalists, guided me to this spot deep in the Great Trinity Forest bottomlands.

▾ White Rock Creek merges into the Trinity.

My boots slip on the slick clay bank. I carefully inch closer to the edge, squat down, and touch the water. White Rock Creek had squeezed into channels and snaked through wild sections for over thirty miles to run through my fingers. From here, it comingles with the Trinity and flows to the Gulf of Mexico.

This creek connects my past to my present and North Texas to the waters of the world. I touch the same water in existence since Precambrian times, repeating without pause through the hydrological cycle. A moment of utter timelessness.

Every child should have a creek. It inspires future careers in biology, hydrology, botany, eco-journalism, and more, bonding them to the earth and their community, fostering a sense of responsibility for the future.

Watersheds

Everyone lives in a watershed. Whether it drips into the driveway and onto the gutter or caresses the leaves of a creek-side tree, every drop of water not absorbed or evaporated must go in one direction or another, obeying its own Continental Divide, to eventually merge with the closest creek and flow to the Trinity.

In rural areas, only a third of precipitation flows into creeks or rivers. The rest is absorbed. Plant foliage and roots slow water and enhance absorption. But urban areas are dominated by impervious surfaces: 70 percent in industrial and commercial areas and 50 percent in multifamily or zero-lot-line developments.

> In the United States, rivers west of the Continental Divide in the Rocky Mountains drain to the Pacific Ocean. Those to the east head to the Atlantic Ocean or Gulf of Mexico.

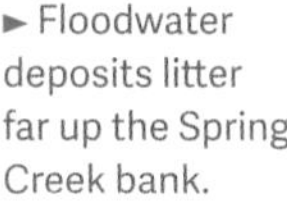

► Floodwater deposits litter far up the Spring Creek bank.

A zip code search at these websites will reveal your watershed: Texas Parks and Wildlife: Texas Watershed Viewer, US Geological Survey: Find Your Watershed, and EPA: How's My Waterway.

Surf your creek on Google maps. Activate terrain and traffic views and follow where it goes upstream and down. Then switch to satellite view and see how much, if any, riparian corridor remains.

Creek kid Julia Catherine Koch, a North Texas Master Naturalist:

"When the family moved to northwest Richardson, we kids were thrilled that it had a nearby pond and winding Prairie Creek. My twin sister, Valerie, and I would wander for hours each day, exploring the creek. Its steep, white rocky banks were full of slivers of rock that made for great skippers across the water. One of my fondest memories was building a little fort with our best friend. The three of us would play Huckleberry Finn all summer long. Now I live two doors down from my childhood home in a house that sits directly on the creek. My husband and I enjoy the birds, turtles, beaver, honeybee hives in old black willow trees, and, most recently, a pair of river otters."

Most impervious surfaces are roadways and parking lots, which the Center for Watershed Protection terms "habitat for cars." Water flows via surfaces and gutters into storm sewers that usually empty into the closest stream. This forces pollutant and litter-laden water into creeks at high velocity, hastening erosion and debilitating riparian corridors.

After reaching the Trinity or a significant reservoir, some water begins the journey again by being withdrawn and sent to purification plants. More pipes relay purified water to users. In turn, wastewater is piped from bathrooms and kitchens to treatment plants. Finally, treated wastewater effluent is released into rivers or reservoirs, and the urban water cycle begins again.

◄ A great egret rests in Julia Catherine Koch's backyard along Prairie Creek.

The Natural Creek

A classic natural creek features a meandering channel of water flanked by gentle terraces where riparian plants grow, restraining erosion and providing wildlife habitat. In rainy periods, water covers the terraces, enabling riparian plants to thrive and keeping the area moist for amphibians and reptiles.

Thick riparian and floodplain greenery slows stormwater rushing toward the creek, enhancing soil absorption while filtering pollutants and litter. During heavy storms, the stream overbanks and spreads into the floodplain with nutrient and silt-rich water.

Wide riparian corridors are the key, stressed Mikel Wilkins of the landscape architecture and engineering firm TBG Partners: "Develop too close to the creek edge and you can't fit in the trails people need. Inevitable erosion threatens streets and buildings nearby. We've spent millions regionally repairing sanitary sewers damaged by erosion."

Get to know your local creek. Take a folding chair to the bank and spend thirty minutes watching birds and other wildlife. Try your hand at sketching in a nature journal. Show your creek a little love by bringing a grocery sack with you and collecting litter.

Riparian corridors also provide travel cover for wildlife. Close access to water is imperative while raising young. Consistent moisture fosters lush riparian plants and larger trees like bur oaks that provide prime nesting habitat and bounteous food.

Creek kid Richard Grayson, with the Aquatic Alliance for the Texas Stream Team:

"A creek, more or less a gully, beside my house flowed into Nix Creek, where I began a lifelong pursuit of whitewater skills. I built rafts that would hardly float. Sails were worthless, so I figured out paddling technique. It was enough to get down the creek, Huck Finn style. Being in the creek offered excitement that you couldn't get on dry land. Back in the day, we skinny-dipped in that creek. When I learned canoeing at scout camp at age 11, that's all she wrote. I was forever hooked on the freedom of going with the flow."

▲ Richard Grayson in his happy place: paddling the West Fork.

▲ A majestic tree will soon topple, taking other trees with it.

Urban Creeks Under Assault

The natural creek is fast disappearing because of poor stormwater management. Rapid runoff scours banks, stripping away stabilizing plant cover. Erosion undercuts, toppling creek-side trees along with the banks. The creek widens—encroaching on streets, buildings, and infrastructure—and deepens.

Urge your city leaders to follow stormwater practices suggested by Tarrant Regional Water District and North Central Texas Council of Governments.

Ultimately, water can no longer overflow into the floodplain except in the most catastrophic floods, depriving those plants of the regular silt-rich infusions on which they depend. It becomes a channel, a mere water conduit, sometimes even lined with concrete, and the natural creek is no more.

Backyards

Cindy Kearney had finally had enough. The president of the Dallas chapter of Native Plant Society of Texas (NPSOT) couldn't tolerate lifeless Bermudagrass another day. She vanquished the grass with layers of cardboard, then installed annuals and finally perennials. Now she says, "I am the only one on the block with fireflies and bees of all sorts, plus butterflies, toads, dragonflies, anoles, garden spiders, hummingbirds and lots of songbirds." Watching from her office window as walkers linger by her yard is a highlight of working from home.

Grow Your Own National Park

Birds and amphibians are declining precipitously. Insects that form the food chain foundation are under siege. Wildlife habitat disappears to development on a massive scale every day. Plant species from overseas fill most yards and run rampant in urban parks, edging out natives that wildlife depends on. What can we do?

Create a new national park—twenty million acres of protected habitat and native plants—one yard at a time. That's the big idea of Doug Tallamy's Homegrown National Park movement. Today's environmental front line is not the wilderness of John Muir and Aldo Leopold. It's the urban ecosystem where the millions of people who can impact change reside.

According to the Xerces Society, turfgrass is the nation's largest crop, around forty million acres.

It all starts with native plants. "In the past, we have asked one thing of our gardens: that they be pretty," writes Tallamy. "Now they have to support life, sequester carbon, feed pollinators, and manage water." Join the movement by rewilding your yard with native plants, wildlife abodes, and nesting sites as outlined in this chapter.

▲ Cindy Kearney's yard: from blah (top) to beautiful.

▲ Forest tent caterpillars are essential food for baby birds.

Oaks and More

Trees anchor the residential ecosystem and oaks are a keystone species. In *The Nature of Oaks*, Tallamy states that oaks are the most critical tree for wildlife in 84 percent of the nation's counties. Acorns are a vital wildlife food for mammals and birds.

More than 900 species of Lepidoptera—most of them moths—depend on oaks. No other tree family comes close. Their caterpillars power the food web. Birds are dependent on soft-bodied insects to feed their young. Moths and butterflies are essential pollinators and themselves serve as food for birds, bats, and more.

Remove these invasive trees and vines right away: Bradford pear, chinaberry, Chinese tallow, Japanese honeysuckle, and paulownia.

If you have room for just one tree, plant a native oak: a red oak for fall color or white oak for sweet acorns. Dry or rocky soil? Try Cross Timbers stalwarts like post oaks. For perennial leaves, plant live oaks, using escarpment live oaks in upland areas.

Create a natural forest effect with understory trees that provide a safe option to plant beneath powerlines. These are attractive, superior berry producers: Carolina buckthorn, cherry laurel, Mexican plum, roughleaf dogwood, and rusty blackhaw viburnum. Eve's necklace has gorgeous pollinator flowers, and Hercules club is host to the giant swallowtail butterfly.

Though dead or dying trees, called snags, can threaten property if they fall, leave them standing as long as possible to provide cavity-nesting sites and wood-burrowing insects for birds.

The final tier is shrubbery. Chances are your landscape shrub hails from Southeast Asia. Remove these invasive shrubs right away: Amur honeysuckle, nandina, and privet. None will please birds and pollinators like native beautyberry, elderberry, possumhaw, flameleaf and smooth sumac, and yaupon holly, or the smaller coralberry and aromatic sumac.

Pleasing the Pollinators

Remove, reduce, or replace lawn grasses. Groundcovers provide better habitat for amphibians and reptiles, keep the ground cooler, and conserve more moisture in hot weather than turf. For lawns, buffalograss and blue grama top out at six inches, require little water and no fertilizer. Or fill the space with garden beds. And you don't have to mow any of them!

Nectar needs of adult bees and butterflies are relatively general. But plants required by the caterpillars that become butterflies, called host plants, can be highly specific and almost exclusively native. Milkweed's superpower is serving as larval host for monarch butterflies while producing prodigious nectar for all.

Let your artistic spirit run free by creating a pollinator garden, blending the different flower colors and leaf textures, balancing their heights and shapes. Make it wildly natural or formal and refined. Select plants so that something's always colorful.

Start your brainstorming with these online databases, many of which include links to native plant nurseries:

- Audubon Society's Native Plants Database (searchable by zip code)
- Dallas Butterflies (select Butterfly Gardening)
- Lady Bird Johnson Wildflower Center Native Plant Database
- Native Plant Society of Texas (select Resources)
- Texas SmartScape (select Native to Texas)
- Xerces Society's Plants for Pollinators (select Southern Plains)

Two books by Doug Tallamy, *Nature's Best Hope* and *Bringing Nature Home*, are essential to rewilding your yard and community.

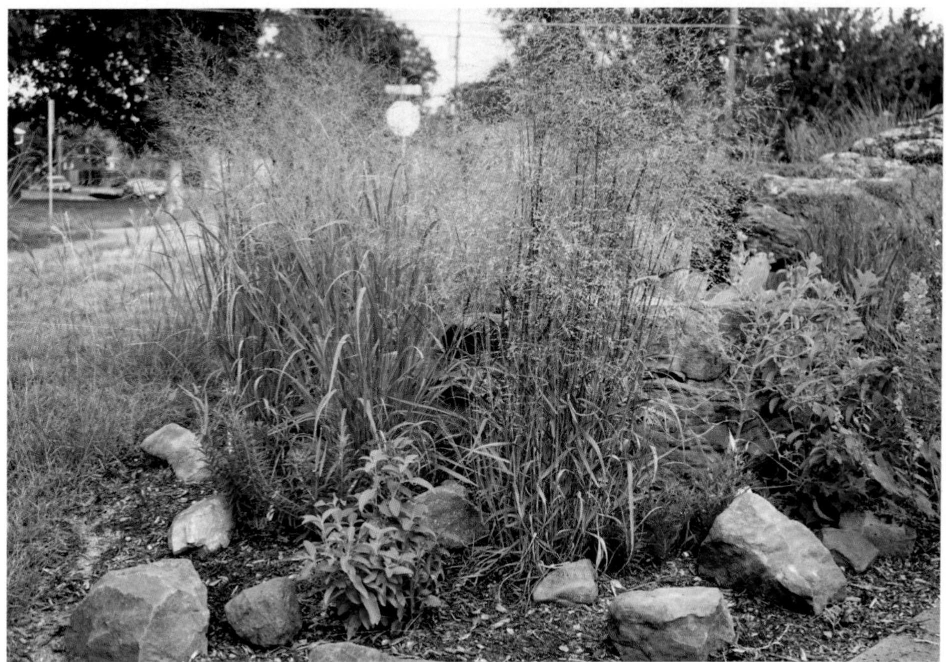

▲ Boulders, switchgrass, and wildflowers make a diverse entrance to an Oak Cliff property in Dallas.

Native Plant Society of Texas chapters and nature centers often have native plant sales and offer lots of local tips. Visiting native plant gardens is a great way to see combinations firsthand. These gardens are a perfect place to start:

- **Texas Discovery Gardens in Fair Park.** Great signage shows how different areas are arranged according to which pollinators and birds they attract.
- **Native Texas Park at George W. Bush Presidential Library in Dallas.** Amble a lovely one-mile path.
- **Botanical Research Institute of Texas in Fort Worth.** Peruse their amazing gardens and pond.

Pint-Sized Prairies

Anyone can do a pocket prairie. Alley, curb, and driveway strips are perfect for unorganized swaths of native grasses and wildflowers and can often be created inexpensively from seed. Make sure plant heights comply with city regulations.

Or construct a naturalistic prairie garden. Little bluestem, larval host plant for many skipper butterflies, holds it down with clumps of delicate, light teal foliage that turns rusty in autumn. Select dramatic plants to go between, such as the bold, silvery rattlesnake master and delicate lavender Gregg's mistflower. Turk's caps bring in the hummingbirds.

Bring on the Birds

Most nutritious for songbirds are native plants: hackberry and beautyberry, sideoats grama and inland sea oats. When birds are rearing their young, they require insects such as oaks' generous production of caterpillars. A garden flush with wildflowers will have more flying insects, attracting insectivores like kingbirds.

But bird feeders bring them in for a closer view. Early spring features migrators exhausted by flying from the tropics and have unique food needs. Suet blends and mealworms help for times like breeding and cold weather, plus attract woodpeckers and flickers. Hummingbird feeders are good when blooms abate.

A key bird feeder issue is deterring squirrels and larger birds like European starlings and white-winged doves that descend en masse, emptying feeders and chasing off smaller birds. For every problem, including rodents drawn by fallen seed, bird enthusiasts have a solution.

Great tips can be found at these websites:

- **Wild Birds Unlimited** gives tips for outwitting squirrels and rodents in "Get Started."
- **All About Birds** from the Cornell Lab of Ornithology covers the art of bird feeders, houses, and baths in "Bird-Friendly Homes."
- **All About Birds** covers what different birds eat and when in their "Bird Guide."

Water: the Universal Attractant

A reliable water source is essential for wildlife. Birdbaths are good, but water containers hung from poles are safer from ground predators. Birds enjoy standing misters, which also provide water for insects, attract dragonflies, and moisten soil for amphibians and reptiles. If you've got a pool and are near a lake, don't be surprised if mallards move in.

Amphibians, reptiles, and mammals need ponds. Keep it shady for most of the day or inhabitants might overheat. Aquatic plants provide shelter for amphibian eggs and decaying matter for tadpoles to eat. Build where water naturally collects. Maybe you'll attract dragonflies to lay eggs, producing generations of mosquito eaters.

But even just a shallow depression of water surrounded by plants helps reptiles and amphibians. Or nestle a water trough or tub into your groundcover for amphibian fun, making sure to install an exit ramp. Set up a game cam by your water feature and check the nightly action.

▲ Collin County homeowner assists a mallard mom by providing a pool ramp.

▲ A koi pond provides much habitat for wildlife.

Amphibian and Reptile Homes

Surround your water source with toad abodes, as simple as sinking an overturned ceramic flowerpot into the dirt and partially propping it up with rocks or wood or knocking a hole in the side. "I have a pile with rocks of different sizes next to my water feature, and snakes and toads hang out in there," says Annika Lindqvist, an amateur herpetologist

An organically maintained yard with lots of compost provides friable soil amphibians and reptiles can dig into. Flat stones or boards laid loosely on top creates prime garden snake habitat underneath, especially in winter. Use no glyphosate herbicides that are harmful to aquatic creatures.

Want more green tree frogs? Cap a three-foot length of one-inch PVC pipe and drill a hole a few inches above the bottom for drainage. Drill another hole near the top and hang from a nail on a fence or structure. Best to locate where it can fill with rain or water.

Outside cats can decimate small reptile populations, as well as songbirds. Consider a catio.

NATURAL HISTORY & ECOLOGY

Leave the Leaves

Even though only 2 percent are pests, bugphobia is fueling an insect Armageddon. A passion for yard neatness, especially fastidious autumn clean ups, are devastating. Many insects overwinter in hollow stems, leaf litter, and soil.

► Some overwintering insects look like dried leaves.

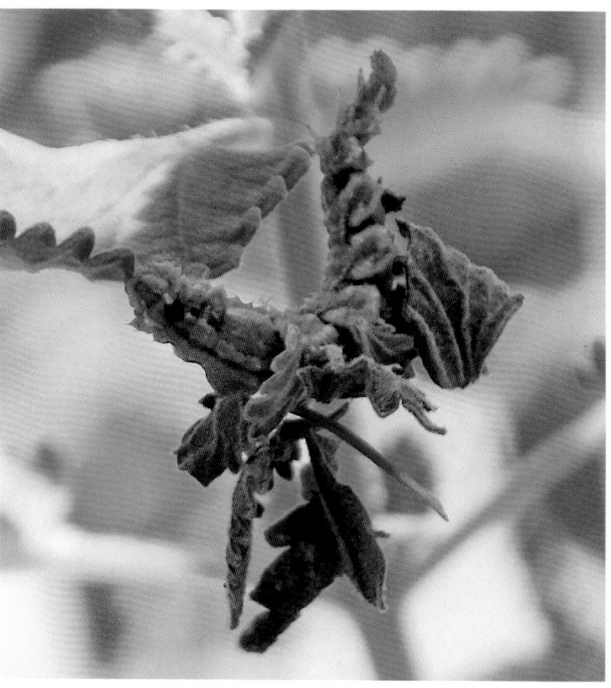

Just like birds, amphibians and reptiles need insects. Xerces Society's Leave the Leaves campaign extols the full gamut of invertebrates sheltering in fallen leaves: spiders, snails, worms, beetles, millipedes, centipedes, and more. These support rodents, reptiles, amphibians, and birds that rely on them for food through winter.

Leave as many leaves as possible without smothering plants. Mulch with leaves for winter warmth. Rake or vacuum excess leaves off to the side, pile in corners, or into the compost pile. Above all, do not shred. Enjoy bountiful butterflies and fireflies next year.

Bat, Bee, and Bird Abodes

Tree cavities for nesting are scarce in residential areas, making birdhouses essential. There's a science to it: the entrance size, perch or no perch, how high off the ground, which direction to face. Many birds are open nesters. Suspend empty hanging baskets lined with coir fiber. Shallow ledges appeal to doves, swallows, and other cliff dwellers. Locate away from rain. All About Birds' Bird-Friendly Homes has excellent advice and even how to make your own.

Bat houses also require fact-based locating and design. Bat Conservation International's website features terrific easy tutorials, plus other advice on encouraging bats. Local evening bats require shelter for the entire colony of a hundred or so, necessitating a group of houses.

Standing dead vegetation provides long hollow spaces where native bees can create compartments and lay eggs. Create bee hotels by drilling holes into woodblocks or bundling narrow PVC pipes or bamboo stems. Or lean logs against surfaces that receive rain and wood-boring insects will make cavities.

Seventy percent of native bees nest in the ground. Help them by providing bare patches of soil in warm but not sunbaked locations or create bee sandboxes. Bumblebees will patronize special nest boxes at tree bases. More on native bee support at Xerces Society.

After Dark

"Look, everyone—bats!" The small dark shapes of evening bats flitting about are barely visible in the low light of dusk, yet still a thrill. A perfect start to a full moon walk hosted by Twelve Hills Nature Center, a five-acre Dallas preserve tucked away in Oak Cliff.

Our group of ten North Texas Master Naturalists, led by center director Marcie Haley, meanders down the loop trail in the moonlight. Then I feel it over my left shoulder, drawing closer—silver light spilling over the school's roofline to the east. I watch my own shadow magically appear before me. Others do as well. Soon we're singing, "I'm being followed by a moon shadow, moon shadow, moon shadow . . ."

▼ Pink evening primrose opens as the full moon rises.

▲ Naturalists examine night creatures under ultraviolet light.

John Wilt shines his ultraviolet flashlight in a copse of trees, hoping to spy the sphinx moth larva that glows in UV light. His son raises and releases them once they emerge from pupas. Amanda Pounds makes a big score. A brown millipede crawling along glows lime green under her UV flashlight. "Its little antenna especially fluoresces," she notes.

Conversation ceases as we walk beneath trees that dim the moonlight to a faint silver mist. Marcie hopes to hear the nocturnal Chuck-will's-widow, its name an onomatopoeia of its call. But the sound, which is incredibly loud for the bird's size, comes from an adjacent neighborhood. A barred owl's *who-cooks-for-youuuu* call drifts down from tall trees.

We gaze at the sky on the edge of Twelve Hills' spectacular re-creation of Blackland Prairie from a refuse-strewn lot where a dilapidated apartment complex once stood. Stalin SM, an astronomy enthusiast from India, points to the ecliptic arc across the night sky, noting the "Dog Star" Sirius. It's so bright—the brightest star visible to us, visible even in cities—because it is a binary star system. The night has a way of revealing wonders.

The larvae of some dragonfly species crawl out of the water only under cover of night and struggle free of their larval exoskeletons to become flying adults.

▲ Lights Out volunteers search for collision-killed birds.

A Night Diminished

Urban wildlife finds freedom in the night. Long after dark, when people sink into their television sets, nocturnal animals like coyotes roam neighborhood streets. Raccoons and opossums emerge from trees and dens to rummage for food. Large trees in the cities' older areas foster a robust population of owl and arboreal bats. If you're lucky enough to be where the soil is damp and few chemicals used, the flashing light show of fireflies is yours to enjoy. Amphibians hold down the nocturnal soundtrack of summer, joined by cicadas and crickets, accented by bird and mammal calls.

How to Help:

Connect exterior lights to motion detectors instead of leaving on all night and use shields that direct light downward. LEDs' blue light is particularly disruptive to circadian rhythms. Participate in Lights Out Texas during spring and fall migrations.

But it's not just city creatures that like the dark. In *The End of Night*, Paul Bogard writes that at least 30 percent of vertebrates and more than 60 percent of all invertebrates are nocturnal. Yet published studies examining night wildlife are few, and those that do are not positive. Light and noise pollution is altering avian reproduction and may be one factor in bird populations' 30 percent decline. Collisions with exterior lights, especially in tall buildings, kill 600 million to one billion birds each year, according to Cornell Lab of Ornithology.

▲ The group gathers beneath a massive bur oak at Twelve Hills and listens to the night.

While artificial lights can adversely impact wildlife, diurnal grackles and other "parking lot birds" have changed their rest and feeding cycles to take advantage of them. Common nighthawks and other flying insectivores hunt well past their usual nightfall period. Multiple spider webs frame many a front door, snaring insects flying to the porch light.

The light at dawn and dusk reduces matter to its essence. Shadows stretch from the west long before sunset, turning objects to silhouettes. The color drains from the environment as the rising night overtakes the light. Many animals emerge in this period, hunting and foraging in the murky illumination's relative safety. Some crepuscular wildlife ventures out on overcast days or bright moonlit nights.

Symphony of Darkness

Step outside one night a few hours after sunset. Go to the darkest area possible, near a riparian corridor or backyard pond if possible. Set your phone aside and let your eyes adjust to the darkness. Notice the lack of definition, texture, and color. In the dark there is no separation. Look for shapes and movement, rather than defined objects. Close your eyes and open your mouth slightly. What do you smell? What do you taste? And mostly, what do you hear?

Your presence may make the amphibians timid. Drape yourself loosely with a blanket or coat so that they don't see your hands or feet fidgeting.

They'll soon accept you and get back to making music. Green tree frogs are the rhythm section, the males' sharp nasal honks blast up to seventy-five times a minute to create a pulsating chorus. The relaxed throaty rattle of leopard frogs add melodic touches to counter the bleating gargle of Gulf Coast toads. Bullfrogs, the amphiband's tubas, bellow low notes. Crickets' relentless chirps join the katydids' odd array, ranging from raspy trills to songbird-like chirps to teeny duck quacks.

Then the big players come in: birds. The deep, rounded hoots of barred owls and the slower, lower, simpler call of great horned owls provide the bass. The surreal harsh squawks, raspy bleats, croaky woc-a-wocs, and utter screams of the black- and yellow-crowned night-herons add sharp accents like cymbals. Northern mockingbirds, notorious blabberbeaks, will continue singing well into the night. No night sound pierces more than the Chuck-will's-widow: an insistent and loud series of two short shouting chirps followed by an ascending swoop. These nightjars have big mouths. Literally.

The vocalists are mammals whose calls convey emotional states. The surreal mystery sound could be a red fox: a nasal chattering play or fighting sound called glekking, a wide range of quirky bark alarms, and thin, high howls. Raccoons emit sequences of high-pitched hisses, chirps, and whistles, and rough growls and snarls. All suddenly fall silent upon hearing the tortured screech of the bobcat or the melodic yips of coyotes, the "song dogs."

Bats, Bees, and Moths

Some night denizens are silent: moths. Most subsist on nectar, aphid honeydew, fruit secretions, and a variety of leafy matter. Some moths like luna and polyphemus don't eat at all. By the front door might be the natty leopard moth with white wings adorned by black rings. Moths are a favored food of bats, amphibians, and night birds. Though some flock to light, studies show that artificial sources lead to a decline in moth populations, which impacts pollination of night-blooming flowers.

Opening only at night, the fragrant white, deep trumpet-bell blooms of big, rangy jimsonweed are irresistible to Carolina sphinx and hawk moths that use their long proboscises to extract nectar while pollinating them. Pink evening, yellow evening, and Missouri primroses have a specialized native bee pollinator: the Texas nocturnal sweat bee.

Moth evangelists like Sam Kieschnick, a Texas Parks and Wildlife biologist, offer mothing nights. Hang up a vertical, light-colored sheet at night, reflect light off it (ultraviolet is best), and watch what lands. Attract more with a paste of mashed ripe fruit and cheap beer on the sheet. The big score

Mothing events are plentiful during National Moth Week, observed in mid-July for over a decade.

▲ A multitude of moths fascinate university student Kaitlynn Davis at a moth week event in Lewisville.

is when giant yellow io or green luna moths show up. Lovely green lacewings and bronze dobsonflies with enormous pincers spice up the fray.

Colonies of Mexican freetail bats in North Texas are small. More often seen are tree nesting evening bats and eastern red bats. Home in on these fast and erratic moving mammals with a bat detector app and echolocation device. Bats avoid being under bright lights where predators can see them easily, so look for them on the fringes of illuminated areas.

Moon Rhythms

This night finds me moonstruck by silver illumination filtering through the clouds. Against this pearlescent glow, the twisted majesty of oak tree limbs create art from the process of life. I feel tugged by this reflective sphere, my emotional tides pulled in its wake along with the sea. At this moment, North Texans line the western sides of lakes and prairies to watch it rise while paddlers slip through the luminous moonlit water of the Trinity.

Even the brightest urban glare can't obscure the moon. The full moon rises over the eastern horizon just as the sun sets in the west. Each night the moon wanes, it rises about forty-five minutes later, peeling a slice of itself each night. By the third quarter, it won't rise until midnight and continues to diminish until it's a shadow without stars suspended against the cosmos, the old moon cradled in the new moon's arms, visible only by light reflected from the earth.

▲ Kristi Kerr Leonard leads a full moon hike.

The new moon rises and sets with the sun, conjunct with it, lost in the coronal glare—a daytime phenomenon. Until it moves away from the light and waxes into the crescent moon seen following the sun as it descends below the evening horizon, sinking forty-five minutes later each night. To find the first-quarter moon, look east at noon.

Become comfortable with darkness by taking a moonwalk with friends. The second quarter leading to the full moon provides plenty of illumination. Ultraviolet flashlights and bat detectors are cool toys but spend most of the time walking slowly and quietly. Prairies with clear sightlines to the east are perfect. Bring a blanket so you can stop for a while, soak in the moonlight, and submit to the night.

In lunar gardening lore, the first two quarters of the waxing moon draw plants upward toward the light and channel energy into leaves and blooms. The third quarter waning moon is when plants bear seed and shunt energy to roots below. The fourth quarter is when lunar energy is at its lowest, making weeding easier. Seeds sprout best when sown at new and full moons.

Citizen Science

"As I pulled into the parking lot, I could see sheets bathed in the ethereal glow of black lights," said Spring Creek Forest Preserve board member Carol Garrison. "Adults and children were flitting from sheet to sheet—not unlike the nocturnal insects they were looking at—with smiles on their faces. And there was Sam, holding a huge beetle and sharing his enthusiasm for insects."

Go in-depth with *The Field Guide to Citizen Science*, by Timber Press.

"An estimated 150 people, including many children small to large, gathered at the Preserve just as night was falling," wrote board member Barbara Baynham. "Sam Kieschnick, a Texas Parks urban wildlife biologist for DFW, brought a team of experts so that every screen had someone to help identify. Many folks stayed until nearly midnight."

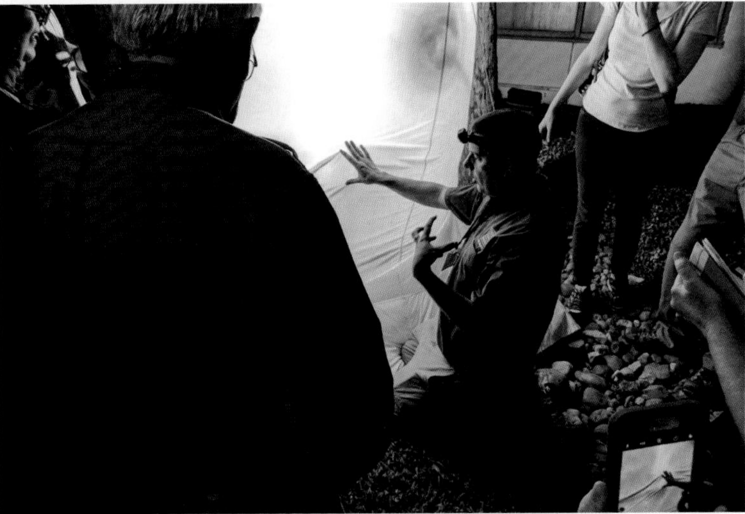

◄ Sam Kieschnick educates and inspires for a night of mothing at another master naturalist event.

The iNaturalist Community

Cellphones bring you closer to nature? What an incongruous thought! Yet most adults and many kids at moth night were wielding one, taking observations for Spring Creek's iNaturalist (iNat) project by photographing plants and wildlife, then uploading to the iNat website (there is also an iNaturalist mobile app), and seeking an identification or verification. Participants racked up over 1386 observations of 357 confirmed species of insects, amphibians, reptiles, and mammals.

Spring Creek Preserve now has over 15,000 observations of over 1700 species recorded in nine years. Did the larval host plants increase moths and butterflies? Have the new native forbs improved the rabbit population? Did forest management techniques broaden diversity? Experiences on moth night confirm, but the proof is in the iNat observations.

Few are better iNat cheerleaders than Kieschnick, who is also the top iNat observer in North Texas with well over 102,000 observations of more than 9500 species. He rallies the troops, drawn heavily from Texas Master Naturalist chapters, to participate in multiple bioblitzes each year. Participants record as many species as possible within a specific location and time.

> "iNaturalist engages the community like nothing else I've seen. Policy makers and public land managers can recognize the constituency of naturalists just by looking at the number of observers on iNaturalist."
>
> *—Sam Kieschnick*

◄ Scott Hudson of North Texas Master Naturalists wades into Bittern Marsh to make an observation.

City Nature Challenge is the biggest bioblitz, a good-natured competition between metropolitan regions. Dallas–Fort Worth took top prize in 2018. In just three years, the challenge went from a two-city state contest with 20,000 observations to an international competition of nearly seventy urban areas and almost a million observations.

The iNaturalist's sound and photo identification system and resulting monster database is managed by the California Academy of Sciences and National Geographic Society. Yet only a human who knows the species and terrain can confirm observations. Some naturalists become renowned for identifying certain species. Debates can get spirited!

Few possess more enthusiasm for iNaturalist than Arlington's Zach Chapman, who has logged over 20,000 observations and 2800 species, some of them seldom seen, in just six years. He uses a camera, rather than a phone, for its photo quality and high-powered zoom. "I've always been curious and iNaturalist feeds that. I also want to do my part to help. And I can keep track of places I've been. It's great to be part of this large, awesome community."

The iNat community—over 2.5 million strong—includes biologists, ecologists, land managers, and others who depend on the data. Meteorologists use it to track the impact of climate change. Officials can lobby for increasing park budgets by proving previously unheralded naturalist patronage. Writers and educators find insight into what lives and grows in an area. It was indispensable for this book.

Bob O'Kennon, aka Botany Bob, is the second most prolific iNat observer, with 45,000 observations of 3600 species. In the process, the research scientist at Botanical Research Institute of Texas discovered a new species of beetle—*Cis okennoni*—that was named for him.

Sky's the Limit

How did the telegraph broaden the impact of citizen science? Skilled amateur weather enthusiasts like Benjamin Franklin and Thomas Jefferson had long kept fastidious records. But once telegraph lines went intercontinental in the 1860s, weather watchers, many of them in the military, were able to quickly relay air pressure, temperature, wind, and rain data. The first weather maps resulted, produced by the US Army Signal Corps, according to David Finfrock, longtime senior meteorologist for NBC 5.

National Weather Service stations now do those tasks, but community weather data collectors still play a valuable role. "Since rain measurements vary tremendously over short distances, it is helpful to have individuals with home weather stations who post their data on the internet," says Finfrock. Participate by connecting your station to Weather Underground.

Citizen weather scientists also safeguard us in monitoring severe storms. SKYWARN classes from the National Weather Service train weather spotters

▲ Cumulus clouds could indicate a potential severe storm.

in cloud formations, wind patterns, and other severe weather signatures, adding critical visual information to weather station data and helping save lives through improved predictions.

Citizen Nature Brigade

They train for forty hours in the classroom with experts in biology, botany, ecology, geology, mammalogy, ornithology, weather, and more. Then they spend hours learning firsthand on educational field trips. Once graduated, they put in a minimum of eight hours of advanced training classes and at least forty hours of volunteer work every year to retain certification. Such is the commitment of Texas Master Naturalists (TMN), sponsored by Texas Parks and Wildlife and Texas A & M AgriLife Extension Service. Volunteers restore habitat from little pollinator gardens to large-scale natural areas, install native seeds and plants, pull out invasive privet, and develop trails. It can be strenuous. And rewarding. Healing the land continues long after we've passed away.

As of 2020, more than 15,200 TMNs have contributed nearly six million hours of community service and created more than two thousand miles of trails, adding up to over $121 million worth of work statewide. Dozens of North Texas nature centers, schools, and gardens depend on TMN volunteers from four chapters: Blackland Prairie (Collin and Hunt Counties), Cross Timbers (Tarrant and Parker Counties), Elm Fork (Denton, Wise, and Cooke Counties), and North Texas (Dallas, Kaufman, and Rockwall Counties).

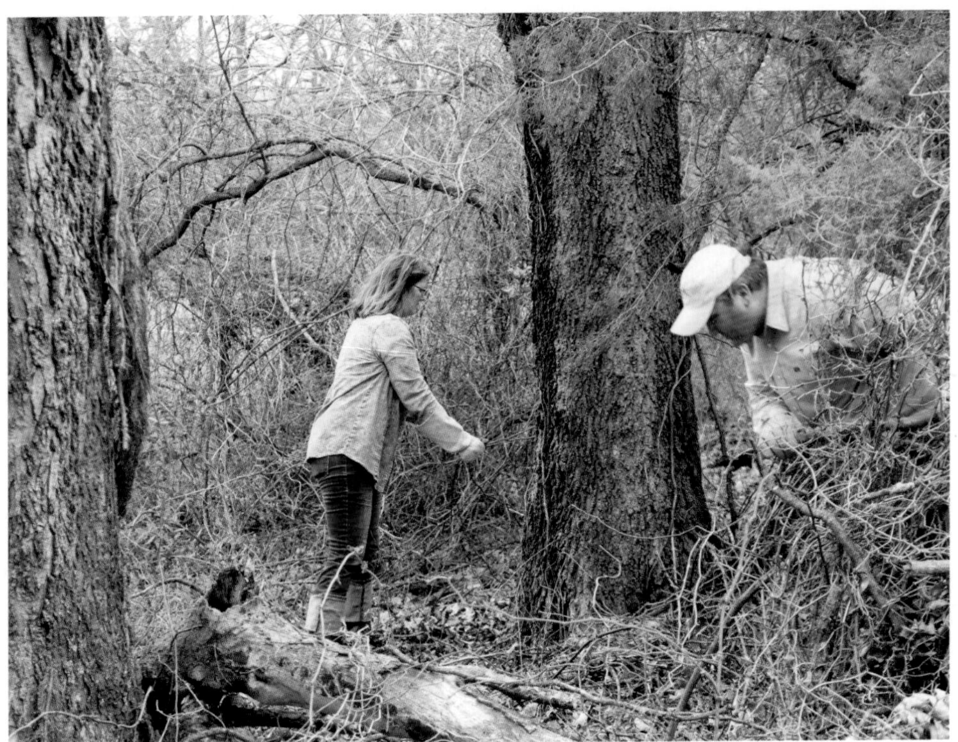

▲ Blackland Prairie Master Naturalists clear a trail.

Scott Kiester exemplifies TMN's powerful impact, with over 7000 volunteer hours for the Elm Fork and two other chapters. A retired petroleum geologist, his projects are many, including breeding bird surveys. But nothing is closer to his heart than being TMN project manager for Lewisville Lake Environmental Learning Area, where he works among a fleet of volunteers.

"Why do I do all this? Long ago, my mom, a widowed schoolteacher, had a saying 'You can rust out like grandpa's old tractor behind the shed, or you can be like the Ford Carryall he drove until it would drive no more. Your choice.' I choose to be the Carryall. I want to leave the world a greener place and I have the honor and privilege of being part of a dedicated bunch of folks who do just that."

TMNs also instigate deep change one conversation at a time, explaining gently and without judgment alternatives to rodenticides that poison owls. They convey why leaving dead trees standing in the parks creates homes and food for songbirds and how letting the grass get a little weedy makes for more fireflies. As citizen scientists, they teach by example.

It Begins with Birds

The world's longest-running community science survey is the Christmas Bird Count (CBC), administered by the National Audubon Society, dating to the early 1900s. The North Texas count, now compiled by Jim and Gretchen Peterson, has been ongoing since the 1950s. A big boon, says Jim, was the

► Birding instructor Shannon Love uses a high-powered scope to identify birds for students at John Bunker Sands Wetlands.

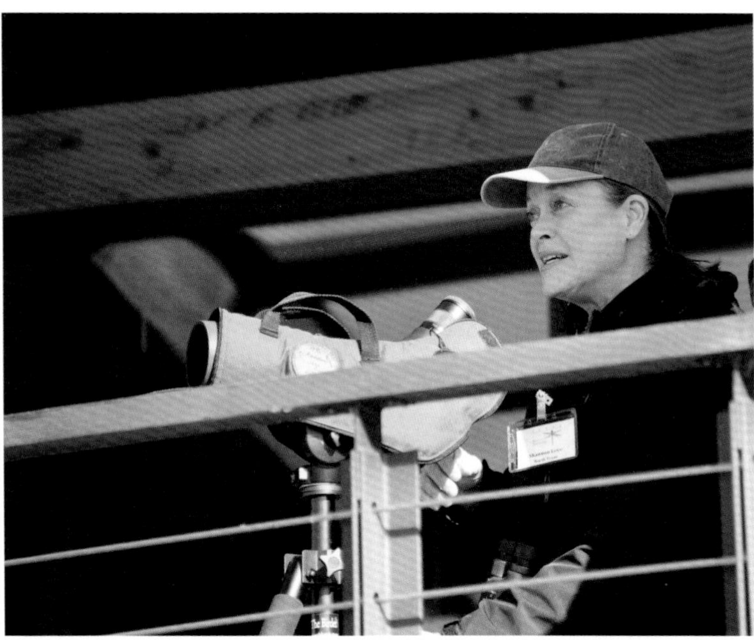

► North Texas Master Naturalists survey birds on the Trinity Forest Trail in Dallas.

Wild Birds Unlimited sponsors Christmas Bird Count, Great Backyard Bird Count, FeederWatch, and more.

Keep up with many of these groups and projects through the GreenSourceDFW weekly email newsletter.

move to online data entry in the '80s. Learn all about the count and more at the North-Central Texas Birds website.

From mid-December to early January, experienced birdwatchers follow assigned routes, counting each bird they see. In the process of tracking bird movements for science, participants sometimes find rare-to-the-area birds such as red-throated loon and long-eared owl. Another top-level census is the North American Breeding Bird Survey, launched in 1966 and coordinated by the United States Geological Survey and the Canadian Wildlife Service.

Individuals and groups can participate in the Great Backyard Bird Count held for four days each February since 1998. Coordinated by Cornell Lab of Ornithology and the National Audubon Society, the program asks participants to watch and identify birds for fifteen minutes or more at least once in the period. Observations feed into eBird, one of the world's largest nature databases. Merlin and eBird apps make it easy.

New to birdwatching? Project FeederWatch is for you. Coordinated by the Cornell Lab of Ornithology and Birds Canada, a small fee grants you a welcome kit with a bird identification poster and activity calendar. More than a bird census, FeederWatch tracks issues such as abnormal plumage, bill deformities, or missing head feathers.

A World of Citizen Science

Whatever your area or species of interest, there's a community science project for you. Odonata Central crowdsources dragonfly and damselfly data and sponsors twice yearly Odonata Olympics. Lost Ladybug Project uses citizen science to determine why some native species are disappearing.

Downwinders at Risk offers training in the use of portable air monitors and helps maintain the SharedAirDFW monitoring network with several partners.

Texas Stream Team trains volunteers in water chemistry and riparian botany who then collect and sample water quality in creeks, rivers, and water bodies. Aquatic Alliance, coordinated by Richard Grayson, oversees several groups, schools, Scout troops, and Texas Master Naturalists, monitoring fifty Dallas and Collin County sites. Many teachers integrate the practice into their curriculum.

Over 11,000 Certified Water Quality Monitors assess more than 400 sites across the state on a weekly to annual basis. Monitors are often the first to report water issues like pollution spills, fish kills, and *E. coli* spikes to state environmental agencies. Stream Teamers also evaluate riparian health, especially the impact of high-velocity stormwater. Nurdle Patrols focus on microplastics pollution.

Members of the Dallas Paleontological Society have discovered fossils, some of them rare. Local science museums display several. Dallas and Tarrant archeological societies add to the historical record through digs supervised by trained archeologists.

Texas Master Gardeners (TMG), a Texas A & M AgriLife program, installs gardens in schools and public places and presents talks and classes. TMGs donate over 40,000 hours statewide for a value of over a million dollars. Citizen scientists are often at the front line of invasives detection. At the young age of ten, Sam Hunt observed on iNaturalist the first emerald ash borer in North Texas.

FIELD GUIDE: NORTH TEXAS SPECIES TO KNOW

Birds
108

Insects and Spiders
120

Insect and Nectar Eaters

Woodpeckers

Downy Woodpecker

Dryobates pubescens

Red-Bellied Woodpecker

Melanerpes carolinus

Pileated Woodpecker

Dryocopus pileatus

WHERE TO FIND THEM: Downies and red-bellieds can be found in most spaces with forest or sufficient trees. You can hear, if not see, pileated on **Adventures 5, 13, 16,** and **22**.

Whatever the type of forest, there is a woodpecker for it. Small downies are frequent visitors in wooded residential areas. The larger and oddly named red-bellieds, whose red crest is far more visible, also haunt backyards. King-sized pileateds are rare sights of the deep woods, particularly along rivers and lakes.

Sensory Clues Downies make light hoarse whinnies. Red-bellied sounds include rolling churrs and rough coughs, and males can drum up to nineteen times per second as a call. Mysterious birds that prefer high canopies, the loud *wuk-wuk-wuk* call of the pileated is definitive.

Habitat Prefer hardwood or conifer forests with large trees with cavities for nesting. Pileateds and red-bellieds have a love of swamps and river habitats. Downies and red-bellieds adapt to open woods, savannahs, and fence lines.

▲ Downy woodpecker inspecting for a nest.

▲ Red-bellied woodpecker searching for insects.

Pileated woodpecker in flight.

Food In addition to burrowing insects, wood-boring beetles, and a variety of caterpillars, woodpeckers eat termites and large ants such as carpenter and harvester ants using their sticky, barbed tongues. These birds consume a considerable amount of berries, seeds, nuts, and tree sap when insects are few. Pileateds and red-bellieds are known to eat tree frogs, bird eggs, and small fish.

Habits Locate insects in trees by drumming loudly on the trunk or branches, causing minute echoes in hollow spaces. Red-bellieds secure acorns and pecans in tree crevices and pound into pieces with their beaks.

Tidbits Deep holes in rotten wood are a sign of pileateds and can be so deep they break trunks apart. • Abandoned feeding cavities are used by other birds for nesting. • Red-bellied and pileated woodpeckers cache nuts and seeds in bark crevices for winter eating. • Downies hang out with flocks of mixed bird species, especially in winter. • Downies and red-bellieds enjoy feeders with suet and peanut butter. • Red-bellied tongues can reach an inch or two past bill tips. • European starlings invade and occupy red-bellied nests.

Hummingbirds

Ruby-Throated Hummingbird

Archilochus colubris

Black-Chinned Hummingbird

Archilochus alexandri

WHERE TO FIND THEM: Any area with sufficient flowers and scattered tree cover, especially **Adventures 1, 2, 6, 7, 8, 9, 14, 15, 21, 22,** and **23.**

Sugar feeders lure hummingbirds.

These flying jewels migrate from the tropics to breed in North America and are precision flyers, able to move up, down, sideways, and backward at high speeds. *Archilochus* means "without feet," because hummingbird feet are too small and weak to do much more than hold a perch. Ruby-throateds are found all over North Texas, with black-chinned favoring the western half.

Black-chinned hummingbird.

Sensory Clues Emit tiny chirps, but wings beating at fifty to seventy times a second make a whirring sound.

Habitat Prefer semi-open habitats with flowers, such as parks and residential areas.

Food Hummingbirds hover over flowers and insert their very long tongues into those flowers for nectar, consuming a surprising amount of insects in the process. They prefer flowers with deep wells where nectar collects and know how long it takes nectar to refill on different flower species. They eagerly patronize hummingbird feeders that are refilled frequently with fresh sugar water. Spider webs are raided for insects and small bugs are plucked from air and off foliage.

Habits Known for their insane aerial-dogfight defense of hummingbird feeders and flower patches as well as spectacular flying courtship maneuvers.

Tidbits Walnut-sized cup nests built by females are lined with spiderwebs and plant down and camouflaged with lichens. Nests expand as chicks grow. • A hummingbird's heart in flight can beat twenty times per second. • Females are usually larger than males.

Songbirds and Passerines

Buntings

Painted Bunting

Passerina ciris

Indigo Bunting

Passerina cyanea

WHERE TO FIND THEM: Lightly wooded parks and prairies with wooded fence lines, especially on **Adventures 1, 3, 6, 7, 8, 10, 14, 15, 17, 21, 22,** and **23.**

The most beautiful birds in North Texas. Male painteds' coloration of blue, green, red, and yellow looks artist designed. The male indigos are a stunning solid light royal blue and have exquisite songs. They migrate to the tropics after fledging offspring.

Sensory Clues Male painted buntings emit long, melodic, short phrases with as many as ten different songs a minute. Males will exchange with each other—definite show-offs. Male indigos boast high-pitched short phrases

Painted bunting surveys the scene.

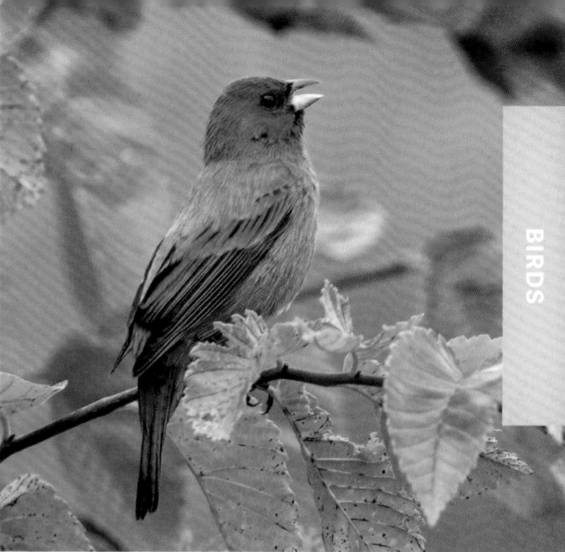

Indigo bunting singing.

often sung in pairs. Young indigos learn from older males where they hatched, making for unique song neighborhoods.

Habitat Buntings favor edge habitats where they can fly from trees and pluck seeds and insects from neighboring grassy areas.

Food Like most seedeaters, buntings consume insects in the breeding season.

Habits Males defend territories of about three acres with song and even fighting, but focus on the nest area during breeding.

Tidbits • Nests are built by females a yard or so aboveground in brushy vegetation. • The tidy cups of dried foliage are bound together with spider webs. • Indigo feathers are not blue tinted but instead have structuring in their feathers that reflect blue waves in sunlight. • Buntings, especially painteds, are trapped for illegal export trade as cage birds. • They migrate at night using stars and other aids for navigation.

Northern Mockingbird

Mimus polyglottos

WHERE TO FIND THEM: A fixture in residential yards and parks with upland forests and wooded fence lines.

The state bird of Texas, they are boastful, singing continuously, even well into the night, especially on full moons. The male taunts birds infringing on territory with almost comical dances and wing moves.

Sensory Polyglot refers to one who is multilingual. This applies to northern mockingbirds because they appropriate songs from other bird species and even dog barks, musical instruments, and mechanical noises like sirens.

Habitat Northern mockingbirds favor dense shrubbery adjoining open areas, making residential lawns a prime habitat, but they can also be found in wooded areas.

▲ Northern mockingbird eats roughleaf dogwood berries.

Food This opportunistic eater favors crawling and hopping insects along with berries and fruits. They also eat spiders, snails, pillbugs, caterpillars, and earthworms. It's large enough to tackle small crawfish and lizards such as geckos.

Habits These birds favor high viewpoints to perch and find other birds to bother and are relentless at clearing birds and mammals, including pets and humans, away from their nests.

Tidbits Northern mockingbirds were popular cage birds in the 1800s because of their song variety. • More common in Texas than in any other state. • Males have over 150 different songs.

Eastern Phoebe

Sayornis phoebe

WHERE TO FIND THEM: Grasslands with brushy mottes and wooded fence lines near water.

A grassland bird found in low-density residential areas as well as larger parks with prairie grasses and creeks. Often seen perching on tall foliage stems and singing relentlessly.

Sensory Its call is a distinct *fee-bee*.

Habitat Eastern phoebe stays close to water and prefers prairies with riparian corridors. Needs brushy areas for breeding and overwintering but makes use of bridges and structures.

Food Perching on tall foliage, eastern phoebe drops down to peck ground bugs. It also plucks bees and other flying bugs off flowers and from the air and eats berries and seeds in times of scant insects.

Habits These are loner birds that don't socialize much with other phoebes, even mated pairs; the females chase males away after egg laying.

Tidbits Female constructs nest, occasionally using old American robin or barn swallow nests, but she also builds on roofed structures. Tends to reuse nests annually. • The first bird to be banded in North America, by John James Audubon.

Eastern phoebe prefers being close to water.

Birds of Prey

Barred Owl

Strix varia

WHERE TO FIND THEM: Forested areas along creeks and rivers in twilight hours and into the night, especially **Adventures 2, 3, 5, 6, 12, 13, 16, 17,** and **22**.

Master of the urban evening, the most prevalent big owl in North Texas. Fly silently as they hunt, a shadow in the night that catches walkers by surprise. Barred owls prowl neighborhoods, but they prefer riparian corridors.

Sensory Its famous call sounds like "Who cooks for you?" but it also makes a wide variety of calls, earning the nickname 'hoot owl," which it shares with great horned owls.

Habitat Requires considerable swaths of mature trees capable of large cavities for nesting; prefers habitat near water for greater prey diversity.

Barred owl making a daytime appearance.

Because they hunt in dim light, owls' hearing is extremely acute. They can detect movement underground or beneath snow. Its asymmetrically placed ears create minutely different sound perceptions that aid in pinpointing sound locations.

Food Barred owls prey on amphibians, crawfish, and reptiles, plus squirrels, rabbits, rodents, and occasionally other birds.

Habits Slightly afraid of humans, sometimes seen napping on tree limbs.

Tidbits Appropriates nests of hawks, crows, and squirrels, sometimes eating the inhabitants. • Prefers natural tree cavities but will use owl boxes if placed high in a large tree. • Will wade into shallow water after prey such as fish.

Bald Eagle

Haliaeetus leucocephalus

WHERE TO FIND THEM: Nesting pairs at **Adventures 2, 4, 5,** and **17**.

The white heads of mature bald eagles make them an unmistakable sight, contrasting with their beautiful chocolate feathers. North Texas boasts at least six breeding pairs that nest in larger preserves adjoining rivers and reservoirs, but they have also been seen hunting in urban parks such as White Rock Lake. The pair at John Bunker Sands Wetlands Center has a considerable nest-cam following.

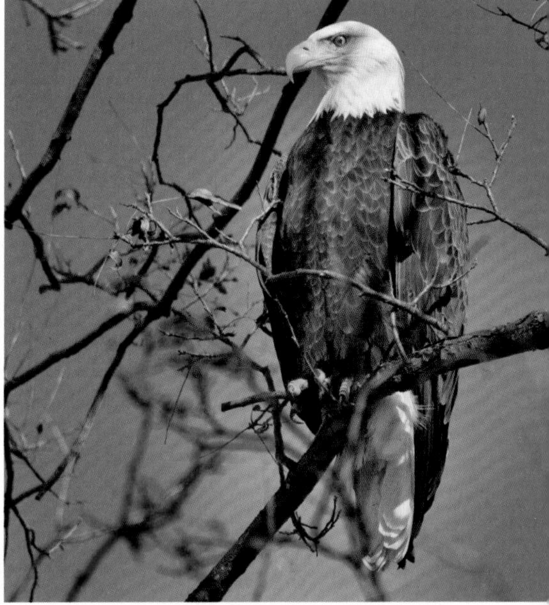

▲ Bald eagle perched at White Rock Lake in Dallas.

Sensory These big birds make surprisingly meek, high-pitched whistling calls. Hikers are sometimes startled by these diurnal hunters' large moving shadows.

Habitat Bald eagles prefer forested areas adjacent to large bodies of water away from heavily developed areas.

Food These are expert fisher birds and snatchers of water snakes, able to see fish deep in the water from several hundred feet up and a rabbit on the ground from a mile away. They eat small mammals, large rodents, and birds. Known for harassing other raptors into dropping prey that they then catch and eat, and even steal from humans who are fishing. Scavenges carrion.

Habits Low tolerance for human interference, especially around nests, but will hunt in populated areas.

Tidbits Builds nests a couple yards across and almost as deep inside a tree crown, on large rock ledges, and occasionally in electrical towers. • Impressive high-flying aerial courtship displays. Females sometimes make surreal noises during copulation. • Can take five years for plumage to become fully white on heads. • Capable of short bursts of swimming. • Lives two decades or more.

Most birds of prey have two centers of focus, enabling forward and side sight simultaneously to create an extremely wide field of vision. Forward-facing eyes create excellent binocular vision able to see accurately at far distances.

Cooper's Hawk

Accipiter cooperii

WHERE TO FIND THEM: Look for them hunting in mornings at forested parks and neighborhoods.

Cooper's hawk is now an urban fixture.

Extremely skillful flier that primarily hunts birds. Short, stout swings and long rudder-like tails enable these woodland hawks to fly through tree canopies at high speed, snatching young from nests and birds on the fly or from feeders. These hawks are becoming increasingly common in cities.

Sensory Silent hunters, they make loud, grating calls to defend their nest and during courtship.

Habitat Wooded residential areas and a wide variety of forests.

Food Prefers larger birds like European starlings, doves, and pigeons, and sizable songbirds such as blue jays and American robins. Preys on woodpeckers and flickers, plucking them right off the tree. Occasionally takes squirrels, rabbits, and bats.

Habits Their classic accipiter flap-flap-glide flying style changes to rapid wingbeats when in pursuit of prey, enabling quick directional changes.

Tidbits Seen perched on limbs plucking feathers from prey, causing a rain of feathers (and feather piles) on the ground. • Kills bird prey by repeatedly crushing with powerful talons or by holding underwater. • Chicks' eyes turn from yellow-green to orange and then red.

Herons

Great Blue Heron

Ardea Herodias

Little Blue Heron

Egretta caerulea

WHERE TO FIND THEM: At most Adventures featuring lakes, wetlands, rivers, and large creeks.

A fixture in wetlands and lake inlets, blue herons stalk the shorelines in slow, careful steps, creating little water disturbance. Great blue herons are wary yet curious and undeniably majestic in size and bearing. Sadly, little blue heron populations declined by over 50 percent between 1966 and 2015.

Sensory Incredibly vocal and loud birds with squawks, honks, croaks, and clucks that are often harsh and extended.

Habitat Marshes, swamps, sheltered bays, lakes, and slow-moving rivers.

Food Herons dine mainly on fish, along with amphibians, baby turtles, snakes, and crustaceans, but will venture out to snatch a rodent, lizard, or small bird. Little blues will forage in damp grasslands, raking the ground to disturb prey.

Habits These elegant birds stand motionless in water while scanning for food. Then they extend their long, curved neck in a flash, nabbing prey. It's thrilling to see a great blue gulp a fish whole or impale it with a sharp bill, flip it into the air and swallow it. Herons will raise their wings and do other crazy things to startle fish.

Tidbits Great blue herons have chest feathers that produce down, which they extract with fringed claws on their middle toes. They use the down to clean wetland residue and food debris from their body. • Great blue herons

▲ Great blue heron flying past reservoir outlet.

▲ Little blue heron stalking prey.

nest in groups, sometimes mixed with great egrets, little blue herons, and others. Heronries are known for their noise levels and overwhelming poop aroma. • Heron chicks have lethal beaks and can be extremely aggressive toward weaker siblings. • Great blue herons can also hunt at night thanks to plentiful rod-type photoreceptors. • Though five feet tall, great blues weigh only five to six pounds. • Beavers craft habitat perfect for blue herons.

Double-Crested Cormorant

Nannopterum auritum

WHERE TO FIND THEM: At places with lakes, wetlands, and rivers, especially **Adventures 2, 4, 5, 6, 10, 17, 22,** and **25**.

▲ Double-crested cormorants gather at White Rock Lake in Dallas.

A gangly, big-boned, sleekly feathered bird that evokes its dinosaur ancestors. Dark gray, lanky necked bird that looks macabre silently lurking in tree canopies roosting as a flock. They spread out their wings to dry after diving for fish, adding to their weird spectacle. Check them out with binoculars to see their colorful faces: orange-yellow face and throat, sparkling aquamarine eyes, and a startlingly blue mouth interior.

Sensory Makes deep grunts when irritated, mating, or taking off and landing.

Habitat Prefers to roost in calm bays and inlets, but adapts to many habitats.

Food Eats a wide variety of fish, crustaceans, small turtles, and snakes. Forages almost anywhere—wetlands, rivers, and lakes of all sizes—and willing to fly long distances from roost to feed. Dives for fish while floating, using its big feet to propel deep into the water, though sometimes uses wings.

Habits Often forages in quiet yet gregarious groups.

Tidbits Cormorants produce a prodigious amount of smelly poop, especially in breeding season, which does not endear them to humans and can even kill roost trees with too much ammonia. • With less preen oil than many birds, their feathers soak up water which may aid in underwater swimming. • When nests get overheated, parents douse the chicks and inject water into their beaks. • The double crest shows only during breeding season.

Pied-Billed Grebe

Podilymbus podiceps

WHERE TO FIND THEM: At places with lakes, wetlands, and rivers, especially **Adventures 2, 4, 5, 6, 10, 17, 22,** and **25.**

Elegant in the water, comical on land and in the air, the Latin *podiceps* refers to this bird's unwebbed feet being located far back near their rear. They spend almost all their time on the water where they are extremely nimble, even building floating nests. These avian submarines can control their buoyancy—sink and hide, or rise to surface in a flash, making them fierce fishers.

▲ Pied-billed grebe wet from diving for fish.

Sensory Their varied vocalizations include a bleat, coo, kuk, chuckle, and whoop; these are truly funny birds.

Habitat Prefers marshy freshwater ponds, quiet lake inlets, and wetlands.

Food Dives underwater after fish from the surface, propelled mainly by large feet. Dines on amphibians, snakes, crustaceans, and small turtles, and grazes aquatic plants. Eats both dragonfly and damselfly water-born nymphs and adults.

Habits Tolerates human activity and blends well with other waterfowl and shorebirds.

Tidbits Build nests so dense, they float. • Chicks hatch and climb onto their parents' backs where they stay a week or more. • These birds submerge themselves with just their eyes and nostrils visible above the water, like alligators. • Parents swallow feathers and regurgitate them to feed their young. • Their stout bills easily crush large crustaceans.

Wood Duck

Aix sponsa

WHERE TO FIND THEM: At places with lakes, wetlands, and rivers, especially **Adventures 2, 4, 5, 6, 10, 17, 22,** and **25**.

▲ Male wood ducks are exceptionally colorful.

Males are stunning from tip to tail, with iridescent colors of green and teal contrasting with warm beiges and rich chestnut, speckles and striping, even individual feathers are ornate. Unique oblong head shape and trailing crest. Near extinction in the early 1900s, legal protections and a nest box campaign brought them back. Resurgence of beaver populations helped craft the forested wetland habitat they need.

Sensory Female makes a repeated rising squawk. Male has a thin, wavering whistle.

Habitat Wood ducks prefer wetlands, wooded freshwater ponds, quiet creeks, and lake inlets. Not often seen on open water expanses.

Food They dabble for aquatic plants, algae, and invertebrates, floating crustaceans, and insects. Will forage on land for nuts and seeds when aquatic plants are few.

Habits Particularly enjoy shade and protection of trees hanging low over water.

Tidbits Wood ducks readily use nest boxes provided and will take over pileated woodpecker cavities when available. • Females frequently lay eggs in other wood duck nests for them to be raised by others. • Strong claws in feet grip aggressively, enabling it to perch on branches and structures. • They nest in tree cavities, sometimes very high, that can be up to a mile from water. • Strong enough fliers to reach speeds of 30 mph. • A rare duck, in that it has two broods a year.

Insects and Spiders

Summer Bugs

Dog-Day Cicada

Neotibicen spp.

WHERE TO FIND THEM: Any wooded park in summer.

The sound of summer, the stuff of nightmares. Cicada comes from the Latin word meaning buzzer. Enough of them at once can hit seventy or more decibels—the level of garbage disposals and vacuum cleaners. But cicadas go on for hours. These are not the Brood X cicadas with seventeen-year life cycles. Dog-day cicadas and their cousins are an annual event, timed to coincide with Sirius the Dog Star's prominence in the night sky. The translucent, open-back carcasses of cicada nymphs clinging to trees have been freaking people out for centuries. The adults' blocky heads with bulging black eyes evoke aliens.

Sensory Aside from hearing the incessant cicada buzz, you can feel the vibrations as they cling to trees. But be careful. Copperheads can also patrol at night in cicada season to climb trees and hunt them.

Habitat Male cicadas cling to trees and produce sounds to attract females by vibrating membranes in their abdomen sides. Females are silent.

Food Nymphs suck sap from tree roots. Adult sucks juices from small twigs.

▲ Dog-day cicada ready to make some noise.

Habits Buzzing. That's it.

Tidbits The female cicada killer wasp paralyzes a cicada (zombie cicadas!) and transports it to her nest burrow, often by heroically flying with the much larger cicada. Females provision a nest tunnel with two or three cicadas and lay one egg before sealing and moving on to the next. Otherwise, the adult wasp is a peaceful consumer of nectar. • Cicada emergence sets off a wildlife dining frenzy. Birds, reptiles, big spiders, and small mammals appreciate the insect's meaty size. • Cicadas cannot hear their own buzzing.

Firefly

Photinus spp.

WHERE TO FIND THEM: Floodplains, drainage swales, and patchy wetlands are prime firefly habitats, as well as wooded areas with generous leaf litter. **Adventures 5** and **9** have open wet fields where they are easily viewable in large numbers.

The rhythmic flashing of the soft-bodied beetle lights up childhood memories of awe and wonder and has inspired numerous works of literature, art, and performance. Yet this iconic summer species is steadily disappearing. Fourteen species in North America are listed as threatened, and 8 percent are at risk of extinction. Lawn chemicals and manicured yards are culprits, as the beetles spend much of their life cycle underground or in plant litter. Light pollution and drought are also factors. One-fifth of the nearly two hundred firefly species live in Texas. You can help by creating firefly habitat at home; details at Firefly.org.

Sensory Look for the lightning bugs at dusk between May and October. The males fly about three feet off the ground and blink regularly. Interested females, which are sedentary, respond with a flash. Each species has a unique flash pattern.

Habitat *Photinus pyralis*, the common eastern firefly and most prevalent firefly species, is a habitat generalist—grasslands, lawns, woodlands, riparian corridors. But the soil must be dependably damp.

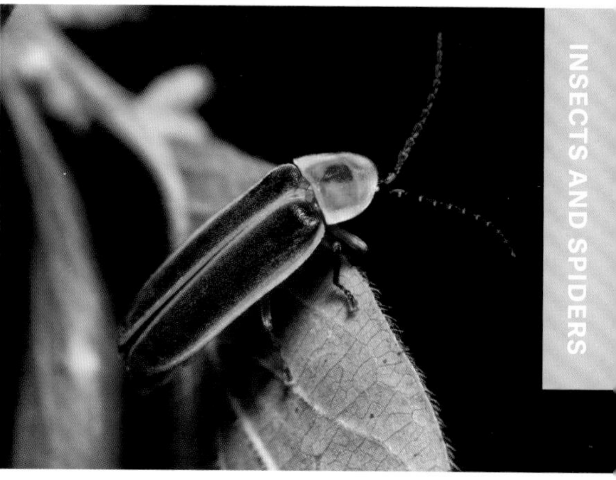

▲ Firefly in a moment of rest.

Food Immature stages are predatory on other small insects, earthworms, slugs, and snails. Adults of some species are also predatory.

Habits Fireflies emerge in the early evening to flash and find mates.

Tidbits Wingless females and many larvae can produce a non-flashing light, making them appear to glow. • Females in the genus *Photuris* mimic *Photinus* males' flashing and lure them closer to eat them, earning the moniker femme fatale fireflies. • A candle produces 80,000 times more heat than firefly bioluminescence of the same brightness.

Mosquitos

Southern House Mosquito

Culex quinquefasciatus

Asian Tiger Mosquito

Aedes albopictus

WHERE TO FIND THEM: Everywhere. No place is immune (except Antarctica).

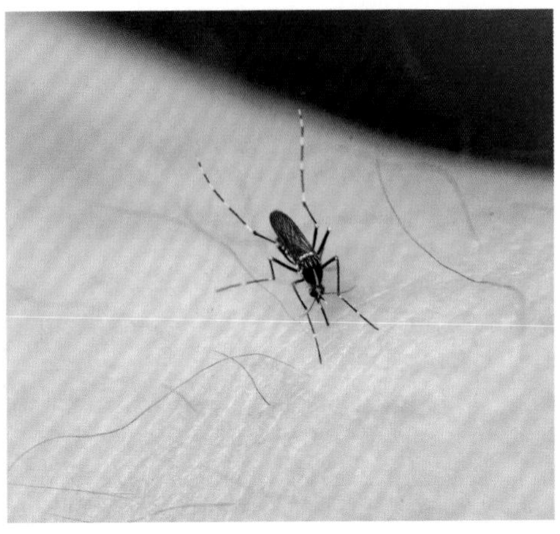

▲ Female Asian tiger mosquito feeding on the photographer.

Everyone hates them and their itchy bites. Southern house mosquitoes (SHM) and Asian tiger mosquitoes (ATM) transmit diseases to humans (West Nile virus) and spread heartworm (the parasitic worm Dirofilaria immitis) to dogs and cats. Quite the tag-team duo, SHMs tend to feed at dawn and dusk, while ATMs are active all day and night. Our exhaled carbon dioxide, laced with body chemicals like lactic acid, lets mosquitoes know human prey is near, and some blood-meal analyses show that they prefer our blood. Known as the bane of outdoor summers, in North Texas they breed almost all year.

Sensory Their whine is a familiar summer sound.

Habitat Wherever there is calm or standing water or even moist soil, there are mosquitoes.

Food Males survive on nectar and sweet plant secretions, as do females who also need blood to develop their eggs. Females live for weeks, repeatedly laying eggs.

Habits Buzzing around the torso at night? Probably an SHM. Biting your ankles and feet in the daytime? Most likely an ATM.

Tidbits Repellents with refined oil of lemon eucalyptus last as long as DEET but do not stain. Treat all standing water and moist soil with Bacillus thuringiensis (BT) granules, known as mosquito bits or dunks. • Lawn mosquito treatments with pyrethrum and related synthetic compounds are detrimental to fish, amphibians, and beneficial bugs. • Mosquito lure and trap devices attract them using carbon dioxide, so place well away from seating areas. Bug zappers do not attract mosquitoes. • Look for the wriggling, centimeter-long larva in water. They are a vital food source for many small fish and amphibian young, underwater dragonfly and damselfly nymphs, and predaceous and scavenger beetles. • Mosquito adults are an important source of food for insectivore birds and insects such as dragonflies that prey on flying insects. • ATMs are exceptionally versatile in finding breeding spots in small water bodies such as plant saucers and gutters. • ATMs invaded the South in the 1980s through imported materials.

Chiggers

Eutrombicula alfreddugesi and *Eutrombicula splendens*

WHERE TO FIND THEM: Only through a magnifying glass

Invisible to the eye, chiggers cling to plant foliage and hitch a ride from passersby, humans and animals alike. The mite's invisible larvae inject victims with a necrotizing compound that dissolves skin that they then slurp up. Dying cells cause quite an itch. By the time the bite is felt, the larvae have dropped off.

Sensory Silent. Invisible.

Habitat *Eutrombicula alfreddugesi* patronizes dry upland areas, while *Eutrombicula splendens* likes it damp. Chigger distribution is erratic—concentrated in one place and scant directly adjacent. Chigger nests are every hiker's nightmare.

Food Mammals, birds, reptiles, and some amphibians get bitten. The larvae stage themselves on the tips of plants and other objects and detect potential victims through vibrations, exhalation, aromas, and other stimuli. Adult chiggers eat small insects and their eggs.

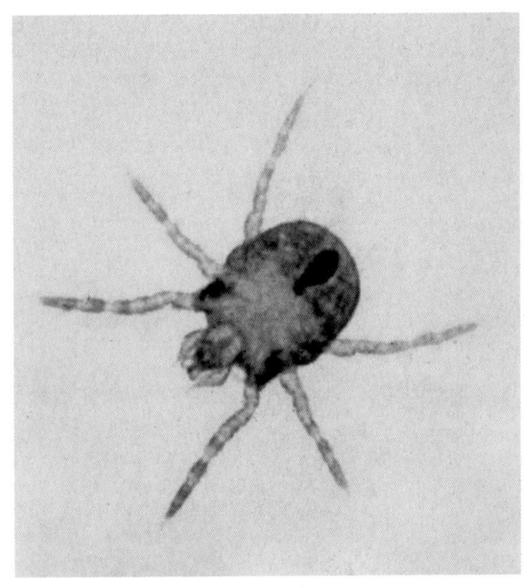

▲ Chigger mite: maker of misery.

Habits Lurking.

Tidbits Snug-fitting clothes—such as bras, waistbands, and socks—and wrinkling behind joints such as knees create minute skin abrasions that make biting easier for chiggers. • Wearing long pants and tucking them into socks help in chigger territory. Apply dusting sulfur (sold in nurseries) or insect repellent to clothes and skin. Dusting sulfur also works on lawns.

Native Bees

American Bumblebee

Bombus pensylvanicus

WHERE TO FIND THEM: Any area with sufficient flowers, especially prairies, at **Adventures 1, 6, 7, 8, 9, 22,** and **23**.

Big, round, fuzzy, boldly yellow and black, and comically loud, the American bumblebee is iconic—the best-known native bee. Unlike solitary native bees, bumbles live in colonies with a complex social structure. Because they can vibrate pollen from flowers—called buzz pollination, required by Solanaceae plants such as tomatoes and peppers—their importance to crop pollination is second only to honeybees. Sadly, Texas Parks and Wildlife lists them as a Species of Greatest Conservation Need.

◄ American bumblebee, feeding.

Sensory Buzzes very loudly. *Bombus* is from the Latin term for "deep roar."

Habitat Prairies, open areas, gardens, open forests—any place flowers grow.

Food Nectar and pollen. Bumblebees mix both with saliva to sustain the queen and developing brood.

Habits Look on their back legs for pollen pouches called corbiculae that overflow with golden granules on a good day. Nests are created in hollows beneath matted vegetation, often in old rodent burrows. Be aware when walking in tall grass to avoid being stung.

Tidbits American bumblebee colonies form anew each spring by an overwintering queen who mates just before hibernation. Emerging in warm weather, the queen feeds, finds a nesting place, provisions it with nectar and pollen "honey pots," and starts laying eggs. • After producing new queens, a colony's old queen dies in the cold weeks of autumn. New queens must feed extensively to put on calories for hibernation. • Bumblebees mostly flap their wings back and forth rather than up and down, aiding the giant bee's aerodynamics. • Only female bumblebees sting and must be provoked to do so.

Metallic Green Sweat Bee

Agapostemon virescens

WHERE TO FIND THEM: Any area with sufficient flowers and shrubbery, such as gardens or developed parks.

Busy and beautiful, these iridescent flying emeralds are pollinator generalists, important to agricultural crops as well as gardens. One of the most visible native bees, like other sweat bees they enjoy sipping mineral-rich sweat off human skin. Don't swat—they impart a tiny sting and only stay a few seconds. These

▲ Metallic green sweat bee with pollen sacs.

ground nesters build communal tunnels for building homes in soil or soft wood. Attract them to your yard by leaving patches of protected bare soil.

Habitat Flowers, flowers, and more flowers.

Food Pollen and nectar.

Habits Look for pollen grains coating the back of female legs. They are quiet little bees that sometimes will surprise you as you sniff flowers.

Tidbits Males sometimes gather in large bachelor groups around big blossoms.

Spiders

Wolf Spider

Lycosa spp.

WHERE TO FIND THEM: Forests and grasslands, urban and rural, wet and dry—wolf spiders are there.

These big spider sprinters can move two feet a second to pursue prey or escape from predators on stout legs designed for walking. Look for them scurrying about at night or in dimly lit woods. Use a flashlight to find their set of exceptionally large eyes that glow teal.

Sensory Some species communicate using a brief purr audible to humans up to twenty feet. Others rub their pedipalps together to make sounds.

Habitat Wolf spiders are habitat generalists that live in wooded areas, grasslands, rock piles, farm fields—anyplace from beaches to mountains. Comfortable around human habitation and chases bugs attracted by lights.

Food Insects and small invertebrates are on the menu, even much larger ones. These spiders mash caught prey into a slurpable mess or inject victims with venom to liquefy for sipping.

▲ Tiny wolf spider babies crawling out of the egg sack and onto the mother's back.

Habits After hatching, spiderlings crawl onto their mother's back and stay for up to four weeks. Look for their tiny burrows beneath rocks or logs.

Tidbits Their scientific (and common) name derives from an outdated assumption that they hunt in packs like wolves.

Yellow Garden Spider

Argiope aurantia

WHERE TO FIND THEM: Prairie preserves and other places with tall grasses and wildflowers.

▲ Yellow garden spiders become huge by the end of summer.

It's hard to miss: a bold yellow and black female spider over an inch long in the center of a complicated circular web two feet across or more. Often erects webs in open, sunny places in gardens and meadows and around houses. For some, they're like a summer pet. Sometimes the much smaller male hangs out with the female. She usually maintains her web in the same location until dying. Watch her grow larger with every large prey (think cicada) she snares. Look for her egg sacs up to an inch across, suspended behind the web.

Sensory Utterly silent.

Habitat Open areas, especially those with flowers that attract insects, locating her web in the busiest flight path.

Food Ensnares flying prey such as flies, beetles, bees, wasps, mosquitoes, moths, and butterflies, but will eat whatever ends up in the web, including small geckos. Upon catching prey, the female wraps it with silk and kills it with venom for later consumption.

Habits Once the smaller brown male finds a female, he builds a small web nearby and plucks her web to create vibrations. When she signals readiness, he approaches but keeps a drop filament ready for a fast escape.

Tidbits The stabilimentum (zigzag of webbing at the web center) helps camouflage the female, warn birds away from the web, and reflects UV light to lure insects. • Females often do web construction and repair at night.

Eastern Giant Swallowtail

Papilio cresphontes

WHERE TO FIND THEM: In the sunlight in woods and fields, where they are beautiful.

▲ Eastern giant swallowtail brings beauty to Clymer Meadow.

The largest butterfly in North America, with a wingspan up to six inches, is a stunning sight. Its larvae, not so much. The caterpillars molt several times and young instars look like bird droppings. Older stages can inflate the osmeterium behind their heads into something resembling a snake's forked tongue and capable of foul-smelling, acidic secretions.

Habitat Enjoys deciduous forests as well as prairies.

Food Hercules club and hop ash trees are a primary food for larvae, but rue or citrus trees in the garden will also attract.

Habits Large wings allow them to float for long distances, making for great photography.

Tidbits Northern expansion of their range is linked to global warming. • They flutter their wings while feeding.

Aren't insects fascinating? Learn more with Texas Master Volunteer Entomology Specialist training by Texas A & M AgriLife Extension Service.

Gulf Fritillary

Agraulis vanillae

WHERE TO FIND THEM: Just about everywhere.

▲ Gulf fritillary is a common sight in summer.

If it's medium-sized and orange and flitting about a meadow, there's a good chance it's a gulf fritillary, which brings happiness on hot days. Its bright orange contrasts with its purple passionflower host plant, though it will host on others in the genus *Passiflora*, causing the caterpillar to be quite toxic to predators. Its caterpillar sports a Mad Max look, with bold orange and black stripes topped by huge shiny spikes.

Habitat Grasslands and forest glens with passionflowers.

Food Flower nectar, especially of asters, lantanas, and verbenas.

Habits Widespread and active butterfly.

Tidbits The males of the species are smaller than their female counterparts and brighter orange. • The chrysalis looks like a folded dangling leaf.

Luna Moth

Actias luna

WHERE TO FIND THEM: Wooded areas away from artificial lights at night.

▲ Luna moths are an exceptional sight.

On a bright moonlit night, the bright green, four-inch wingspan of a luna moth seems to glow. Oval eyespots on its wings resemble crescent moons. Elegant long teardrop extensions off the hindwing are twirled in spirals to confuse the echolocation of bats that prey on them. Light pollution and pesticides are decreasing their population. They lack mouths for feeding and live only for about a week.

Habitat Found only in North America, the luna moth favors hardwood forests.

Food Caterpillars dine on hickory, persimmon, sumac, sweetgum, and walnut leaves. The adult lives for about a week and does not consume sustenance.

Habits Being beautiful.

Tidbits Mating occurs in the deep hours of the night. Females release pheromones that male luna moths can sense from miles away with their large feather-like antennae. • Caterpillars click their mandibles in defense and regurgitate unpleasant intestinal contents. • A member of the family Saturniidae: silkworms or giant silk moths.

Aquatic Insects

Dragonflies and Damselflies

WHERE TO FIND THEM: Wooded parks with ponds, lake inlets, and slow streams.

North Texas is rich in dragonflies (who generally hold their wings out to the side) and damselflies (who typically hold their folded wings up), with at least a hundred species from tiny one-inchers to those with wingspans of over five inches, all in spectacular colors. Dragonflies are generally larger and stouter, with huge eyes close together. Damselflies have a long, slender body and smaller eyes.

Nature's deadly drones can move at 35 mph, spin 180 degrees, fly straight up, straight down, and backward, as well as hover. Their wings beat at twenty to forty-five times per second and are individually controllable. A nearly 360-degree field of vision makes them difficult to sneak up on.

Eggs laid in water hatch into predatory underwater nymphs with lightning-fast pincers—reportedly inspiring the creature in the movie Alien. They consume large amounts of mosquito larvae, water bugs, tadpoles, minnows, and crustaceans.

Habitat Denizens of shady ponds, marshes, and slow, wooded streams. Floating leaves, algal mats, and aquatic vegetation aid in egg laying.

Food These expert fliers can snatch prey from the air, including mosquitoes, earning them a huge fan base. But every flying insect is fair game—gnats, crane flies, small moths, and butterflies—even other dragonflies and damselflies.

Habits When a dragonfly or damselfly lifts its lower body erect in the air, it's called an obelisk posture and aids in cooling. Will stalk large mammals and humans to hunt the biting insects following them.

Cyrano Darner

Nasiaeschna pentacantha

The logo animal of the Texas Master Naturalists, this darner's bulbous frons evokes the immense nose of literary character Cyrano de Bergerac. One of the first darners to become active in spring. It tends to glean prey that is resting on vegetation rather than in flight, then take it to a perch for consumption. Males patrol territory by flying slowly with flickering wings held up at an angle. Cyrano darners prefer the protection of forests and rarely forage out in the open.

► Cyrano darner at rest.

Ebony Jewelwing

Calopteryx maculata

▲ Ebony jewelwing at Lewisville Lake Environmental Learning Area.

A large species of broad-winged damselfly with a brilliant aqua body. The male's wings are intensely black, while the female's are smoky bronze. Most often found in Collin and Denton Counties, the dappled forest creek crossings on Blackjack Trail at Lewisville Lake Environmental Learning Area are a dependable place for viewing. Languid fliers, they flit between perches, making them easy to observe. Males and females communicate with each other by snapping their wings together. Females prefer to wedge eggs into aquatic plant stems, rather than release them loose in the water.

Mammals

Woodland Creatures

Bobcat

Lynx rufus

WHERE TO FIND THEM: Bobcats are most active in spring, when they are hunting to feed young, and in fall, putting on calories for winter, sometimes out in the open and during daylight. Since their prey is more diurnal during cold weather, they are as well..

If your neighborhood has big trees and a nearby creek, step outside at sunset. Chances are a bobcat is watching you. And listening, too, with its prominent ears tipped with tufts of black hair to aid hearing. Secretive, solitary, and usually unseen, they emerge at dusk to hunt. Highly adaptable to urban environments, their ubiquitous presence was confirmed by a Carnivores of DFW study on iNaturalist managed by Texas Parks and Wildlife. They are active year round and do not hibernate. If rodents eat rodenticide and then are consumed by bobcats, accumulation of rodenticide can cause bobcats to develop notoedric mange and sometimes die.

Sensory The bobcat vocal repertoire includes raspy barks, caterwauls, short screeches,

▲ Bobcat lounges in a suburban yard.

and extended ones that sound like a woman screaming. The breeding yowls are surreal and very loud.

Habitat A secret inhabitant of wooded neighborhoods, especially near creeks, and sometimes beneath decks, sheds, and houses. Rests in thickets and in larger trees. Enjoys rocky outcroppings where it can get a good view, but roofs and wooden fences will do. Look for bobcat tracks where creeks cross beneath bridges.

Food Rodents, rabbits, squirrels, ground-feeding birds such as doves and robins, waterfowl chicks, and the young of coyotes, opossums, and raccoons are on the menu, along with occasional roadkill. Preferred prey is generally much smaller than most house cats.

Habits Look for trunk shredding where they sharpen their claws and climbing marks on favored lookout trees. At good vantage points, they will create a circular bed of compressed foliage—the result of changing crouching positions frequently to get a 360-degree view, sometimes leaving paw prints on the edge.

Tidbits As density-dependent breeders, bobcats produce only the amount of young an area can support by making smaller litters when food resources are low. • Closely related to lynx as noted by their facial features and bobbed tail. • Round tracks with four toes and no claw marks due to retractile claws. • Named for their short tails, about seven inches long. • There are no legal protections for bobcats.

Northern Raccoon

Procyon lotor

WHERE TO FIND THEM: Almost every large park, **Adventures 1, 2, 3, 4, 8, 9, 10, 11, 12, 13, 16, 17, 18,** and **22,** and along the Trinity River.

Its devilishly dexterous five-digit paws led to its Indigenous names, such as its Algonquian term *arakun*, meaning "he scratches with his hands," which became raccoon. These hands, developed for opening crawfish and bivalves, help it unfasten latches and open trash and other containers. They pass their tricks on to future generations. *Lotor* is Latin for "washer," but that's not why it wets its food. Raccoons depend on touch to forage. Water softens and makes pliable the thin, horny layer covering their paws, enhancing tactile responses. These trash pandas flourish in the city, growing bigger and making larger litters than their woodland country cousins.

Sensory Raccoons vocalize their many emotions with a repertoire of over 200 sounds which include hissing and snarling when fighting each other (which is a lot of the time), irritated mothers barking, and general enthusiastic screeching. The high-pitched chattering of baby raccoons is a surreal sound that descends from trees.

Habitat They prefer wooded areas with brushy cover near streams, ponds, or lakes, developed or not. In natural spaces, they'll be wherever crawfish reside and amphibians lay eggs. But they can live almost anywhere with cover, food, and water.

Food Some of the most opportunistic of omnivores, raccoons eat 40 percent invertebrates (crawfish, bivalves, worms, caterpillars, grubs, large insects like cicadas and grasshoppers), 27 percent vertebrates (mice, lizards, the young of mammals and squirrels, bird eggs,

▲ Northern raccoons are adorable and mischievous.

carrion), and 33 percent plants (berries and nuts, food scraps, produce trimmings).

Habits Look for them during daytime snoozing in tree hollows or branch crotches. Often seen coming and going from storm sewers in cold weather. Raccoons select level sites raised off the ground as raccoon latrines where family members deposit feces that unfortunately contain raccoon roundworm eggs. If accidentally inhaled or swallowed by humans or other animals, larvae hatch and infest the host's organs, causing serious damage or even death.

Tidbits Their front paws have ten times more nerve endings than human hands. Almost two-thirds of their brain's sensory perception is devoted to interpreting tactile impulses. • Now also distributed across much of Europe and Japan, where they are considered serious pests. • Can both sweat and pant for heat dissipation.

Grassland and Woods Mammals

Coyote

Canis latrans

WHERE TO FIND THEM: All natural areas, especially around lakes and creeks, and wooded riparian neighborhoods.

All too often on social media is posted: "I heard a pack of coyotes last night, celebrating a kill, probably some poor cat." Let's unpack this. Coyotes have over ten vocalizations, making three coyotes sound like a dozen. They have family units of parents and kits, but it's not like a wolf pack. They don't vocalize after a kill. Why advertise to the competition a new food source is available? Besides coyotes preferring prey without sharp teeth and claws, domestic

▲ Coyote and offspring enjoying a sunny day.

cats weighing seven to fifteen pounds are on the large side for them. Rabbits and rodents are their target. The prairie "song dog" is a full-time urban resident now. Neighborhoods with large trees adjoining riparian corridors are prime habitat, providing cover during the day and roaming range for the one to four miles they travel a night. Their most active period is from after sunset to midnight. A mated pair claims a modest two square miles, so there can be numerous coyotes in surprising places. They've even raised pups atop parking garages, preying on pigeons and rats.

Sensory *Canis latrans* means "barking dog" in Latin. Coyote sounds are its social media, mainly family units communicating with each other and occasionally other units. Some calls show alarm and aggression against territory invaders: barks, growls, howls, huffs, and whines. Greeting and contact sounds tend to be rolling and yip howls by individuals and units.

Habitat Able to survive in rapidly changing environs, they live in open to dense woods, grasslands, thickets, scrubland, and more. Only limitation is that the den needs to be within six miles of a permanent water source.

Food Rabbits are a big favorite, along with squirrels and other rodents, reptiles and lizards, large insects such as grasshoppers and cicadas, ground-feeding birds such as doves and robins, and young waterfowl around lakes. Vehicle encounters cause about 80 percent of outdoor cat deaths, and as avid opportunists, coyotes happily scarf those bodies up. But some suffer mange from eating rats that ingested rodenticide. Being omnivorous, they eat fruit (especially persimmon and Mexican plum), nuts, mesquite beans, pecans, and whatever they find in unsecured garbage bins.

Habits Coyote tracks can be distinguished from those of dogs by their narrower, more elongated shape and visible nail marks. Most visible around Valentine's Day (peak of the mating season) and mid- to late spring (young to feed). In late summer they depart thickets for breezier spots. Privet transpires about 20 percent more than native plants when temperatures are over eighty degrees, making most urban thickets too humid to tolerate.

Found an injured mammal? Search for "wildlife rehabber" in your city. Use only licensed rehabbers. Seek advice from the DFW Wildlife Coalition website.

Tidbits These density-dependent breeders produce only the amount of young an area can support by making fewer and smaller litters when food resources are low. • The prominent trickster character in Native American folklore uses deception and humor to thwart the status quo. • Runs with its tail down instead of raised like wolves and dogs or swishing horizontally such as foxes.

Eastern Cottontail

Sylvilagus floridanus

WHERE TO FIND THEM: Abundant in Adventures with a mix of grassy areas and trees, especially **Adventures 1, 2, 3, 4, 5, 6, 7, 8, 9, 14, 15, 16, 17,** and **18**.

In some neighborhoods, cottontail rabbits are plentiful, nibbling on constantly growing grass, making themselves unwelcome in vegetable gardens, and hiding in dense shrubbery. Or they're at the neighborhood park, venturing out from wooded edges to dine on grass. Most often seen around dawn and dusk, especially in breeding peaks. You may come across an unattended nest of baby bunnies tucked in dried foliage beneath a bush. So that her smell doesn't attract predators to the young, mom visits just once or twice a day to rapidly dispense milk through high-pressure teats. So don't disturb! They breed like, well, rabbits—up to forty babies per year. Only 15 percent will reach adulthood, despite being able to run up to eighteen miles per hour, sometimes leaping eight feet in crazy erratic zigzag patterns, changing direct in a second.

▲ Eastern cottontail at rest.

Sensory Very vocal, but you must listen closely for distress cries and grunts that warn off predators. Squeals during mating are loud.

Habitat Grasslands with wildflowers featuring densely wooded fence lines and copses, and forested riparian corridors with thickets adjoining meadows, are perfect cottontail terrain. Its burly cousin, the swamp rabbit, inhabits poorly drained bottomlands.

Food Eastern cottontail favors tender green herbaceous vegetation such as new growth, especially of native grasses and legumes. In winter it chews on woody plants. Indigestible matter is given a second life by the rabbits' cecum, where bacteria and fungi transform the plant material into nutrient-packed pellets called cecotropes, which are ingested.

Habits These bunnies sleep by day in hollows under logs or rocks or in a thicket or brush pile. They emerge in times of limited visibility such as rain and fog. In winter, they travel farther distances and are easier to see. When they stand on their hind legs to survey for predators, you might see their ears peaking above tall foliage.

Tidbits Cottontail courtship entails racing around, hopping wildly, and even sparring, a ritual called "cavorting." Otherwise, cottontails don't socialize or feed together. • In hot weather, blood vessels in their ears dilate, helping them to cool off.

If you find an injured rabbit or an apparently abandoned nest, check the WildRescue, Inc / Rescued Rabbits website for advice.

Nine-Banded Armadillo

Dasypus novemcinctus

WHERE TO FIND THEM: Elm Fork of the Trinity River, Where the West Begins Adventures, and **Adventures 16, 17, 18, 19, 20,** and **21** have the sandy soils they prefer, but they'll be anywhere sparse grass cover meets forested areas.

The State Mammal of Texas, Spanish for "little armored one," this humpbacked South American crossed the Rio Grande in the 1800s and kept heading north, limited only by intolerance to cold weather. It still prefers a warm, rainy environment like that of its homeland, but will make do. Armadillos have poor eyesight, but great hearing and smell alert them to predators on the move. If startled, the solitary mammals zip to one of their many burrows, from three to sixteen feet deep, and arch their backs to make removal by predators difficult. Or they head to a water body, since they can hold their breath for up to six minutes while they scamper along, an adaptation that helps when its snout is deep in soil while grub foraging. Plus, they love a good mud bath.

Sensory The dried leaves and grasses of autumn aid in hearing them rustling about, after bugs. Mating pairs exchange raspy chortles.

Habitat Armadillos prefer sandy and silty soils where they can easily dig, which unfortunately can include lawns. They are more active in summer during twilight hours and night, and tend toward diurnal in winter.

Food Known for their love of caterpillars, earthworms, and grubs, armadillos can make short work of ant and termite mounds. With their sticky tongues, they happily lap up any insects (especially beetles), centipedes, and millipedes they come across, plus right-sized amphibians such as crawfish, reptiles, and reptile and bird eggs. An animal carcass infested with maggots is a feast. They will eat seeds, roots, and fungi when preferred food is low.

▲ Nine-banded armadillo is the State Mammal of Texas.

Habits When startled, they jump straight up—and sadly, often right into the bottom of passing cars. To avoid predators, they can inflate their intestines and float across or down creeks and rivers for long distances.

Tidbits Females bear four identical quadruplet babies of the same sex that develop from one egg and share a womb placenta. • Known to carry the leprosy microbe strain (*Myobacterium leprae*) that infects humans. • Only two armadillo species, both three-banded, can roll up completely into a ball.

White-Tailed Deer

Odocoileus virginianus

WHERE TO FIND THEM: Dependably seen at **Adventures 6, 17, 18, 19** and **22.**

Walk quietly some early morning through large swaths of forested land sheltered from rampant human activity. Look for well-worn, narrow trails through the greenery. A rustle, a rush of motion, and then a flash of white—an oval flap of fur from the deer's rear bounding away through tangled, forested terrain at speeds of up to thirty miles per hour. If other deer are nearby, they'll see the white and flee, too. Deer are our megafauna here, found in the largest riparian and reservoir preserves, performing necessary forest maintenance by browsing saplings and brush. They become integral to their domain, spending their entire lives within three miles of their birth. When mom is off feeding, fawns are hidden in brush or tall grass for hours, so leave them be. Females often remain with their mother for two years.

White-tailed doe and fawn

Sensory Bucks and does grunt and snort. Bucks mix both with loud wheezes for their personal dominance song. Does develop a guttural concern call. Fawns make thin bleats and squeals.

Habitat There are few places deer love more than open oak woodland adjoining meadows, where they can work the edge between tender shade greenery and woody browse with acorns and sunny grass and sweet forbs. But they'll need a domain of ten to twenty acres per deer, a strong creek for water, and a riparian corridor with cover for travel.

Food Deer enjoy woody browse of saplings, brush, and vines (they love greenbrier!), but like to nibble just about everything, as frustrated gardeners can attest. Acorns, pecans, and seed-bearing plants add heft.

Habits Look for territorial rubs on tree trunks. Bucks tear through bark with antlers and hooves scrape to move away greenery, exposing dirt which is then rubbed and urinated on. Sometimes compressed bedding spots in tall grass are visible.

Tidbits Bucks jettison antlers after fall rut. Dropped antlers are nibbled by many critters for minerals. • Deer were second to bison in importance to Indigenous tribes of the Great Plains and then by frontier explorers and settlers. • More white-tailed deer—an estimated four million or more—live in Texas than any other state. • A soft skin called velvet covers antlers. It's rich in blood vessels that help cool the deer in hot weather.

Aerial and Aquatic Animals

Bats

Eastern Red Bat

Lasiurus borealis

Evening Bat

Nycticeius humeralis

WHERE TO FIND THEM: In residential areas, look for them along the fringes of streetlight illumination or around aerial landscape lighting in trees. They favor the airspace above parks and preserves with native grasses and flowers that attract plentiful insects, especially those with ponds and lakes.

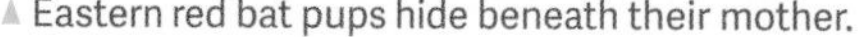

▲ Eastern red bat pups hide beneath their mother.

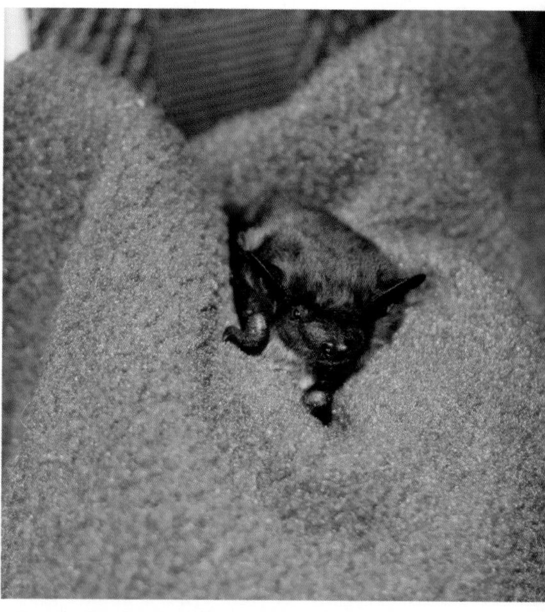

▲ Evening bat in rehabilitation at Bat World Sanctuary.

With the giant Texas colonies of Mexican free-tailed bats getting all the bat bandwidth, it's easy to overlook North Texas's arboreal bats. Evening bat (EB) females form seasonal nursery colonies, and both sexes will congregate by the hundreds in winter. Eastern red bats (ERB) are solitary. Both species also seem to gather and migrate south when weather turns too cold. Medium-sized eastern red bats are burly and furry, while the small, sleek EBs are sometimes confused at dusk with insect-hunting birds like western kingbirds. ERBs put on a great acrobatic show, somersaulting while closing tails and wings about their prey, then consuming on the fly. Most of the time, these arboreal bats roost in tree hollows and bark openings, but will make do with chimneys, eaves, attics, garages, and even folded-up patio umbrellas. Fewer old-growth forests and removal of snags (dead trees) has slashed nesting places and habitat, as has replacing old buildings and barns with modern structures that bats can't access.

Sensory Echolocation entails bats emitting high-pitched squeaks and using their highly sensitive ears to detect variations in the reflected soundwaves. You can track them in bat-detector apps for your phone.

Habitat Arboreal bats need mature forests for roosting. For hunting, they favor open spaces with native grasses and flowers that attract plentiful insects.

Food Bats munch mostly on moths and beetles, but also cicadas, flies, leafhoppers, katydids, and occasionally mosquitoes.

Habits Look for the ERBs resting or sleeping in the day, hanging on tree branches by one foot and resembling dead leaves by wrapping up in their tail membranes. Both emerge at dusk, with EBs the first to fly. ERBs can soar upward and dive down to skim seven to thirteen feet above ground. Both are active for several hours, though nursing mothers feed longer. Bats are a boon to pest control, especially agricultural fields.

Tidbits ERBs can have up to five pups, while most bats have one or two, and will frequently carry the pups with her. • "Blind as a bat" is a misguided term. Though reliant on echolocation, they have adequate sight. • ERBs are known to survive temperatures as low as twenty-three degrees. • ERBs have the second-greatest bat mortality from wind turbines. • Rabies in bats is rare and even more rarely transmitted.

Encountered an injured bat? See the website of Bat World Sanctuary in Weatherford for advice.

River Otter

Lutra canadensis

WHERE TO FIND THEM: Otters can be elusive but look for their trails and slides in **Adventures 4, 5, 6, 13, and 22,** as well as sections Elm Fork of the Trinity River, Great Trinity Forest, and West and Clear Forks of the Trinity (except **Adventure 23**).

The resurgence of muscular yet slinky river otters is one of North Texas's best wildlife success stories. In the last decade, scattered sightings along the Trinity forks and larger creeks like White Rock spread to reports in larger Collin County creeks. Even more were seen at Lavon Lake and Lake Worth. Now many reservoirs in eastern DFW have them, especially downstream from dams, as well as wetlands and large creeks with lush riparian cover, but they are scattered in DFW's western half as well. Watching them during sunset hours is endless fun, the way that play and hunting overlap and merge. But they're underwater much of the time, able to hold their breath for nearly four minutes and swimming up to 7 mph. They prefer clear water with a mild current and a sloped bank suitable for their favorite game: sliding.

Sensory A rather aromatic species, they do much scent marking with feces, urine, and secretions.

Habitat A constant source of food is vital for this hungry beast. Reservoirs (their crawfish-rich headwaters and river exits flush with fish) and rivers (especially those flanked by wetlands) are rich in shelter and sustenance. Otters are sensitive to pollution and depart tainted waters. Look for nests made in

▲ River otter swimming in a Garland creek.

tangled exposed tree roots and burrow den entrances on banks and dams.

Food For as cute as they are, river otters are voracious killers. Adults consume two to three pounds of food a day, favoring fish, mussels, and especially crawfish. They eat amphibians and reptiles such as small snakes and turtles and snack on snails, damselflies, and dragonflies.

Habits River otters are active year round, mostly at night and twilight hours. They are always on the move, swimming about, poking noses and paws in crevices and tight spaces, stirring up invertebrates in mud, and chasing whatever swims. They trace the shore, looking for unwary amphibians, small mammals, and birds.

Tidbits Otter group latrines serve as newspapers for the community. The poop is frequently shiny from crawfish shells. They also expel various stinky intestinal and anal substances. • They happily reside in beaver ponds and coexist with vegetarian rodent residents.

Reptiles

American alligator

Alligator mississippiensis

WHERE TO FIND THEM: Most often seen at **Adventures 17** and especially **22**. Will venture out to outlying areas during high rains.

Alligators have been recorded in North Texas since the late 1800s when they were seen in the West Fork near downtown Fort Worth. The Trinity's broad floodplain fosters wetlands and sloughs they favor. Dallas County Open Space has an alligator preserve (not open to the public) in southeast Dallas. They are fast! Alligators can swim up to twenty miles per hour and run up to 35 mph for short distances. Never get between an alligator and water.

Sensory Listen for grunts, snorts, and hisses. Male alligators bellow loudly to assert territory, causing aquatic vibrations that attract females.

Habitat Slow-moving rivers, reservoir headwaters, and inlets with plentiful riparian foliage for cover.

Food These apex carnivores eat everything and stalk prey while mostly submerged, often with only nostrils and eyes visible.

▲ American alligator eating a ribbon snake.

Habits When the water temperature is cooler than the outside air, alligators will bask in sunlight to warm their body. Alligator wallows create habitat for other wetland creatures and help extend water availability.

Tidbits By altering their lung position to shift their center of buoyancy, they can adjust their position in the water. • The distance in inches between eyes approximately equals their body length in feet. • Tracks are four to six inches long and wedge-shaped with four to five pointed toes. • Decomposing vegetation in the nest provides warmth for eggs.

Lizards

American Five-Lined Skink

Plestiodon fasciatus

WHERE TO FIND THEM: Parks and preserves with wooded areas along creeks and rivers.

This sleek reptile's males have natty stripes and steel-blue coloring that can fade with age to an attractive bronze. Five-lined skinks scamper through vegetation debris searching for rotted wood and other hollow spaces to hide in, moving rapidly and erratically to avoid predators and surprise prey. Males aggressively defend territory and engage in complex courtship behaviors to lure females.

▲ American five-lined skink can be heard skittering among leaves if you listen carefully.

Sensory Listen very closely for their rustling in fallen leaves.

Habitat Prefers moist forests with ground foliage but needs sunny spots for basking. Found in rocky and wooded areas along shores, log and brush piles, and neglected outbuildings with plentiful insects.

Food On the menu: spiders, small invertebrates, crawling and burrowing insects, and the young of rodents, amphibians, and other lizards.

Habits Look for them skittering up tree trunks in bottomlands, but hiding around fallen logs is more their thing. Usually solitary, sometimes will cluster in small groups for warmth during cold weather.

Tidbits They hatch with an electric cobalt blue tail that turns brown as they mature. • Nearly indistinguishable from the broad-headed skink as adults.

Texas Spiny Lizard

Sceloporus olivaceus

WHERE TO FIND THEM: A fixture at **Adventures 14, 15, 18, 19, 20, 21,** and **22**.

These arboreal lizards blend with tree bark, thanks to their spiky rough texture and gray coloring with black stripes. Their long toes tipped with sharp claws are perfect for climbing. Well suited to the dry Eastern Cross Timbers' mosaic of woodlands and prairie glens containing plentiful insects and sunny spots for basking.

Sensory Listen for skittering on tree bark, often at head level.

Habitat While upland woods are their native terrain, they adapt to developed areas and large residential yards.

Food Insects, such as beetles, cicadas, grasshoppers, and especially crickets, plus the young of rodents, amphibians, and other lizards.

Habits Look for them searching for insects among fallen leaves. Zips up trees or scampers noisily through leaf litter when approached.

Tidbits Can break off part of its tail if grabbed roughly but can grow a new, shorter tail. • Females are larger than males.

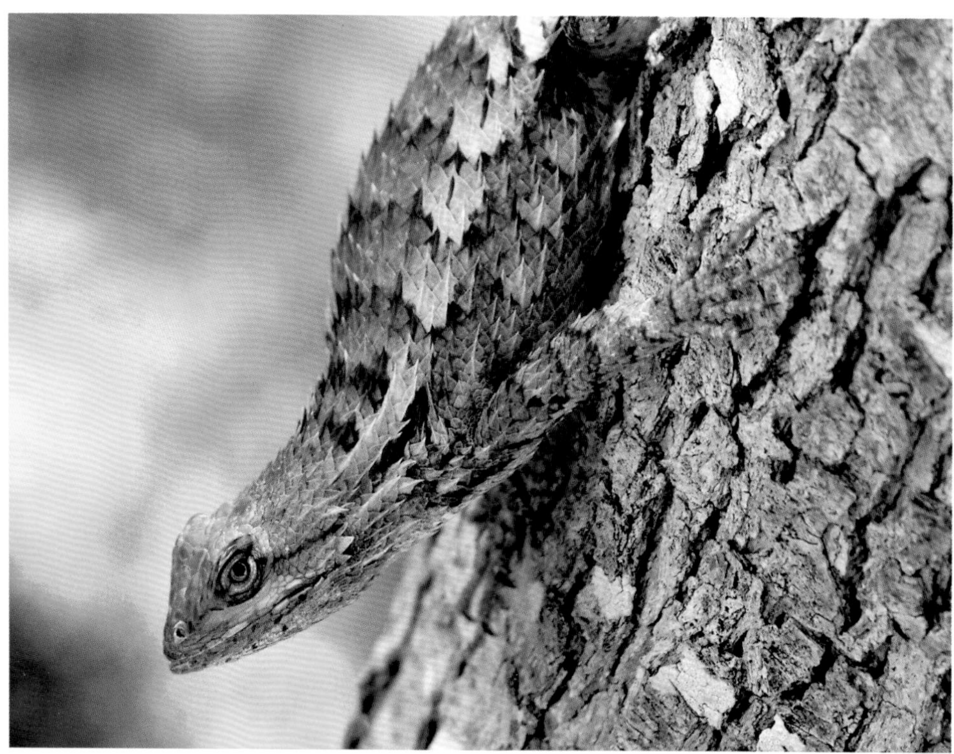

▲ Texas spiny lizard blending in at Sheri Capehart Nature Preserve.

Snakes

Copperhead

Agkistrodon contortrix

WHERE TO FIND THEM: Parks with wooded and relatively well-drained riparian corridors.

This riparian resident dines on frogs, toads—and occasional toes if stepped on, which is a prime reason not to wear sandals in the woods. Its hemotoxic venom is rarely life threatening, though. These ambushing predators hide (often curling into a tight ball) and wait for prey to pass. In mid- to late summer, they station themselves at the base of trees, especially oaks, and snatch emerging new cicadas. They will climb trees to pursue adults.

Sensory If threatened, anxiety displacement can cause their tail tip to vibrate, true of many snakes.

Habitat Copperheads live in rocky outcroppings to swampy terrain, but prefer lightly wooded habitats with a full-time water source, plentiful leaves, and ground foliage for cover.

Food These snakes prey on small rodents using heat-sensitive facial pits. They also eat caterpillars and cicadas, lizards, and the young of rodents, amphibians, and reptiles.

Habits Diurnal hunter during spring and fall, switching to crepuscular or nocturnal during hot weather.

Tidbits Males sparring over females will raise their bodies vertically, lunging and twisting to try and force the other male down—serpent arm wrestling. • Will brumate (hibernation for warm-blooded animals) in winter with other species for warmth.

▲ Copperhead coiled and waiting for prey.

The Big Snakes

Western Rat Snake

Pantherophis obsoletus

Diamondback Water Snake

Nerodia rhombifer

WHERE TO FIND THEM: Western rat snakes are abundant, especially in forested areas of **all Adventures** except 24 and 25. Diamondback water snakes are abundant in creeks, lakes, and rivers, especially in **Adventures 1, 2, 4, 5, 6, 7, 8, 9, 10, 11, 12, 13, 16, 17, 18, 20, 21, 22, 24,** and **25.**

Stout and reaching four feet or more in length, western rat snakes are surprisingly common in residential areas, favoring large trees. They're able to go straight up a trunk, raiding birds' nests for eggs and chicks. But they'll give your yard a quick pass through at nightfall for rats and mice. Western rat snakes reside in every wild park, especially those with prairies, dining on grasslands' considerable population of rodents. The young of mammals like opossums are also on the menu, which they squeeze like a boa constrictor. Battles between large birds of prey that try eating western rat snakes can be epic struggles, with the famously agile snake whipping its muscular body around in attempting a fatal squeeze.

The equally sizable diamondback water snake is found in just about every lake and river, making quick meals of fish and amphibians. These eating machines have no interest in humans but will vigorously attack if capture is attempted. They'll bite if necessary or release a truly nasty musk they can smear around with their tails.

Sensory In addition to the acrid musk, diamondback water snakes will defensively defecate awful-smelling feces due to their fish diet.

Habitat Western rat snakes live anywhere from rocky hillsides to river bottoms, but moist hardwood forests are a favorite. Look for them around barns and outbuildings where rodents congregate.

▲ Western rat snake wandering down an East Dallas sidewalk.

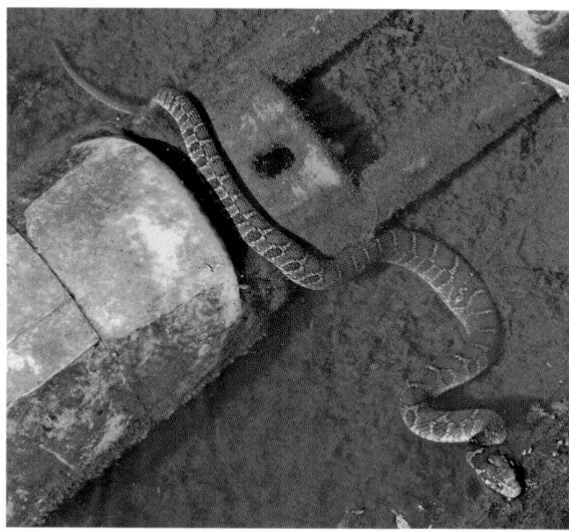

▲ Diamondback water snake searches for bird eggs at Village Creek Drying Beds.

Diamondback water snakes love a good slough and also inhabit ponds, lakes, and slow-moving rivers.

Food Because western rat snakes squeeze prey into cardiovascular collapse, they can take on sizable animals and swallow huge meals, including an entire clutch of waterfowl eggs. Diamondback water snakes favor fish and amphibians, but also crawfish, young turtles, and small snakes. Look for them draped from low shoreline branches, darting their heads into the water to snatch prey passing by.

Habits Both patrol often, hoping to surprise prey.

Tidbits Diamondback water snakes are sometimes mistaken for cottonmouths or diamondback rattlesnakes and killed. • Western rat snakes will brumate (hibernate) in winter with copperheads and other snakes. • While large, western rat snakes are not bigger than bull snakes or coachwhips.

Western Diamondback Rattlesnake

Crotalus atrox

WHERE TO FIND THEM: Southwest Dallas Escarpment, Where the West Begins, and **Adventures 18, 19, and 22**.

This iconic snake evokes a strong fear response and rightfully so. It is responsible for more human fatalities than any other snake, yet you're five times more likely to be killed by lightning. Venom is a defense of last resort, as it does not immediately disable the attacker.

▲ Western diamondback rattlesnake blends into leaf litter.

That's why the diamondback developed a warning rattle. Mainly a resident of Tarrant County, western Denton County, and southwestern Dallas County. One of the largest diamondback rattlesnakes in the state was recorded in the Cedar Hill area at a whopping 92 inches—over seven feet! Awareness is vital. Wear hiking boots and long pants to deflect bite strikes. Be especially aware around rock outcroppings and sunny places where rattlesnakes might be basking.

Sensory Can shake its rattle over sixty times per second. If you hear it, freeze, locate the snake, and back away slowly.

Habitat Found on rocky canyons and hillsides, mesquite grasslands, and upland forests.

Food Active during the day, it hunts at night during hot weather. This snake eats a sizable meal—such as a rabbit or large rodent—every two to three weeks. Snacks on large insects like grasshoppers. Occasionally eats fresh carrion of small mammals.

Habits Since they eat so seldom, diamondbacks spend a lot of time resting, often coiled in the shade of shrubs or the bases of trees, tucked away in piles of debris or rocks, or waiting in animal burrows.

Tidbits As a member of the pit viper family, possesses facial pits that sense minute temperature changes to aid in finding prey. • Rattles are formed of keratin, like human nails and hair. • A group of rattlesnakes is called a rhumba.

Yard Snakes

Rough Earth Snake

Virginia striatula

Rough Green Snake

Opheodrys aestivus

WHERE TO FIND THEM: Forests, grasslands, and more, but you must look closely.

Lift a paving stone in your yard, especially one warmed by sunshine. A small and slender rough earth snake may slither out and seek immediate cover under leaf litter or foliage. Part of every garden and forest, utterly nondescript and able to blend in anywhere, this snake uses its pointed snout to burrow through soil for earthworms, its favorite food.

◄ Rough earth snake in its element—dirt.

► Rough green snake imitating a branch to surprise prey.

Photogenic and docile, rough green snakes spend most of their time in vegetation, posing as vines and branches, waiting for prey, even sleeping there.

Sensory Both expel foul secretions if mishandled.

Habitat Rough earth snakes favor moist wooded terrain, either wild or residential, where leaves and small branches remain on the ground, but will live in rocky and grassy areas. Rough green snakes prefer areas with thick greenery, especially along waterways.

Food Rough earth snakes methodically search for earthworms, pillbugs, and other insects in soil. Rough green snakes pluck insects, caterpillars, and spiders from greenery.

Habits Rough green snake is strongly diurnal. Being mostly fossorial, rough earth snake prefers dim light.

Tidbits Rough earth snakes give birth to exceptionally thin live young.

Turtles

Box Turtles

Ornate Turtle

Terrapene ornate

Three-Toed Turtle

Terrapene carolina triunguis

WHERE TO FIND THEM: **Adventures 1, 5, 6, 7, 8, 16, 17, 18, 19, 20, 21, 22,** and **23** have prime box turtle habitats.

Ornate and three-toed box turtles are quite a sight, stomping about with upright heads, looking like little mobile helmets. Unfortunately, until recently, this made them easy prey for commercial trappers who sold them, often overseas, a practice ended by a 2018 Texas law. Children find these trekkers irresistible and take them home, then release them. But box turtles do not recolonize outside their home range—a mile across or less—and usually perish trying to return. Because they take between five and ten years to mature, don't produce many offspring, and tend to get hit by vehicles and field machinery, their numbers are in decline. University of North Texas students are studying three-toed box turtles at Lewisville Lake Environmental Learning Area.

Sensory The dried fallen leaves of autumn aid in hearing them stomp around.

Habitat These terrestrial turtles prefer unmowed grasslands and pastures, and open woodlands with grassy glens. They prefer being near streams or ponds, or areas that collect rainfall.

Food Omnivorous eaters, they dine on snails, slugs, earthworms, caterpillars, crawfish, amphibian and reptile eggs, and various insects. They avidly consume berries, fungi, and succulent plant growth. The ornate box turtle is particularly fond of dung beetles that are plentiful in cow pastures.

Habits Box turtles are more active after rain, particularly following dry spells. In hot weather, they hide under foliage or in animal burrows or submerge themselves in mud, and forage in the hours before nightfall. In spring and fall,

Three-toed box turtle with tracking device as part of a study at Lewisville Lake Environmental Learning Center.

This ornate box turtle blends beautifully with its surroundings, thanks to its camouflaged markings.

they are fully diurnal and bask in the sunlight. When feeling threatened, they retract head and limbs and clamp their shell shut. If food is unavailable, they retreat into their shells to wait for better times.

Tidbits The ornate box turtle has a nearly statewide distribution, while the three-toed tends toward the eastern half. • Eggs that incubate above 82 degrees Fahrenheit are more likely to be females. • A female can lay fertile eggs for up to four years after mating.

Snapping Turtles

Alligator Snapping Turtle

Macrochelys temminckii

Common Snapping Turtle

Chelydra serpentina

WHERE TO FIND THEM: Rivers and lakes in **Adventures 2, 5, 6, 13, 16, 17, 22,** and **24**, and Fort Worth Nature Center and Refuge.

The largest turtles in North Texas certainly can snap. Male alligator snappers can weigh more than 200 pounds with powerful beak-like jaws possessing a bite force of 1000 pounds. But they swim away from conflict, saving their bites for prey, preferring to rest unseen on the river or pond bottoms. The common snapper buries itself in mud, exposing only nostrils and eyes. The alligator snapper rarely leaves the water, often developing a coat of camouflaging algae, and can stay submerged for up to fifty minutes.

Habitat Both snappers live in the Trinity River, as well as wetlands, reservoir headwaters and inlets, and significant creeks. Aquatic plants and fallen vegetation provide cover for when they surface.

Food Snapping turtles dine on fish, amphibians (mmm, tasty bullfrogs), reptiles (including

▲ Alligator snapping turtle expresses discontent.

◄ Common snapping turtle in Fort Worth's Clear Fork.

baby alligators and small turtles), crawfish, and mussels. They snatch small mammals, birds, or rodents from the water's edge and make meals of nutria and beaver infants and waterfowl chicks. Alligator snappers extend their tongue—which is tipped with a dangling red, worm-looking appendage to act as a lure—then close their jaws upon any curious prey.

Habits Females of both species leave the water to lay eggs, with common snappers traveling a good distance from water. Common snapper's Latin species name *serpentina* refers to its long neck and flexible head. Look for its nostrils thrust to the surface for the occasional inhale.

Tidbits Texas laws enacted in 2018 forbid commercial trapping of snapping turtles. • High temperatures after egg laying result in more females. • Common snappers can be remarkably tolerant of cold. • Alligator snapper tails are as long as their carapace.

Amphibians, Fish, and Crustaceans

Amphibians

Green Tree Frog

Hyla cinerea

WHERE TO FIND THEM: On trees and foliage in riparian corridors, bottomland forests, near ponds, and in well-watered yards.

These are exceptionally attractive, glossy, bright green frogs with beautifully sculpted heads, yet they are more often heard than seen as an integral anchor of the night chorus. Any time it rains in summer, the males get loud in search of females who will go on to lay a couple thousand eggs in shallow water under the cover of aquatic plants.

Sensory Hundreds or even thousands of male green tree frogs will gather in near water sites and try to appeal to females all night long in a miasma of calls, overlapping and pulsating, peaking and ebbing, coming from all directions

▲ Green tree frog resting in daytime.

and levels, repeated up to seventy-five times per minute. At the appearance of a predator, all will fall silent at once.

Habitat These frogs prefer habitats with plentiful floating vegetation, as well as trees and foliage in riparian corridors, bottomland forests, near ponds, and well-watered yards.

Food Green tree frogs feed on all types of insects, flying and crawling, as long as the bugs are alive and moving. The frogs seem to enjoy the hunt.

Habits They spend daytime attached to plant stems, seemingly defying gravity, using their large and utterly cute red toe pads.

Tidbits Skin color changes green tones with temperature and activity. • Males will mate with as many females as they can attract.

Gulf Coast Toad

Incilius nebulifer

WHERE TO FIND THEM: At night, floating in ponds and creeks, on riparian edges, and hopping around well-watered lawns, often after rains.

Current reigning toad of North Texas, edging out Woodhouse's toad due to its extended and late-starting breeding season and its ability to do better in clay soils. Its croaky trill is sedate compared to Woodhouse's distressed-goat bleat, irritating homeowners with backyard ponds because males gather in a breeding chorus that goes on all night. While they prefer being near a constant water source, they can venture quite far for their size when foraging.

▲ Gulf Coast toad shows off its beautiful texture.

Not unusual to find them catching bugs under porch lights.

Sensory Males call for mates during the breeding season from March to September, making a signature sound of the summer chorus, especially after rainfall. Find one calling and watch how large its throat vocal sack expands.

Habitat Warm, moist areas like riparian corridors and wetlands but they also make use of backyard ponds.

Food Any flying, crawling, or swimming insect or arthropod it can swallow.

Habits Experts at hiding in dark, confined spaces during the day, such as dugouts beneath rocks and logs. Will sneak naps in crawfish burrows. See Backyards for how to make amphibian homes.

Tidbits Birds, snakes, and turtles prey on toadlets emerging from water sources. • Parotid (salivary) glands excrete toxins to deter predators.

Small-Mouthed Salamander

Ambystoma texanum

WHERE TO FIND THEM: Turn over a rock or log in places with terraced creeks, ponds, and wetlands and one might scurry out.

The small-mouthed salamander raises its tail and waves it back and forth when disturbed, trying to appear ferocious but instead looking completely cute, even if a sizable six inches. This salamander takes advantage of ephemeral woodland ponds, prairie gilgai (water holes), roadside ditches, flooded areas, and water sources without fish that prey on

▲ Small-mouthed salamander in the woods.

their young to breed. Will venture quite far in search of prey.

Sensory Very quiet and aroma free.

Habitat Forested bottomlands, riparian corridors with terraces, damp prairies, and around wetlands and ponds.

Food Insects, spiders, slugs, worms, and small crustaceans.

Habits Scurrying around for a meal. Appropriates burrows dug by other small animals.

Tidbits Most visible late January to April, when they travel to suitable breeding habitat.

Fish

Gars

Alligator Gar

Atractosteus spatula

Spotted Gar

Lepisosteus oculatus

WHERE TO FIND THEM: Spotted and alligator gars live in rivers and lakes in **Adventures 2, 4, 5, 6, 13, 16,17, 18, 22,** and **24,** with the Trinity in **Adventure 13** being especially favorable for large alligator gar.

Alligator gars are gargantuan, the largest freshwater fish in Texas—up to ten feet long and weighing up to three hundred pounds. These voracious predators can live twenty to fifty years. Their less massive cousin, spotted gar, grows about a yard long and sports

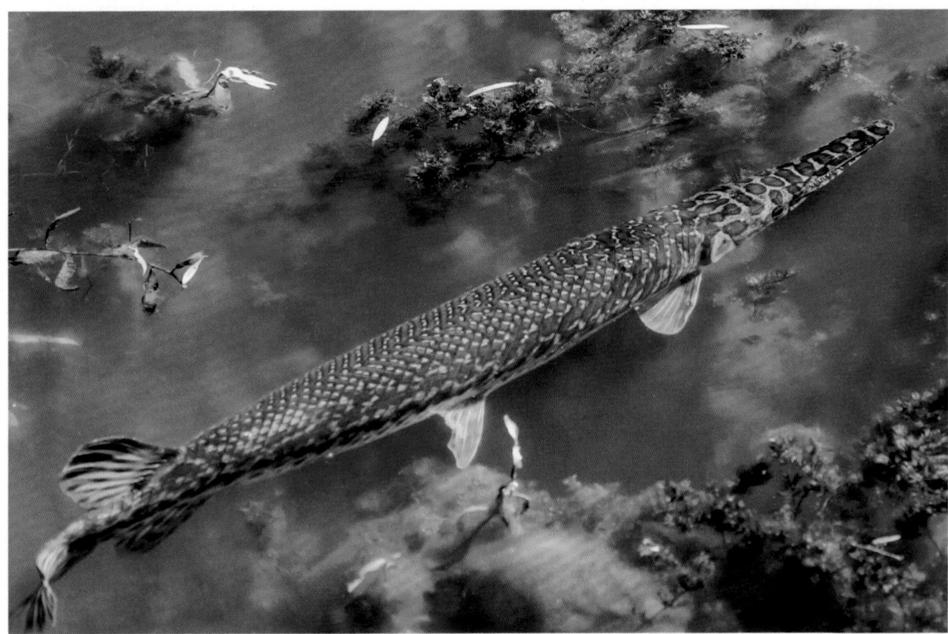

▲ Spotted gar cruises the wetlands at the Heard in McKinney

Alligator gar, in its full glory.

camouflaging dots. Unchanged since the Cretaceous era, these living fossils look dinosaurish, covered in armored scales and with snouts containing double rows of razor teeth. Gulping air into a modified swim bladder enables tolerance of low-oxygen waters like the Trinity River and periods of drought or low-river flows. Gars require floodplains or slow-moving water to spawn, environments greatly reduced by channelization and downcutting.

Sensory Much noisy splashing when gars mate.

Habitat Gars prefer slow rivers, quiet lakes, and reservoir backwaters.

Food These nocturnal predators mainly eat fish, also reptiles and turtles, plus animals floating on the surface such as juvenile waterfowl.

Habits Alligator gars come together in groups during their pre-spawning period and while overwintering.

Tidbits North Americans used gar scales for arrowheads, breastplates, and covering tools. • Gars are euryhaline, which means they can live in fresh and saline waters.

Crustaceans

Red Swamp Crawfish

Procambarus clarkii

WHERE TO FIND THEM: Bottomland woods and riparian corridors.

You can see crawfish (or crawdad or mudbug or crayfish—all are the same crustacean) "chimneys" around their burrow entrances and their empty exoskeletons after some critter has had them for a meal much more often than the live crawfish itself. Yet the crawdad or mudbug is an anchor of the bottomland food chain.

▲ A red swamp crawfish strikes a defensive pose.

On the dinner menu for raccoons, opossums, owls, and predatory fish, turtles, and reptiles. Below the ground are deep burrows where the young reside with a mother crawfish through two molts, for up to eight weeks. Since she can produce 500 eggs, it gets crowded.

Habitat Prefers low-flowing creeks and rivers, wetlands, and reservoir headwaters, but adapts to human development, living in golf course and retention ponds, ditches, and low-lying areas that are frequently flooded.

Sensory Tunnels have a peculiar smell. Take a sniff!

Food Omnivorous diet of insects, invertebrates, small crustaceans and reptiles, and general detritus.

Habits Look for them wandering about, sometimes in speedy bursts, in twilight hours.

Tidbits Their burrows are shared by amphibians, crustaceans, and insects. • Despite their big eyes, their vision is poor. • Crawfish racing—it's a thing.

Wildflowers

American Basket-flower

Centaurea americana

WHERE TO FIND THEM: Any place with prairies, especially **Adventures 7, 8, 9, 14, 21,** and **23**.

Everyone should experience the peak bloom of basket-flowers. First there is the pure sight of prairie slopes packed with three- to six-foot-tall plants sporting five-inch-wide lavender blooms with cream-colored centers. The aroma wafting from a blooming mass is divine. Containing plentiful pollen, they attract so many pollinators that fields audibly buzz and visibly vibrate. They are especially beloved by bumblebees but attract hummingbirds and butterflies as well. Light tan bracts below each bud look woven, making the bloom appear as if it's in a basket.

▲ American basket-flowers spread widely as the blooms conclude.

Flower Peak bloom in May and June, continuing through August.

Seed Profuse amounts of large sunflower-like seeds mature in summer and sustain grassland birds.

Home Help Plant where they can reseed annually. Suitable for fresh and dried flower arrangements.

Tidbits The botanical name *Centaurea* derives from the Centaur Chiron who in Greek mythology taught mankind about botanical healing plants. • Campgrounds near historical Native American bison kill sites often have extensive basket-flowers. • Native Americans used the plant to treat venomous bites, wounds, and other ailments. • Stamens contract when touched and push pollen onto pollinators.

Arkansas Yucca

Yucca arkansana

WHERE TO FIND THEM: Any place with prairies, especially **Adventures 7, 8, 9, 14, 21,** and **23**.

Its two-foot spires rise above spring wildflowers, bedecked with large, globular, greenish ivory blossoms that hang downward—a stunning sight. A useful and iconic plant of the Southwest, yucca is found in Native American ruins dating back 2000 years. Soap was crafted from roots high in saponins. Fibers in leaves turned into very tough rope, fencing, and thatch. Sharp leaf tips served as needles for yucca thread used to craft shoes, hats, mats, and more.

Flower Its waxy, globe-shaped dangling blooms are home to yucca moths that solely pollinate the plant and live most of their lives inside the bloom. Yuccas bloom every year, unlike agaves.

Seed The hard, dark seeds are a food source for wildlife, although toxic to horses, cats, and dogs.

Habitat Well-drained limestone or sandy soils in sunny locations such as rocky outcrops and prairies.

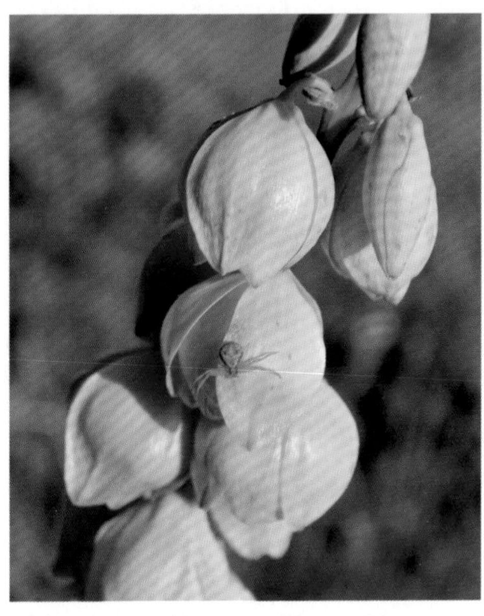

▲ Arkansas yucca blooms on a Plano prairie.

Home Help Excellent specimen plant for pots and low-water xeriscapes, though keep the sharp leaves far from paths.

Tidbits Yucca flowers taste lightly of artichokes with a sweet edge. Very attractive in salads and as a garnish. Check for moths first. Only eat one or two due to saponin content. • Used as a foaming agent in beverages before widespread carbonation.

Milkweed for Monarchs

Green Milkweed

Asclepias viridis

Antelope Horns Milkweed

Asclepias asperula

WHERE TO FIND THEM: Any place with prairies, especially **Adventures 7, 21,** and **23**.

Sturdy, two-foot-tall wildflowers feature large, eye-popping flower clusters up to four inches across. Each flower has a fantastic star-like array of five prominent purple structures. While antelope horns milkweed favors the drier west, and green milkweed enjoys the rainier east, DFW is where east meets west and both

Green milkweed is a sturdy plant.

Antelope horns milkweed blooms are elaborate.

species flourish. That's fortunate, because the area falls in the major migratory route of the milkweed-dependent monarch. The butterfly lays its eggs on the plant for its caterpillars to eat upon hatching. Glycosides in milkweeds give monarch caterpillars a bitter taste and protection from predators. A radical decline in milkweed imperils monarchs. Plant this plant!

Flower From a distance, the flowers look like baseball-sized green spheres. Look closely. Each one is composed of many individual green, waxy blooms with purple accents. Generally, these milkweeds bloom from April to June, with profuse nectar appreciated by many pollinators.

Seed The seedpods mature, taking on the pointed appearance of an animal horn. As the Texas sun beats down, the pods dry and split, revealing flat seeds wrapped in delicate fluff that catch the wind and sail long distances, not unlike newly hatched monarchs. Songbirds use these seed puffs to line their nests.

Habitat Antelope horns prefers sunny, well-drained, even dry, soil, while green likes a bit more moisture. Significant roots aid their hardiness, allowing them to survive even on disturbed land. Found in pastures because cattle won't eat them due to glycoside content.

Home Help Milkweed is required in every pollinator garden. Avoid nurseries that buy plants from growers that use systemic insecticides poisonous to monarchs. Instead, patronize local native plant sales or buy from Monarch Watch. Milkweed's strong taproot makes transplanting challenging, so buy young plants and don't move once planted. Can also be started from seed.

Tidbits During World War II, the buoyant silky down of mature seedpods was used in life jackets. Many collected it as a civic duty. • When abraded or broken, milkweed oozes a milky sap that can aggravate skin, especially in those with sensitive skin. • Native Americans and settlers used the milky sap to treat warts, ringworms, and other skin ailments. • The genus name *Asclepias* refers to Aescupalius, Greed god of medicine and son of Apollo.

Nuttall's Sensitive Briar

Mimosa nuttallii

WHERE TO FIND THEM: Any place with prairies, especially **Adventures 7, 8, 9, 14, 21,** and **23**.

▲ Sensitive briar puffball blooms are psychedelic.

Able to instantly respond to environmental disturbances, sensitive briars have entertained young and old for centuries. A slight touch or breeze makes the mimosa-like leaves fold like they're ready for sleep, just as they do at sundown. While the pink puffball flowers look sweet, handle these miniature briars carefully. Hooked prickles coat the sprawling ground-hugging vines and seedpods, though herbivores like rabbits find them tasty.

Flower April to June is the season for these pompon flowers, which are composed of bright pink stamens with yellow tips, making them look like miniature fireworks explosions.

Seed Its bulging disk seedpods are prickly as well, yet relished by wildlife.

Habitat Nuttall's sensitive briar prefers prairies, fields, dry hillsides, woodland edges, and fence lines. Their presence indicates a lack of disturbance.

Home Help Perfect for xeriscapes and rock gardens. Doesn't spread aggressively. As a bonus, this pea family member fixes nitrogen in the soil. Easy to start from cuttings.

Tidbits If you keep touching a sensitive briar, it will cease to respond.

Stiff Greenthread

Thelesperma filifolium

WHERE TO FIND THEM: Prairies of western Dallas–Fort Worth, especially **Adventures 21, 22,** and **23.**

Enjoy stiff greenthread's extended bloom period as the abundant annual coats western DFW highways in brilliant golden waves, often adorned by butterflies. It adapts to almost any soil, reseeds itself without being aggressive—a perfect beginner's wildflower. The dried thin leaves and stalks make a nice spot of tea—Navajo tea, that is, with a mild green tea flavor perfect with a bit of honey.

Flower Urn-shaped buds open and embrace the petals like a vase. Abundant in April and May when its golden wave blankets roadsides and old prairie remnants, but blooms into November. Great bloom surges after summer rains.

Seed Painted buntings and other songbirds relish its plentiful seeds.

Habitat Needs good drainage, but grows in many soils, with a taproot made to survive drought.

Home Help Perfect for pocket prairies and wild corners where you need a reseeding annual.

Tidbits Navajo tea is considered helpful for joint pain, upset stomachs, and kidney issues.

▲ Greenthread blooms, up close.

White Rosinweed

Silphium albiflorum

WHERE TO FIND THEM: Fort Worth Prairie and Eastern Cross Timber prairie enclaves of western DFW, especially **Adventures 21, 22,** and **23.**

The thin limestone soil of the Fort Worth Prairie and nearby areas creates a unique habitat for this endemic and endangered plant existing nowhere else. Its white, daisylike flowers on a three-foot stalk stand out on the prairie. The large, stiff leaves are deeply lobed and very hairy. This slow-growing perennial forms massive root systems with a taproot piercing ten feet or more. So long-lived that larger clumps become landmarks, befitting a plant that aligns its leaves in a north-south direction, garnering it the nickname compass plant.

Flower Peaks in June but continues to bloom in hot weather when few flower resources are available.

White rosinweed flower stalks are a striking sight on the prairie.

Seed Sizable domed discs provide good seeds for birds.

Habitat On slopes and in well-drained areas of medium grass prairies, in gravelly limestone soil.

Home Help Impressive specimen plant for yards with limestone soil with good drainage.

Tidbits Binomial name refers to the sticky resin exuding from the stem when abraded. • Indigenous communities used the resin from compass plants as chewing gum.

Native Grasses

Big Bluestem

Andropogon gerardii

WHERE TO FIND THEM: Any place with Blackland Prairies, especially **Adventures 6, 7, 8, 9, 14,** and **17**.

Native grass roots pierce six to fifteen deep into the ground, enabling them to survive heat and drought. With growing nodes inches below the surface, they defy fires, too. Native grasses once sustained vast herds of bison.

Big bluestem is the "King of the Prairie," reigning royalty of the "Big Four" native grasses that anchor the Blackland Prairie and include Indiangrass, switchgrass, and little bluestem. Big bluestem's teal-tinged, long, broad blades soar to six feet or more, turning mauve as they mature. Strongly rhizomatous, big bluestem creates colonies of foliage thick as a jungle. Craved by cattle.

Big bluestem in a prairie restoration at Lewisville Lake Environmental Learning Area.

Seed Big bluestem's purplish, tri-pronged seedhead, stretching up to ten feet, resembles a turkey foot or three skinny fingers.

Habitat A denizen of the Blackland Prairie, where it thrives in deep clay soils and full sunlight, it also grows in vales and riparian corridors of Fort Worth Prairies. Provides superb cover and browse for deer, and nesting sites for grassland birds.

Home Help Big bluestem makes a dramatic large plant (use instead of pampas grass) and anchors larger prairie gardens that have deep soil.

Tidbits Larval host to several skipper butterflies.

Indiangrass

Sorghastrum nutans

WHERE TO FIND THEM: Any place with Blackland Prairies, especially **Adventures 6, 7, 8, 9, 14,** and **17**.

One of the "Big Four" and the "Queen of the Prairie" to big bluestem's king, Indiangrass also has broad blue-green-gray blades that reach six feet or more. Spectacular bronze seed plumes soar above burnt orange to purple foliage in fall. Savored by livestock.

▲ Indiangrass at Clymer Meadow.

Seed Plumes of fluffy, soft, golden-brown seeds with a purple tinge and metallic sheen are stunning well into winter. Excellent in dried arrangements. Essential to grassland birds.

Habitat Tolerates some shade, occasional poor drainage, and various soils, but thrives in deeper bottomlands and lower slopes.

Home Help Desirable accent plant for its seed plumes but tends to flop over in rich soils.

Tidbits Attracts grasshoppers that are an essential food source for wildlife. • Larval host to several skipper butterflies.

Little Bluestem

Schizachyrium scoparium

WHERE TO FIND THEM: Any place with Blackland Prairies, especially **Adventures 6, 7, 8, 9, 14,** and **17**.

Little bluestem is the glue of the prairie—its delicate appearance belies its strength. This is a prime example of a bunchgrass with foliage rarely topping four feet. It historically comprised 30 to 40 percent of total prairie vegetation. Presenting an ever-changing palette, its vegetation emerges bluish in spring, turns grayish green in summer, then progresses to a radiant, bronzed brick-red in fall, mellowing to brown in winter.

Seed Shiny, white seed tufts make a showy display through winter.

Habitat Characteristic of the prairies and Eastern Cross Timbers, versatile little bluestem takes some shade, prefers well-drained soils, and grows in sand, loams, or clay—from open fields to wherever a pocket of prairie arises. Its dense clumps are prime grassland bird-nesting sites.

Home Help Little bluestem accents rock gardens and easily fills wild corners where it can reseed.

Tidbits Larval host to several skipper butterflies.

▸ Little bluestem is the bedrock of many prairies.

Sideoats grama

Bouteloua curtipendula

WHERE TO FIND THEM: Prairies of western Dallas–Fort Worth, especially **Adventures 21, 22,** and **23**.

Sideoats grama is the State Grass of Texas. It's tougher than its dainty looks, much like Texas women! The grass grows one to two feet tall and gets its name from the oat-like seeds. Excellent cattle and deer browse. The hairy foliage turns purple or maroon in fall. Related to blue grama, (which is excellent for native grass lawns), and Texas grama (which has seeds on both sides of the stem).

▴ Sideoats grama works well in landscaping.

Seed The wavy stalks of sideoats grama produce spikelets on just one side of the seedstalk, which droop downward like oats and become seeds that birds avidly consume.

Habitat Grows well in a variety of well-drained soils. It takes full sun to dappled shade. Successful colonizer of disturbed land.

Home Help Mixes well with spring wildflowers because it stays short in spring and grows taller after wildflowers have finished blooming.

Tidbits Larval host to several skipper butterflies.

Vines

Eastern Poison Ivy

Toxicodendron radicans

WHERE TO FIND THEM: Forests and shady areas everywhere.

Many a forest hiker never feels the soft, lush leaves trail across their skin, nor see the leaves of three they're told to let be. Then a couple of days later, a horrible, itchy rash erupts. The culprit is urushiol, a potent allergen that about 60 percent of the population reacts to, some intensely. Only humans are allergic to urushiol. Sadly, it gives many people a negative impression of nature. Poison ivy protection is simple: cover up skin with long pants, a loose overshirt, and closed-toe shoes. Use Ivy-X Precontact Solution on exposed skin and wash skin thoroughly once you are back home with Dawn dishwashing detergent. Wipe down your dog and gear after hiking or it'll spread through the house. Additional defense tips in the book *Itchy Business*.

▲ Eastern poison ivy is every hiker's peril.

Habitat Wherever there is shade, there is poison ivy, a primary plant of many forests. It grows amid ground foliage and sends vines up trees that sprout extensive side branches. Underground rhizomes send up thickets of yard-high stems. It grows along fence lines, on the sides of structures, even in prairies where it gets shade from tall grasses. Makes many areas unpassable in summer.

Flower Tassels of tiny greenish white blooms. Nectar and pollen are the only parts of poison ivy without urushiol.

Seed Drooping dangles of ivory berries feature dark lines of urushiol canals—rash super-carriers.

Home Help Not a plant for around the house.

Tidbits A superb plant food for urushiol-immune wildlife: birds love the berries, rabbits and deer browse the high-protein leaves, and tree vines provide nesting areas for arboreal wildlife. • Vigorous root and rhizome systems provide excellent erosion control for creeks and slopes. • Red fall foliage is beautiful and aids in finding hidden patches to avoid.

▲ Purple passionflower possesses elaborate beauty.

Purple Passionflower

Passiflora incarnata

WHERE TO FIND THEM: Adventures featuring prairies and unmowed meadows.

Beauty, healing, and spirituality—all in one plant. Jesuit missionaries used the New World native around the globe as a teaching aid for the story of Christ, earning it the name Passiflora—flower of the passion incarnate, evoking the crown of thorns, nails, and wounds. Its ornate and effuse flowers, a true marvel of nature, contradict the plant's utter toughness.

Flower This showstopper peaks in July and August, each flower lasting a day. Hummingbirds fight over the blooms with a tropical fruit aroma. As bees gather nectar, stamens bonk their heads, depositing a healthy dab of pollen, which they transfer to the next bloom.

Seed Fruit the size of a squashed tennis ball turns yellow as it ripens. The pulp, with plentiful sticky seeds, turns into juices, jellies, jams, and flavoring that tastes both sweet and slightly tart, with overtones of orange and mango. No surprise that many songbirds and mammals, humans included, go for this treat.

Habitat Grows with plentiful sunlight in prairies and unmowed pastures, and along rivers, roads, and railroads—a delight to find in degraded places.

Home Help Beautiful along fences that get at least a half day of sun and have lattices to help tendrils attach. Spreads vigorously by rhizomes, so if space is tight, grow purple passionflower in a large container. Vines die back in winter.

Tidbits Some South American Indigenous groups term it *maraca-cui-iba*, because seeds rattle inside the dried fruit. • Unique leaf colorations discourage egg laying by butterflies. • Nicknamed maypop because blooming begins in May. • Extract used in relaxation and sleeping supplements.

Junipers

Ashe Juniper

Juniperus ashei

Eastern Red Cedar

Juniperus virginiana

▲ Ashe junipers get enormously wide.

WHERE TO FIND THEM: Scattered through most upland and some riparian forests. Juniper-oak ecosystems are part of the Western Cross Timbers in **Adventures 22** and **23**.

The area's native conifers, commonly called cedars, provide superb winter cover and windbreak for birds and small mammals. But cedar is loathed for producing avalanches of pollen that turn male trees—and anything that walks past them—yellow. Cedar fever season runs from December to February. While valuable in forests, they can be aggressive invaders of pastures and prairies. Eastern red cedar branches grow high on a solo trunk. The squatty Ashe juniper branches close to the base and often has multi trunks.

▲ Eastern red cedar can take on unusual shapes.

Habitat From deep prairie soils to eroded limestone bluffs, junipers will take root. They prefer good drainage.

Flower When the leaf tips turn orange, the males are about to blow!

Seed Wildlife consumes the light-blue cones which resemble berries.

Home Help Excellent for blocking wind and views; leave lots of room.

Tidbits Eastern red cedar heartwood is deeply maroon or reddish brown and very aromatic. Baton Rouge—"red stick" in French—is named for it. • Endangered golden-cheeked warblers weave shreds of bark from older Ashe junipers to build their nests. • Junipers resists decay, making it great for fence posts and outdoor structures. • Fresh twig tips can be steeped to create respiratory tea. • Larval hosts for olive juniper hairstreak butterfly.

Bois d'Arc

Maclura pomifera

WHERE TO FIND THEM: Along creeks and rivers, especially **Adventures 1, 2 6, 8, 9, 10, 11, 12, 13, 16,** and **17**.

Wherever the Blackland Prairie reigned, bois d'arcs were there, flourishing along creeks and rivers. Native Americans prized the strong, flexible wood for bows, earning the name "bow-wood" by French explorers. From this narrow home range, it traveled up the Great Plains by Native Americans carrying the large, wrinkled fruit, garnering osage orange as a name. Settlers took it across the South and Midwest, using the squat, thorny tree for hedgerow fencing.

Habitat This iconic tree prefers deep and fertile soil. It is a relatively rare find in riparian corridors. Distinctive curving branches, sometimes reaching to the ground, create shelter domes for deer.

▲ Bois d'arc in spring.

Seed Grapefruit-sized "horse apples" from female trees are an evolutionary anachronism, meant for distribution by Pleistocene period megafauna such as giant ground sloths. Pulp surrounds edible, oil-rich seeds eaten by squirrels.

Home Help Requires space to sprawl and plenty of moisture.

Tidbits Bois d'arc wood resists decay and is renowned for use as fenceposts and foundation piers. • Its dense wood also creates superb woodwind instruments and game calls. • Female trees make pom-shaped lime-green flowers.

Pecan

Carya illinoinensis

WHERE TO FIND THEM: Riparian corridors, especially **Adventures 1, 2, 3, 6, 8, 9, 10, 11, 12, 13, 16, 17, 21, 22,** and **24.**

The majestic State Tree of Texas, this riparian wonder can grow to mammoth size and live three centuries or more, acquiring a delightful, shaggy bark and broad canopy. Pecan nuts are essential to sustaining birds, mammals, and two southern traditions: pecan pie and pralines.

Habitat Pecans grow best in deep alluvial soils but will adapt with steady moisture.

Seed Tend to alternate years of abundance with small or no crops. Native pecans are tastier but more challenging to shell than papershell cultivars.

Home Help Pecan trees create superb, dappled shade and excellent wildlife watching.

▲ Heritage pecan tree starting to show fall colors at Quanah Parker Park in Fort Worth.

Tidbits Popular for infusing smoked meats with a sweet, nutty flavor.

Oaks

Post Oak

Quercus stellata

Blackjack Oak

Quercus marilandica

WHERE TO FIND THEM: **Adventure 20** has an astounding collection. Also seen at **19, 22,** and **23.**

Century-old post oak in Pioneer Park next to Dallas City Hall.

Some call them scrubby for their short stature and contorted branches; others regard them as survivors. The signature trees of the Cross Timbers endure poor soils, scant rain, and high winds. Slow growing and drought resistant, even century-old oaks might not top twenty feet and a foot in diameter. Post oak is the most common oak in Texas, even has an ecoregion named after it: Post Oak Savannah. The eccentric branching makes for exceptional winter beauty.

Habitat Known for taking hold in rocky, upland sites, post oaks will grow straighter and taller in deep, rich soils. Blackjack oak is intolerant of shade, so much so that its canopy can cause its lower limbs to die. Limbs persist on the tree and look a bit macabre.

Seed Squirrels and birds enjoy the small blackjack and post oak acorns.

Home Help Sensitivity to root disturbance limits post oaks' commercial sales and urban suitability, but blackjacks appear in larger nurseries.

Blackjack leaves are notable for their spiny lobes.

Tidbits Dense wood produces a hot flame, making blackjack and post oak timber superb for barbecues and wood-burning stoves. • Post oak's leathery leaves have hairy undersides, while blackjack leaves have pointed tips. • Blackjack serves as larval host for southern and white hairstreak and Horace's and Juvenal's duskywing butterflies. • Post oaks' thick bark resists fires.

Shumard Oak

Quercus shumardii

WHERE TO FIND THEM: Widely found, especially in riparian areas, but less so in western Dallas–Fort Worth. Along Trinity forks and creeks, appearing less frequently farther west.

The top red oak of North Texas has a classic branching structure and scarlet fall color that landscapers love. It's a stunning forest tree that grows to majestic size, often found solo, almost as if it wants adoration. Hosts thousands of caterpillars for nesting birds. Produces fall acorns for birds, squirrels, and mammals. Provides nesting locations for winged wildlife from songbirds to raptors and abodes for opossums, raccoons, and squirrels. What's not to love? Highly regarded in Doug Tallamy's *The Nature of Oaks*.

Habitat An anchor of the riparian forest, favoring alluvial soils with good drainage such as on slopes. Drought resistant, yet tolerates short-term flooding. Look for its similar, smaller relative, Texas oak (*Quercus buckleyi*), in upland forests.

Seed Acorns take two years to mature. Highly tannic, usually eaten late in the season.

Home Help Superb landscape tree if given plenty of room.

Tidbits Wood is close-grained, hard, and treasured for woodworking. • Larval host to Horace's duskywing butterfly.

▲ Shumard oak in splendid fall foliage.

Understory Trees

Plums

Chickasaw Plum

Prunus angustifolia

Mexican Plum

Prunus mexicana

WHERE TO FIND THEM: Widely found in forested areas, especially in riparian corridors. Impressive chickasaw thickets at **Adventures 17, 20,** and **23**. Mexican plum concentrations at **Adventures 14, 17, 19,** and **22**.

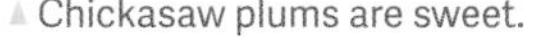

▲ Chickasaw plums are sweet.

▲ Mexican plum blossoms.

First sign of spring: clouds of bright flowers on native plum trees, fragrant enough to smell from many yards away. Forest edges, fence lines, and meadows are home to Mexican plum trees and thickets of Chickasaw plums, whose thorniness enables safer bird nesting.

Habitat These plum trees tolerate low water and a variety of soils if drainage is good. Mexican plum thrives in the dappled light of forests.

Flower Plums produce aromatic and profuse small white and pale pink blossoms.

Seed Chickasaw plums are small and sweet, changing from red to yellow when fully ripe. Eat one right off the tree, make into preserves, or even ferment into wine. Mexican plums go from yellow to purple as they ripen, a larger fruit that makes a superior jam. The fruit often have a white dusting of wild yeast.

Home Help With its compact size, unique branching, and attractive dark and wildly textured bark, Mexican plum excels—a perfect replacement for Bradford pear. Chickasaw plum thrives in wild areas where it can spread.

Tidbits Mexican plum is a larval host for tiger swallowtail. Chickasaw plum supports elm sphinx, hummingbird clearwing, imperial, io, and polyphemus moth larvae, among others. • Native Americans dried plums on hot rocks for winter use.

Roughleaf Dogwood

Cornus drummondii

WHERE TO FIND THEM: Widely found in forested areas, especially in riparian corridors.

▲ Roughleaf dogwood berries brighten fall.

Its fuzzy, rough leaves are a delight, but it's the bold, white berries consumed by over forty species of birds that make this small tree a wildlife star. It's a fast grower that suckers profusely, much to the appreciation of deer and rabbits who browse tender shoots. Its extensive roots stabilize creek banks and it provides gorgeous maroon fall color.

Habitat Roughleaf dogwood favors riparian corridors and bottomlands where it can form massive thickets. It grows robustly on forest edges and fence lines with some sunlight, becoming a woody pest in prairies.

Flower Native bees and butterflies adore the clusters of small white flowers.

Seed White berries ripen during early fall migration. Flocks can strip a thicket in minutes.

Home Help Good selection for wild shaded corners where it can sucker. Able to be contained and pruned.

Tidbits Native Americans used the extremely hard wood for arrows, pegs, and smoking pipes.

Sumacs

Flameleaf Sumac

Rhus lanceolata

Smooth Sumac

Rhus glabra

WHERE TO FIND THEM: Widely found, especially along woodland edges.

From the bounteous pyramids of claret berries to the shockingly crimson autumn foliage, these fast-growing sumacs impress. They form thickets of curved, elegant stems that branch at the top for abundant flowers and fruits. The glossier smooth sumac is the only native woody plant found in all forty-eight contiguous states.

Habitat Able to cling to steep slopes and thrive in poor soil but appreciates a comfy place to grow. Likes it sunny and tends to encroach on prairies. Privet displaces it in many spaces.

Flower Pointed bundles of yellow-green flowers stand out in spring and attract bounteous amounts of native bees.

Seed Beautiful pyramids of claret berries persist on the branch into winter, benefitting birds. Use to make tart, refreshing pink sumacade, or dry and grind the berries for a tangy, peppery spice.

Home Help Great as a garden backdrop or beneath shade trees. Contain roots to prevent spreading.

Tidbits Larval host to many hairstreak butterflies. • Roots make a yellow dye.

▲ Flameleaf sumac's famous fall color.

ADVENTURES

WILD WATERS OF THE EAST

WILD LANDS OF THE NORTH

BIG CREEKS OF SOUTHERN COLLIN COUNTY

GREAT TRINITY FOREST

Adventure Advice

Adventures range from paved paths to backwoods bushwhacking, even places to camp, swim, and ride horses.

▲ Scott Hudson, president of the North Texas Master Naturalists, and the author watch wildlife in a slough beneath electrical lines.

Be Aware

Unless noted, all places listed:

- Are free to enter. (Donations to preserves stewarded by nonprofits are appreciated.)
- Are open dawn to dusk.
- Allow dogs on leashes.

Follow accepted trail protocol:

- Take only photos; leave only footprints.
- Plant and animal harvesting are not allowed.
- Leave all artifacts in place. Please collect trash on trails when possible.
- Facilities listed do not include sports fields, fishing, hunting, playgrounds, or children's attractions.

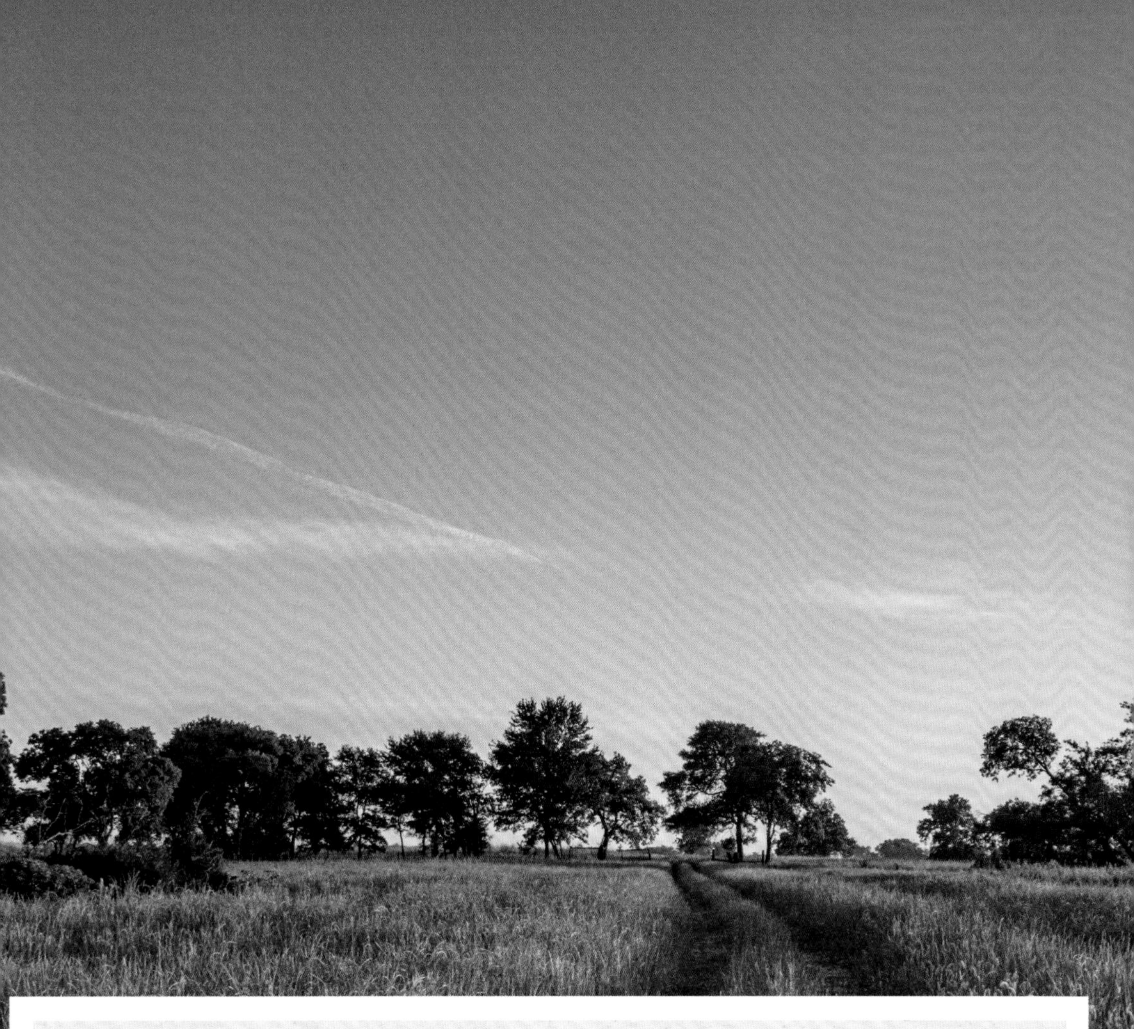

Stay Safe

Urban nature explorations require special considerations:

- Park only in brightly lit and very visible locations. Don't leave valuables in the car.
- Before leaving the vehicle, check your cell reception, battery power, and surroundings.

Southern weather has risks:

- Dressing to walk a nature trail is much different that preparing for a paved park path. Dress for sun and heat with hats, sunscreen, and cooling devices. Ants, snakes, thorny plants, and poison ivy make closed-toe shoes and long pants necessary.
- Carry plenty of water. Drink one-half liter an hour in moderate conditions, one liter an hour in summer heat.
- Carry backup power for your phone. Set to airplane mode to save power.

Hiking Seasons

Botanical and wildlife rhythms will affect your hiking experience:

- There are three peak pollen seasons. Junipers, mistakenly called cedars, release from December through February. Native grasses peak in May, while imported grasses continue through August. Ragweed begins in late August and releases through mid-October.

- In midsummer, wildlife movement is muted, notably among birds—a great time to watch dragonflies and damselflies. Even diurnal animals shift to dawn and dusk because of the heat.

- Privet transpires significantly more humidity than other shrubs in summer temperatures, making an area with this plant feel much hotter—not even wildlife tolerates it.

- The pretty white blossoms of hedge parsley, an invasive, turn into a multitude of burs in summer that cling obnoxiously to clothes and pet fur.

- Giant ragweed can reach twelve feet by fall, turning some trails into tunnels. Learn to recognize this tall plant when it is young in spring and avoid those areas in summer.

- Winter is prime hiking time in North Texas—fewer snakes and bugs, poison ivy leaves have dropped, and trails are more visible.

What to Keep Handy in Your Car

It's a good idea to clean up a bit after getting up close with nature:

- Keep a towel for drying off, in case you had an unexpected water crossing.

- Pack a container for muddy hiking shoes and bring a pair of sandals for driving home.

- Bring premoistened towelettes or containers of soapy and clean water to wash and rinse hands.

- Pack a change of pants, especially if you hike in poison ivy or chigger territory.

Citizen Science

Cellular signals are strong throughout most of North Texas, so:

- Fire up your iNaturalist, Merlin, Rockd, and other nature identification apps.

- Turn off automatic uploads to save power and time.

- Don't forget your power block.

Go Wild

Go Wild adventures are trail-free or difficult-to-navigate trails. Read these two sections first.

How Not to Get Lost

Understand your terrain:

- Mark your intended location on Google or other map apps. Switch to satellite view and study where you'll be going. Where is the parking? How much tree cover is there? Are there drainage channels or creeks to get around?
- Many map apps, including Google, mark popular trails. Search using "trail" or "trailhead." Best to verify these paths with another source.
- Before you start hiking, orient yourself to the directions. Smartphones contain compass apps, but manual compasses are cheap and necessary.
- A trail GPS app such as Gaia or Strava can track time, mileage, and trail route, allowing you to follow your route back out if lost.

How to Not Get Hurt

Hiking in wild areas, even in cities, takes preparation and awareness:

- Hike with a buddy and let a third party know where you've gone hiking. Have a plan for how you'd seek help and describe your location in case you get hurt.
- Check a weather app before you depart. If hiking along waterways, make sure there aren't big storms upstream.
- Riverbanks can be soft and prone to collapse, so stand back from the edge. Shorelines can have "quickmud," able to dangerously mire dogs and people.
- In warm weather, stay aware of venomous snakes.
- Poison ivy grows in shady areas as shrubs as well as ground and tree vines. Wear long pants and closed-toed shoes. A long-sleeved shirt with ventilation panels worn open over clothing helps keep poison ivy and mosquitoes off. Wash all exposed skin with Dawn dishwashing detergent after hiking. Wash all clothing and wipe down pets, shoes, and packs.

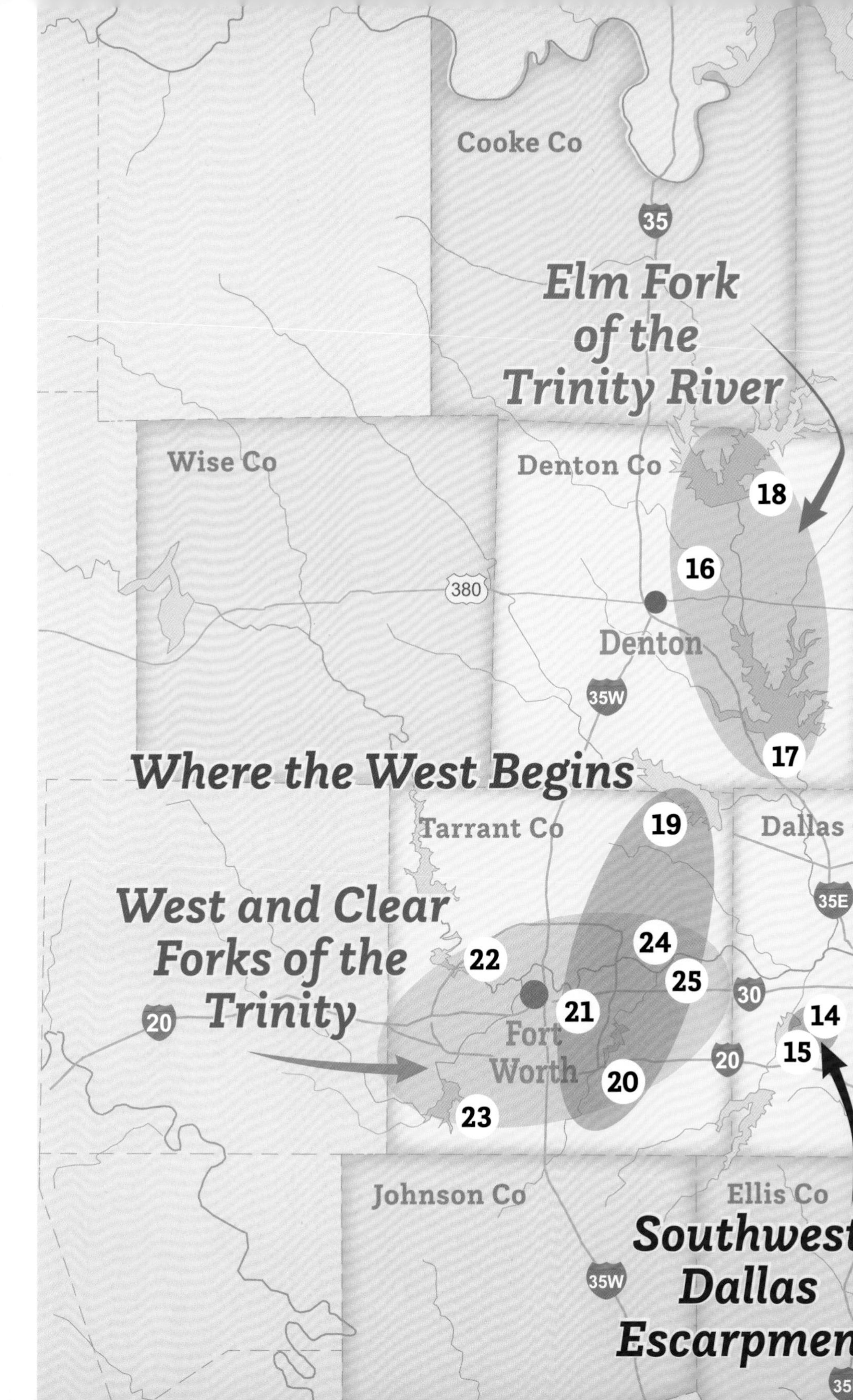

Cooke Co
35
Elm Fork
of the
Trinity River
Wise Co
Denton Co
18
16
380
Denton
35W
17
Where the West Begins
19
Tarrant Co
Dallas C
35E
West and Clear
Forks of the
Trinity
24
22
25
30
21
14
20
Fort
Worth
15
20
20
23
Johnson Co
Ellis Co
Southwest
Dallas
Escarpmen
35W
35E

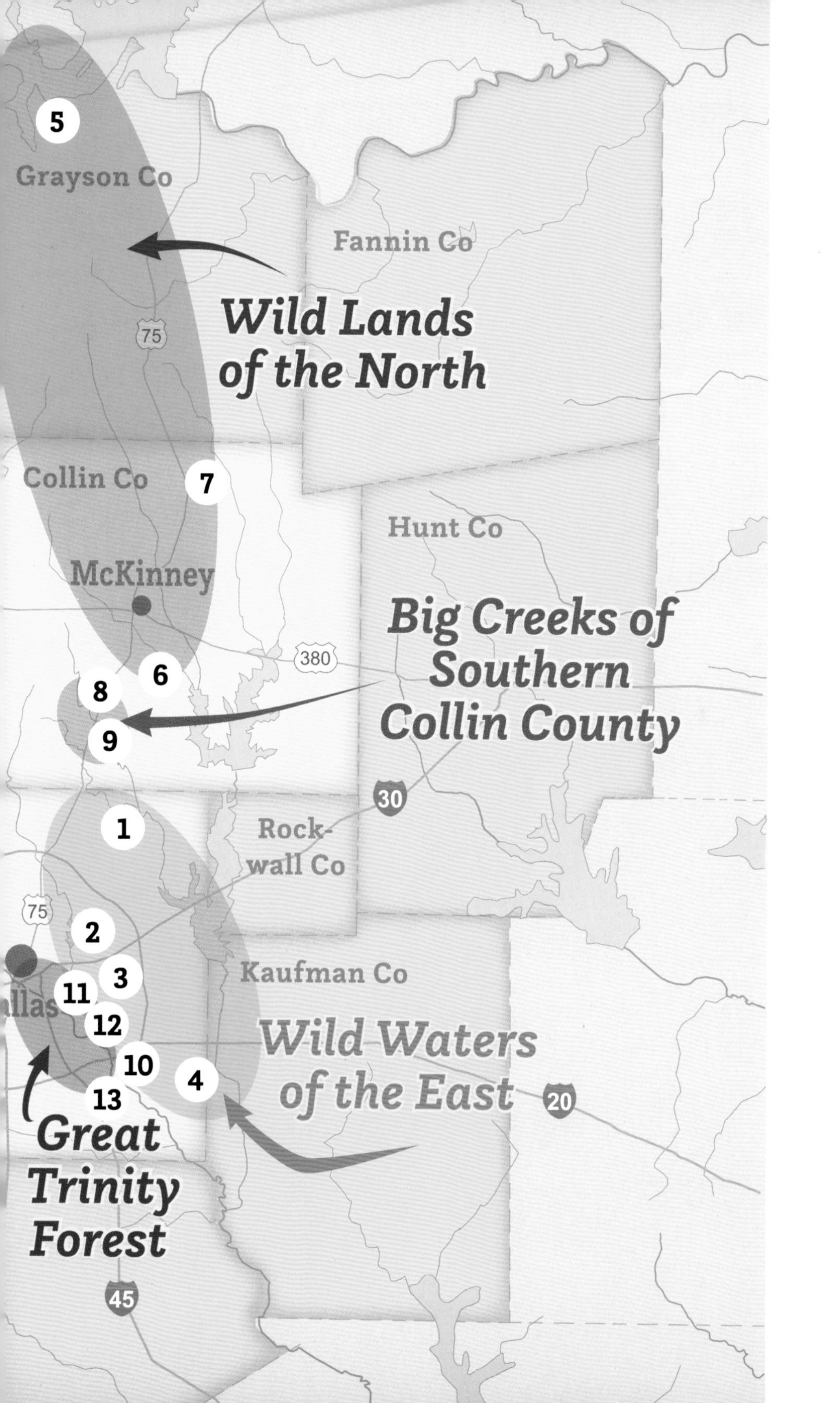
5
Grayson Co
Fannin Co
Wild Lands of the North
75
Collin Co
7
Hunt Co
McKinney
Big Creeks of Southern Collin County
380
6
8
9
30
1
Rock-wall Co
75
2
3
11
12
Kaufman Co
Wild Waters of the East
10
4
13
20
Great Trinity Forest
45

ADVENTURE 1 **WILD WATERS OF THE EAST**

Spring Creek Forest Preserve

An old-growth forest flanking a deep, sparkling Spring Creek creates a diverse riparian corridor in the shadow of development.

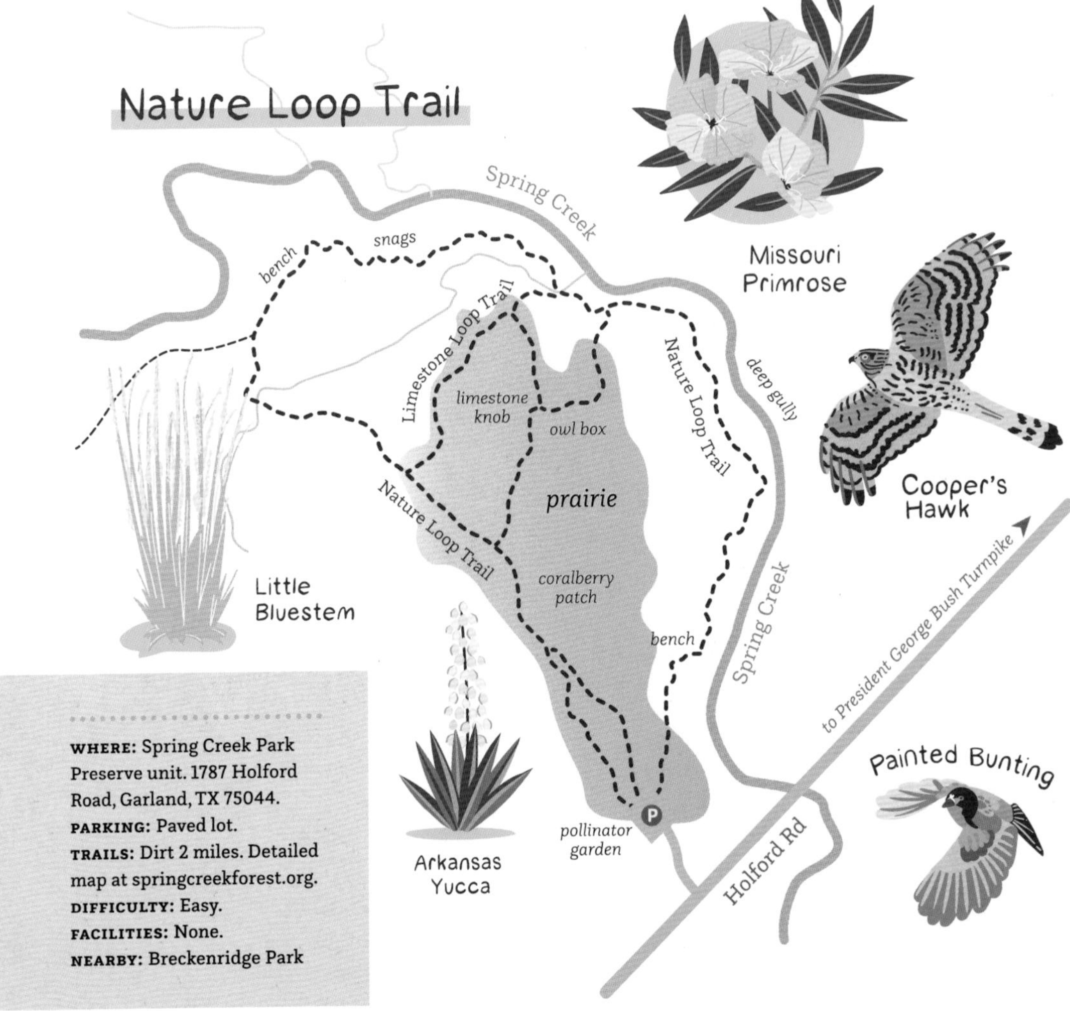

WHERE: Spring Creek Park Preserve unit. 1787 Holford Road, Garland, TX 75044.
PARKING: Paved lot.
TRAILS: Dirt 2 miles. Detailed map at springcreekforest.org.
DIFFICULTY: Easy.
FACILITIES: None.
NEARBY: Breckenridge Park

▲ The preserve flanks sparkling Spring Creek.

Learning While Walking

The Nature Loop Trail at Spring Creek Forest Preserve (SCFP) helps walkers understand the outdoors thanks to interpretative stops researched and created by a team of North Texas Master Naturalists. Access the webpage on your phone or download and print the brochure. Look for narrow, brown, numbered posts about a yard high, and let's go.

WEALTH OF WILDFLOWERS

Once you're past the tiny, wooded knoll and picnic table with a great view, notice the edge habitat plants that grow where the prairie meets the upland forest (#3 on website map). Red-tailed hawks frequently perch in the trees to hunt the open spaces. Extra points if you spy a painted bunting!

Take a side wander on the Limestone Loop Trail, through a fine chalk prairie of shallow soil over limestone too rocky for cultivation, preserving the prairie. Spectacularly colorful with wildflowers like Missouri primrose's extravagant yellow blooms. In fall, little bluestem creates a carpet of bronze. Listen for eastern phoebes with their strident calls: *fee-bee, fee-bee.*

Back on the Nature Loop Trail, enter the forest (#5 on website map) with trees over seventy feet tall. SCFP volunteers cracked down on invasive Chinese privet and honeysuckle, creating a healthy, diverse understory. Notice young trees growing up to replace older ones. Do you see signs of armadillo digging in the soft soil?

▼ Through all seasons, the prairie is splendid with color.

▲ Spring Creek volunteer leads a guided hike.

FOREST CREATURES

As you cross a small feeder creek, notice the lush and inviting vale. Listen for the rat-a-tat tapping of small downy and larger red-bellied woodpeckers. In winter, you're sure to see the butter-butt flash of a yellow-rumped warbler. Spring into summer, you might spy some coralroot orchids with tiny, speckled blooms on burgundy stems.

Continue right on Nature Loop Trail to follow Spring Creek. Take the dirt side path into a meander lobe with a very diverse and healthy forest (#7 on map). So many birds and squirrels! Abundant seeds, nuts, and berries support a variety of forest mammals. Watch for creek overview spurs.

Look for the occasional standing dead tree called a snag (#8 on map). Some look macabre! Insects burrow into the wood, providing a buffet for birds, and fungi and lichen help decomposition while serving up tasty morsels for wildlife. Woodpeckers utilize cavities in the decaying wood for nests.

Are you feeling like a naturalist? You should be! Treat yourself to a mindfulness walk. When the trail rises toward the prairie, does light filtering through the trees change? Listen for the creek. You'll pass a patch of invasive honeysuckle. (#10 on map) Can you still embrace SCFP's beauty?

Continue down the Nature Loop Trail and take a detour to look at beautiful but embattled Spring Creek (#12 on map). Paved developments nearby funnel high-velocity stormwater into the creek. Notice the collapsing banks, exposed tree roots, and litter marking the high-water level.

Once out of the forest, take a moment on the bench to reflect on your experiences and the hard work of dozens of people who made your walk possible, including the wealthy landowner's artist daughter, who sought its preservation, the activists who lobbied the city to purchase the land, and all the SCFP volunteers who keep their dreams alive.

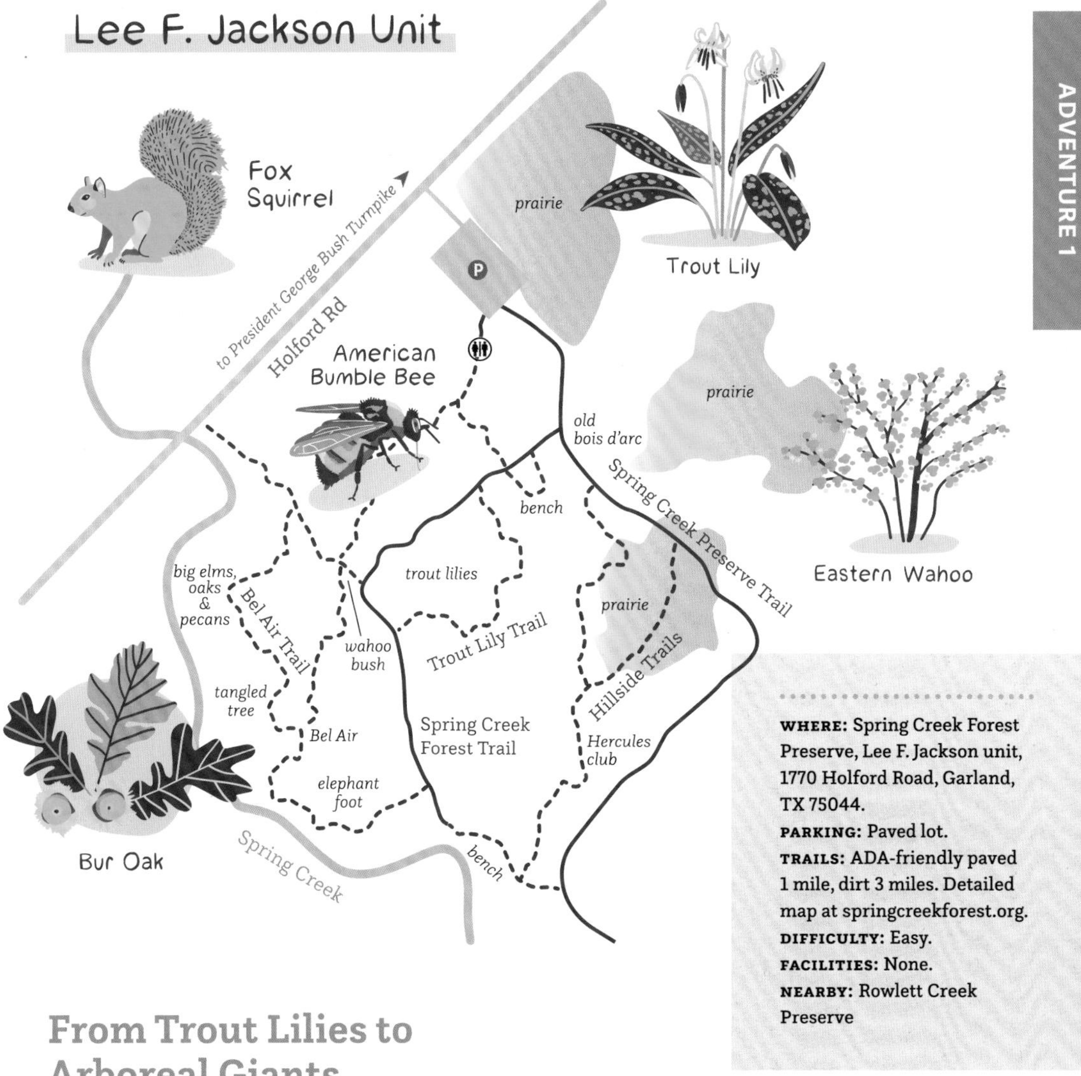

WHERE: Spring Creek Forest Preserve, Lee F. Jackson unit, 1770 Holford Road, Garland, TX 75044.
PARKING: Paved lot.
TRAILS: ADA-friendly paved 1 mile, dirt 3 miles. Detailed map at springcreekforest.org.
DIFFICULTY: Easy.
FACILITIES: None.
NEARBY: Rowlett Creek Preserve

From Trout Lilies to Arboreal Giants

President of Spring Creek Forest Preservation Society and retired from the Environmental Protection Agency, David Parrish is young at heart. As he heads into the giant trees of Spring Creek Forest Preserve (SCFP), a smile erupts and he almost skips. True to the Boy Scout he's always been, nature is a place of joy and endless projects for him. His enthusiasm is contagious.

On a beautiful fall day, we head down the paved path toward Spring Creek. It curves cool and shady through the trees, passing through occasional sunlit glens, and slopes down to the creek. It's a lovely ramble, even easy for the ambulatory impaired.

We depart the pavement for narrow trails lacing through a sizable block of old-growth forest, a magical expanse with an awesome hush that holds birdcalls aloft. Thanks to monthly Preservation Society for Spring Creek Forest workdays, it's surprisingly free of invasives.

◄ A group of naturalists pause to study the forest.

"There's the Trout Lily Trail," he says, gesturing to our left. The society hosts popular walks each February to enjoy the petite wildflowers that carpet the woods. The ceremonial winter emergence is a big social event.

SCFP is a biological museum, home to some of the oldest trees in the county. The towering trees offer dappled light to a radiant understory. I point and David's attention follows to a patch of elephant's foot, whose broad leaves lie flat on the soil like a foot. Spring brings bright yellow swaths of golden groundsel and delicate dangling heads of purple meadow rue.

"Oh, so many wahoos!" I exclaim. The slight, shrubby eastern wahoo trees burst into a mass of dangling, red, strawberry-shaped fruit each fall. We note a mature cedar elm leaning over the trail and wonder how long it'll last. A few maroon leaves linger on rusty blackhaw viburnum plants.

We slip onto the Bel Air Trail, repaired by David's Boy Scouts after 2015's record-breaking rains. "When you have a bunch of young Scouts, they just zoom right through it," says David. Then we come to the trail's namesake Chevy Bel Air. In this pristine forest, the abandoned car in a ravine gets much attention, particularly from youth who paint it periodically. Makes a terrific condo for rat snakes.

Once again, I squeal like a kid, this time at bear's foot, with its enormous, coarse leaves. Close by is a pecan tree that fell against a bur oak, creating a perfect niche for a honeybee hive. But it's time to head back to where to-do lists await. We wander up the slope to the paved trail.

Dedicated volunteers with the Preservation Society for Spring Creek Forest work closely with the City of Garland to oversee the preserve. The group organizes workdays and a variety of events, while monitoring the land's ecological health.

▼ Trout lilies put up a solo leaf in the first year, followed by flowers in the second.

Go Wild: Riparian Woods

Our group, including David Parrish, president of the Preservation Society for Spring Creek Forest, and photographer Daniel Koglin, ambles the paved path squeezed between Spring Creek Forest Preserve and a shopping center, heading for the entrance to Ranger Trail that takes us into the bottomlands.

Quiet settles like fog, the surrounding bustle on this winter day blocked by a thick swath of large trees. Spontaneous laughter emerges as we relax into this new reality. The trail swings close to the creek, allowing a glimpse of water sparkling over white limestone.

The four- to six-story trees look impossibly tall. Scattered acorns mark a faint circle beneath a towering Shumard oak. A creek-side bur oak nearby is the elephant of trees: wide, massive, and firmly grounded. On the floodplain slope, a chinkapin oak grows slowly into ancienthood.

WHERE: Albert H. Halff Park, 4695 Ranger Drive, Garland, TX 75040. Northeast Dallas County near N. Garland Avenue and Pres. George Bush Turnpike.
PARKING: Paved lot.
TRAILS: ADA-friendly pavement 1 mile, dirt 1.5 miles. Detailed map at springcreekforest.org.
DIFFICULTY: Moderate.
FACILITIES: None.
Nearby: Breckinridge Park, Rowlett Nature Trail, Woodland Basin Nature Area.

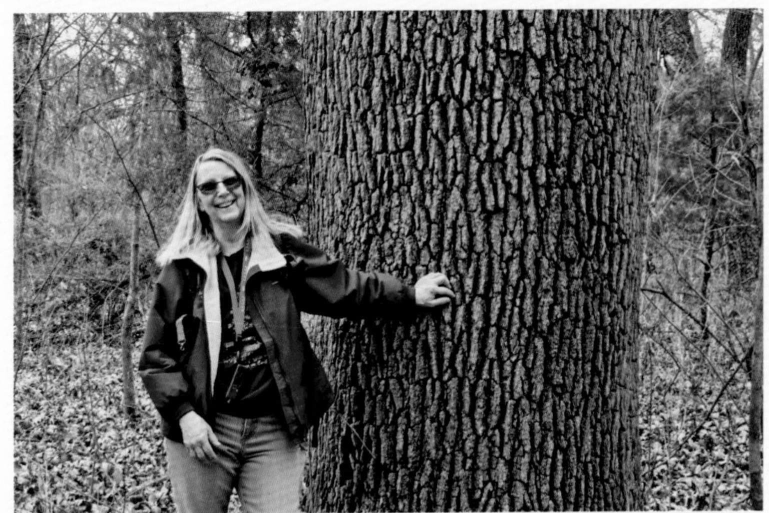

◄ The author next to one of Spring Creek's immense hardwoods.

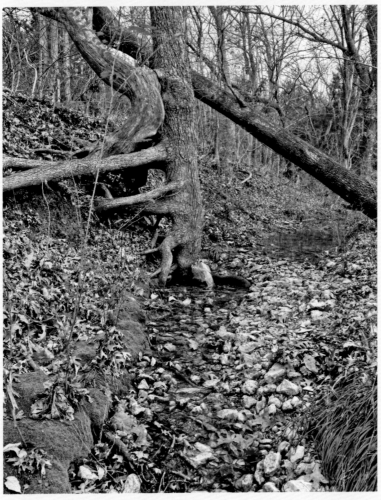

◄ A tree clings to the slope of a small creek.

▲ Spring Creek awakens the creek kid within.

We continue past a gigantic pecan with delightfully shaggy bark, whose tumultuous fallen leaves show evidence of creatures rooting for nuts. The canopy of astoundingly tall green ash, sycamore, and black walnut titters with the laughing cackles and piercing *skee-ews* of northern flickers in conversation.

Small wet-weather creeks furrow their way to Spring Creek, creating moist vales coated with moss in brilliant greens and filigreed sage-green lichens, where a tree clings with roots as thick as branches. Squatty bois d'arcs hold the slope and sport curved, springy branches.

The trail dips into a lush lobe created by a broad creek bend. A multitude of tiny ruby-crowned kinglets and towhees make quite a racket. The robins with their loud swooping calls compete for hackberries with cedar waxwings, whose delicate, high-pitched peeps belie their raucous nature.

A wide gravel bar adorns the creek bend. If the weather were warmer, we'd all scurry down there and while away the day, enjoying the orange and turquoise flashes of longear sunfish in the clear water and looking for tunnel-nests that belted kingfishers have made in the banks. It's been a perfect morning. A path peels off to the left and we join the paved trail.

ADVENTURE 2

WILD WATERS OF THE EAST

White Rock Lake Park

Dallas's urban oasis attracts runners and cyclists, extensive boating activity, superb birdwatching, great vistas, and occasional wild spots.

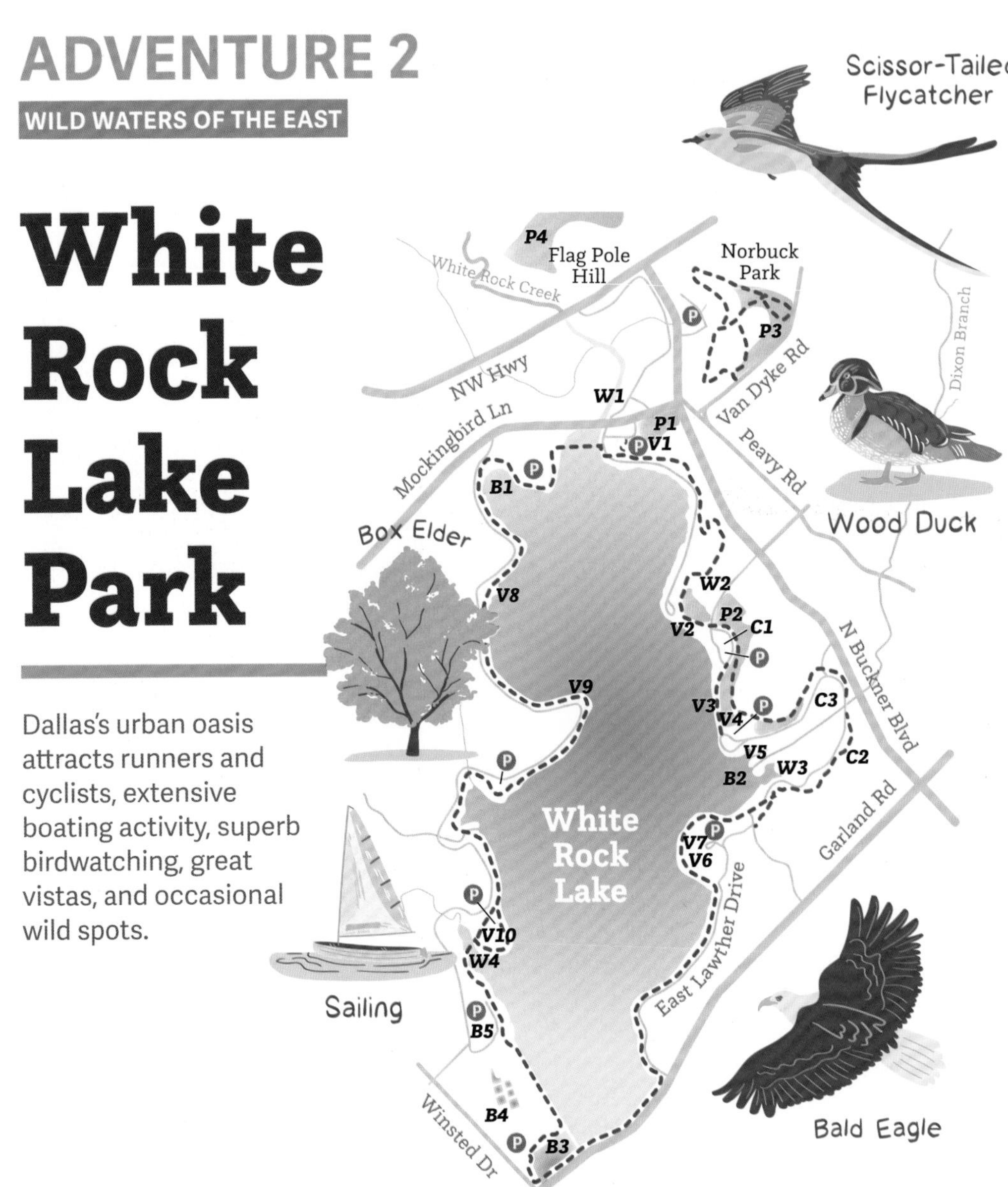

Dairy farms once flourished on the limestone hills forming White Rock Creek's deep valley, with cows grazing on verdant native grasses. Impounded in the early 1900s to create White Rock Lake, the over 2200 acres of what is now lake and green space is Dallas's most beloved park. But popularity has its price. It's challenging to find the wild at White Rock. Challenging, but not impossible.

▲ A great blue heron waits on a moored scull.

Birdwatching Bonanza

More bird species are at White Rock Lake than anywhere else in Dallas County—at least 294 species—due to migrating birds and waterfowl that winter here. Bald eagles hunt here, and currently a young pair of bald eagles nests annually at the lake. White pelican flocks are an anticipated harbinger of the holiday season.

B1: Cormorant Corner. Every winter, visiting double-crested cormorants and a few neotropic ones hang out in the tall trees when not diving for fish. Trees of dark, long-necked birds with startling aqua eyes are a macabre spectacle. Sit at the nearby bench and watch the show.

B2: Sunset Bay. Over 175 species of birds patronize this sheltered inlet, including Muscovy ducks, blue-winged teals, American coots, and Canada geese raising young in summer. Winter brings flocks of white pelicans, earning it the nickname Pelican Point. A favorite place for the resident bald eagles to hunt waterfowl and fish. Take the paved trail north for a lovely small waterfall at Reinhardt Branch.

B3: Spillway. White Rock Lake's outflow tumbles over a terraced spillway. In early winter mornings, ring-billed gulls amass on the spillway. The shallow water attracts wading birds such as black-crowned night herons, great and little blue herons, and great egrets. You might even see a river otter. Watch from scenic overlooks atop the dam and along Garland Road.

WHERE: 8300 East Lawther Drive, Dallas, TX 75218. Northeast Dallas off Garland Road and Buckner Blvd.
PARKING: Paved lots.
TRAILS: Paved 10 miles.
DIFFICULTY: Easy.
FACILITIES: Restrooms and chemical toilets, trail water stations, Bath House Cultural Center.
NEARBY: Flag Pole Hill Park, White Rock Creek Greenbelt.

▲ It's a mallard party at Sunset Bay.

Sunset Bay is a popular place to feed waterfowl. Unfortunately, bread is often what's offered, and it provides little nutrition. Preferable are raw shelled peanuts, greens, melon chunks, and green peas. Or spread nut butters or suet on whole grain bread. But the lake keeps them well fed.

B4: Old Fish Hatchery. Ponds for raising fingerlings closed in the 1950s and became seasonal rain-filled wetlands. Water-loving cottonwoods and pecan trees grew in the basins, draped with vines. The scene evokes Mayan ruins swallowed by jungle. Its reputation as an excellent birding site grew. Trails developed on dikes, some of the few dirt ones at White Rock, enabling closer looks at birds.

Although the forest became clogged with privet, during spring migration the area is "dripping with migrating warblers and thrushes in April and early May," says birder Chris Runk. Even in summer heat, herons and other wading birds feast on crawfish, amphibians, and reptiles. Be prepared for mosquito hordes in summer.

Trees and brush in an electric power corridor west of the ponds were razed in 2020, destroying habitat for wildlife, including beavers. After public outcry, Texas Discovery Gardens was tapped to lead restoration, with native grasses and privet control, so more productive natives like elderberry can flourish.

▲ A great egret shows off its breeding plumage.

B5: Monk parakeets. Native to South America, monk parakeets roost at an electrical substation, sustained by the warmth. The lime-green birds feed around the lake and are known for their loud, often harsh, calls.

Wild Areas

W1: White Rock Creek. The wildest area at White Rock is the north end, where the creek enters. Multiple channels in bottomland woods foster habitat for turtles, water snakes, gar, and more. A frog and toad cacophony is constant in summer. Immense trees harbor barred and great horned owls. Coyotes and bobcats hunt the woods. White blooms of elderflower shrubs line the banks in spring and trailing autumn clematis fills the space in fall. Explore by kayak or canoe.

W2: Northcliff Spring. A healthy seep in a copse follows a roadside rock channel to a lakeshore area favored by amphibians.

W3: Dixon Branch. Swampy inlets mark Dixon Branch's channelized stretch and original path. The wet creek-side terrain nurtures the lake's most enormous cottonwoods and pecans. Nature enthusiast Mark Clive advises, "If you're there just after dark, you're likely to see a beaver or two sneaking by. Notice the teeth marks on some of the trees. Meander down the creek edge for a raucous amphibian chorus. It's glorious!" Try access by canoe or kayak.

For the Love of the Lake organizes Second Saturday Shoreline Spruce-Ups and raises money to fund improvements to the park.

W4: Boomerang Boathouse. The low-slung Art Deco boathouse at T & P Hill sits on an inlet frequented by the friendliest ducks and sweetest ducklings in Dallas. From the paved trail's picturesque bridge, you can view numerous sliders and coots lazily floating or perched on driftwood. Cross to the stone benches of Plaza Solana to watch the cove's bird action.

Prairie Parcels

About 250 acres of rare Blackland Prairie, mainly on the lake's east side, escaped destruction because it was too shallow to till. Some parcels feature coveted prairie plants like Arkansas yucca, rattlesnake master, and a host of delicate wildflowers, thanks to restoration by volunteers from Native Prairies Association of Texas, North Texas Master Naturalists, and other groups. In other parcels, the prairie struggles. Brett Johnson, Dallas Parks and Recreation urban biologist, plans to restore them all.

Here's where you can view some of the better prairies.

P1: Boy Scout Hill. View the downtown Dallas skyline amid the wildflowers on the tall limestone knob. Favored by scissor-tailed flycatchers and barn swallows. Pass underneath Mockingbird Lane for more prime prairie, known for its spring wild hyacinth blooms.

P2: Bath House Cultural Center. The slopes around the Art Deco building feature the most accessible prairie. A disconnected block of Luna Place

▸ Scissor-tailed flycatchers hunt for bugs from an Arkansas yucca perch on Boy Scout Hill.

▾ A young boy finds delight in a White Rock Lake prairie.

provides a chigger-free stretch. A narrow rock trail just to its north gets you up close, so prairie glories like Drummond's skullcap can reveal themselves.

P3: Norbuck Park. Park at the tennis courts and walk east into a brilliant prairie remnant hidden from public view. Walk rock trails on the high slope along Van Dyke, until the trail dives into the woods. From there, take a Go Wild route through the prairie and look for Arkansas yucca.

P4: Flagpole Hill. A high limestone prairie on the hilltop along Lanshire has rare, albeit degraded, gilgai formations.

Contemplative Enclaves

C1: Bath House Pollinator Garden. Overflowing native wildflower beds surround a swirling metal sculpture. Sit on benches and watch butterflies. Designed and maintained by Dallas County Master Gardeners.

C2: Celebration Tree Grove. Meditative quiet place beneath a tree canopy. Stone structures feature bronze plaques that honor, remember, and celebrate lake lovers. Gifts to the grove raise funds for lake trees. Songbirds and northern flickers frequent surprisingly large trees nearby.

C3: Stone Tables. A popular place for gatherings, this collection of sandstone structures adjoins Dixon Branch's tall trees. In the quiet hours of dusk, watch foxes and owls hunt.

White Rock Lake Conservancy stages large events to raise funds for major lake amenity improvements.

◄ Bald eagles are frequent visitors to the lake.

▲ Pelicans gather with mallards at Sunset Bay.

Vista Benches

The lake's east side is known for views of sunsets and downtown lights, while docks lining the west are perfect for sunrises and moonrises.

V1: Boy Scout Hill. Picnic shelter for watching sunsets and storms amid splendid wildflowers.

V2: Bath House to Big Thicket. Serene picnic table and benches near the circle. Listen for barred owls in the evening hunting along the shore.

V3: Old East Lawther. Midway between Bath House and Dreyfus Point on an abandoned stretch of Lawther exists a quiet bench with lake and downtown views. Easy to do in business or date clothes.

V4: Lakeview Bench. On the hilltop at the sharp curve on E. Lake Highlands, enjoy the sun setting and the downtown lights coming on.

V5: Dreyfus Point. Watch birds at Sunset Bay from a bench on the lower parking lot's south side.

V6: Winfrey Hill. Several benches on the slope have sunset and downtown views with great breezes. Lots of bird action on the prairie slopes.

V7: Winfrey Porch. Sit on the porch beneath large live oaks and watch the sunset.

V8: West Lawther and Chapel Hill. Quiet green space swaddles a dock.

V9: Jackson Point. Prominent point to watch sailboats ply the lake. Amble north for a lovely stone circle of benches.

V10: T and P Hill. Popular locale has a hilltop picnic shelter and plenty of benches for moon gazing. Site of annual June Full Moon gathering.

ADVENTURE 3 WILD WATERS OF THE EAST

Piedmont Ridge

The Austin Chalk escarpment that rises above Oak Creek is known for its epic vistas, diverse ecosystems, and Native American and pioneer history.

WHERE: 2725 N Jim Miller Road, Dallas, TX 75227. Southeast Dallas, southwest of Jim Miller and Scyene.
PARKING: Paved lot.
TRAILS: Dirt 1 mile.
DIFFICULTY: Moderate.
FACILITIES: None.
NEARBY: Crawford Memorial Park.

Scyene Overlook

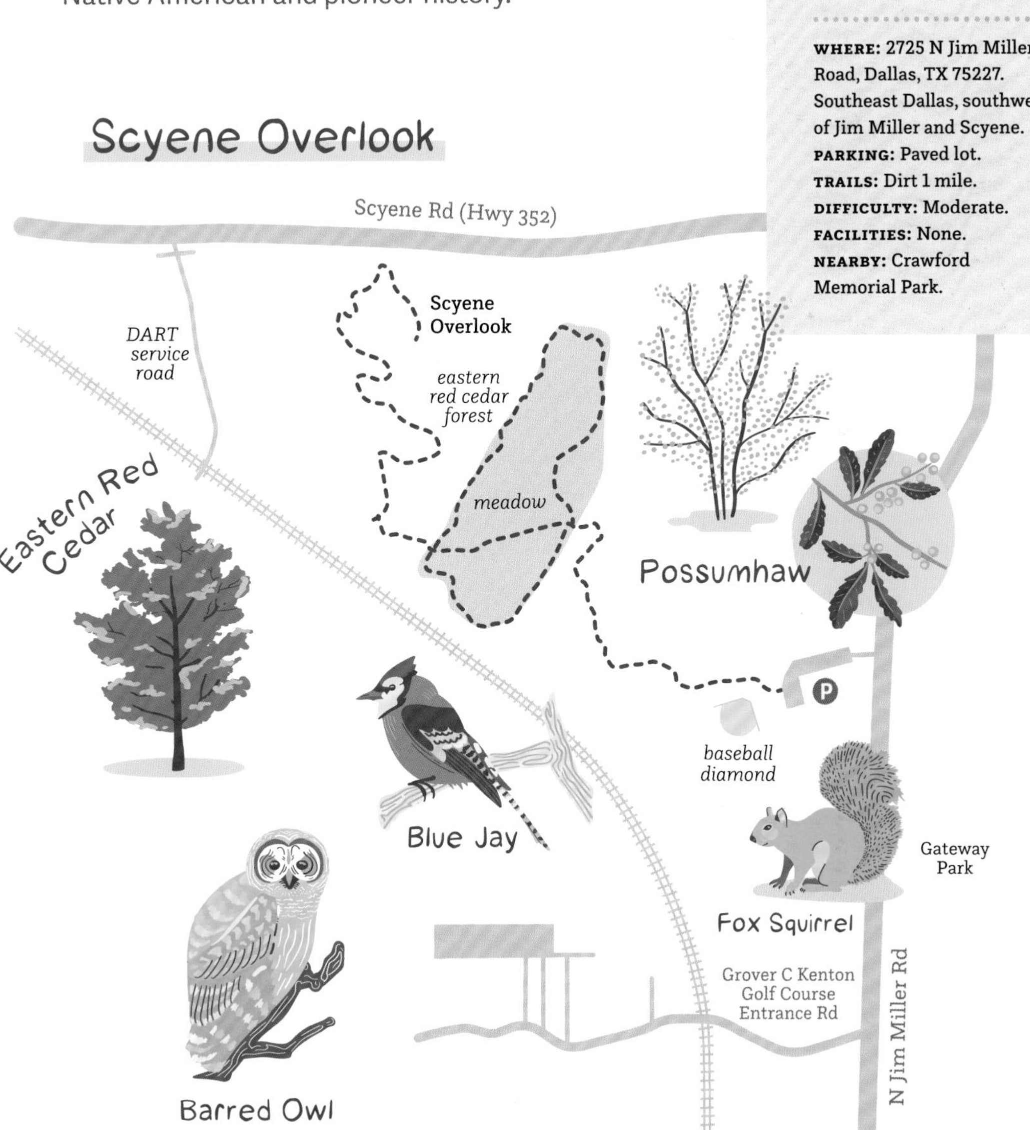

▲ Kristi Kerr Leonard, of North Texas Master Naturalists, ascends to the overlook.

Scyene Overlook

A hot summer day is a good time for a short hike if there's hope for a breeze at the end. Inveterate hiker Scott Hudson, president of the North Texas Master Naturalists, and I set out north from the parking lot, hop over a metal barrier for keeping out ATVs, and walk until an overgrown meadow with a maze of citizen-made trails opens before us.

We hew to the left through the woods that flank a DART rail line. It takes a bit of searching for the path as we tiptoe through a boggy draw rife with Cherokee sedge and wander through a cathedral-like grove of eastern red cedar. Keep heading north-north-west toward the highest point near Scyene, keeping the DART line generally to your left.

The Scyene Overlook knoll juts to 480 feet. Citizen-made trails up the face have eroded into barren channels. It seems the makers were out here to enjoy nature. So why inflict permanent damage?

A sustainable nature trail requires geology, geometry, and hydrology to create inclines, dips, and curves that slow stormwater yet drain effectively. Avoiding sensitive plants and wildlife nesting areas takes botany and wildlife biology. Learn more at American Trails and the International Mountain Bicycling Association.

▲ The most epic sunset views in Dallas.

We approach the overlook on the west side through a series of switchbacks. The shift from lowland to upland woods startles. Buckley's oak, as broad as it is tall, spreads its low crown's tangle of twisty limbs. Similar to its Shumard oak relative, leaves turn vivid auburn in autumn.

The North Texas chapter of Texas Master Naturalists trains well-informed volunteers to provide education, outreach, and service dedicated to enhancing nature in Dallas, Kaufman, and Rockwall counties.

The peeps of American cardinals and sharp trills of Carolina chickadees and tufted titmice are continuous. Possumhaw shrubs' pale bark and sage-green leaves contrast with rusty blackhaw viburnums' ruddy stems and dark green foliage.

Scott orients me to the view as I cool in the breeze. In the Great Trinity Forest below ambles the Oak Creek corridor and then the more dynamic White Rock Creek. Almost twenty miles away, the narrow silver lines of Cedar Hill broadcast towers are visible.

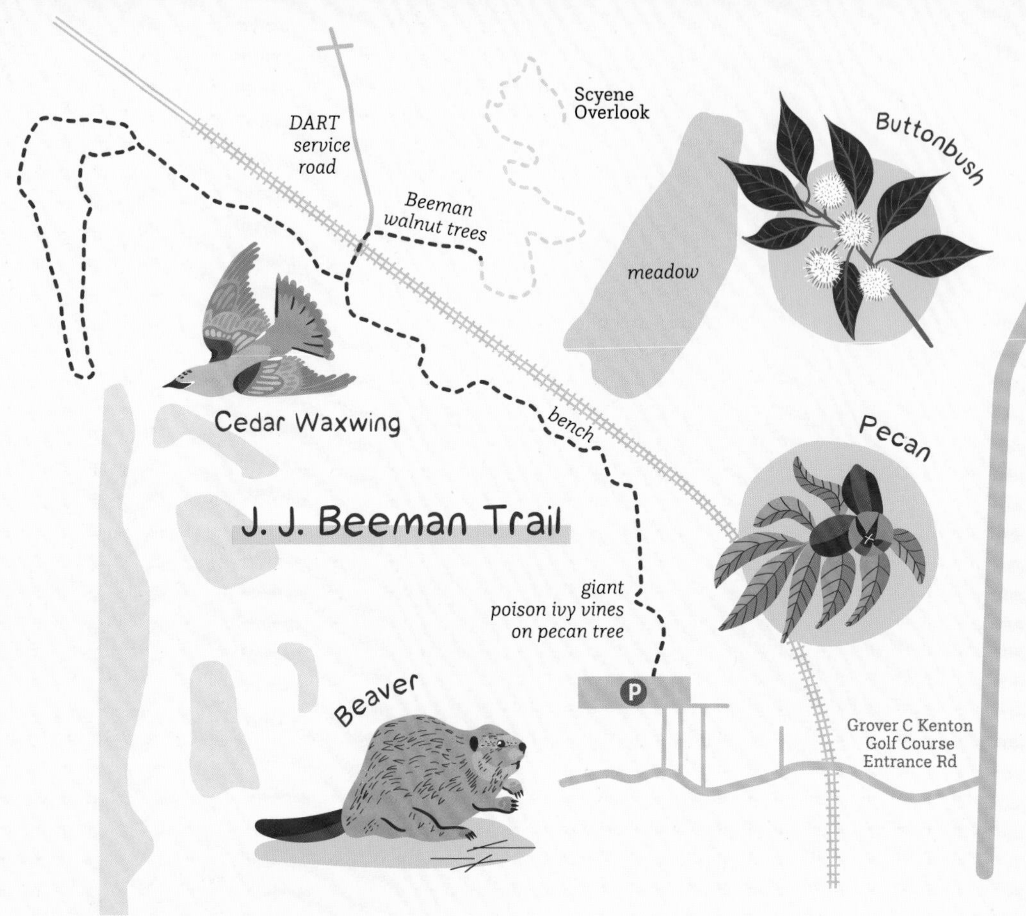

Go Wild: J. J. Beeman Trail

The J. J. Beeman Trail is the least traveled of the Piedmont trails. When hiking unfamiliar territory, best to go first with someone who knows the terrain. Scott Hudson of the North Texas Master Naturalists leads us on our trek.

The ridge blocks traffic sounds, making the trail feel calm and remote on this spring day, until the DART train passes. Towering cottonwoods four feet across, oaks almost as high, and squatty, dense bois d'arcs greet us. A massive pecan tree hosts a rustic log bench. Virginia wildrye and inland sea oats flourish in the shady understory, creating a carpet of green.

The DART crossing comes into view and our reverie breaks. We decide to Go Wild. Using Gaia GPS and Google Maps, we depart the trail and head for a long skinny pond. Scott spies a communal latrine of the elusive swamp rabbit on a log. We feel lucky.

The woods are a wildlife haven. Armadillo, coyote, fox squirrel, and eastern cottontail thrive, along with Cooper's and red-shouldered hawk, and barred owl. Dragonflies and damselflies are abundant, as are moths.

A pastoral waterway with the aromatic yellow blooms of swamp privet comes into view. Bare branches of buttonbushes still bear seed balls on

WHERE: Grover C. Keeton Golf Course, 2323 N Jim Miller Road, Dallas, TX 75227. Southeast Dallas, on Jim Miller between Scyene and Bruton.
PARKING: Paved clubhouse lot. Park next to woods.
TRAILS: Dirt 3 miles.
DIFFICULTY: Moderate.
FACILITIES: Full restrooms inside clubhouse.

▲ A massive red oak soars to the sky.

▲ Dense woods support a diverse array of wildlife.

dangling stems. Chewed young trees and dam remnants show beavers at work. We absorb the tranquility.

Retracing our route, we cross DART and continue on the Beeman Trail to the Scyene Overlook Trail. History abounds: a red cedar grove perhaps coveted by local Indigenous communities for lodgepoles and bois d'arc used for making bows. We take in the overlook view and retrace steps to the clubhouse.

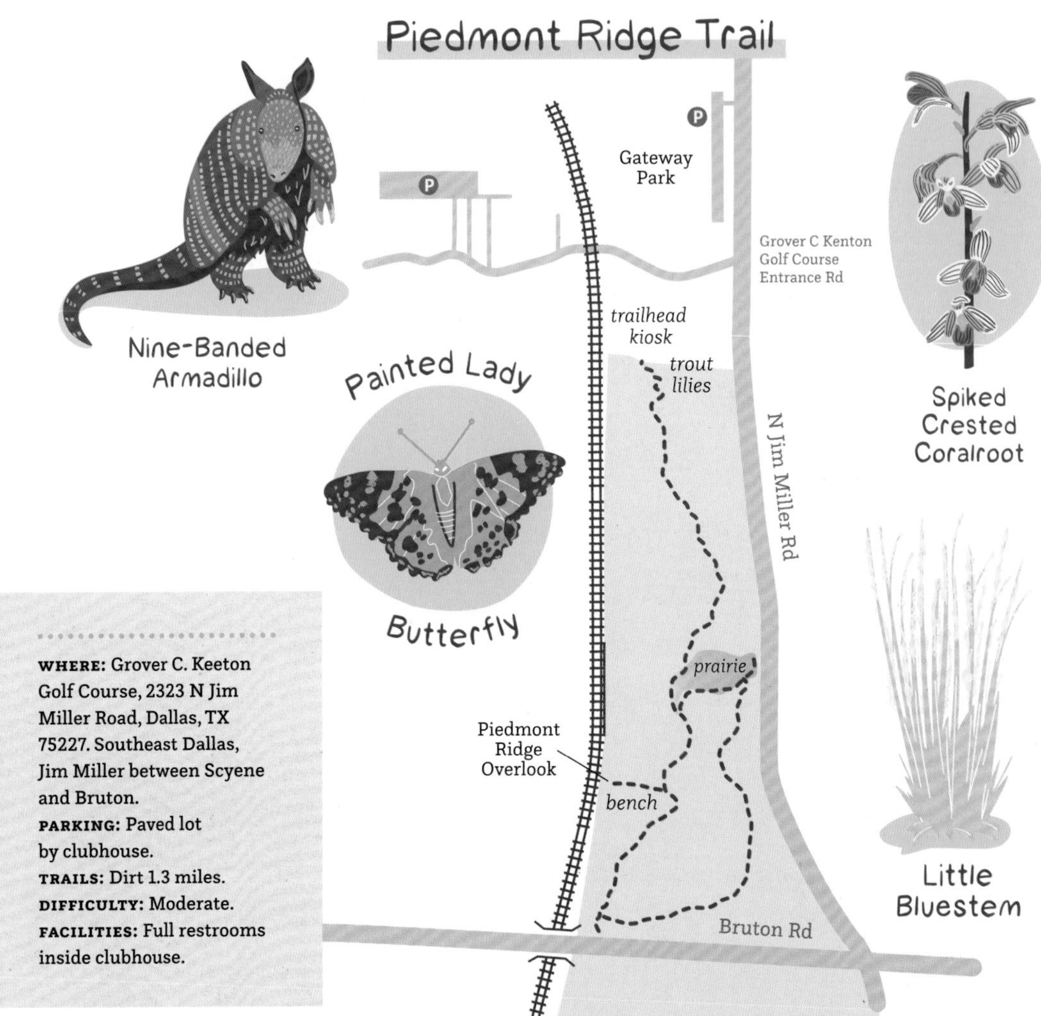

WHERE: Grover C. Keeton Golf Course, 2323 N Jim Miller Road, Dallas, TX 75227. Southeast Dallas, Jim Miller between Scyene and Bruton.
PARKING: Paved lot by clubhouse.
TRAILS: Dirt 1.3 miles.
DIFFICULTY: Moderate.
FACILITIES: Full restrooms inside clubhouse.

Piedmont Ridge Trail

A couple dozen excited Texas Master Naturalists depart the van on this fine autumn day and follow Kristi Kerr Leonard of North Texas Master Naturalists and Bob Richie of Foraging DFW to a field dotted with large Ashe junipers. Bob regales us with the evergreen's medicinal qualities, such as its vitamin C–rich leaf tips, which were essential to Indigenous communities surviving winters.

The group enters the woods, angling up a series of switchbacks to the 500-foot ridge top. We fling curses at amur honeysuckle shrubs that are taking over. Hackberry and cedar elm shade our path, giving way to Buckley's oak at the top.

"Oh look, a beautyberry, hanging in there," notes Bob. Bright globes of purple berries weigh down graceful arching stems. They make a spritely jelly, he notes, but leave plenty for birds. These woods should be purple with beautyberries, but instead invasives dominate.

Suddenly we walk into a Blackland Prairie glade flush with little bluestem gone ruddy with fall color. Between them, tufts of sideoats grama still have seeds clinging to stems. Wildflowers abound here in spring. A rocky ridge seems inhospitable for a prairie, but slightly acidic rain dissolves the limestone's calcium carbonate to create rainwater-holding cavities.

Bob regales us with the healing properties of New Jersey tea—natives use the root for blood clotting, and the settlers made passable tea from the leaves—and purple coneflower, a great immune booster. He points out eastern prickly pear cacti whose mucilaginous pads treat burn wounds and grill up as nopalitos, while the red fruits make jelly and flavor beverages.

▲ Downtown Dallas disappears into the sunset.

▲ Texas Master Naturalists pass through a prairie glen.

A flurry of movement draws us to a Buckley's oak. Orange and gray hairstreaks flit around its splayed, multiple trunks, having been larvae on the tree. Titmice and ruby-crowned kinglets find safety and shade, noisily hopping among limbs.

We crowd into a small overlook facing west toward downtown skyscrapers. Great Trinity Forest spreads for miles. Below in the Oak Creek bottoms, river

Piedmont Ridge is home to native orchids in the genus *Hexalectris*. These plants include crested coralroot, which acquires its energy through a specialized three-way relationship with soil fungus and juniper and oak roots. Five of the six *Hexalectris* species in Texas reside in Dallas County.

otters cavort in beaver-engineered ponds, white-tailed deer roam and wild hogs cause havoc. Beyond it, White Rock Creek heads for the Trinity. "Is this really Dallas?" someone asks. Soon the woods will be glorious in the oaks' carmine foliage, accented by brilliant yellow ash and golden elm.

Comanche Storytelling Place

It's an odd entrance to a sacred place: a gap into the woods just past the playground. North Texas Master Naturalist Kristi Kerr Leonard and I slip through the obligatory privet corridor and pass through Buckley's oak and cedar elm, alternating with sunny Blackland Prairie patches, turning south at the trail intersection toward the Comanche Storytelling Place.

WHERE: Devon Anderson Park, 1700 Eastcliff Drive, Dallas, TX 75217. Southeast Dallas, off Jim Miller between Bruton and Lake June.
PARKING: On street.
TRAILS: Dirt 0.5 mile.
DIFFICULTY: Moderate
FACILITIES: None.

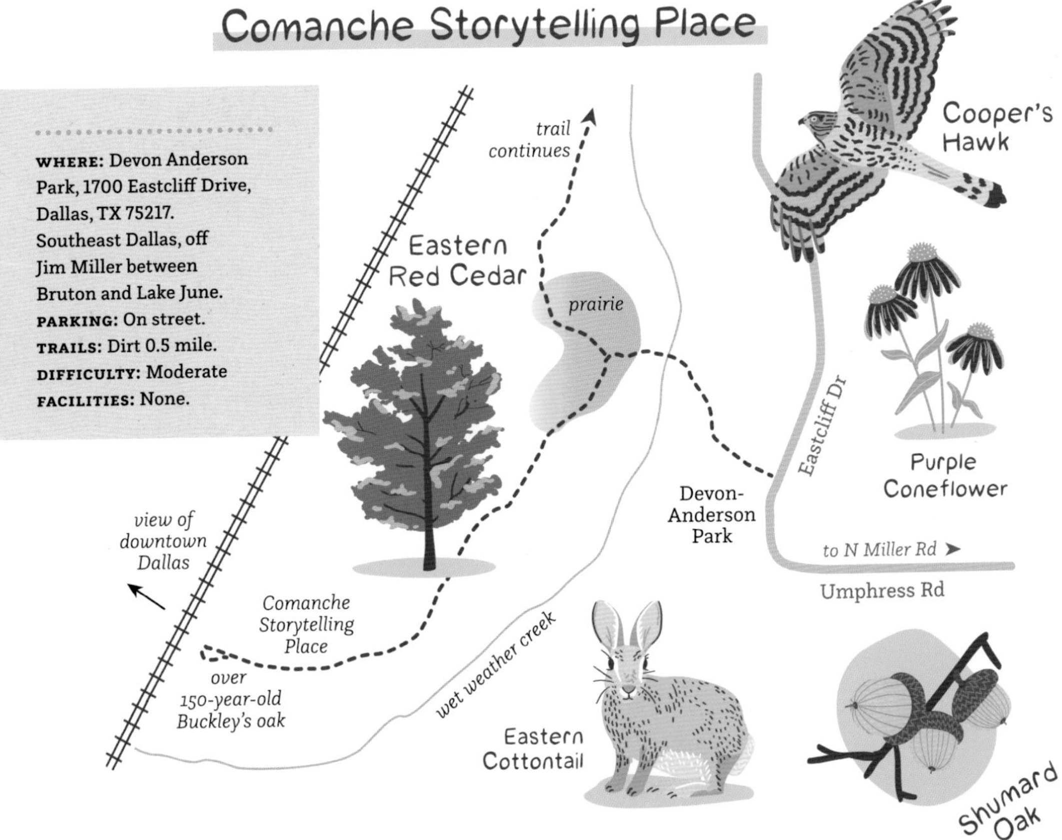

▲ The arbor elder is deemed a Comanche cultural property.

Soon it comes into view: a descending series of broad white limestone terraces. Comanche stories still echo here, especially when the full moon's light reflects off pale limestone. Comanche occasionally visit for ceremonies.

At the trail intersection, turn north to take a trail to Bruton. Large trees, intimate folded ravines, and sweet vistas compete with extensive privet infestation.

As a naturalist, Kristi bonds deeply with this place. The skills she hones are like those on which the Indigenous peoples who visited here depended: plant identification, animal tracking, natural navigation, and the reading of terrain, water, and weather.

We continue in silence on this still, quiet summer afternoon, up a chalk rise that abruptly ends at a tall retaining wall for the DART line. Clinging to a limestone knob before us lives one of the oldest trees in Dallas, yet the Buckley's oak is barely over twenty-five feet tall.

Arborists like Steve Houser, coauthor *of Comanche Marker Trees of Texas*, know its fifty-six-inch-diameter base indicates its age. Tenaciously holding on, the sacred sentinel of the stories it has heard persists, through decades of drought and fire, insect hordes, and hungry deer.

Yet if not for citizen heroics, it would not be. Linda Pelon, coauthor of *Comanche Marker Trees of Texas*, interrupted plans to run the DART line over the tree by rallying forces with Jimmy Arterberry, Comanche Nation Historic Preservation Officer, who awarded the tree Comanche Traditional Cultural Property status. The DART line was rerouted and stories are still able to whisper.

ADVENTURE 4 WILD WATERS OF THE EAST

John Bunker Sands Wetland Center

Almost two thousand acres of human-made wetlands along the East Fork of the Trinity process municipal wastewater and provide habitat for wildlife.

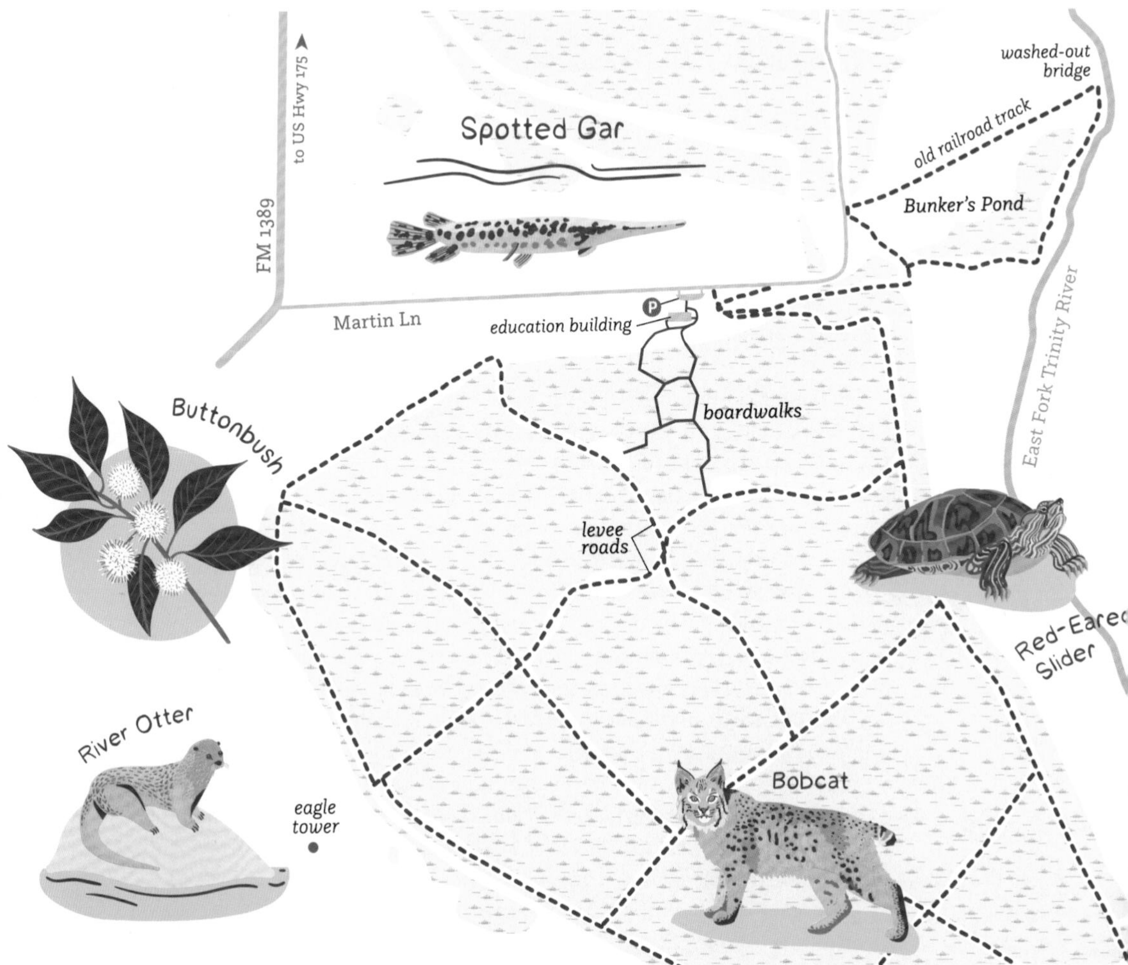

Bob Richie of Foraging DFW is eating the trail.

But he shares. The tender growing tip of a smilax vine (currently wrapped around a barbed-wire fence) is tasty, like asparagus. Knowing more about plants, especially ones that can feed or heal you, makes any hike more fun, a reason why Bob's foraging hikes here are so popular.

Bird photographer Nick diGennaro and I walk with Bob on the Bunker's Pond Trail. It's a beautiful autumn morning. We cross a country lane that separates the north and south halves of John Bunker Sands Wetland Center's 1840 acres of wetlands. A concrete silo once used for storing fermented corn crops (silage) looms two stories tall. The trail continues down an abandoned rail line, now flanked by a thick row of woods, for an easy, level, shady path.

Elevated on a levee, we can see into the tree canopy. Bob points out aging, hollowed-out trees favored by raccoons for nesting. On our right is Bunker's Pond, a shallow expanse once used for growing aquatic plants to create the wetlands. Now it's an ephemeral pond, capturing rain until it evaporates. In moister times, it would be loud with red-winged blackbirds and a variety of herons.

Bob whispers: "Look! A pair of great horned owls, there at the end of the trail. They're often around, but not on the ground." Nick pulls out his camera with a long lens, but they're hard to see in dim light. Heads down, the big birds busily devour a creature and then fly off silently. We see no trace of prey at the spot; the birds will later regurgitate owl pellets with bones, fur, and other nondigestibles.

WHERE: 655 Martin Lane, Combine, TX 75159. Combine, Kaufman County, near US-175.
PARKING: Gravel lot.
TRAILS: Dirt 2 miles, boardwalk 0.5 miles, levee roads 8 miles. Detailed map at wetlandcenter.com/maps.
DIFFICULTY: Easy.
FACILITIES: Visitor and educational center.
NEARBY: Post Oak Preserve.

▲ Boardwalks bring you up close to Bunker's wildlife.

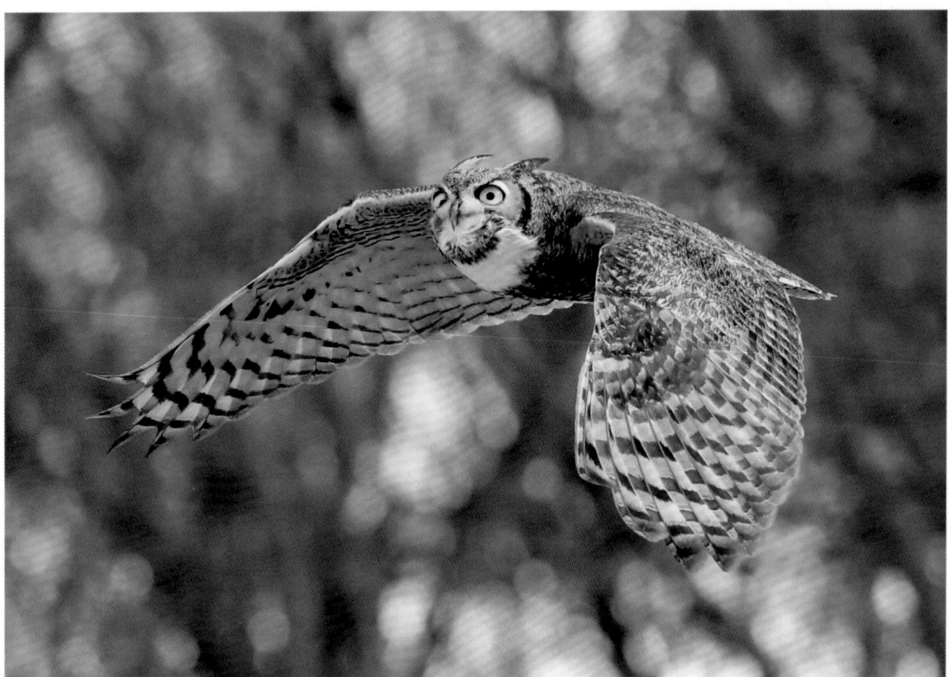

▲ Great horned owls are powerfully intense.

Trained volunteers from the North Texas chapter of Texas Master Naturalists help provide trail upkeep and guided hikes.

Wetland Woods

Continuing into bottomland woods along the Trinity's East Fork, pecans are everywhere. Bob notes their leaves are flush with tannin for processing leather and treating head lice. A gum bumelia or chittamwood tree produces a gum that's chewable but not as savory as chicle (remember Chiclets?) from a related tree in Mexico.

The sound of tumbling water draws us to the river. A concrete weir forces the river into a narrow opening, raising the level upstream. Scant land adjoining the East Fork is publicly accessible, so it's a treat to see the river, even if the banks are too steep to visit up close. Nick scans for waterfowl, but it's quiet.

We trek through a sunny section, snacking on the leaves of bastard cabbage that taste like tough kale, and search for much tastier chickweed and corn salad rebounding in cool weather. Bob finds eighteen-inch string bobcat scat hidden in the grass, which he holds up proudly. It must have eaten something fibrous to stay so connected, he says.

A rowdy tangle of peppervine is already stripped of its navy berries, proof that birds had fun. Nearby, a clump of black willows, a quick grower found on many ponds, prompts Bob to chat about the salicylic acid in the bark's cambium layer. "Its genus is *Salix*, from which salicylic acid draws its name. It helps beavers with the pain caused by constantly growing incisors."

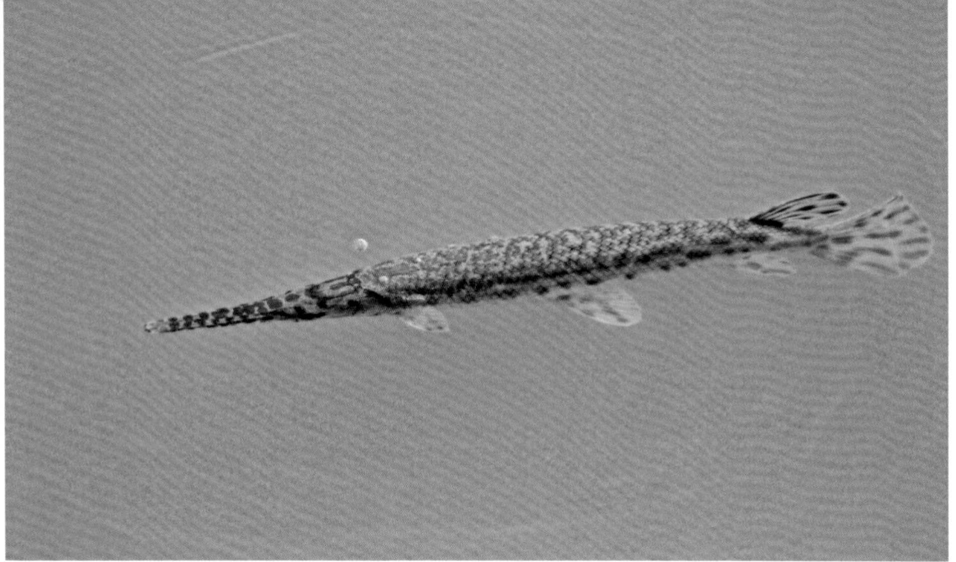

▲ A spotted gar searches for a meal in the wetlands.

Mosaic of Water and Plants

The trail turns along the base of the wetlands' outer levee. Vertical stripes of compressed grass mark the short, steep slope. Bob informs it's where river otters slither to a wetland cell particularly rich in crawfish and mussels.

Atop the levee, the wetlands' southern section unfurls nearly to the horizon, a muddled mosaic of muted green foliage islands laced with sinews of Aegean water. From this distance, waterfowl flocks look like amorphous dark blobs moving around. Shadows of cumulous clouds trace the surface on this bright and breezy day, further softening the scene. Literal watercolors.

Nick pulls out his telephoto lens camera and starts clicking away. Bob teaches me how the wetland system takes in water from the East Fork and moves it between cells, going through the various stages of water purification such as removal of sediment, nitrogen, and phosphorus. From here, the beginning of a more than forty-mile-long pipeline path is faintly visible, transferring polished water to Lavon Lake for storage until needed.

Squawks of Franklin's gull fill the air while shores peep with spotted sandpipers. Ahead lies the sleek, modern outline and gleaming metal roof of the wetlands' education and visitor center. Adirondack chairs on its lawn beckon a break for sandwiches.

The wetlands are the centerpiece of the East Fork Water Reuse Project, a public-private partnership between North Texas Municipal Water District and The Rosewood Corporation. The late conservationist John Bunker Sands began the conversion of Rosewood ranchland into wetlands.

▲ A diamondback water snake hides from prying eyes.

The visitor center's eco-building houses extensive displays. Over 5000 middle and high-school students visit each year for education on wetland and river ecosystems, bird migration, and water conservation.

On the Boardwalk

A half mile of boardwalk takes walkers close to birds and directly over the wetlands to peer in. The wilderness of water plants is dizzying. Some float on the surface; others sway in the current. Occasional aquatic wildlife paths slice through the greenery. In summer, the air is thick with dragonflies and damselflies hunting aerial insects.

Bob points out a diamondback water snake slithering into the reeds. The heads of red-eared sliders and river cooters pop out of water that is busy with bugs skittering about the surface. With all the crustaceans and other invertebrates thriving in the wetlands, it's a river otter paradise.

Tucked in a boardwalk bend, we discover a pile of mixed wildlife scat, reminding us wetlands are also habitat for raccoons, bobcats, and other mammals. The prevalent poop on this day is river otter, shiny with crustacean shells.

We depart the boardwalks for the levee roads. The network leads deep into wetland cells. Soon, waterfowl by the thousands will take rest here on their long flight to wintering grounds. But today there are few. We head for a high levee on the west perimeter, hoping to glimpse the bald eagle nest nearby.

In 2011, an American bald eagle pair began nesting in a nearby electrical tower. Concern for the eagles' safety and potential power disruptions led to an adjacent faux electrical tower being constructed while the eagles were away. Their nest was carefully moved to the fake tower, and upon their return, the eagles accepted the new location.

▲ Cattails provide prime nesting habitat for birds.

▲ Duckweeds of the genus *Lemna* are the smallest flowering plants known.

ADVENTURE 5 WILD LANDS OF THE NORTH

Hagerman National Wildlife Refuge

An 11,320-acre US Fish and Wildlife Service refuge known for its numerous waterfowl, wading birds, and shorebirds during migration periods, plus excellent birdwatching and hiking all year.

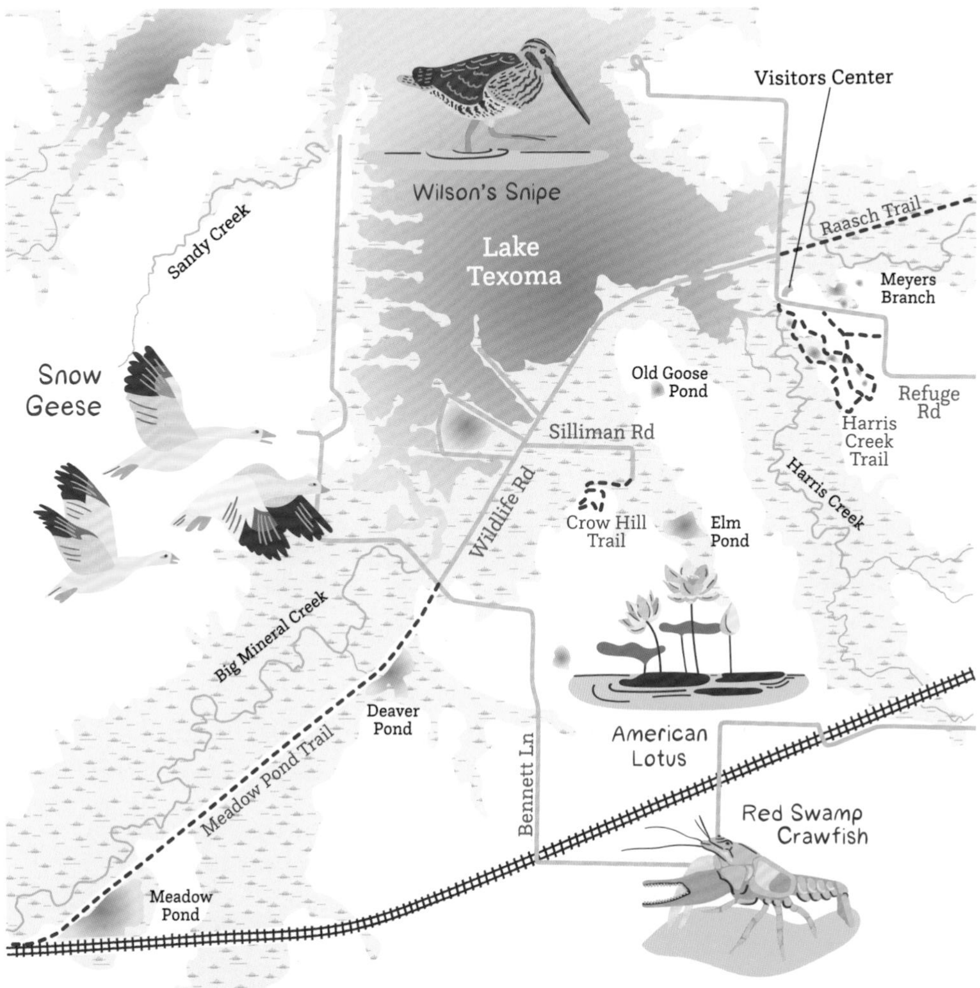

▲ Sunrises are prime time for wildlife watching at Hagerman.

A main stop on the Central Flyway is Lake Texoma, an 89,000-acre impoundment of the Red River and one of the nation's largest reservoirs. Hagerman National Wildlife Refuge wraps the long inlet of Big Mineral Creek. Its calm waters attract waterfowl, wading, and shorebirds, along with a variety of songbirds and raptors, including a pair of nesting bald eagles nicknamed Lucy and Ricky. The refuge enjoys over 230,000 visitors annually.

Some migrators stick around for winter, congregating along the aptly named Wildlife Road along the shoreline. During migration, thousands of white pelicans wheel above the water, fold wings and deftly swoop, scooping up fish—endless fun to watch. In winter, spectacular numbers of snow and Ross's geese, sometimes as many as 15,000, coat the offshore waters a fluffy white. Cacophonous does not begin to describe it.

WHERE: 6465 Refuge Road, Sherman, TX 75092. Big Mineral arm on Lake Texoma at the Oklahoma border in Grayson County.
PARKING: Paved and gravel lots.
TRAILS: Dirt 16+ miles, ADA one-third mile. Detailed map at fws.gov/refuge/hagerman.
DIFFICULTY: Moderate.
FACILITIES: Visitor center. Restrooms at day use areas.
NEARBY: Cross Timbers Hiking Trail, Blackland Prairie Raptor Center, Trinity Trail at Lavon Lake.

Having thousands of geese and their allies as winter houseguests requires planning. The refuge farms hundreds of acres in winter wheat and other grains, plus water-loving plants such as sedges and smartweed. Some fields produce clovers and sunflowers for white-tailed deer, wild turkeys, and songbirds in warm seasons.

The visitor center's eco-building houses extensive displays. Over 5000 middle and high-school students visit each year for education on wetland and river ecosystems, bird migration, and water conservation.

▲ The snow geese spectacle is not to be missed.

Aquatic Avians

Farther south on Wildlife Drive, fingers of old oil-field roads extend into the sound, creating contained marshes. They brim with reeds and aquatic plants fostering a healthy supply of invertebrates, amphibians, and small fish—a perfect environment for dabbling ducks and wading birds. Drive the berms and enjoy being close to the birds, who generally ignore vehicles but flee pedestrians.

When their butts aren't pointing upward while dabbling for dinner, enjoy the garnet tones of cinnamon teal and ruddy and redhead ducks, or the sleek cocoa head of the northern pintail. Ever-abundant northern shovelers sport the males' shiny green tops and the females' comically large orange bill. The black and white (male) and silver-gray (female) feather Mohawks of hooded mergansers are always delightful, as is the giant noggin of the male bufflehead in iridescent purple, blue, and teal with a bold white splash.

The winter shoreline bustles with greater yellowlegs boasting mottled platinum feathers. They stride confidently deep into water, swinging their long beaks back and forth catching small fish and invertebrates. Far subtler is the rotund Wilson's snipe, with its mottled brown feathers and ridiculously long, striped beak. Well camouflaged and utterly still, it flushes at the last minute with a series of raspy "scaipe" calls. Like the American woodcock, which favors the brushier areas, its eyes are set far back on its head so it can watch for predators while its head is down eating.

◂ A Wilson's snipe rests on rocks.

Hagerman is an immense preserve. Speed limits are low, allowing cars to serve as rolling bird blinds, but don't create dangerous conditions by stopping on the road. Orient yourself first and discover the best viewing spots through the self-guided auto tour. Get equipped for audio at the visitor center or find the narration online. Or visit on weekends for guided tours led by experienced naturalists in the open-air Wildlife Explorer electric tram, with frequent stops for photography. Bring binoculars or borrow from the visitor center.

Ecosystem Sampler

Hagerman is renowned for its aquatic wonders, yet 8700 of its 12,000 acres are upland woods and prairies. Over sixteen miles of trails traverse gentle hills of Eastern Cross Timbers and bright open meadows, tracing along a plethora of ponds. Off-trail Go Wild wandering is endless, but only in cooler seasons for experienced hikers who bring plenty of water and phone power.

Two volunteers from Friends of Hagerman—Bert Garcia, 76, who pilots the Wildlife Explorer, and Jack Chiles, 80, who leads the weekly bird census—are hiking me down Meadow Pond Trail. It runs along the former Katy railroad line for a six-mile round-trip, which does not faze these two. Their predecessor, Karl Haller, conducted the bird census until age 98—volunteering at Hagerman keeps you young.

The well-drained and graveled Meadow Pond Trail is an easy amble due to the level railroad bed—perfect for kids or if you love nature but prefer it at a distance. The views are grand. To one side, upland woods, meadows, and some gorgeous ponds unfurl, and to the other are Big Mineral Creek's lush bottomland forest and swamps.

Bert and I chat about his former life as US Attorney for Puerto Rico. Jack's always looking up as he walks, yet never stumbles; his feet possess eyes.

"Friends of Hagerman provides education and outreach at the refuge and throughout the community that has greatly increased our visibility and led to more understanding of the natural resource conservation goals of the refuge and national wildlife refuge system."

—Kathy Whaley, refuge manager

▲ Meadow Pond Trail entrance in spring.

◀ Yellow-headed blackbirds are a striking sight.

A birdcall catches his ear and binoculars rise to his eyes as he swivels, gets the bird in sight, and reels off its name, all within a few seconds—bird-watcher gymnastics.

With a variety of habitats in one trail, it's a birding smorgasbord. On this and other late-winter excursions, Jack's seen Bewick's wren, dark-eyed juncos, pine siskins, and white-eyed vireos, along with the ever-present Carolina chickadees, Carolina wrens, northern cardinals, titmice, and a variety of sparrows.

Deaver Pond comes into view, hugging the trail berm and bringing wildlife up close. Canada geese and blue-winged teal float nearby, unperturbed. A red-headed woodpecker taps in swampy woods on the water's edge. Yellow-rumped and prothonotary warblers are no doubt close, pursuing insects. A wooden bench made by Boy Scouts invites a rest.

Watery Woods

We walk the Meadow Pond Trail along exceptionally deep bottomlands. Glints of still water and lazy rivulets sneak through. The air is moist and still. Amid the woods' timeless quiet, an occasional splash and crackle of wildlife rise from the underbrush. No doubt, barred owls are sleepily monitoring us; it's owlet-fledging time.

I soak in the way birdsongs harmonize and echo in the woods and how sounds from more open areas differ from upland. Big Mineral Creek swings close to the trail, bringing some light to the woods and shifting the birdsong once again. We hope to see Lucy the bald eagle on a favorite riparian perch, but not today.

Our goal, Meadow Pond, comes into view, nearly fifty acres of smooth expanse, oddly quiet with birds today. I imagine it in summer, when thousands of American lotuses, the nation's largest native blossom, rise on stalks above their large, round leaves, bedazzled by jewellike dragonflies, drawn to

the still, shaded waters. Native Americans ate the unripe lotus-pod seeds like chickpeas and cooked the roots like potatoes.

We look up at a kettle of turkey vultures working the updrafts. "There's a bald eagle in there!" exclaims Jack. "Juvenile. Two of them," noting they're possibly offspring from one of the refuge's two breeding pairs. Jack mentions that sometimes a train will pass on the track at the pond's end, making for a nice picture. As if on cue, a rumble draws closer and a long Union Pacific locomotive passes by.

▼ A train passes Meadow Pond in lotus season.

▲ White-faced ibises are a rare winter visitor.

Roaming the Refuge

I sit in one of the charming pergolas at the visitor center and watch grandparents squire their grandson around the quarter-acre pollinator garden as he squeals in delight. Friends of Hagerman raised an estimated $84,000 to construct it with US Fish and Wildlife Service help. Stroll the easy ADA paths and use your phone to click and identify plants. Join the group's activities at the visitor center: talks, guided tours and walks, children's education, and a tasty gift shop.

After the hike, I treat myself to the self-guided auto tour. The route touches on the area's history and ecology, stops at Goose Point, and takes a loop through the bird-rich marshes, pausing at a gravel observation deck amid the action. Back on land, the tour passes Chiles Marsh (named for Jack), visits the Big Mineral Public Use Area where a small oil pumper still operates, and concludes at Crow Hill.

Find delight in the superb Eastern Cross Timbers ecosystem of Crow Hill Trail, just under a mile. Placards along the way convey native plant details. Once up a moderately steep slope, the trail circles the hilltop with perfectly placed benches and short spurs to various refuge views. A surprising prairie glen promises wildflowers in spring and summer.

My hiking urge unmet, I head to the nearby Harris Creek Trails around a chain of ponds in a savannah setting, including a one-third mile ADA loop. I follow the wide dirt paths to Crawfish Pond until a foot injury flares up. A bench surrounded by Missouri violets beckons, so I lie back and watch the sky. The rest of the trails looked so inviting, dotted with bluebird houses and benches, but I could not go on, a reason to return for another fine day.

Heard Natural Science Museum & Wildlife Sanctuary

From dynamic limestone escarpment, to rolling Blackland Prairies, to deep bottomland forest surrounding a wetland, the Heard captures the essence of North Texas ecology.

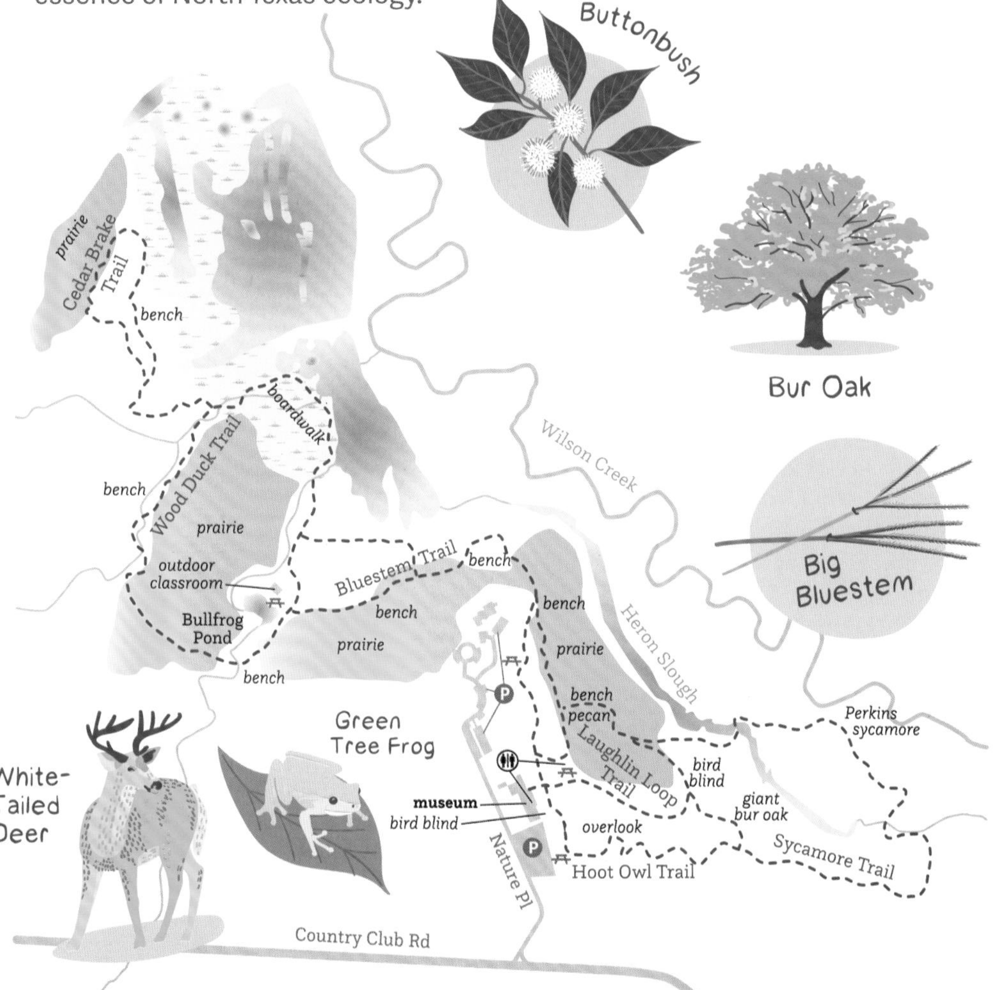

WHERE: 1 Nature Place, McKinney, TX 75069. McKinney, central Collin County, near US Route 75 and Texas State Highway 5.
PARKING: Paved lot.
TRAILS: Soft surface 6 miles. Detailed map at heardmuseum.org.
DIFFICULTY: Moderate.
FACILITIES: Museum and educational center.
DOGS: Not allowed except service animals.
COST: $10–$12, discounts for children and seniors, free for Heard members and children under 2.
NEARBY: Blackland Prairie Raptor Center, Erwin Park, McKinney Greens Nature Preserve.

▲ Heard's mix of prairies, woods, and wetlands inspires.

Rick Travis says about the 289-acre Heard Natural Science Museum and Wildlife Sanctuary: "It's got a lot of topography which creates diversity." From this overlook, past the upland woods, a prairie stretches to a slow-moving slough. Exceptionally tall trees beyond it indicate a bottomland forest and riparian corridor that frame a sprawling wetland.

The Blackland Prairie Chapter of Texas Master Naturalists stewards the Heard with a deep passion and commitment. Rick is their forestry point person and my companion today. We descend the Hoot Owl Trail, wide and surfaced with decomposed granite, as it curves through widely spaced trees barely two stories tall. Bigelow and Buckley's oak dominate, with their narrow, stiff, dark green leaves; thin, twisted branches; and slender trunks.

We stand in bright filtered sunlight, absorbed in a symphony of birdsong, admiring a generous understory of forbs and short, shrubby plants. "This is a perfect environment for deer," Rick whispers. On cue, three young white-tailed deer appear and wind among the trees, unafraid of us and disappearing into the dappled light.

At age 80, Bessie Heard decided to create a preserve where future generations could experience and learn about nature. It's the only privately operated nature preserve in North Texas, open since 1967.

◂ Deer are integral to the Heard landscape.

Arbor Insights

Midway down the slope, Rick notes, "Trees are getting bigger. You've got some big ashes, starting to see the bur oaks. As we get into deeper soil that holds moisture, you're going to see some mega-size burs." Once in the floodplain of Wilson Creek, a forest of bur oaks seems to absorb all sound. Golf ball-sized acorns dot the ground.

Heard offers a variety of walks and educational programs, after-hours date nights, a Dinosaurs Live! animatronic installation, and Halloween and Christmas events.

Rising before us is Heard's star bur oak, at least 250 years old. We view the sentinel from a wooden deck and ponder what it's witnessed. Fifteen feet around at the base, its branches are as large as tree trunks. "This is a rich woodland," says Rick. "Spots here are as good as anything in North Texas."

Rick teaches how to discern black walnut trees from pecans, two riparian stalwarts, by comparing their pinnate leaves along a stem. Pecans are pale underneath. Walnuts are more pointed and seem to spin off the stem. Both young barks have deep furrows with diagonal breaks, but the pecan's become shaggy with age.

The Cedar Brake Trail passes through an almost pure stand of eastern red cedar. Densely packed trees block the sunlight, causing lower limbs to drop needles. The bareness traces spooky skeletal shadows on the forest floor. We instinctively become quiet and whisper. A breeze barely penetrates, doing nothing to break the near silence.

Boardwalk Birds

▼ Songs of the swamps include those of the prothonotary warbler.

▲ The food-rich wetlands produce a lot of turtles.

We walk the Wood Duck Trail's rambling wooden boardwalk through swampy woods. Shimmering wetlands with marshy edges come into view. Buttonbush, still dangling its button seeds, lines the trail. Clumps of pickerelweed blades pierce floating smartweed that adapts to changing water levels.

Groups of birders listen intently, scanning slowly for movement, a splash of color, a silhouette on a trunk. Birdsong is melodic and intense. Woodpeckers and flickers tap relentlessly, extracting insects from the soft swamp timber. American green tree frogs cling to plants with spatula toes and emit croaks. Everything makes music.

Late spring through early fall, native butterfly caterpillars munch on host plants, pupate, and emerge at the Native Texas Butterfly House and Garden.

At the end of a short spur, we watch great egrets flying back and forth to the deep woods across the pond. A pervasive squeaky clattering rises from the trees. "What you hear is the rookery," says Rick, describing hundreds of great egrets and others in large nests raising their young. A group of young schoolchildren and their teachers get curious. "It's like school for egrets, getting fed and learning how to be a bird," says Rick.

Prairie Pride

Dave Powell knows prairies. At 77 years of age, his work with the Blackland Prairie Chapter of Texas Master Naturalists is legendary. "A third of this place is prairie," says Dave, "all laboriously crafted from former pastureland." First up is Restoration Prairie at the escarpment's base, reseeded two years ago after a planting effort failed.

◂ The rookery is more often heard than seen.

"In this last year, we had tremendous growth," says Dave, noting that native plants focus on making roots the first growing season. A grassland matrix holds a yellow and orange weave of Indian blanket, black-eyed Susan, and lanceleaf coreopsis. "We've got all the Big Five out here now," says Dave proudly, referring to big bluestem, eastern gamagrass, Indiangrass, little bluestem, and switchgrass.

"Look at this eastern gamagrass," I squeal, surveying a clump about six feet across, long emerald blades arcing from a brawny bundle of rhizomes. Related to Mesoamerican teosinte, from which cultivated corn arose thousands of years ago, it is North American history in a plant. Like corn, its male and female reproductive parts are on the same seedhead.

We continue up the Bluestem Trail and diversity disappears. "This is where the restoration ends," says Dave, noting where the foliage suddenly becomes uniform. "What do you see?" he asks. Just a few green milkweeds stand out, the sturdy little buggers. "Their seeds are wind-blown and drifted from the restoration," notes Dave. "That's how the prairie grows."

▾ Dave and the author check out his restoration work.

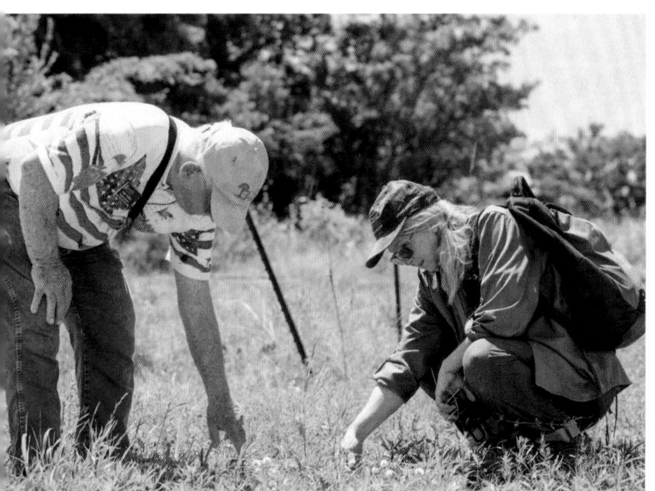

Blackland Prairie chapter of Texas Master Naturalists provides education, outreach, and service to benefit nature by training a cadre of well-informed volunteers.

◄ Brushy bluestem soaks up moisture with its deep roots.

Prairie as Sponge

The trail dips into a wooded area rich with thirsty pecan trees and slippery elm along a rivulet. We stop at a bench and mini-bridge over a trickling stream. Beyond a broad, sunny slope thick with native grasses and forbs, the roofs of houses rise behind a tall fence.

"Hear that water?" asks Dave. "This prairie stays wetter than others because of runoff. Several storm sewer drains empty into it. It rained days ago. Next week, water is still going to be trickling through, the grass is that thick. Think about if that were a parking lot, what would happen."

Heard's Science Resource Center serves as a community hub for native plant and naturalist groups, Audubon and archaeological societies, and other entities.

The trail dips down into the forest, crosses a little creek, and passes by a tiny pond of strangely lurid seafoam-green water. The nearby neighborhood dyes their show ponds blue. "Blue blocks sunlight, so it keeps the plants from growing," Dave says.

Prairie Wisdom

In West Bullfrog Pond Prairie, the Heard's largest grassland, we admire rattlesnake masters' spiky yucca-like leaves thrusting through a tangle of foliage. "In a prairie at different times, the flowers, the grasses, everything changes. You just don't get that with forests."

"All the prairies here had some form of restoration done," says Dave. "A team of Heard Sanctuary staff and volunteers work from a master plan for

▲ Sturdy prairie plants like eryngo (left) and prairie parsley (right) adapt to development.

both prairie and forest developed over many years. Together they implement solutions that often entail grueling work."

Saving prairies requires all hands on deck. Dave points to a rectangle of prairie downslope that stands out in its vibrancy. "A Boy Scout troop purchased their own seed and worked it in. They can stand up here with pride and see what they've done."

Dave's dedicated to helping land remember its prairie past. The imperiled grasshopper sparrow and eastern meadowlark live here as they always have. Eastern phoebes perch on last year's Maximilian sunflower stems, filling the field with strident *fee-bee* calls.

Pipeline Prairies

A massive sewage line on Heard's west side passes through Blackland Prairies noted for their limestone ecology. Years of Dave's sweat infuse every inch. These prairies have his soul. When speaking of Dowell's Prairie damage during pipeline construction, his voice quakes.

Dowell's is radiant today. Opulent sweet pea–like blooms of blue false indigo are forming hard round seeds encased in shells that rattle like mini-maracas. At broad Ken's Prairie, framed by trees, a Mississippi kite swoops after bugs while another alights on the nest.

Dave stands in the sunlight, looking across the expanse. You can almost hear the prairie to-do lists

On the Wildlife Animal Encounters Trail, each one has a story, including bobcats rescued from a burning brush pile and a white-tailed deer injured by a dog.

◄ Blue false indigo is beautiful yet aces drought conditions.

Find excitement in the trees with the Heard's ropes course and zipline located on the sanctuary's southeastern edge.

forming in his head. He radiates happiness. "Now I'm doing what I always wanted to do, but I didn't know it," he says.

Fossil Fun

The closing bell calling in hikers off the trails rings. "We have just enough time to see the museum," says Dave. The small museum attracts over 90,000 annually. The centerpiece is a fourteen-foot-long marine reptile fossil called Texas Nessie, discovered in Collin County.

Joining Nessie is an 85-million-year-old mosasaur, another giant marine reptile from the Western Interior Seaway of the Cretaceous epoch, and a pair of 34-million-year-old tortoises known as Tootsie and Peanut, plus more. Exhibits showcase local geology and ecology, passenger pigeons, and global rocks and seashells.

ADVENTURE 7

WILD LANDS OF THE NORTH

Parkhill Prairie

WHERE: 17100 County Road 668, Blue Ridge, TX 75442. Blue Ridge, northeast corner of Collin County.
TRAILS: Dirt 1.5 miles.
PARKING: Paved lots.
DIFFICULTY: Moderate.
FACILITIES: Restrooms (often locked).
NEARBY: Clymer Meadow, Sister Grove Park.

Experience a rare Blackland Prairie remnant unchanged for thousands of years, with vistas for miles.

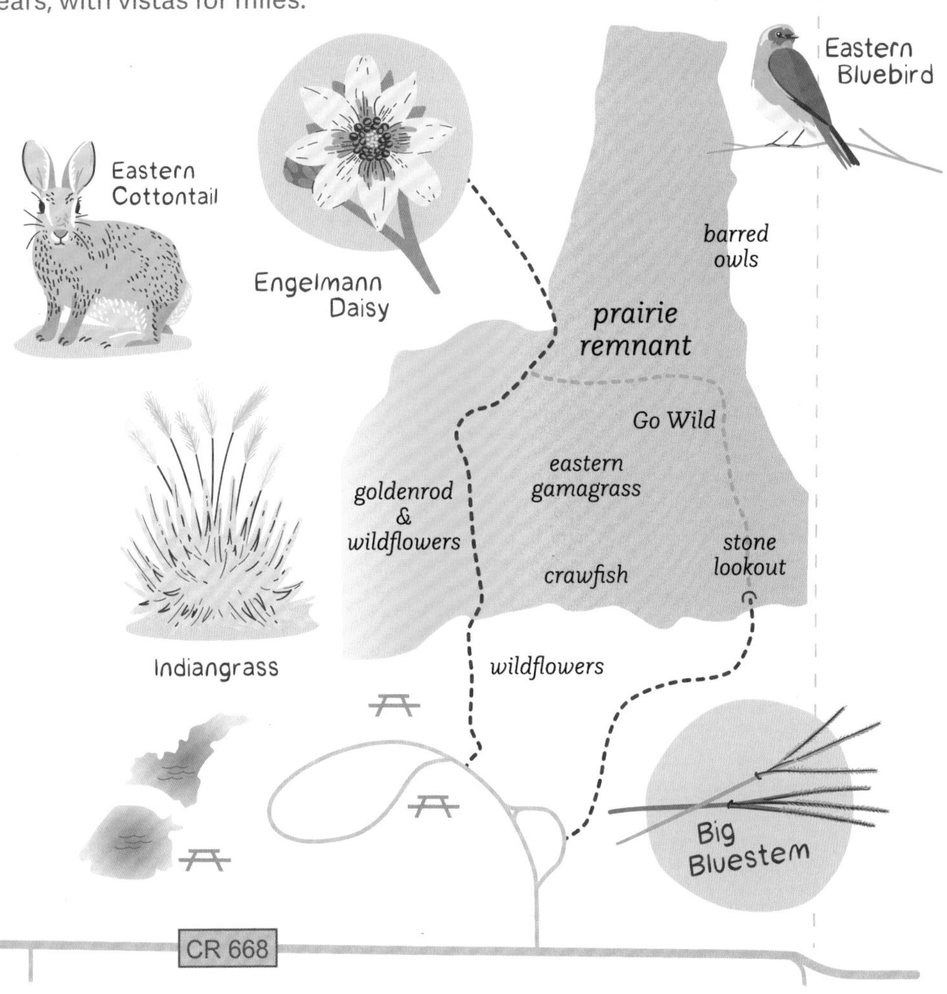

▼ Maximilian sunflowers bring joy after a long, hot summer.

▲ Parkhill evokes pioneer-era prairies.

If you desire to experience the way North Texas looked for many thousands of years, Parkhill Prairie is the place. Miles down a rock road and surrounded by ranches, its 436 acres offer a remoteness and quiet unexpected in a public park. Less than 1 percent of Blackland Prairie remains and in the center of Parkhill is a rare fifty-two-acre remnant.

On this warm, overcast autumn day, a mild, steady wind sets the prairie's rolling hills into motion. The long, strappy leaves of native grasses undulate in waves. Patches of yellow Maximilian sunflowers bob in the breeze on stiff stems while the more flexible goldenrod bends. From the foliage rises the buzzing of bugs.

Standing there in its midst is Rich Jaynes, the native grass go-to guy for the Texas Master Naturalists Blackland Prairie chapter and other groups. An environmental scientist by day, prairie is his passion. Rich and I amble with photographer Stalin SM up the mowed path through the prairie, flanked by native grasses nearly five feet tall, their plentiful itchy chiggers safely at a distance.

Wide open spaces and steady, mild winds make Parkhill Prairie a perfect place for flying kites.

▲ A mowed prairie path is an immersion in native grasses.

The Dynamic Prairie

The Nature Conservancy manages Parkhill. A couple years ago, North Texas preserves manager Brandon Belcher led a prescribed burn of the remnant and rehabilitated acreage. In centuries past, wildfires swept through the Blackland Prairies, incinerating woody plants that can turn productive grassland into useless brush. Native grasses regrow from nodes safely below the surface.

The Blackland Prairie chapter of Texas Master Naturalists is renowned for its prairie enthusiasm and outreach.

The positive effects of the prescribed burn are apparent. The Indiangrass is robust with seedstalks topped with tight bundles of inflorescences not yet opened. Stimulated by recent rains after a dry spell, the shorter sideoats grama strives for another round of seed, even though spent June husks are still visible. No brush incursion is visible.

"Prairies are so dynamic," says Rich. Unlike forests that change slowly, prairies are responsive, quickly able to take advantage of opportunities. "These are warm-season grasses. There's a genius to it, waiting for the season when nobody else dares to grow to put on your growth."

The tall grasses and wildflowers are flush with seed and cacophonous with birdcalls—the dickcissel's *dic-thiss-sul* and eastern phoebe's piercing *fee-bee*. Eastern bluebirds flit about in party mode. Cliff swallows swoop about after the prairie's prodigious insects.

Go Wild: Into the Prairie

▼ Related to teosinte, the progenitor of corn, eastern gamagrass makes large seed kernels on a stem.

▲ Rich and the author contemplate where to go next.

The mowed path ends at a curious brick half circle at the top of a rise. The virgin prairie remnant spreads out on the hillside below us. Naturalists know this hilltop for its *Procambarus steigmani*, a rare crawfish found mainly in two Texas counties, Collin and Hunt, and named for local prairie pioneer Kenneth Steigman, who discovered it.

From here, we must take a trailless Go Wild segment into the prairie. Avidly absorbing Rich's grass-nerd knowledge, photographer Stalin SM and I follow him down the slope. Prairie hiking is calisthenics, navigating a tangle of waist-high foliage by high stepping between grassy clumps while waving your arms for balance. Onlookers would think we walk like drunks.

We stop before dozens of glossy, emerald-green eastern gamagrass clumps about two feet tall. The gnarly roots burst through the soil surface with great power. Stalin, who's from India, thinks they look like ginger. "These are decades old. They've withstood fire and drought. Just look at them," says Rich with awe.

Looking as if clouds landed on the prairie, heath aster scrambles over taller plants to form airy mounds of tiny white blooms. Here in the untilled prairie, goldenrod grows in sprawling clonal colonies connected by rhizomes a plow has never sundered. The low afternoon sunlight sets them ablaze. We admire the sight like an exquisite work of art.

Most crawfish prefer moist bottomlands or areas adjacent to standing water. Procambarus steigmani burrows yards deep into the soil and finds moisture from perched water tables that accumulate above an impermeable layer.

Prairie Car Tour

Hiking not possible? Treat yourself to a prairie wildflower drive past two of North Texas's most pristine prairies: Clymer Meadow and Paul Mathews Prairie. Both are private property, open by invitation only, but the view from the road is great.

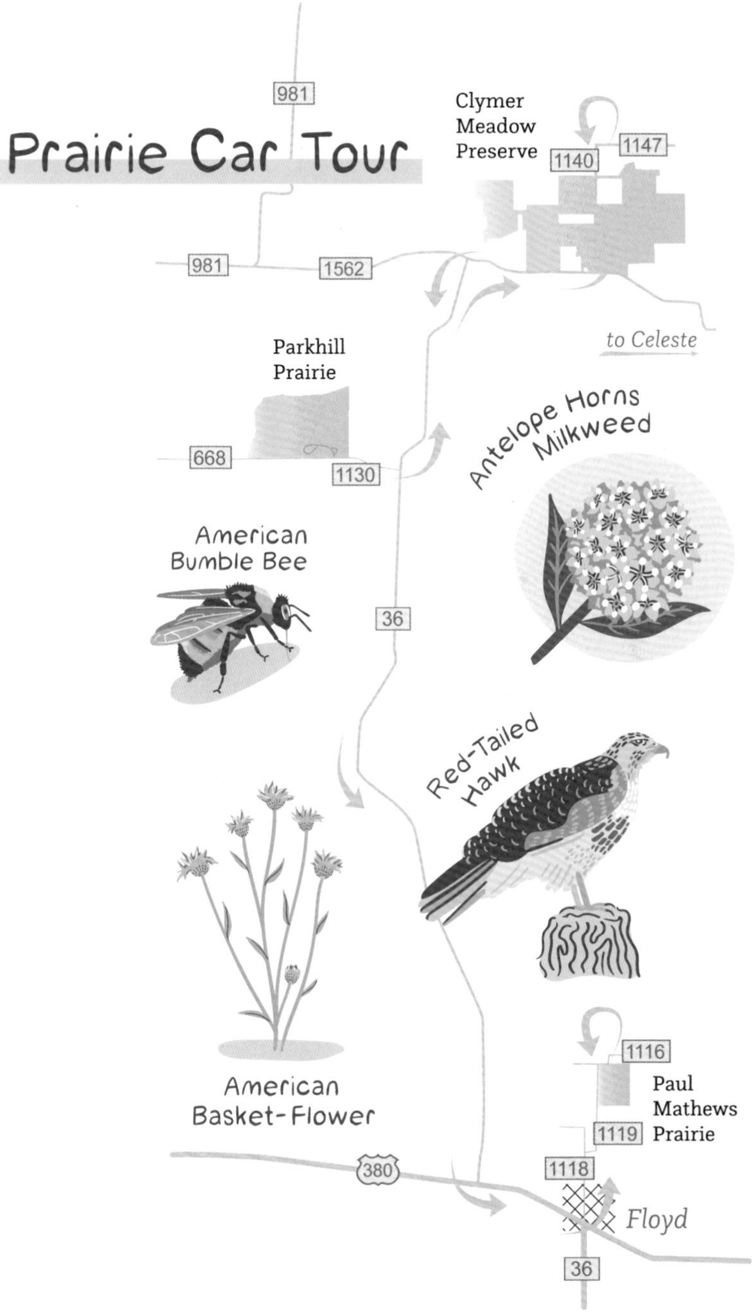

◄ Deep in the grasses, a prairie rose blooms and sets seed.

Go Wild: Prairie Understory

A prairie is as intimate as it is expansive. We shift our gaze to the ground. Prickly dewberry vines hidden in the grass snag our shoes as we ramble down the hill. Eastern poison ivy winds among the grass clumps, shaded by their leaves. Clamoring for light between grass clumps, the diminutive, sensitive briar closes its mimosa-like leaves when touched.

It is an understory as rich as any jungle. Rich finds a vining prairie rose with mature hips. We each take a firm, pea-sized fruit to nibble. "It tastes like mild coconut, same texture too," says Stalin. Rich and I proclaim it entirely pleasant, if unremarkable.

Down in the grass jungle, small wildlife prowls. A long sinew of pressed-down leaves indicates the path of a large western rat snake, preying on little deer mice who weave tunnels of dried grass. But the much larger hispid cotton rat is a better meal.

It's perhaps the smallest wildlife here that are the most important. A tallgrass prairie produces about five tons of surface biomass per acre. Without frequent wildfires or herds of hungry bison, it accumulates too much. It's up to the detritivores, creatures that primarily live off dead organic material to stem the accumulation. On the prairie, that means tiny globular drop snails and larger, conical decollate snails.

Decollate snails from the Mediterranean also consume other snails and were imported decades ago to California to control brown garden snails, yet found their way into a remote Texas prairie.

▲ Rich finds amazement in a prairie plant.

Sunset on the Prairie

Sunlight is ebbing. But we keep finding things to see. "Is that a clump of big bluestem over there?" Rich asks. On our way, we find the tall, silvery dried skeleton of a starkly branched rattlesnake master and a spent stalk of an Arkansas yucca, both indicators of prime prairie.

Hoots of a barred owl, that denizen of the twilight hour, remind us it's leaving time. Coyotes yip in the distance. Yet we must stop to appreciate a giant, yellow garden spider, fat and happy from prairie insects. She appears suspended, her web invisible in the pale light.

The mowed path resumes at the bottom of the slope, and we make our way back, ending up about a hundred yards down from where we parked. As we draw close, a white truck zips by on the park road blasting its horn—a Collin County Open Space employee clearing folks out so he can lock the gate. The prairie is endlessly fascinating, but we must go home and shower off these chiggers.

ADVENTURE 8

BIG CREEKS OF SOUTHERN COLLIN COUNTY

Connemara Meadow

Open space amid residential development, transforming into tallgrass prairie, with wide, mowed paths and room to ramble on seventy-two acres along Rowlett Creek.

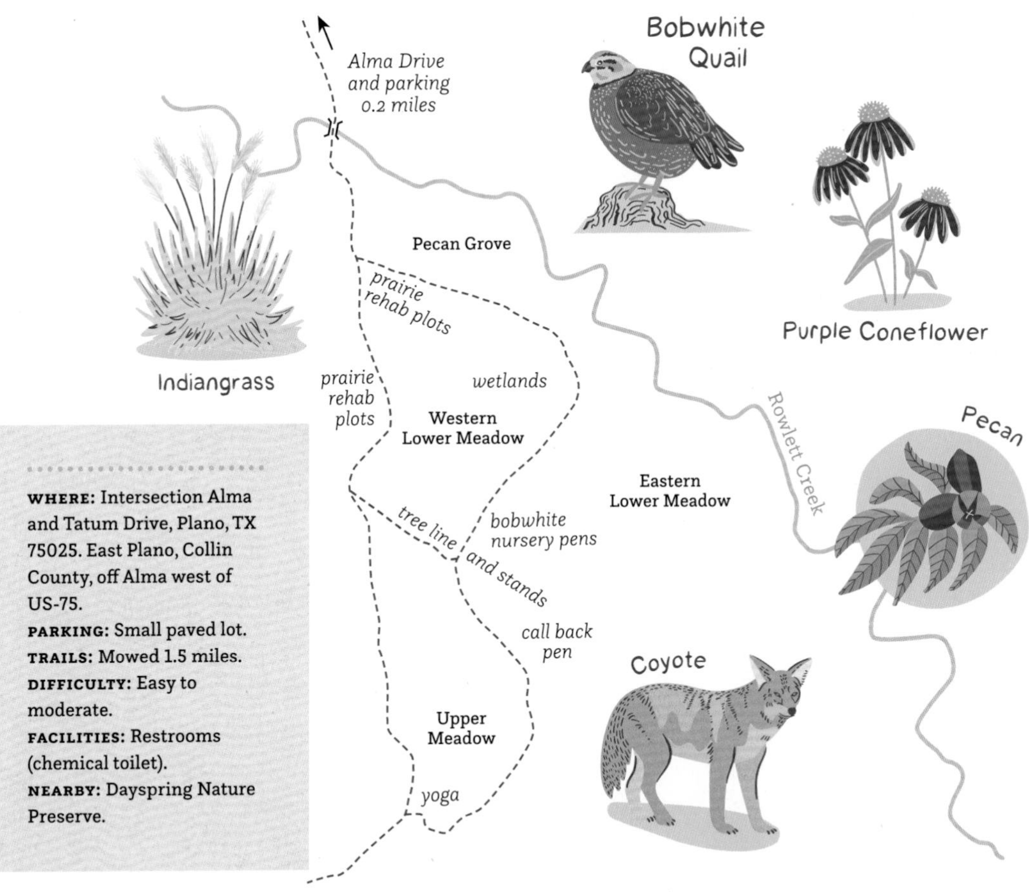

WHERE: Intersection Alma and Tatum Drive, Plano, TX 75025. East Plano, Collin County, off Alma west of US-75.
PARKING: Small paved lot.
TRAILS: Mowed 1.5 miles.
DIFFICULTY: Easy to moderate.
FACILITIES: Restrooms (chemical toilet).
NEARBY: Dayspring Nature Preserve.

▲ From pasture to beautiful prairie.

Frances Williams enjoyed decades of horseback riding and woods wandering at her family's Montgomery Farms. When a young visitor picked up a pecan and asked Frances what it was, she realized many children did not experience a childhood shaped by nature. In 1981, she founded a land trust, Connemara Conservancy, to preserve seventy-two acres of the farm as green space, writing, "'Come forth into the light of things, let nature be your teacher.' So sayeth Wordsworth and methinks he speaks of Connemara."

On this sunny spring day, a mother walks the mowed path at Connemara Meadow as her two young children squeal with delight at wildflowers. One points excitedly at an orange and brown pearl crescent butterfly working the Indian blanket flowers. The mom directs their attention to a bumblebee gathering nectar on green milkweed but misses the rabbit watching from behind a little bluestem clump.

"Every day I come in, I thank Frances for having such a vision. Grateful her daughter Amy Monier carried it on," says Bob Mione, Connemara Nature Preserve Manager since 2011. Before that, his career had been in IT with the US Department of Defense. Frances's fondness for gatherings continues with Connemara's many special events, including concerts and yoga in the pecan grove. Amy's passion for art lives on through the annual Arts in the Meadow event.

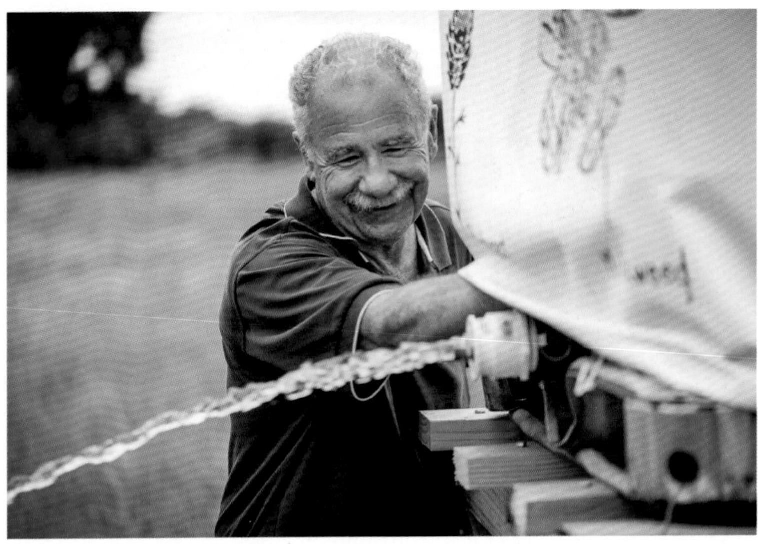

◄ Bob works the irrigation system.

A People Place

Connemara rests in a community embrace. Neighbors drop by to walk Bob's Labrador. A steady stream of young families and retired couples amble past the wildflowers. People walk their leashed dogs. A jogger eschews numerous paved trails nearby for a run on the grass paths. The place is busy with volunteers fixing equipment, watering newly installed plants, and pulling invasives. Blackland Prairie Texas Master Naturalist Sue Kacines, who is surveying the preserve's plants, joins Bob and me for a walk.

After Connemara's establishment, the meadows grew back wild, but not productively. Invasives took over, creating monocultures. Flowers were few and wildlife almost nonexistent. In 2012, the Connemara board endorsed efforts to restore native grasses and wildflowers. "We learned quickly from early failures that irrigation and working in small patches was the key," says Bob.

A series of small agricultural plots spread up the Lower Meadow slope, raising native plants to populate the prairie. Purple coneflowers with long, drooping lavender petals surrounding bright orange centers are thriving, as are clasping coneflowers, named for cone-shaped centers protruding from yellow and maroon petals. Tiny yellow butterflies flitting from plot to plot bounce against us.

Creating Diversity

We stroll up the slope, a former Bermuda pasture now glorious with color and texture. Each section has a story. Prickly thistles once covered one; pulling up thousands was a huge chore. Another was solid Johnsongrass, eradicated by an expensive selective herbicide. "This used to be a cotton field," says Bob, his arm sweeping across a hilltop with lines of trees where

▲ Monarch butterflies almost outshine Connemara's wildflowers.

◄ Painted buntings add to Connemara's rich color palette.

► Sensitive briar's leaves fold up when touched.

fences once stood. "It was Frances's favorite place. Now we have yoga classes up here."

In response to restoration efforts, tall stems of Berlandier's yellow flax and standing winecups in bold magenta join the lavender of American basket-flower. Petite, pointed yellow stars peek out between native grasses along with the pink puffs of sensitive briar blooms. The diversity engenders a smorgasbord of insects. The yellow chests of eastern phoebes and western kingbirds glint in the sunlight, framed by gray feathers, as they swoop for bugs.

The hilltop fosters expansive peace and oneness with the sky. The vista of grassy fields dotted with color rolling down to the creek is breathtaking. Terracing of the hillside where irrigation can't reach, done for cotton cultivation, now collects moisture to nurture an astounding array of wildflowers. "One reason we have so much milkweed," says Bob, "is that when the seedpods are ready, we take a tennis racket and smack 'em," sending the fluffy seeds over a wide expanse.

▼ A mature quail hides in a juniper.

▲ A coyote runs past switchgrass clumps.

Leaving a Legacy

We stop at a tree copse, admiring the vibrant roughleaf dogwoods, when a chortled clucking catches our ear. Then the unmistakable ascending whistle-like call: poor-bob-WHITE. After being gone for many decades, bobwhite quail have returned to the meadow. Untold hours of volunteer effort go into raising farm-bred quail chicks to maturity for release.

Bob leads us to a wire pen about fifteen feet long containing a few dozen bustling, young bobwhite quail. For their first five weeks, volunteers mist chicks with water to stimulate feather preening. They play Cooper's hawk calls to awaken predator responses and release live crickets to teach them to catch. At ten to twelve weeks, the prairie becomes the birds' home. Even with all that effort, chicks' survival skills are poor. The goal is for enough to survive and breed a new generation with wild instincts.

Resuming our trek down the slope, the sprawling Eastern Lower Meadow spreads on our right to Rowlett Creek. The last pasture parcel slated for conversion to prairie, coyotes and bobcats favor it for rodent hunting. "Do you see out there where the vegetation changes color?" asks Bob. "That's my dead line. I plan to restore up to that. Then someone else must carry on." No doubt it will continue, aided in some part by Bob's cremains.

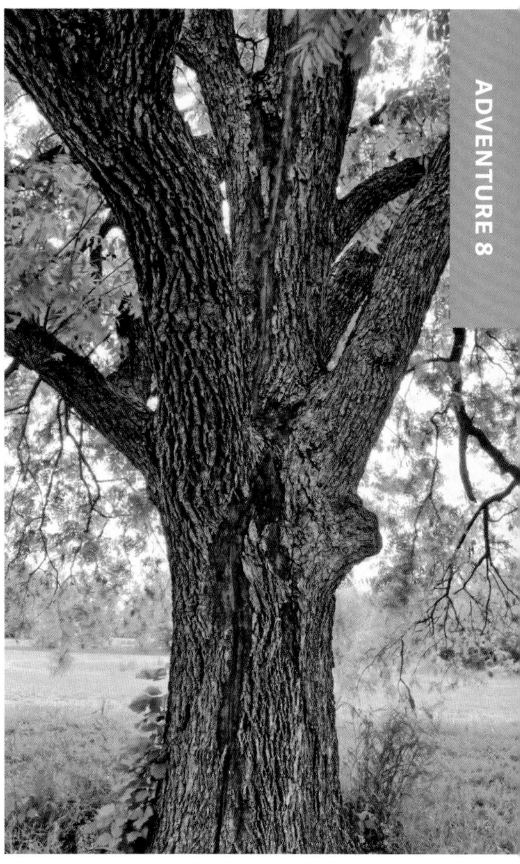

▲ Trees hang on against erosion in Rowlett Creek.

◀ This older pecan has so far survived a lightning strike.

Creek Conversations

Rowlett Creek forms Connemara's riparian corridor. As it flows twenty-six miles to Lake Ray Hubbard, it drains over one hundred thirty square miles. It now floods multiple times a year because of poor stormwater management by upstream cities, causing damage to the low prairies that a volunteer calls heartbreaking. We pass the cool, shady Lower Meadow Wetlands and detour to a view spot overlooking the creek. On the side of a chasm ten yards deep, a pair of tenacious trees hang on against erosion.

The crew gathers in the low prairie beneath The Twins, a pair of massive pecan trees. Lightning struck one, so all nervously worry about its fate. Bob stops for a minute to look at the volunteers. "When Jack was killed in 2017," says Bob referring to his son, "I don't know what I would've done if I wasn't able to work with these people. It helped me realize I could continue."

We sit on pickup tailgates, share sandwiches, and discuss the day. Mike and Barbara Wilson catch Bob up on their efforts to keep invasive hedge parsley from going to seed. Rick Park exults over a successful mower repair. Sue uses the break to upload iNaturalist observations. "So," says Bob. "What are we doing next?"

ADVENTURE 9

BIG CREEKS OF SOUTHERN COLLIN COUNTY

Oak Point Park & Nature Preserve

Plano's largest park at 800 acres stretches for two miles along Rowlett Creek with old-growth riparian forest and some vibrant Blackland Prairie remnants.

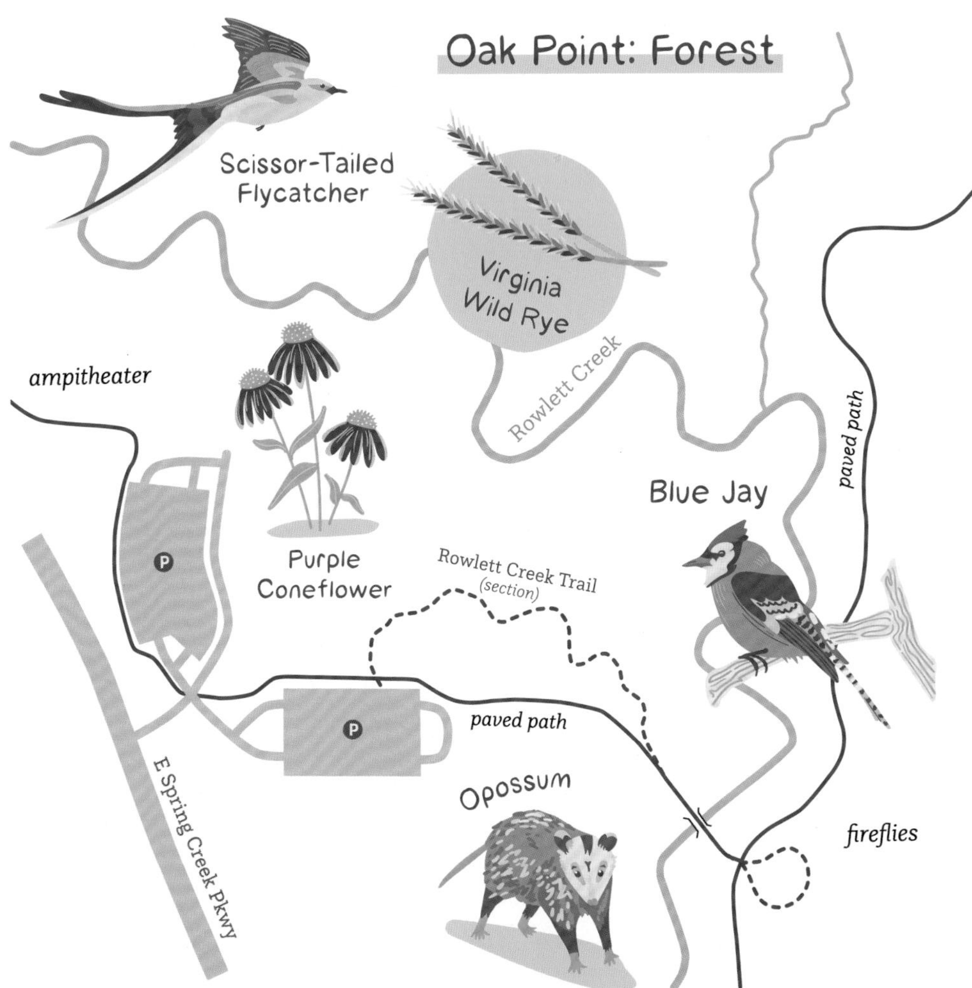

▲ Full moon rises over Oak Point.

WHERE: 2801 E Spring Creek Pkwy, Plano, TX 75074, and off Los Rios Blvd., between Cloverhaven and Parker.
PARKING: Paved lots.
TRAILS: Dirt 5 miles, paved 8 miles. Detailed map at plano.gov/800/parks.
DIFFICULTY: Easy to moderate.
FACILITIES: Retreat and educational center with full restrooms at 5901 Los Rios Blvd.
NEARBY: Bob Woodruff Park, Rowlett Creek Nature Preserve, Rowlett Nature Trail.

Sally Evans is a legend. Retired as a nature educator at Plano Independent School District Holifield Science Learning Center on Rowlett Creek, she knows these riparian woods well. On my visit with her, Oak Point's paved trails are busy with walkers and bicyclists, leaving the dirt ones entirely to us. We enter the forest, greeted immediately by a massive American elm, its branches lifting in a perfect Y.

I'm raring to move, but Sally invokes a venerable safety slogan: stop, look, and listen. Breathe deeply, notice the light, shift into forest time. She asks, "What do you hear?" I stop and listen—birdsong, a breeze moving leaves, a fussy cardinal, a cricket—and soon the traffic noises fade from awareness.

An ephemeral pond nurtures a huge pecan tree and purple meadow rue. Virginia wildrye's long, light green leaves glow like an impressionist painting. Sally asks, "Can you count how many seeds are on one?" Playing this game causes me to look closely, and I discover the tiniest grasshopper, no bigger than a grain of rice. Sally pulls a leaf blade off and shows me how to hold it tight between my thumbs to make a whistle.

It takes us fifteen minutes to walk ten yards. We marvel at a tangle of thick grapevines and muse about lizards that use it as a highway. She

"My mom, the nature lady. Close your eyes, listen to the wind, the birds, and the spaces between. I dare you to open your eyes and see nature the same way. She spent her life teaching and mentoring folks from four to ninety-four. God created it; my mom lives it."

—Sally Evans' son, Bryce Evans

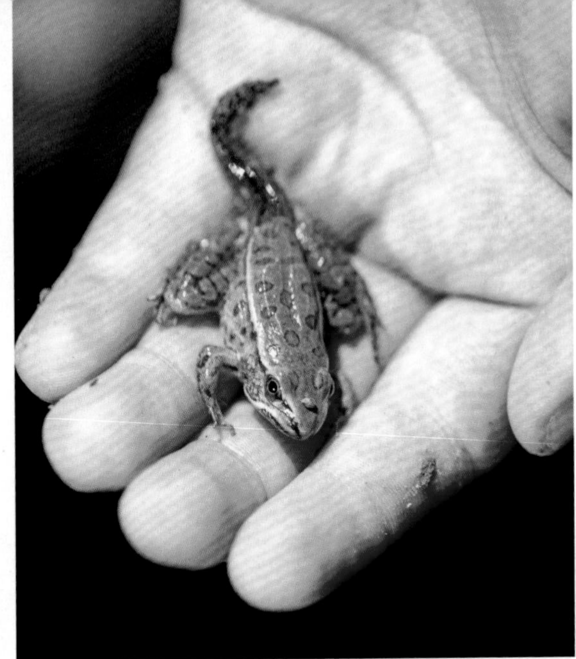

▲ A very young leopard frog still retains its tadpole tail.

◄ For later study, Junior Master Naturalists net insects attracted by wildflowers.

► The big meadow hosts spectacular firefly displays in summer.

carefully peels open a distorted leaf on a hackberry to show the insect eggs inside—a bug nursery, she calls it. Deep in the woods a cacophony of screaming blue jays suddenly lets loose. "Trouble," she says.

Worlds at Play

We emerge from woods near the paved trail into brightly lit drifts of floating white cottonwood seeds. "Look above the trees!" Sally exclaims. A dozen Mississippi kites swoop high in the air. "Do you see the smaller bird?" A dark shape slices among the gray kites, seeing how close it can get. A kestrel perhaps?

The paved path leads to a picturesque bridge over Rowlett Creek, green from algal blooms caused by lawn fertilizer runoff. A Cooper's hawk bursts from the forest chased by vociferous blue jays and lands on a tree, screeching in defiance. A jay skims the hawk's head with its claws—a warning to stay away from its nest. The hawk flies back into the trees and the battle for blue jay babies continues. Dozens of people pass by, unaware of the drama.

We depart and walk out onto a vista almost too big for our eyes. A vast meadow dotted with colorful wildflowers stretches before us. The paved trail circling the meadow is full of people walking, jogging, and bicycling. Our eyes are pulled to the sky above where the Mississippi kites still engage in aerial games. Parallel worlds at play.

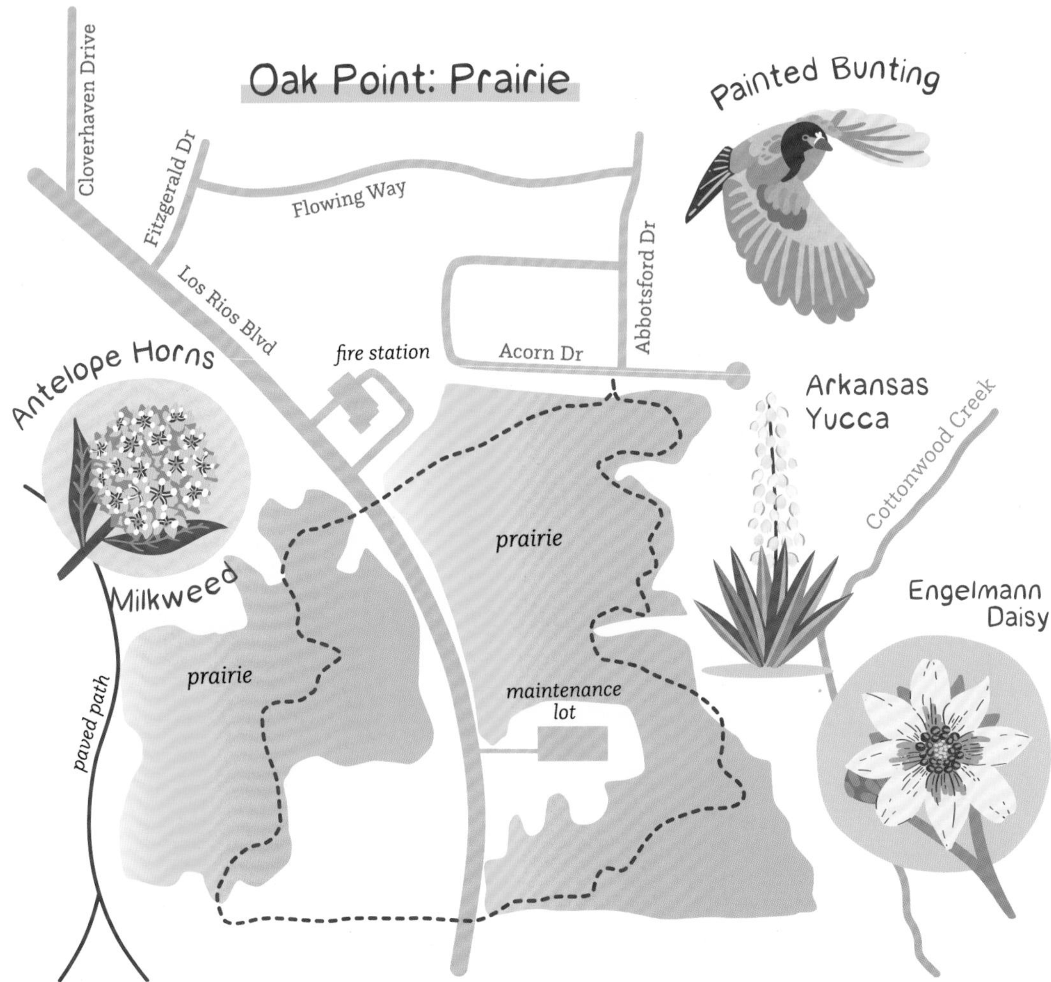

Secret Prairie: Los Rios East

Few driving on busy Los Rios notice the prairies atop the broad limestone ridge. Carol Clark, of the Collin County Native Plant Society, knows them well, both as a native plant expert and as someone who lives nearby. Many a time she has stepped up to defend them from wanton development plans.

Although Blackland Prairie is most associated with deep, dark soils and massively rooted tall grasses, those composed of shallow soil over limestone—sometimes called prairie barrens or chalk prairies—favor shorter, finely bladed grasses. The sparse plant arrangement, with some flowers just a few inches tall, creates a Lilliputian landscape.

It's almost a secret prairie, this flower-filled delight. Once downslope toward Cottonwood Creek, it's invisible from the street—so dotted with small, white prairie bishops it looks like a sky with stars. Engelmann's daisy thrusts yellow blossoms from ornate gray-green leaves. Wooded drainage channels furrow the slope, creating private nooks that are worlds into themselves. "All you have to do is stand in one place for a while and notice," says Carol.

▲ A praying mantis seeks insects on a sunflower.

Prairie Bees

"These limestone prairies, some find it hard to see value in them," says Carol. "But you'll find plants that you don't see elsewhere, like bluets and Barbara's buttons." We set off on this late-spring day, curious how native bees fared after North Texas endured nearly two weeks of below-freezing temperatures. Our walking disturbs a big bee. "Not sure if that was a carpenter or a bumblebee," says Carol. "If they're shiny on their hiney, they're not a bumblebee."

We turn into a particularly thick patch of prairie bishop and Carol lights up. "Here are the bees!" I lean over to watch a buzzing maroon speck no bigger than a grain of rice fly off. "I had no idea they could be so small," I say. "Look, the flowers are just full of them. See the pollen clinging to their legs?" Carol replies. "In this little patch, we've got at least a dozen bees of various kinds that are almost invisible unless you're really, really looking."

But mostly, bees are scarce. Carol informs that some species have an overwintering prepupa stage in the soil, yet can sense surrounding conditions. "They can make rudimentary predictions about whether their plants will be available or not," she says. The freeze delayed some spring blooms. Out there, the prairie is full of sleeping bees.

Saved Prairie: Los Rios West

We leave the Cottonwood Creek watershed and cross Los Rios onto Old Morton Vale Road. We turn through a gap in the trees and a rampant mix of yellow and red wildflowers coats the upward slope. "There are bluebirds,

▼ Milkweeds draw monarchs to Oak Point.

▲ American basket-flowers and Indian plantains adorn a prairie parcel.

scissor-tailed flycatchers, western kingbirds, dickcissels. Painted buntings nest over there. You name it, they're out here," says Carol. Plans to replace this rare prairie with a concert amphitheater were thwarted.

We continue up the slope, past a split rail fence encircling a prairie remnant, to an active restoration area, where native grasses battle it out with imported King Ranch bluestem. The bold persist: the Engelmann's daisy, Maximilian sunflower, and Arkansas yucca. Liatris, with its roots that are yards deep, provides spires of purple blooms in fall. "It's full of wand milkweed, which isn't very common, and three other kinds of milkweeds, too," says Carol, boding well for migrating monarchs.

Before us unfurls a slope covered in Arkansas yucca, indicating it was never heavily grazed or plowed. In our walk, we've passed through parcels of former dairy farms and horse ranches. Through prescribed burns, judicious mowing, and selective seeding, the City of Plano is bringing it back to life—a commendable effort.

Prairie Wisdom

Reflecting back on our quiet morning enjoying nature, Carol comments, "People with boomboxes and beachballs aren't better than those with binoculars. Introverts need outdoor recreation space, too. And there are a lot of us."

We head back to Los Rios, passing one of thirteen artistic metal gates capturing nature vignettes, and cross near the fire station. Taking the paved path to our cars, we are charmed that a patch of prairie bishop dances in a light breeze, graceful and animated like ballerinas in white tutus.

Collin County Chapter of the Native Plant Society of Texas promotes the conservation, research, and utilization of native plants and plant habitats through outreach and education.

ADVENTURE 10 GREAT TRINITY FOREST

Trinity River Audubon Center & Trinity Forest Trail

An Audubon environmental education center serves as entry to the largest urban bottomland hardwood forest in the nation, while a system of paved trails offers access to the mobility impaired.

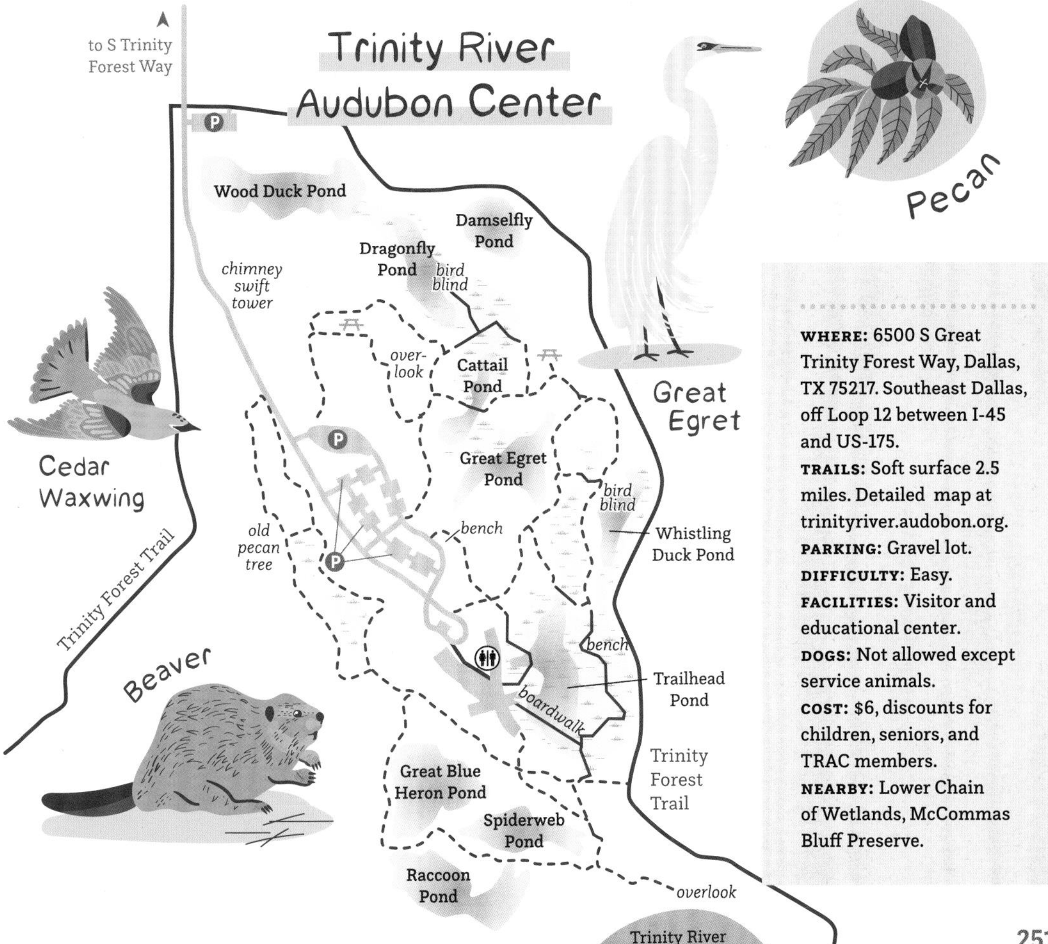

WHERE: 6500 S Great Trinity Forest Way, Dallas, TX 75217. Southeast Dallas, off Loop 12 between I-45 and US-175.
TRAILS: Soft surface 2.5 miles. Detailed map at trinityriver.audubon.org.
PARKING: Gravel lot.
DIFFICULTY: Easy.
FACILITIES: Visitor and educational center.
DOGS: Not allowed except service animals.
COST: $6, discounts for children, seniors, and TRAC members.
NEARBY: Lower Chain of Wetlands, McCommas Bluff Preserve.

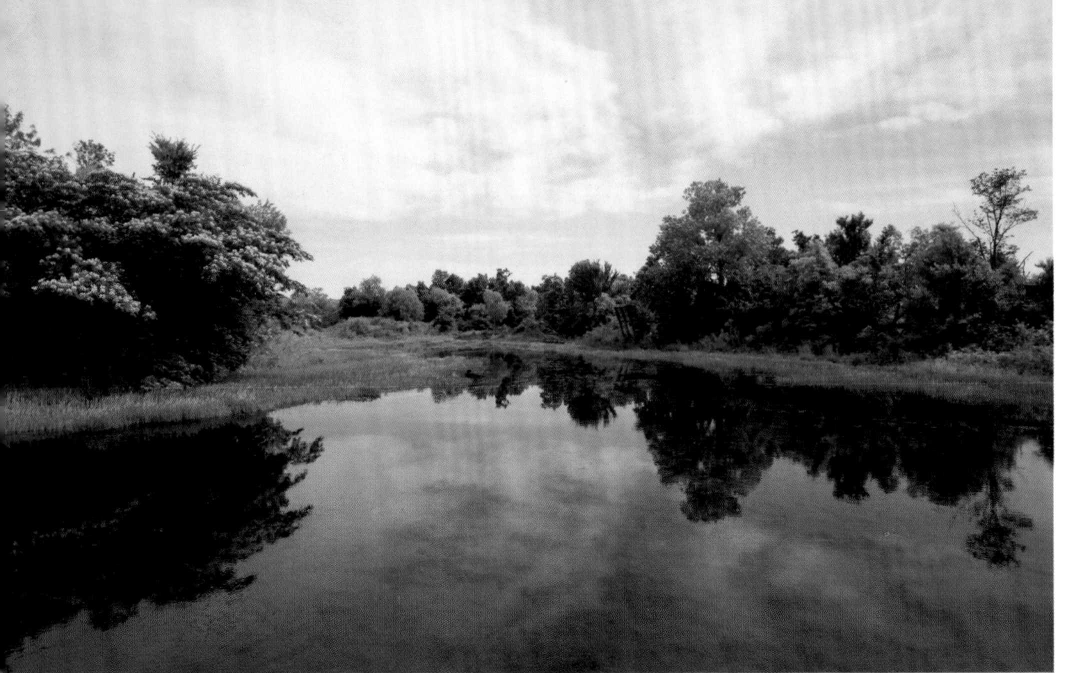

▲ The size of wetlands varies with precipitation.

TRAC hosts the North-Central Texas Master Birder course for intermediate-level birders. Participants receive advanced training in field ornithology in exchange for volunteering in service to birds and their habitat.

The 6000-acre Great Trinity Forest (GTF) spreads south from near downtown Dallas. The Trinity River slices it from north to south, bringing alluvial richness and moisture. Mostly former ranch and farmland that began returning to forest in the mid-1900s, many trees were located in difficult-to-develop areas or preserved for shade.

GTF abounds in contrasts: serene nature beneath overpasses, white-tailed deer within shouting distance of ball fields, a barren golf course plopped in a forest. Economically struggling neighborhoods wrap around gleaming developments. Crime continues to be a problem in some areas. Naturalists worry how plans for future Trinity River engineering and wide, paved trails will damage the besieged forest.

Trinity River Audubon Center (TRAC) is a sampler of North Texas ecosystems. Boardwalks skim over wetlands, chipped granite trails thread through prairies and upland woods, and dirt trails pad through riparian woods for five miles of paths. All are securely contained within 130 acres, and a modern educational center presides at the heart.

Jake Poinsett and Marcus Cole share their knowledge as Trinity River Audubon Center educators on this warm spring day. We take the boardwalk across the big Trailhead Pond. The shady Wetland Trail wanders among seasonal ponds, with small bridges spanning rivulets and providing side trips to bird blinds.

Wetlands Wonderland

It's a wet spring, so ponds named Cattail, Dragonfly, and Great Egret ooze into one long bayou. In drier times, they'll be distinct ponds, at times very small. The topic quickly becomes a beaver that Jake says, "is doing his own wetland engineering."

The beaver fells young black willows but leaves enough bark so the tree survives. "It makes its own food," says Jake, noting that the rodent grazes young willow shoots emerging from the now-reachable trunk. Marcus observes the beaver's broad, muddy path through reeds. I share that the salicylic acid in black willow bark soothes beaver incisors. With this nature nerd triple swap, we are now fully bonded.

Jake and Marcus hear birdsong, raise binoculars, and identify birds one after another, training for the national Bird Bowl, a birdwatching count competition hosted annually by the Audubon Society around World Migratory Bird Day. Thickets of roughleaf dogwood abound with short-lived umbels of white flowers that pop in the dim, dappled light. Birds will flock here in early fall for the white berries, eaten by over fifty species.

TRAC's wetlands attract migrating waterfowl such as coots, shovelers, and teals, and shorebirds including greater yellowlegs and the very loud, ring-billed gull. Over a dozen sparrow species pass through, notably Harris's, LeConte's, and savannah, along with towhees, warblers, and wrens. Migrating along with them are birds of prey, including the northern harrier and sharp-shinned hawk.

Toxic Dump to Eco-Treasure

Dwarf palmettos grow in an open glen, an homage to deep parts of the Great Trinity Forest where they still grow in the wild. The trail swings into the

▼ Bird blinds allow sneak peeks at wildlife.

◄ Beaver engineering.

▲ Birds like great egrets now thrive where a toxic dump once stood.

Blackland Prairie restoration. Beyond TRAC fences sits a massive, two-story slope dotted with landfill monitors—reminders that the area was once the largest illegal dump in Texas, containing 1.5 million tons of industrial refuse.

Over two decades, the dump leaked toxic chemicals and caught fire twice, smothering an adjacent African-American neighborhood in black soot. Finally, a federal court case ordered restoration by the dump operators, who then abandoned the property. "It decimated the ecosystem far beyond here," says Marcus. A $37 million environmental remediation led by the city of Dallas ensued.

Designers crafted a 130-acre swath of excavated land into TRAC's wetlands, woods, and prairie. The 21,000-square-foot, LEED-rated education center sits in its midst, radiating ecological stewardship with its recycled materials, vegetated roof, rainwater collection, and energy efficiency—a fitting coda to an environmental crime.

Where surface waters once ran in toxic neon colors, healthy waters now flow. Small-mouthed salamanders slither through damp leaf debris. Blanchard's cricket, as well as green tree and southern leopard frogs, cling to pondside plants. Green anoles skitter about nervously, hoping to find a meal without becoming one.

Savannah Knoll

Rising out of the wetland, we ascend a small knoll into a short motte of post oaks, Eve's necklace, and Mexican plums. I remark about the red, sandy soil. "It's a finger of Post Oak Savannah," says Jake. "Eco divisions aren't as clear as maps make them." We absorb the view of the wetland ponds, lush in a myriad of light, spring-green tones.

I imagine the wetlands gradually receding as hot weather evaporates the water, greenery diminishing to a wisp of its former self. Small fish, tadpoles, and crustaceans become stranded in the muck, providing a feast for

▲ TRAC's education building melds with the landscape.

◀ The old pecan tree is a TRAC landmark.

shorebirds, barred owls, raccoons, and opossums, before summer thunderstorms fill them again.

As we depart the knoll, I spot an Eve's necklace tree growing out of the steep slope, placing opulent dangles of lavender flowers at face level. I inhale robustly. Native plant gardens separate the parking lot sections on our way back, providing seed for future prairie rehabilitation.

About 20,000 school children visit TRAC annually. Younger students play with pond life and educational animals. Older ones learn scientific methods of water quality evaluation and study wildlife in the field.

Forest Stroll

Jake and Marcus go back to work, leaving me to stroll the forest trails. The well-shaded path starts wide and travels along two shallow ponds lost in the trees. Then the trail narrows, and a sense of the Great Trinity Forest emerges.

Scattered immense pecan trees stand like teachers among younger trees only a few decades old. The forest floor is a brilliant green sea of Virginia wildrye and broad-leaved forbs. As the path widens again, I come to TRAC's most significant tree: a pecan twelve feet around and towering three stories tall. With over two centuries of life under its bark, it commands respect.

I depart the woods for the Great Blue Heron and Spider Web ponds, taking the forested backside trails for new views and more big trees. Cottonwoods flap their leaves noisily in the wind. Soon I'm at the Trinity River overlook, a rare chance to picnic right on the river and a fine place to rest before heading home.

WHERE: Off the road before you reach the Audubon Center.
PARKING: Paved lot.
TRAILS: Paved 8 miles. Detailed map at trinityrivercorridor.com/recreation/great-trinity-forest.
DIFFICULTY: Easy.
FACILITIES: None.
NEARBY: Lower Chain of Wetlands, McCommas Bluff Preserve.

AT&T Trinity Forest Trail

The pavement corridors of AT&T Trinity Forest Trail (TFT) make it easy for anyone to experience the Great Trinity Forest (GTF). Most weekday mornings at dawn, lawyer Bill Holston takes a two-mile walk to the Trinity River pedestrian bridge and back, readying himself for another stressful day as executive director of Human Rights Initiative, defending resilient immigrants.

The dawn chorus of indigo and painted buntings from the treetops, the barred owl calling to its mate, restores him. "I started doing it a year ago because you are surrounded by birdsong. This morning, I watched about twenty nighthawks feeding in the dawn sky. Occasionally I see white-tailed deer."

▲ A yellow-crowned night heron strides the shore.

Woods Dark and Deep

There are other trails in the area. Joppa Preserve is set in a lovely historical park. Note that Lemmon Lake only holds water seasonally. Though right on the Trinity, Loop 12 trailhead is challenging to access. Eco Park provides quick river access.

Michael Cook, botanist and manager of Sammons Center for the Performing Arts, and I are traversing the TFT on a late-winter afternoon. Long weekend hikes are essential for his mental health. We depart from the AT&T Trail trailhead off the road to TRAC.

We are awestruck by the architectural majesty of large cedar elms, green ash, and red oaks in winter. Just past TRAC boundaries, hundreds of robins set up a peeping commotion in the woods. The rich redness of a northern cardinal flock pops in the trees.

Michael observes a compact, sharp-shinned hawk dive-bombing songbirds and white-winged doves. A red-tailed hawk eats its meal in a tree close by, unimpressed by observers. Eastern phoebes swoop after flying insects, showing soft yellow bellies.

The trail skirts the edge of McCommas Bluff Preserve, held by Dallas County Open Space. An enticing dirt trail leads into the forest. The pecans

▲ Pecan trees grow huge in the bottomlands.

and oaks are noticeably larger, the understory dense with briar and vine. The woods lightly crackle as coyotes and armadillos emerge at dusk.

The land becomes rich with inland sea oats as we approach the pedestrian bridge spanning the river. It grants a stellar view of the Trinity River, close enough to see the water's turbulent surface. Stone benches provide a nice rest.

Once on the river's south side, the wildness abates in favor of a parklike appearance, honored by aged pecans topping three stories tall. The ground beneath them is covered in nuts, hard to shell but deliciously sweet. We stuff our pockets and head back home.

ADVENTURE 11 GREAT TRINITY FOREST

Ned and Genie Fritz Texas Buckeye Trail and Bonton Woods

A section of the Great Trinity Forest noted for its Texas buckeye tree grove, Bart Simpson Lake, the confluence of White Rock Creek and Trinity River, and nearby Bonton Farms.

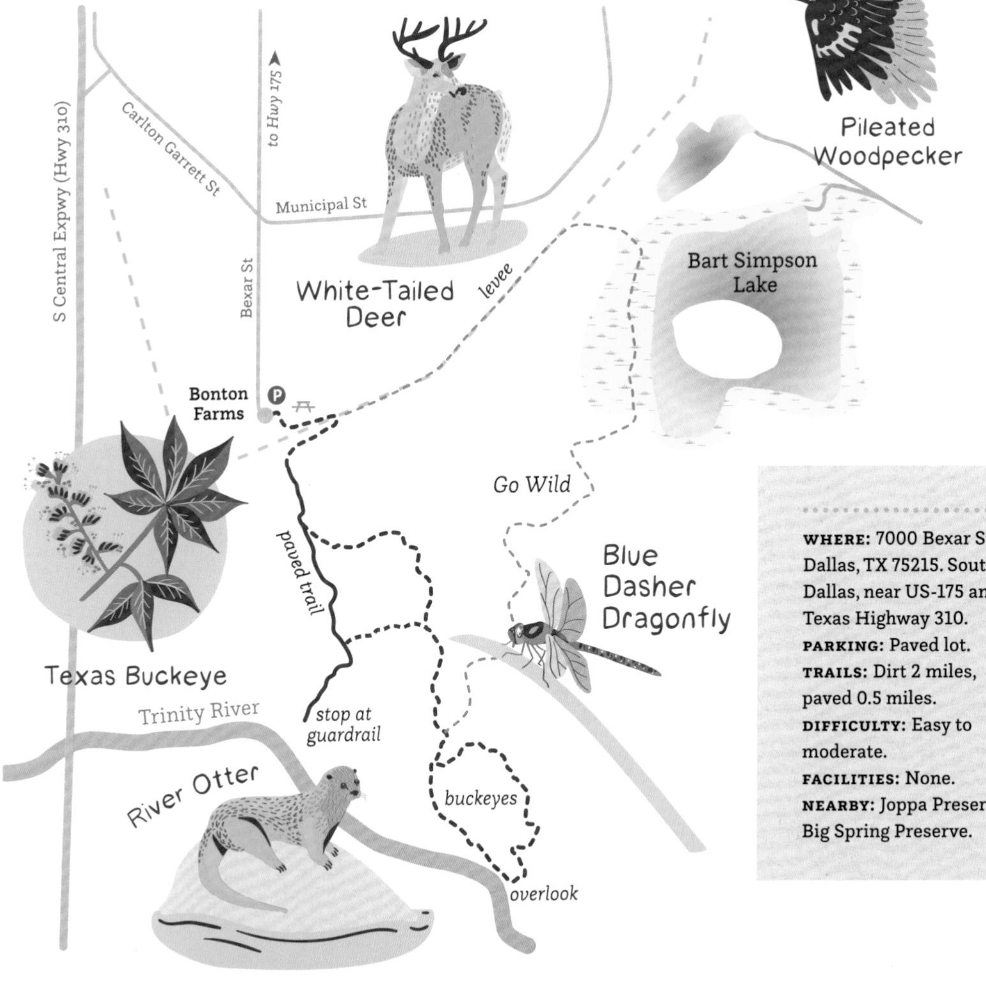

WHERE: 7000 Bexar Street, Dallas, TX 75215. Southeast Dallas, near US-175 and Texas Highway 310.
PARKING: Paved lot.
TRAILS: Dirt 2 miles, paved 0.5 miles.
DIFFICULTY: Easy to moderate.
FACILITIES: None.
NEARBY: Joppa Preserve, Big Spring Preserve.

▲ Sunrise at Bart Simpson Lake.

Ned and Genie Fritz Texas Buckeye Trail

At the end of the Ned and Genie Fritz Texas Buckeye Trails, Eileen McKee gently inhales the conical spire of cream-colored blooms from the Texas buckeye, a stout understory tree, and smiles—the aroma of family. Her father, Ned Fritz, discovered this grove of Texas buckeyes in the 1970s while exploring the Great Trinity Forest (GTF), as it's now known. It was a first glimpse into what wonders the forest might hold.

Fritz brought his wife Genie and family to share his excitement over the blooming buckeyes. "There was no trail and it was always muddy. You had to jump over ravines. Definitely an adventure hike," says Eileen. "He wanted to share what he'd found and people follow that kind of passion." I was one of them, joining some of Ned's early annual spring hikes through the Trinity River bottomlands. A left boot of mine is still there somewhere, deep in the muck.

The Deep Forest

Kristi Kerr Leonard, representing the Trinity Coalition, joins us with photographer Jennifer Weisensel of North Texas Master Naturalists. The first part of Ned's original footpath is now a ten-foot-wide paved span—odd, since users must scale a twenty-foot levee on a dirt path to reach it. A barricade blocks the end. The city built an overlook atop the soft riverbank and it collapsed into the Trinity.

Trinity Coalition dedicates itself to transforming the Trinity River and its natural spaces into a national nature destination with everything from forest hikes to river floats.

▲ The paved trail stops short of the Trinity River.

◀ Forest tent caterpillars are an important food source for birds raising young.

We quickly exit for TBT's dirt paths, much like those Eileen's father once trod. The forest soon swaddles us in the classic Great Trinity Forest mix of two- to three-story-tall American and cedar elm, green ash, and red oaks. Sunlight streams through early spring leaves of translucent green, infusing the forest with a verdant atmosphere. Kristi exclaims with delight upon seeing a small grove of eastern wahoo shrubs, announcing her intent to return and enjoy the sight when strawberry-shaped fruits dangle from stems.

The bottomland forest spreads in a low floodplain from the Trinity, occasionally inundated for weeks after big rains. The hardwoods are majestic, even though they only grew up after dairy farm operations ended post World War II. In this moist place, shelf fungi march their way up many a trunk. Fallen logs are bright green with mosses. Fruticose lichen, which only thrives where the air is clean, clings to barks. These deep woods radiate a sense of life uninterrupted.

A large fallen tree opens up a sunlit glen in the dim forest, dotted by hundreds of tiny yellow buttercups. Between them, petite crow poison's delicate white flowers contrast with those of the blue-eyed grass. Crawfish tunnels extend in the soft, deep bottomland soil, the larger ones marked by six-inch-tall mud chimneys. Barred owls hide in the trees most evenings, waiting for crawfish to emerge. A gentle symphony of sounds enthralls us, from songbirds singing in the canopy to the slight rustling of leaves on the forest floor.

▼ A rough green snake merges into foliage.

▲ Without preservation efforts, this elder bur oak would never have existed.

We come upon a tantalizing trail, its faint path marked by tattered orange tapes, heading east toward White Rock Creek, the watery heart of the GTF. The trees unfurl endlessly. No wonder white-tailed deer and bobcats make their home here. We stare in awe, tinged with sadness and gratitude. Eileen's parents battled developers and governmental entities to thwart efforts in the 1970s to channelize the Trinity into a barge canal. One plan was to level these woods for a turning basin.

The Buckeye Grove

The multiple trunks of a giant swamp privet lean over the trail. A sign of undisturbed woods, it's renowned for its highly aromatic, fuzzy yellow blooms in spring. Swamp privet would be dominant along with possumhaw and Texas buckeye if not for the invasive Chinese privet. Water-loving bois d'arcs become more frequent, and giant bur oaks begin to appear.

As we draw closer to the river, privet worsens due to berries carried by floodwaters into the woods. Brush swarms the trail, creating green tunnels. "None of this used to be here," bemoans Eileen. In some sections, Kristi's workday volunteers have cut privet and widened the trail. Trained naturalists from North Texas Master Naturalists first rerouted paths around delicate ecological areas and marked important native plants to prevent harm.

"There's one," Kristi proclaims. A subspecies of the better-known Ohio buckeye, a multi-trunked understory tree with a broad spreading crown, the Texas version is more compact, with a touch more tolerance for heat. Above them tower bur oaks and pecans, massive at their bases. They seem like protectors of the small trees.

▲ Volunteers clear privet and widen the buckeye trail.

► Eileen McKee inhales the buckeye aroma of her childhood.

Close to the river, the buckeyes swell in number and height. We dive our heads into lower branches, inhaling the gentle, sweet aroma, marveling at the native bees working busily even on this chilly day. Eileen describes the grove in its pre-privet days: a cloud of creamy blossoms in the dappled shade of giant hardwoods, an understory of inland sea oats and shade-tolerant wildflowers around their trunks, with clear sightlines to the river.

Go Wild: Bonton Woods

Scott Hudson, president of the North Texas Master Naturalists, and I traipse down the levee from the Ned and Genie Fritz Texas Buckeye trailhead. Daniel Koglin, photographer, wanted sunrise shots, so we're here on a fall morning to meet him at Bart Simpson Lake, nicknamed for its aerial resemblance to the cartoon character's profile. We scramble down and wade into rising fog. Daniel motions us to stop. A young white-tailed buck grazing in tall grass looks at us and returns to feeding as it slowly moves toward the forest. Yet we're just a few miles from downtown Dallas.

It's morning rush hour for birds. A squadron of white pelicans swoops in and lands on the lake. Dozens of cormorants keep up a clatter overhead as they depart the river to fish at White Rock Lake. Songbirds on the forest edge keep up a steady dawn chorus, even while a red-shouldered hawk works the sky. A smattering of dabbling ducks floats peacefully on the lake, unperturbed by the commotion.

Red-winged blackbirds screech in the cattails as we gather near a black willow on the shore. Lingering sunrise orange reflects off the lake. A large roadless section of the GTF and home to the mighty White Rock Creek-

▼ A pelican floats in a misty Bart Simpson Lake.

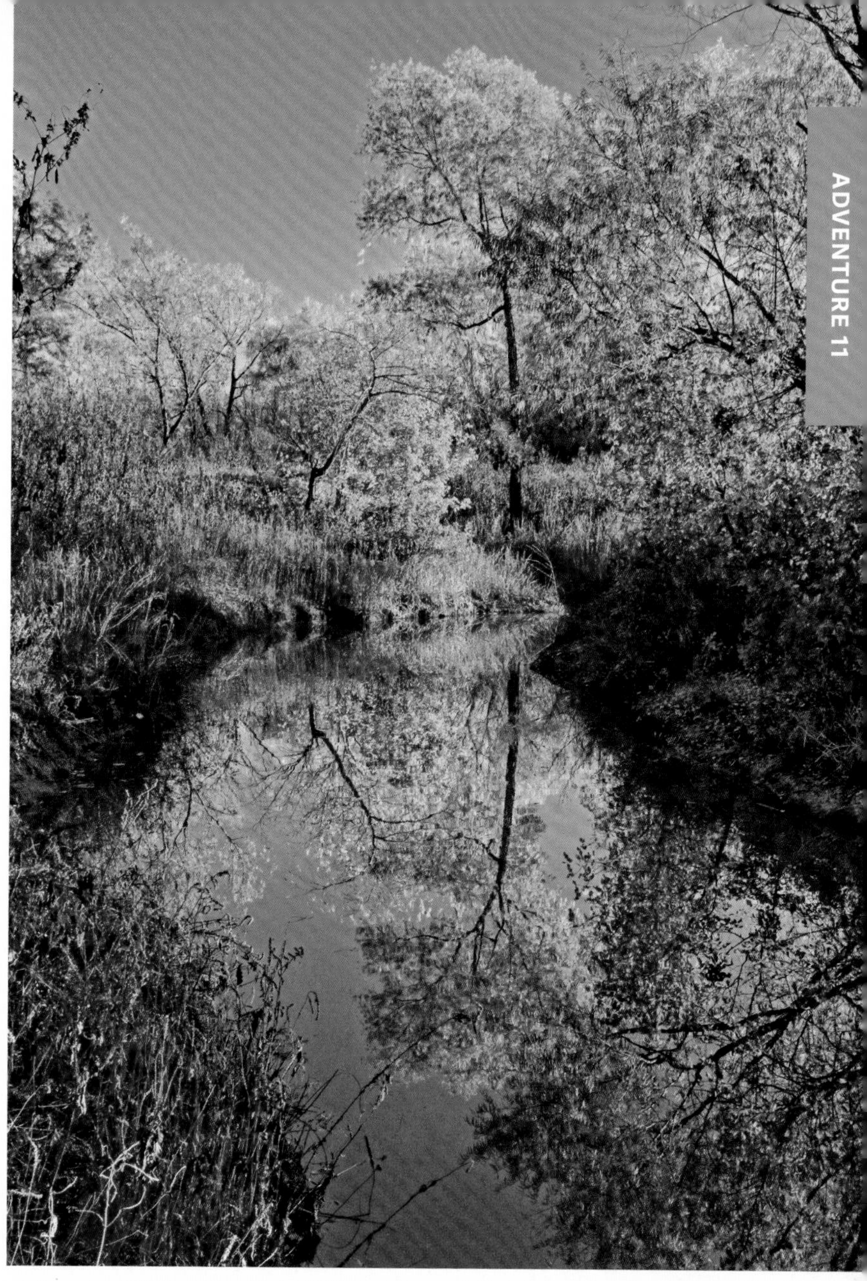

► Fall brings beauty to the Bonton Woods.

Trinity River confluence, this wild place—sometimes termed Bonton Woods after the adjacent historic neighborhood—are its core.

We follow Bart Simpson's nose into the forest, hoping to find some old trails. With every breeze, small yellow cedar elm leaves flutter down like snow, covering any path. Green ashes and American elms sport an array of golden tones. Our footsteps crackle in fallen leaves where rough earth snakes and DeKay's brown snakes hibernate. The loud cackling peal of a pileated woodpecker high in the canopy, ever heard here yet rarely seen, grabs our attention.

The Market Cafe at Bonton Farms offers delightfully fresh meals with produce straight from the field, while empowering the neighboring community with economic opportunities and healthy options in an urban food desert.

Wandering the Wild Woods

The unusually arid autumn dried up the forest's many ephemeral ponds and creeks, creating bare dirt stretches that make handy paths. Just as we think we're making headway, a huge gnarly briar thicket blocks us, forcing us to swing wide. Scott uses a phone GPS app to keep us on a general southwest bearing. Google Maps' satellite view shows we'll ultimately intersect the buckeye trails. Modern bushwhacking requires a phone.

Occasional arboreal giants soar so we appreciate them by their trunks: the tight, elongated diamond pattern of green ash; the shaggy, blockish bark of pecans; the rectangular strips of cedar elm. The slick, stout cord of an Alabama supplejack vine, adorned with bundles of dark purple berries, drapes from one tree to another. Drifts of fluffy white seedheads from late boneset seem to hover above the forest floor like fog.

Yet for each stunning sight, there's another bramble patch to conquer, and we wander off course again. There seems to be no pattern to the frayed trail tape markers we come across. We're not lost, says Scott, just temporarily misplaced. And happily so. Going off trail (where permitted) allows you to take in new landscapes, ones few people see. It feels like a privilege to visit a place where wildlife takes priority and the signs of humanity are minimal. Yet we're within walking distance of a sandwich at Market Cafe.

Scott sets another bearing via GPS. A privet patch blocking our way indicates we're getting close to the river. We punch through rather than risk getting off course again. "There it is!" says Daniel as we emerge, relieved to come upon the Ned and Genie Fritz Texas Buckeye Trail after miles of slogging heavy equipment through rough terrain. We stride the dirt paths to the river, grateful for the easy hike.

North Texas Master Naturalists train volunteers to perform education, outreach, and service to benefit natural areas and resources.

ADVENTURE 12 GREAT TRINITY FOREST

Holland Trail

Honoring a veteran who perished in Iraq, the Holland dirt trail system explores the Great Trinity Forest between White Rock Creek and Big Spring Preserve.

WHERE: 5850 Elam Road, Dallas, TX 75217. Southwest Dallas, off Elam north of Loop 12.
PARKING: Paved lot.
TRAILS: Dirt 2.5 miles.
DIFFICULTY: Challenging.
FACILITIES: None.
NEARBY: Big Spring Preserve.

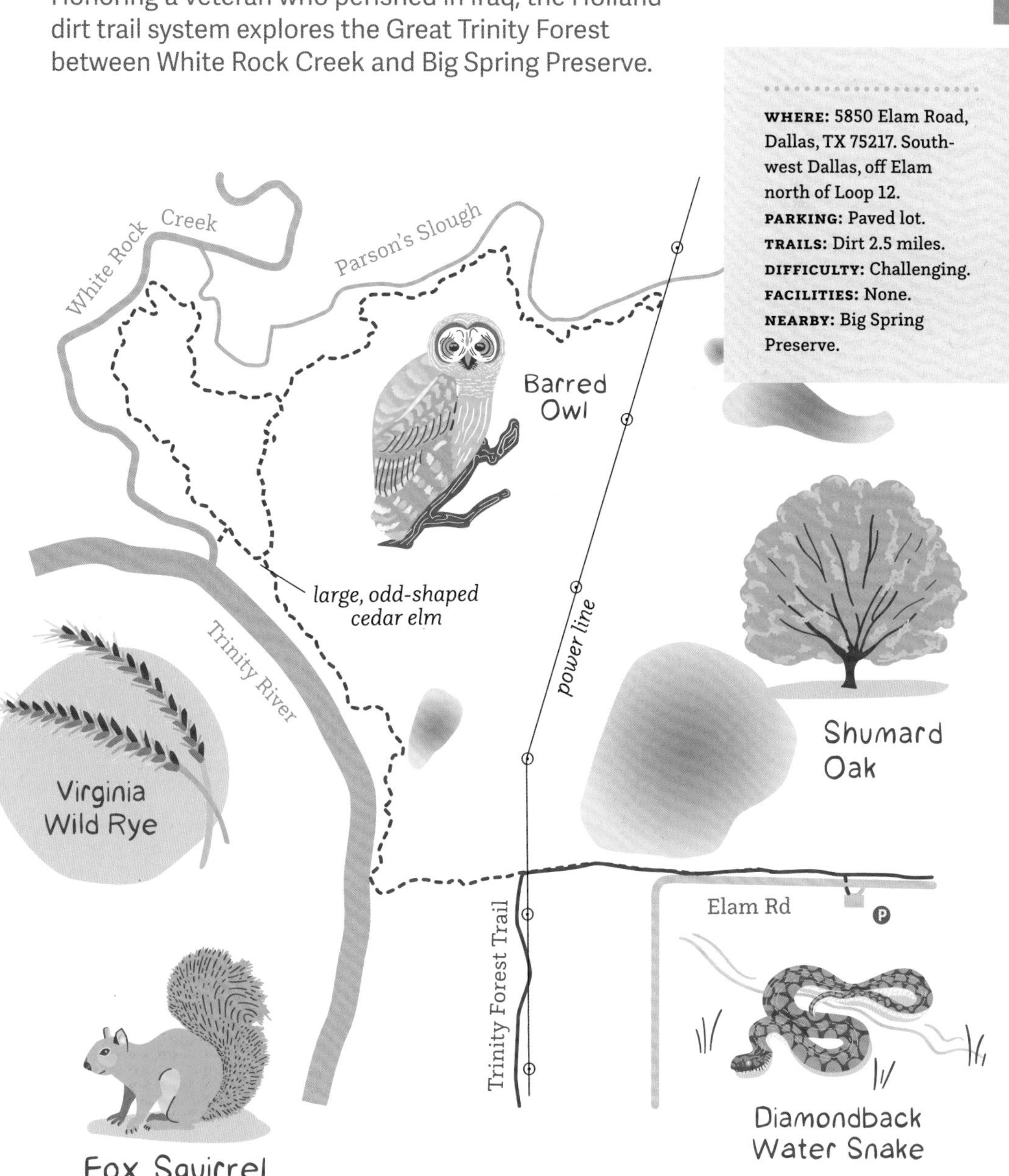

▲ Great Trinity Forest ponds are wildlife hotspots.

Go Wild: Holland Trail

Lieutenant Colonel Daniel Holland, killed in 2006 by an improvised explosive device while serving in Operation Iraqi Freedom, will never know the trail that bears his name. Horse-related veterans groups created this winding path through the Great Trinity Forest (GTF) to honor Holland and other fallen veterans and hold regular events such as Carry the Load to continue the remembrance. The trail's history has significance for photographer Daniel Koglin, a civilian who's worked in the military most of his adult life and joins us for today's hike.

Joining us is North Texas Master Naturalist Scott Hudson, a frequent hiker of the GTF. It's a good thing he's with us, since the initial stretch of trail along the Trinity is challenging to find among the flood debris and alluvial sands. These are wet woods, bottomland forests shaped by river and rain. The deep, rich riparian soil arises from uncounted decades of decaying leaves and fertile river silt deposited by floods. Following Scott's lead, we penetrate the forest and arrive at a shallow pond. Flags for the upcoming Independence Day holiday decorate a bench dedicated to Holland.

A mowed path extends out from the bench. Scott notes that an equestrian who keeps his horse at the nearby Texas Horse Ranch sometimes cuts the trail, which by summer can be obscured by thick foliage. We follow it, pleased for the ease, the older, larger oaks and pecans to our west along the river, and younger cedar elms and green ash to our east. Giant ragweed is thigh high; it will tower on either side in a month, turning parts of the trail into a tunnel.

The Confluence

Trail tangents enhance every journey and we take a narrow side path west to the confluence of White Rock Creek. Its waters traveled an epic thirty miles to reach this point. The Trinity, flush with water released from Lewisville Lake, has backed up into it. As a result, the once-crisp confluence looks more like a lake. In the distance, we can hear the squawks of great blue herons nesting in the canopy. A bench overlooking the confluence would invite a respite if the air wasn't thick with mosquitoes.

Returning to the Holland Trail, the forest unfurls as far as we can see through an idyllic sea of Virginia wildrye beneath scattered large trees. It radiates with the pastoral spaciousness of woods that get regularly swept by floodwaters. The trail swings into a deep bend of the creek where a lighter hand with prior agricultural operations left many majestic-sized trees, such as bur oaks with trunks so massive they could withstand a hurricane. A plethora of native swamp privets, distinctive with their splayed array of multiple thin trunks, grow as large as pickup trucks. Scott mentions he visits every spring for their intoxicating spring floral aroma.

White Rock Creek's sprawling riparian corridor is the lifeblood of the northern GTF. Its banks brim with history, from the Indigenous communities that camped there for the forest's abundant hunting and food-bearing plants, to the settlers drawn by the same, to the formerly enslaved people who carved agricultural homesteads from the forest where they hoped to stay free. The creek's massive floods infuse the bottomlands with nourishing fertile silt.

▼ The serenity of a forest pond and bench invites introspection.

At a Slough's Pace

The trail curves west and soon we follow Bryan's Slough, the tail end of the slow, wide waterway that runs from Piedmont Ridge along the eastern edge of the GTF. Occasionally the slough spreads into ponds that evoke a primeval wildness. Abundant with turtles, crustaceans, and small fish, and rimmed by sizable crawfish burrows, the secluded wetlands are a prime feeding ground for many forest creatures and fundamental to GTF diversity.

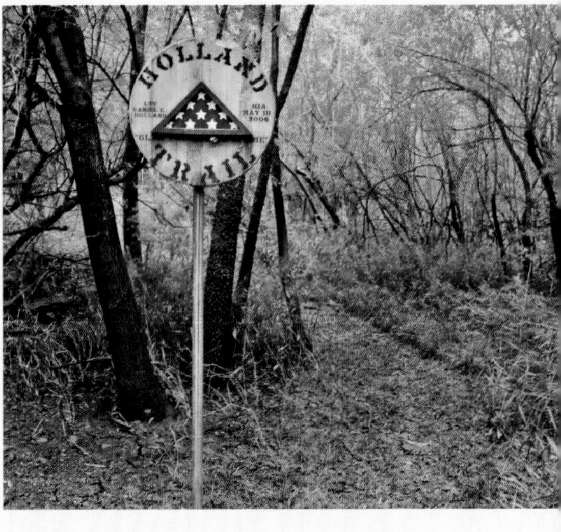

▲ The narrow Holland Trail sometimes disappears into the forest.

The elegiac hush of the dim forest dissipates as the trail crosses into a treeless power corridor. Scott guides us over to the service road's low-water crossing, a concrete pad across the slough that beavers sometimes modify with stick dams to hold more water. Boisterous halberd leaf hibiscus and buttonbush shrubs line the slough. In a few weeks, they'll be profuse with white blooms savored by butterflies and pollinators.

We take in the slough's hypnotic beauty as it disappears into the forest, its slow, meandering pace a reminder of how our life paths should be. We could continue farther, but the summer heat is catching up with us. We break for sandwiches beneath a bois d'arc and trade commentary on the many botched attempts to commercialize the GFT and its vast unrealized potential for urban nature tourism.

Restored, we retrace our trail and then head south to complete the Holland loop. We pass an ephemeral swamp of young trees, the shallow water coated in floating, lime-green duckweed, a reminder that every corner of GTF holds wonders just waiting for discovery.

▼ Sloughs are integral to bottomland forests.

ADVENTURE 13

GREAT TRINITY FOREST

Goat Island Preserve

A lush bottomland wilderness fronting the Trinity River south of Dallas beckons with quiet and shade.

WHERE: 2800 Post Oak Road, Hutchins, TX 75141. Southeast Dallas County, east of I-45 near Belt Line Rd.
PARKING: Paved lot.
TRAILS: Dirt 12 miles.
DIFFICULTY: Moderate to challenging.
FACILITIES: None.
NEARBY: Cottonwood Creek Preserve.

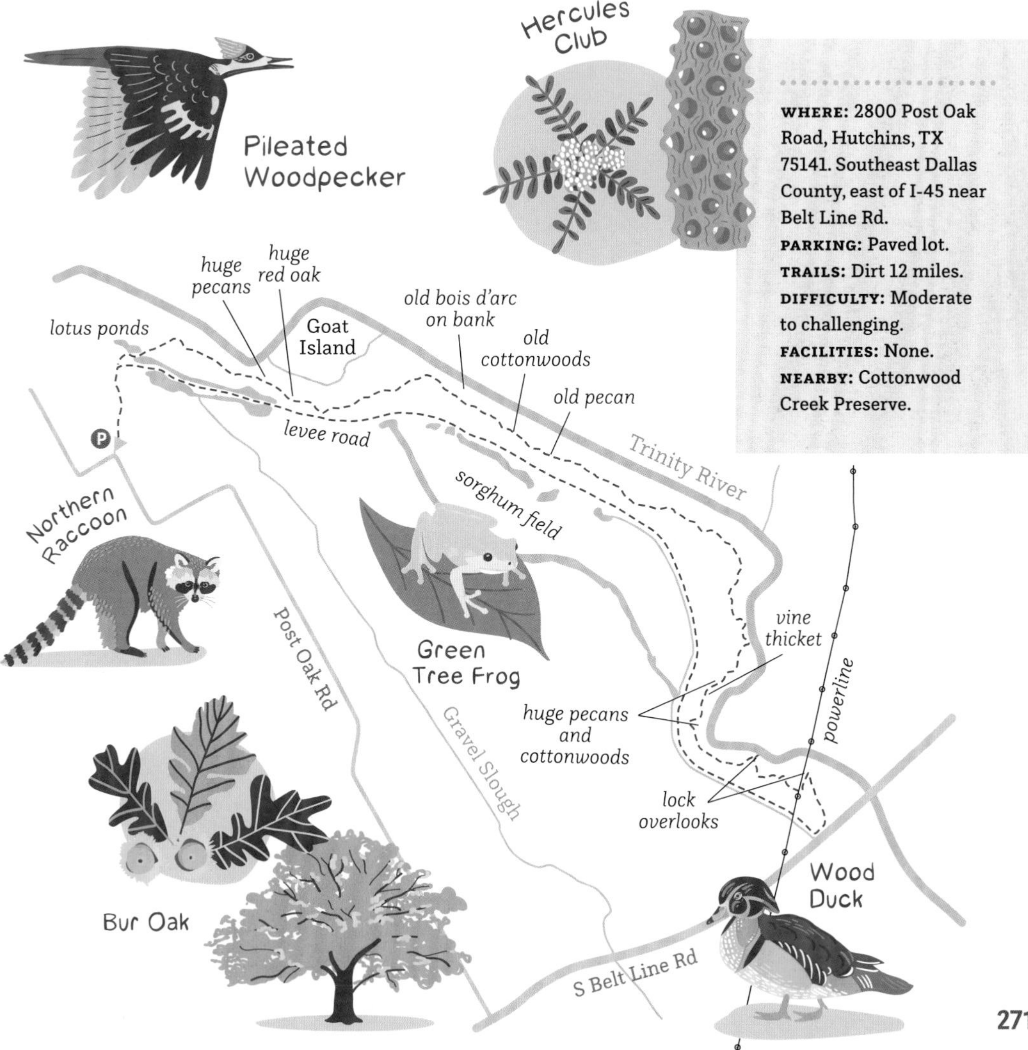

The woods of Goat Island Preserve are dark and deep. Contained between a dike and the Trinity River, the 500-acre slice of hardwood forest stretches for three miles. Massive bur oak, red oak, and pecan, along with their smaller kin, forge a knitted canopy of seamless shade—a true boon in hot Texas summers.

Hiking enthusiast and Goat Island steward Joe Johnson toured the world as a US Navy mechanic, but yearned for a place to roam that was closer to home. He discovered Goat Island when Dallas County Open Space (DCOS) granted Dallas Off-Road Bicycle Association (DORBA) permission to start a trail system. Now over ten miles of wide trails lace the woodlands, though it's more popular with hikers than bikers.

On this summer day, Joe is giving me the grand tour of the former ranch returned to woods. We make our way down the Roadrunner Trail along a two-story dike. It's fun to look into the canopy on both sides and see birds up close. Joe marvels that some people come out just to walk the dike: "Scared of the woods, I guess."

We visit a short walkway extending into the canopy and peer into the forested darkness. It looks wild and tantalizing. We linger at a utility corridor to watch for edge-habitat birds. Moist, slightly fetid air rises from adjacent bogs along with the piercing *skeow* of green herons. Yet we're just twenty minutes from downtown.

▲ The levee trail gives a canopy view of the forest.

When the River Raged

We head to a trail aptly named Joe's Riverside, to the remnants of an early 1900s lock and dam system meant to aid navigation upriver. "This used to be one of our main attractions here. People came to see it," says Joe. Low concrete partly spanned the river, creating a slight waterfall.

In 2015, storm fronts inundated North Texas. Reservoirs filled to the brim and gushed into the river. After rains ceased, water that fell hundreds of

Dallas County Open Space operates over twenty preserves totaling more than 3600 acres. Most feature little or no development and protect a variety of special habitats.

▲ The 2015 floods forever changed Goat Island.

miles away continued its resolute route to the sea, past Goat Island Preserve.

According to eBird, more than 150 species of birds reside at or make migratory stops at Goat Island Preserve.

Joe found Goat Island impassable for many weeks and returned to find the flood had shoved much of the lock and dam's immense, thirty-ton, concrete structures to the side. Yards of riverbank had sloughed into the channel and swept off to sea. Many trails were gone. "You can't believe how bad it looked," says Joe. Over many months, volunteers resurrected the trails.

Canopy Royalty

A high-pitched brittle whinny with jazzy syncopated skips and extensions resonates through the hardwood canopy three to six stories high. "Hear that?" yells Joe. The pileated woodpecker, the largest one in the woods, announces our entry into its realm.

Rather than a scolding territorial *cuk-cuk-cuk*, another pileated, probably its lifelong mate, echoes from deep in the forest. A series of sharp raps indicates our bird has resumed hammering square holes in trees to extract carpenter ants and burrowing bugs.

When they find a bug-ridden piece of timber, often a dead snag, pileateds persist, making cavities several inches deep. Some later provide homes for arboreal bats, woodpeckers, and songbirds such as the prothonotary warblers. Larger ones might harbor barred owls or wood ducks.

The trail building and maintaining prowess of Dallas Off-Road Bicycle Association is renowned. Volunteers from DORBA work with municipal park departments and land trusts to enable access to nature through dirt paths.

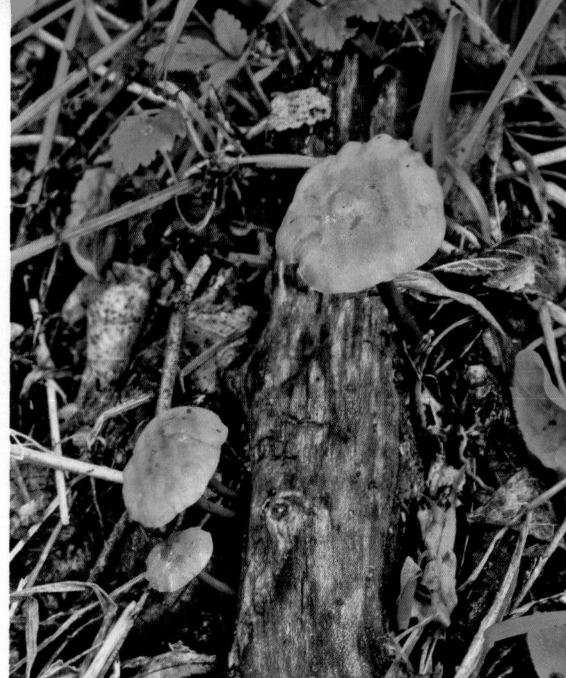

▲ Fungi are essential to fallen tree decomposition.

Land of Giants

Joe and I walk the trail in contemplative silence, through the forest's core of giants that escaped being cleared by ranchers. The trees clamor for sunlight; their shade is dense. Splotches of light from fallen trees puncture the darkness. It is moist and dank with fungus decomposing abundant leaves. Lichen in tones of green adorn nearly every tree.

We pass a massive bur oak that would take three people to encircle. Its roots fiercely burrow into the soil. A colossal, stocky bois d'arc makes a dome with its curved branches, creating a cozy room. Corky thorns adorn the bark of a modest-sized Hercules club, also known as toothache tree for its mouth-numbing qualities.

Massive pecan trees dominate, their bark shaggy with age. A cottonwood pair towers, limbs interlocked and looking contentedly married. Joe halts next to a massive, bulbous log on the edge of a gentle, shady vale. The black willow was 150 to 200 years old when it perished. "It was a landmark of this place. Still is," he says, bending in respect.

River Wisdom

At one of the frequent side trails to overlooks, I absorb Joe's river wisdom. He's been exploring the Trinity bottomlands since he was a boy. Then the river lost its pulse. With each reservoir to serve a growing metropolis, the flow became controlled. "It used to fill and drain and fill and drain. Not anymore," says Joe. Now a constant surge of water strips scours banks, causing collapse.

Treated effluent from wastewater treatment plants—millions of gallons—adds to the flow, even keeps the river running in dry periods. Dallas's

▲ Treated effluent gushes from the treatment plant.

Southeast Wastewater Treatment Plant is just a few hundred yards away, a hotspot for bird activity.

Joe commiserates about the decline in fish quality. But birds are not as picky. Cormorants and many kinds of herons work the river for fish. Brown, sparrow-sized least sandpipers crowd the shoals in search of tiny crustaceans. White great egrets stride the shore, hoping to spear a meal.

"What shocks me is the erosion in the twelve years since I started coming out," says Joe. "We went for thousands of years without it becoming as wide as the Mississippi. I remember this thing used to be a wild river. It was awesome."

Actual Goat Island

Sitting on a bench next to a wide, wet vale, Joe says, "That's the actual Goat Island over there. When the Trinity floods, this fills up with water and makes an island." He tells the story of Parson's Slough and a mammoth dam now lost in the mud—river engineering gone bad. "The more we try to make the river do what we want, the more it does what it wants."

We take a concrete crossing and pass a small pond en route to the majestic, well-watered forest nestled in a crook of the river. Here in the deepest part of the preserve, the hush is intense, the river omnipresent yet invisible. Leaves on the forest floor crackle with critters; birdcalls entwine like a chamber ensemble.

It's a delightful diversity. Joe's most recent trail system is on the island, including a narrow path especially for birdwatchers. "I wanted to do it right, some special places had to be avoided."

▼ A variety of birds call Goat Island home.

▲ Rare dwarf palmetto still grows in the Goat Island area.

Bird by Bird

We ease out of the deep bottomland forest into low spots rich in emerald-green sumpweed with hop-like blooms. "I've been through here when it's wet and covered with big, white lotus flowers," says Joe.

The swampy forest percolates with the insistent "peep-peep-peep-peep-peep" and bright yellow chests of male prothonotary warblers. We head up the slope to a new ecosystem: brushy upland woods. Titmice, Carolina chickadees, and other nesting songbirds flit about a toppled tree taken over by vines.

We pass into the bright sunlight of yet another ecosystem—meadowlands—to see a roadrunner in search of grasshoppers. Bright yellow partridge peas promise hearty seeds for ground-feeding birds. Yet hidden in the woods just yards away is a small wetland that great blue herons enjoy. A panoply of ecosystems capping a perfect woodland hike.

ADVENTURE 14

SOUTHWEST DALLAS ESCARPMENT

Cedar Ridge Preserve

A massive Austin Chalk escarpment furrowed by creeks features the county's best views, with upland woods, Blackland Prairies, spring-fed pond, and riparian corridors.

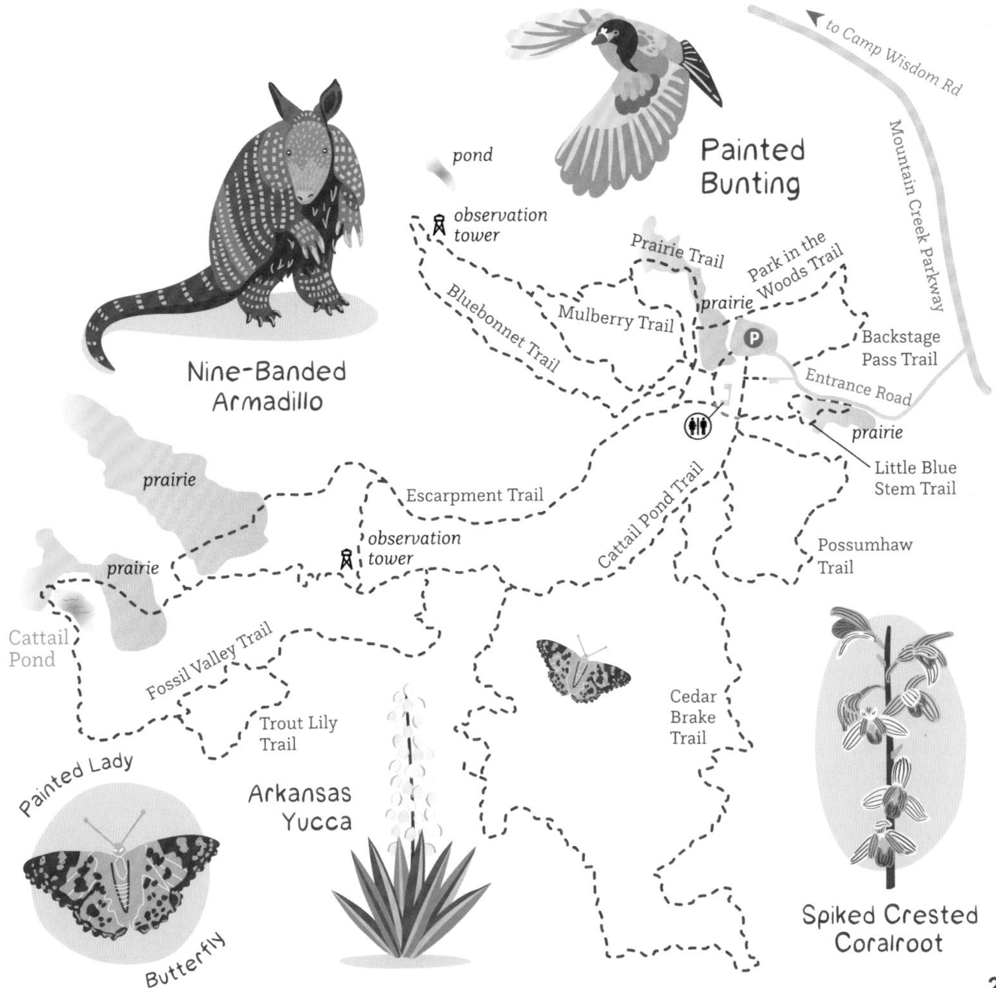

WHERE: 7171 Mountain Creek Pkwy, Dallas, TX 75249. Southwest Dallas County, near US-67 and FM 1382.
PARKING: Paved lots.
TRAILS: Dirt 9 miles. Detailed map at website.
DIFFICULTY: Easy to challenging.
FACILITIES: Restrooms.
COST: $3 donation requested.
NEARBY: Cedar Hill State Park, Elmer W. Oliver Nature Park, Paul S. Dryer Preserve at Windmill Hill.

▲ Cedar Hill's vast escarpment greenbelt includes forest, prairie, and lake.

A limestone escarpment stretches fifteen miles across southwest Dallas County as the older, more erodible Eagle Ford shale grades into the rising Austin Chalk bedrock. The resulting soil variety helps create incredible biodiversity. A more than 200-foot drop from the peak elevation of 750 feet to the surface of Joe Pool Lake creates scenic vistas. The rugged cedar-rich ecology draws comparisons to the Hill Country near Austin.

Along the escarpment and FM 1382, a 3000-acre green space corridor features two large Audubon preserves: Cedar Ridge Preserve and Dogwood Canyon Audubon Center. Joining it are a few smaller preserves and the very popular 1826-acre Cedar Hill State Park. The paved Balcones del Norte trail system links many of them.

Tom Willard grew up on the flat coastal plains, but these limestone hills have his heart. For nearly a decade—sometimes as sanctuary manager, sometimes as volunteer—he has restored prairies and woods at Cedar Ridge Preserve (CRP). Though it is a phenomenally popular place to hike, "First and foremost, conservation is what we're about here," says Tom. "It is an Audubon preserve. The hiking is just a way to enjoy and appreciate the ecology, the plants, and the geological features."

Cedar Ridge Preserve's Quiet Side

Most CRP hikers focus on the trails south of the education center that boast significant elevation changes. We instead stay atop the plateau and head west on the Prairie Trail. Framed by blazing red Indian blankets, a plethora of pale yuccas boasts five-foot spires of large, creamy blossoms that hang like bells. Pale yuccas are pollinated solely by yucca moths. "We're concerned because last year we don't think we got any seeds. It may mean the yucca moth is no longer here," says Tom.

ADVENTURE 14

▲ Sunrise across Cattail Pond.

This small slice of Blackland Prairie is home to what author Ricky Linex calls the Big Four forbs (broad-leafed, nonwoody plants): Maximilian sunflower, bush sunflower, Englemann's daisy, and Illinois bundleflower. Radiant yellow dominates the meadow spring through fall. Only by examining it closer are its smaller jewels revealed. Stiff greenthread's simple yellow blossoms show amid leaves as narrow as spaghetti. Just inches tall, bluets' four-pointed pinkish petals are barely a quarter inch across.

In addition to managing CRP, Dallas Audubon Society advocates for birds and other wildlife and offers field trips and classes, including the lauded Master Birder program, to help everyone enjoy and appreciate birds.

Farther down at another prairie patch, Tom recalls doing battle with hedge parsley, an invasive annual whose seed can cling so thoroughly to clothing there's no option but to throw them away. "About three years ago, we put in a concerted effort to pull it up now there's hardly any left," says Tom. He points to a seep muhly grass clump that resurged. Its super slender, gray-green leaves arising from a curly mass of spent foliage are testament to a prairie reborn.

Mulberries and Bluebonnets

Now on the Mulberry Trail, we quickly dive into deep woods and down stairs made from large timbers painstakingly dug into the slope. "All done by volunteers," Tom notes. The preserve's largest trees thrive here, soaring three stories and more: Shumard oaks, green ash, and American elm. Seeps on the slope and moister soils at the base foster bur oaks and the trail's namesake, red mulberry.

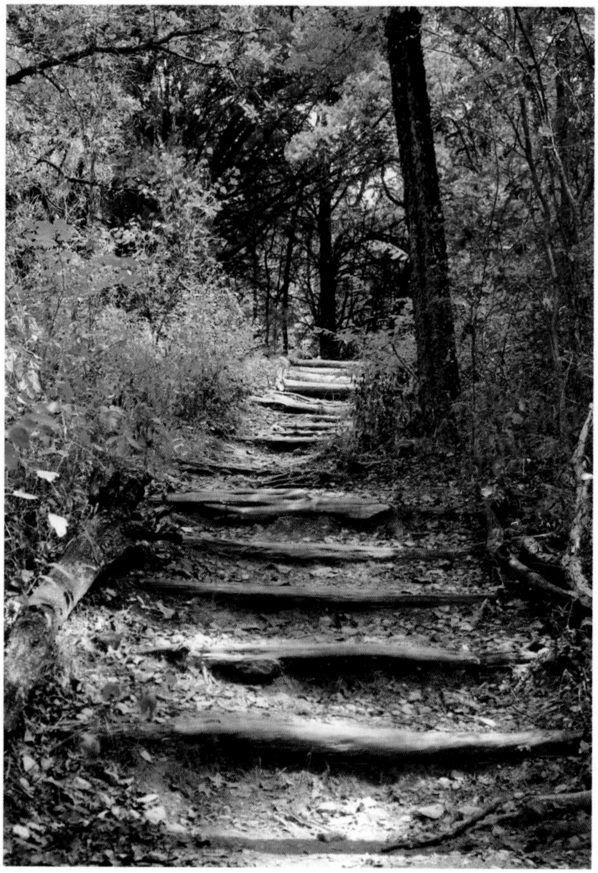

The trail undulates up and down folds of the slope. "This ravine is just a different world," says Tom. We stop at benches flanking a huge bur nurtured by one of CRP's last remaining wet-weather springs. The din of birdsong almost makes conversation difficult. The varied high-pitched tweets of tufted titmouse and Carolina chickadee, and continual peeps of northern cardinal, contrast with the tiny trills of Carolina wren and simple lilts of the eastern wood-pewee. Birds flitting through the shifting mosaic of shadows and light make the forest seem in motion.

The trail merges with the Bluebonnet Trail, oddly named for a forested path. But decades ago, when this was Dr. Geoffrey Sanford's Dallas Nature Center, far more land was still the original prairie, and acres of bluebonnets covered the slopes. Cattle grazing, and before that, wildfires and bison herds kept trees restricted to riparian corridors. When agricultural operations ceased in the mid-1900s, trees began to take over. The region's vast, once-flourishing prairie almost disappeared.

▲ Mulberry Trail is one of CRP's quieter paths.

At the plateau's edge, a one-story observation tower rises above the trees, affording a view of the FM 1382 greenbelt and Joe Pool Lake. The complicated song of a painted bunting emerges from an escarpment live oak. Below us, a grove of petite Mexican buckeyes sports rosy, pink blooms. Finishing out the Bluebonnet Trail loop, we pass by a clump of bluebonnets straining to survive in the shade, a reminder of what was lost, though patches still survive.

Escarpment Forest

Cynthia Bennett, CRP preserve manager, joins us for the afternoon excursion. After a long career in zoology, Cynthia is enjoying "getting to know local wildlife for a change." She is the visionary glue uniting Dallas Audubon Society, which manages the preserve; Dallas city and county, which owns

► Orchids of the genus *Hexalectris* require oak and juniper for the right mycorrhizal fungi.

most of the preserve; and a cadre of volunteers. She also oversees the longtime groundskeeper Domingo Mendez, who rides herd on infrastructure.

Join the team for CRP's monthly Conservation in Action Workdays for habitat restoration and trail maintenance. Get on their email to learn of special projects like prairie planting.

The wide Escarpment Trail offers a study in contrasts. On one side, invasive privet and excess cedar elms congest young woods no more than twenty years old. On the other, volunteer Brett Schubauer made a personal project of eradicating privet and thinning trees. Virginia creeper and other shade understory plants now cover what was once bare ground, providing habitat for reptiles, amphibians, and small woodland mammals.

Occasionally in the young forest, older trees left standing by prior ranchers assert themselves. Squatty shin oaks, wider than they are tall, boast limbs contorted by wind and grapevines. "That is an old tree. It could tell you some stories," says Tom about one. The dry juniper and oak forest

▲ The prairies' spring color is worth seeking out.

on limestone ridges provides a perfect habitat for spiked crested coralroot, a leafless *Hexalectris* orchid that is nourished not by photosynthesis but through mycorrhizal fungi in adjacent tree roots. It sends up striking stems of amber blooms in late spring.

Prairie Survivors

Midway down the Escarpment Trail, a large prairie swath spreads on either side. Stepping through the thin line of trees flanking the trail, we're awe-struck by a vista resplendent in purple American basket-flowers. Each one seems to host a native bee dusted with pollen busily collecting nectar. Tiny yellow butterflies flit among blossoms. Eastern phoebes perch on the taller flowers and proclaim territory.

Across the trail, the prairie continues to a riparian corridor. It glows with large clumps of eastern gamagrass and big bluestem, plus an abundance of green milkweed and other wildflowers, even large showstoppers like white rosinweed—most planted by CRP volunteers and allowed to spread through the once degraded prairie.

Cedar Ridge Preserve is popular with distance hikers intent on making their miles. Hundreds pass within yards of these beautiful grasslands every open day. How many think to look beyond the trees and see this splendor? CRP volunteers have put many hours of care into these private prairies solely for wildlife's benefit—a true conservation preserve.

▲ Cattail Pond is a perfect rest stop between vigorous trails.

The trail dips into the coolness of the riparian corridor, a delightfully shady enclave. A trickling stream harbors little nooks of reeds. The clicking of Blanchard's cricket frogs is almost deafening. Limestone boulders sit atop slick shelves of dark gray marl, the intersection of Austin Chalk and Eagle Ford Shale. We rest nearby at Cattail Pond's covered deck. People of a wide array of ages, races, and interests stop by and chat with us about nature.

Scaling the Heights

As we continue up the Cattail Pond Trail, it climbs straight up the escarpment—or at least it feels that way. The afternoon heat catches up with me, and I douse myself with water. On top of the plateau's edge, we're too tuckered to climb the observation tower and grateful to see some well-placed benches. CRP's riparian corridor is a ribbon of dark green and beyond it unfurls the splendid ecology of Cedar Hill's green space corridor.

If you have only a couple of hours to explore Cedar Ridge Preserve, the ADA-rated Little Bluestem Trail and adjacent pollinator garden offer a glimpse of prairie life, while the Possumhaw Trail provides a concentrated experience of CRP's wooded ravines.

▲ Volunteers created a pollinator garden at the entrance so that even non-hikers could enjoy the ecology.

Continuing back, we stop at the Fossil Valley trailhead. A big pile of brush blocks the path. Tom explains to a frustrated hiker why the trail is closed after a week of rain. Walking wet trails creates ruts that collect water, and walking around muddy areas widens trails and kills vegetation that stems erosion. Yet some irresponsible hikers ignore the request. "For us to close a trail," says Tom, "we can't just put a trail closed sign on it or even put a fence across it. People won't honor it. We have to make it a physical impossibility."

Once again where we started, at the education center, people are streaming in after work. "It's gone from 12,000 visitors in 2003 to 600,000 a year," says Tom. Only 10 percent donate the requested three-dollar fee. "We definitely need a bigger budget," says Cynthia. "We're doing miraculous things now with what we have. But we could do so much more."

ADVENTURE 15 SOUTHWEST DALLAS ESCARPMENT

Dogwood Canyon Audubon Center

A modern Audubon Society education center and sanctuary with over 200 acres of deep canyon and soaring limestone escarpment provides prime bird habitat and hosts a rare grove of flowering dogwoods in their range's western edge.

WHERE: 1206 FM 1382, Cedar Hill, TX 75104. Southwest Dallas County near I-20 and I-35E
PARKING: Gravel lot.
TRAILS: Dirt 3 miles.
DIFFICULTY: Canyon Floor Trail—easy; Dogwood Trail—moderate; West Loop Trail—strenuous.
FACILITIES: Audubon educational center.
DOGS: Not allowed except service animals.
NEARBY: Cedar Mountain Preserve.

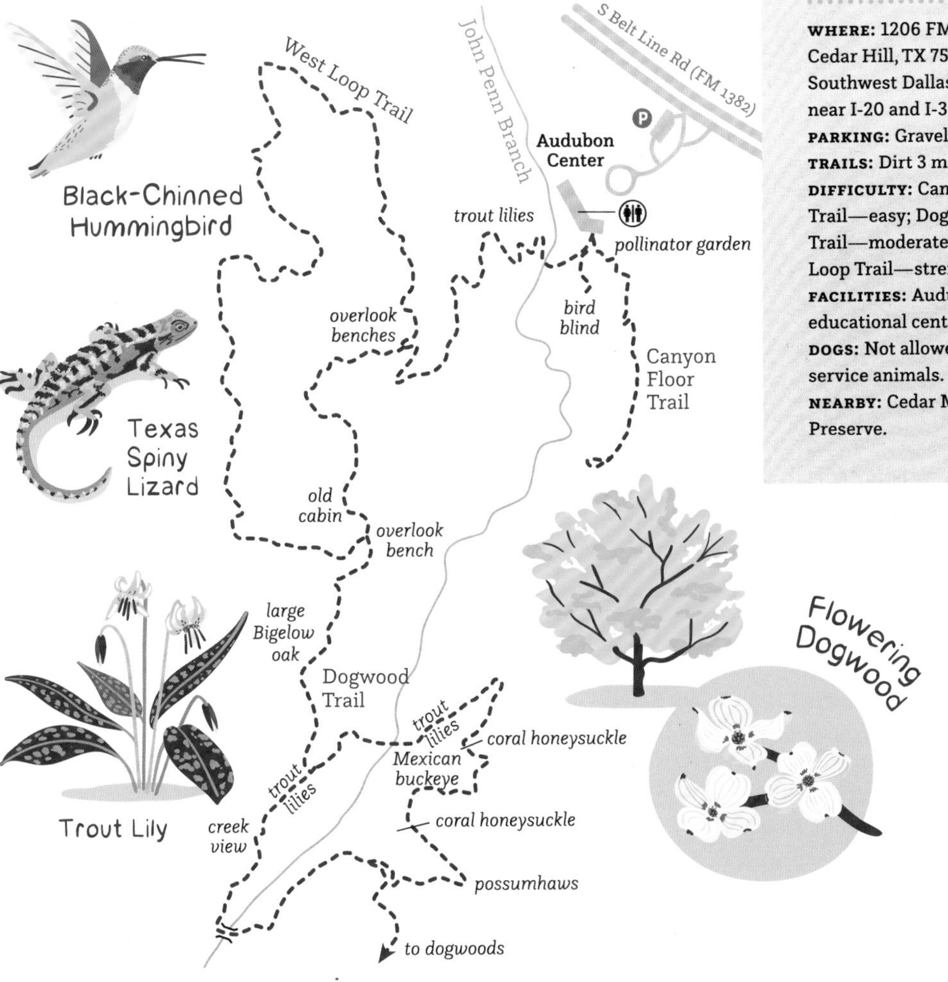

▲ Flowering dogwoods give the center its name.

Cedar Hill's Southwest Escarpment, a massive hunk of Austin Chalk with dramatic elevation changes, is home to Dogwood Canyon Audubon Center. There, deciduous forest from East Texas meets limestone ravines of the Central Texas Hill Country, with touches of Blackland Prairie and western plateaus. In this modest canyon, the black-chinned hummingbirds more common to West Texas are found alongside flowering dogwood trees of East Texas.

The sanctuary's compressed mix of habitats—upland and riparian woods, canyon, Blackland Prairie, and a touch of Eastern Cross Timbers—create "a diversity of plants that draws the insects that draw the birds," says center director Julie Collins. Over 160 species of plants attract more than 250 species of insects and spiders that help support at least 140 resident and migratory bird species. Dogwood's abundance of birds during migration periods is aided by its location on the Central Flyway.

More species of plant and wildlife rare in North Texas, many at the edge of their range, make their home here. White trout lily, on the edge of its range, is bounteous at the sanctuary. The limestone outcroppings support three species of *Hexalectris* orchids. The canyon is the last known nesting spot of the imperiled golden-cheeked warbler in Dallas County.

Naturalist and master birder David Hurt, known for his popular Wild Birds Unlimited store, purchased acreage here with Kim Shuler for a future home and personal refuge. He discovered a grove of old-growth dogwoods in 1997 and began identifying exceptional plants and birds. An old friend and skilled botanist, Matt White, helped verify several unique plants and dubbed it Dogwood Canyon.

▲ Migratory songbirds including hermit thrush (left) and red-breasted nuthatch (right) find a safe place at Dogwood Canyon.

A passion arose in Hurt that protecting the ecosystem was more important than a home with views. He reached out to Audubon Dallas and his customer base, offering over 500 guided hikes to introduce supporters to Dogwood Canyon, and the coalition grew to include the National Audubon Society and City of Cedar Hill. The 200-acre sanctuary opened in 2011.

Jewel of the Greenbelt

Located in the middle of a 3000-acre, recreation-based greenbelt along FM 1382 in Cedar Hill, Dogwood Canyon is its contemplative jewel, preserving wildlife and native plants while providing peace for visitors. Cedar Hill intends to set aside 30 percent of its land in green space. The greenbelt includes Cedar Hill State Park and a portion of Cedar Ridge Preserve, plus a handful of smaller nature spaces, eventually connected by the Balcones del Norte multiuse trail.

Dogwood's C. E. Doolin Visitor Center, dedicated to the inventor of the Frito chip that built Frito-Lay, occupies an elegant modern building constructed to LEED Gold specifications. It is located on former industrial land fronting the highway. The center's Canyon View birdwatching and education loft is a popular relaxation spot. Over 5000 students visit Dogwood each year.

On a perfect spring afternoon, Julie and I head out for the preserve's trail to the dogwood grove. We pass through the center's charming backyard with bird blind, native garden, and benches, pausing to say hello to the educational birds of prey in their enclosure. After passing the Canyon Floor Trail, we wind our way up the canyonside, a 200-foot rise from the creek bottom.

◄ David Hurt's passion for Dogwood fuels its development.

Canyon Floor Trail is a half-mile, round-trip trail made of packed decomposed granite. It's suitable for wheelchairs and strollers, making the lush riparian canyon bottom accessible to all.

Like the Blackland Prairie around it, over a century of wildfire suppression shaped Dogwood Canyon. The area once bore native grasses such as little and silver bluestems and drought-hearty forbs like Leavenworth's eryngo and western ironweed, with scattered shrubs in crevices and riparian corridors fire couldn't reach. Now it's home to a climax plant community dominated by Ashe junipers and smaller, tenacious white oaks such as Bigelow.

Climbing the Canyon

Hiking quietly up the rocky trail, snaking through tangled trees, we try unsuccessfully to dodge dozens of small green oak leaf rollers hanging from filaments. Near the plateau, highway noise disappears. "Listen," says Julie, "you can hear the frass." So many dangling caterpillars are defecating that the air resonates with the tick-tick-tick of minuscule poop pellets hitting the ground—and us. I feel gritty. But the caterpillar abundance only lasts a short while during nesting season when birds need them to feed young.

We reach the trailhead of the West Loop Trail, a charming place. Eagle Scout–made benches provide a place to rest after the steep canyon climb and enjoy an expansive view. At times, the mile-long plateau loop reaches an elevation of 750 feet, providing vistas across the canyon and neighboring Joe Pool Lake, with cities to the west visible. It's perfect for painted and indigo buntings.

Continuing on the West Loop, we pass the old tin summer cabin used by the L. C. Mobley family when they owned the land. David is fond of noting how golden-cheeked warblers might use the loose, peeling bark of a mature Ashe juniper that grows here to build their nests. Soon we come to the preserve's favorite photo opportunity: a vista across the heavily forested canyon.

We depart West Loop for the Dogwood Trail. Knowing we enter a wooded refuge with scant human interference, we grow quiet. Dogwood Canyon fosters a vibrant understory tree community. Mexican buckeyes and Eve's necklace dangle cascades of delicate, aromatic flowers. Downy, light-green leaves adorn graceful, small coralberry shrubs. Sporting broad emerald exoskeletons, fiery searcher beetles fulfill their name, zipping about everywhere in search of fallen caterpillars.

▲ A view across the canyon in early spring.

▲ Dickcissels live most of the year at Dogwood Canyon.

The forest percolates with the tapping of woodpeckers and northern flickers, perhaps a yellow-bellied sapsucker, too. The pine siskins' rapid, garbled *breet*, punctuated by an ascending buzz, are plentiful in this irruption year. Yellow-rumped warblers' strident cheeps accent the din, their bold yellow markings peeking through the dim forest light. Tendrils of eastern poison ivy blossoms peek from beneath leaves, someday to be berries sought avidly by fall migrators.

◄ A dogwood flower's "petals" are actually modified leaves called bracts, which guide pollinators to the minute pale-green flowers in the center.

Discovering the Dogwoods

Few understory trees mark Dogwood Canyon more than common hoptree, also called wafer ash. Beer-making German immigrants used its papery seeds in place of hops. Thick, pliable roots pierce the limestone, allowing it to thrive on inclines. Branches sport charming, downy buds of the trifoliate leaves. Many humans find its aroma and warty, rough bark unpleasant, but giant swallowtail butterfly larvae depend on its leaves for food.

The Dogwood Trail loop, expertly made by S & S Trail Services, naturally hugs the canyon's contours. It unfolds before us, swinging us past interesting trees and compelling views. Julie and I amble at naturalist speed, slow enough to see, hear, and smell as much possible, sensing wind, humidity, air pressure, and the quality of light. Dogwood Canyon is truly a place for curiosity and contemplation, with something new to explore around every curve.

In the dappled light, leaves of tiny trout lilies persist. Yellow carpets of golden groundsel are fading. I search for the strong, singular stems and tropical-looking palmate leaves of the green dragon, but it's not yet pierced the vigorous carpet of Virginia wildrye and inland sea oats. We hear Texas spiny lizards skitter through the leafy forest floor.

I follow Julie down a short spur deeper into the forest; the canyonside rises steeply to our right. From the intimate adjoining vale rises a surprising grove of flowering dogwoods—at least a couple dozen! Some are at least a hundred years old. Today the display is fading, but a week before, on one of David's hikes, clouds of white blooms-bracts appeared suspended against brilliant young green. An elevated observation deck will bring viewers even closer.

▲ A lush feeder creek creates impeccable songbird habitat.

Finding Home

We resume the loop and undulate along the canyon walls. In the folds, we see nature up close—Carolina buckthorns and possumhaws striving for enough sunlight to set fruit, the old nests of tiny birds. As the trail scales a jutting knob, the sky comes into view, and an arc of coral honeysuckle vine extends toward it. Julie scans intently for a pair of broad-winged hawks that raise their young in summers at Dogwood Canyon.

The conservation powerhouse Audubon Texas oversees four education centers in the state, including two in Dallas County—Dogwood Canyon and Trinity River—that offer classes, lectures, nature walks, and other activities.

The trail descends to follow a significant feeder of John Penn Branch. In the moister environs, birdsong is crazy loud. Crossing the creek on a bridge that effortlessly melds into nature, Julie is observant enough to notice a small ant on the rail. It tries to move a comparatively giant beetle, gives up, and departs, leaving a trail of pheromones, she notes, so that it can return with mound mates.

We return to the West Loop Trail, knowing our forest bathing soon must end. Julie draws my attention to Bigelow's oak, with its unusual shaggy bark and tendency to grow in clumps, and the vaguely lemon smell of aromatic sumac in bloom. We could have only experienced this because of those who

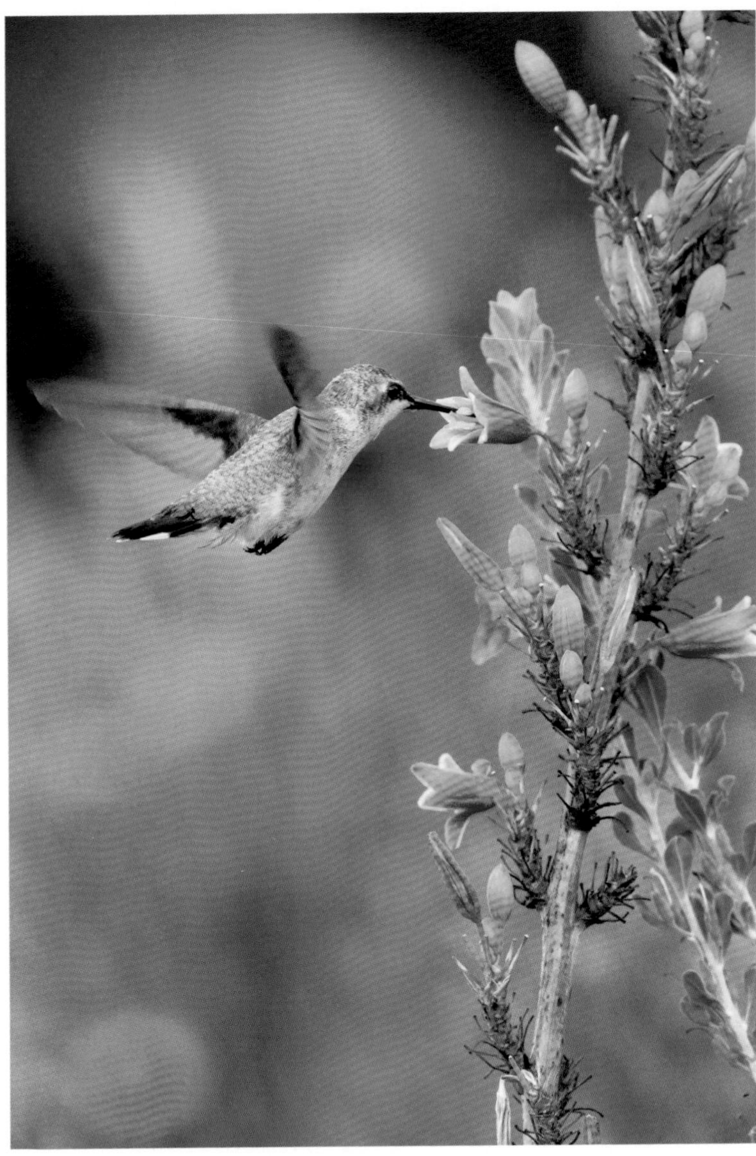

◄ Black-chinned hummingbird is a favorite at Dogwood Canyon.

supported David and his vision. They believe, as he does, in these lines from Rudyard Kipling's poem *Sussex*:

> *God gave all men all earth to love,*
> *But, since our hearts are small*
> *Ordained for each one spot should prove*
> *Beloved over all . . .*

David says, "Dogwood Canyon is my one spot."

ADVENTURE 16 ELM FORK OF THE TRINITY RIVER

Clear Creek Natural Heritage Center

Vast preserve with extensive bottomland woods and wetlands along the Elm Fork of the Trinity River.

WHERE: 3310 Collins Road, Denton, TX 76208. East of Denton, north of US-380.
PARKING: Gravel lot.
TRAILS: Dirt 7 miles. Detailed map at website.
DIFFICULTY: Moderate to challenging.
FACILITIES: Restrooms (chemical toilet).
NEARBY: Lewisville Lake's Elm Fork and Pilot Knoll Trails, Discovery Park's Pollinative Prairie, Ray Roberts Lake State Park Greenbelt.

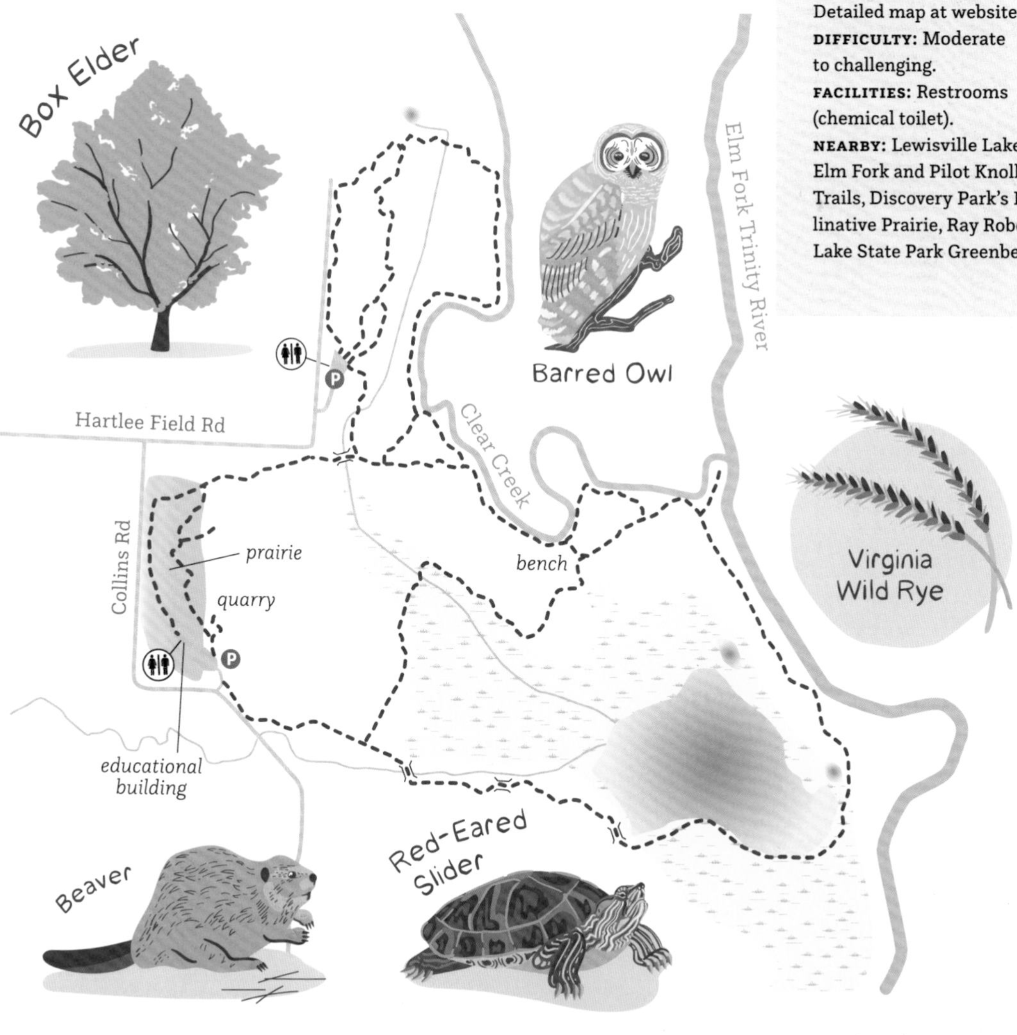

▲ Elm Fork Texas Master Naturalist Project Manager Clay Thurmond demonstrates how large Clear Creek trees grow.

▲ Penstemon (left) and evening primrose (right) brighten the prairie.

Located where Clear Creek merges with the Elm Fork, Clear Creek Natural Heritage Center is a watery place; wetlands compose almost half its area. Its 2900 acres are kept undeveloped for flood control by the US Army Corps of Engineers. The City of Denton now leases the property.

The mix of Blackland Prairie and bottomland woods is a home base for Elm Fork Texas Master Naturalists. Their project manager, Clay Thurmond, guides our journey, along with Diane Wetherbee, a delightful naturalist working on a forestry PhD. We're here shortly after a rain to see this botanical sponge in action (with management permission, because trails are closed for hiking) and to make observations for the City Nature Challenge, a citizen science competition.

The Lower Prairie Trail is waking up for spring. Low-growing pink puffs of sensitive briar flourish below Texas star, with its simple yellow blooms of five-pointed petals. The yard-high Texas prairie parsley brings joy with its lime-green foliage and giant yellow umbel of flowers.

Fish in the Fisherman's Trail

We head north to the preserve's latest acquisition: a corridor of upland woods sloping to Clear Creek. Light filtering through the young tree leaves and bouncing off the understory grasses infuses the air with luminous green. Occasional red oaks and pecan trees six feet around at their bases stand like Goliaths in a green sea.

So much water fills Fisherman's Trail that a current flows. Clay hikes carefully in his waders; Diane and I walk the more elevated woods to the side. Evaluating how to get around a particularly wet area, we hear loud splashing and three carp swim by, their orange back ridges visible as they weave among fallen branches.

"They're just happily swimming with their bodies half out of the water," says Diane. The omnivorous fish eagerly explore newly flooded territory for

▼ A gentle current flows in the trail.

▲ Cottonwoods and pecan trees grow huge in the wet woods.

crustaceans and mollusks. "They're equipped with teeth inside their throat. They can eat anything." Farther down the trail, dead carp stranded by receding floodwaters have had their evidently tasty eyes pecked out.

Cathedral Woods

We turn north on Big Cottonwood Loop along Clear Creek and find dry land. As far as we can see are scattered giant trees swathed in a lush understory of coralberry, elderberry, and poison ivy. Towering cottonwoods soar into an arching canopy radiant in filtered light. "It's like a cathedral," I observe. Yet amid the colossi, a young bur oak is just a couple feet tall, fresh green leaves sprouting from a stout stem, someday to be a giant—an emblem of hope.

Briar vines hang down from four-story trees, aerial thickets that vibrate with bird activity. So many songbirds are calling, it's hard to tell them apart. Some stake territory, others look for mates. A few sound like they're just bragging. The extended hoot of a barred owl resonates. Silently, a dark shape flies through the canopy.

Creeks carry privet berries, and where the trail swings next to the banks an invasive thicket ensues. Diane notes how the woods become dark and absent of birdsong when privet dominates. Then grand old cottonwoods, bur oaks, and pecans come back into view. It's like seeing old friends.

The arching branches of a graceful bois d'arc wrap around a towering cottonwood fifteen feet around. The woods are awe-inspiring. Except for birdcalls, all we hear are cottonwood leaves rustling wildly, hinting of a storm front to come. Deep in nature, one with the elements and weather, lacking in artifice and disconnected from time, I feel fully human.

Creekside Reverie

Box elders flourish in the wet riparian earth, their dancing, triangular leaves responding to the lightest breeze. They swarm the path with a multitude of slender trunks, pushing out all the privet. The caterpillars of nearly three hundred moth and butterfly species depend on box elder leaves.

A trail spur takes us to a favored fishing spot on Clear Creek where Clay wants to install a bench. The view is quintessential Texas riparian. On the opposite bank grows an immense box elder with a hearty girth and low, spreading crown. The surging creek riffles over snags, creating swirling eddies that hypnotize.

We resume hiking as a light rain starts to fall. Diane notices rolled-up cottonwood leaves stuffed with webbing: "The leaf roller moth lays its eggs inside. See how they stitch it up?" How do the leaves get onto the ground, I ask. Does the caterpillar bite it off? "That's a good question," she says, no doubt planning to look it up.

> The Elm Fork chapter of Texas Master Naturalists helps craft a nature preserve from raw US Army Corps of Engineers land. They conduct plant and wildlife surveys, create an evolving trail system, provide naturalist hikes, and plan restoration projects.

A patch of elephant's foot, with its broad oval leaves that lie flat on the ground, delights us. It's popular in Southeast Asia for treating pain. Nearby is a tall stalk of wild lettuce with prickly ten-inch-long leaves known for nerve-soothing qualities. I break a leaf and acrid aroma and milky sap exudes. The woods are a medicine cabinet.

Water Goes Where It Flows

We find the Clear Creek–Elm Fork confluence is an amorphous, wet mess. Even with rain and reservoir releases, water shouldn't be this high. A mammoth logjam here that once blocked the Elm Fork is now small. Only one place for the logs to go: downstream. We break with sandwiches of peanut butter and mayhaw jelly, a Southern swamp fruit, appropriately enough.

▲ There's a trail here somewhere.

Over 5000 Denton ISD students visit the preserve each year. Projects from local universities include research on pollinators, bumblebees, and air quality impact on native plants.

Now on the last leg of an enormous loop around the preserve, we debate our choices: backtrack to our starting point or continue forward. "This way is the Wetlands Trail. It's going to be wet," says Clay. With a soaked shirt and soggy shoes, I reply: "And what are we now?" Clay gallantly loans me his walking stick.

Around a curve, the trail becomes a long ribbon of water flanked by submerged reeds. An overflowing Elm Fork has merged with an adjacent large, marshy wetland, turning riparian woods into a swamp. "This is more than a release from Ray Roberts Reservoir," says Clay. "The logjam at US-380 must be pushing the river back."

Water spreads from horizon to horizon. This is my most insane hike ever, and I've done many. But I came to see the refuge act as a sponge, stemming the rush of floodwater into Lewisville Lake that strains the reservoir and exacerbates flooding downriver.

One with the Water

Turning back would add many miles, so we wade on up to our thighs, well over Clay's waders. It's worth it for the City Nature Challenge observations. Snails, crawling bugs, and tiny frogs cling beneath leaves, trying not to float away. A gooey ball of black amphibian eggs drifts by—Diane calls it frog jelly.

▲ A raft of fire ants.

While Clay and Diane observe a mother beaver and babies atop a lodge, I shuffle forward, feeling for a trail with my feet. Half-submerged black willows and buttonbushes mark its edges. Caked mud on trees indicates water once reached well over my head. That's sobering.

Diane asks excitedly, "Did you see the floating fire ants?" Yes I did, and moved away as fast as I could. Fire ants weave their bodies together so tightly that water can't penetrate, forming a raft. Many drown. "You don't want to be in a kayak and have your paddle hit one. They'll swarm the boat." Horrifying!

Clay assures us we're almost done: "There's a bench not too far ahead." We take one last look across the wetlands. "It's truly wild on the other side, no trails at all," says Diane. "It's kind of nice to know it's over there, just being wild."

We come across the promised bench, most of it underwater. We slog on. The water level slowly drops from over our knees and finally dry land appears. Clay leans against a tree and empties his waders. We all laugh at a fitting end to our watery escapade.

ADVENTURE 17 ELM FORK OF THE TRINITY RIVER

Lewisville Lake Environmental Learning Area

View white-tailed deer, wild turkeys, river otters, American beavers, bobcats, and even American minks on trails through a variety of habitats in a massive preserve below the Lewisville Lake Dam.

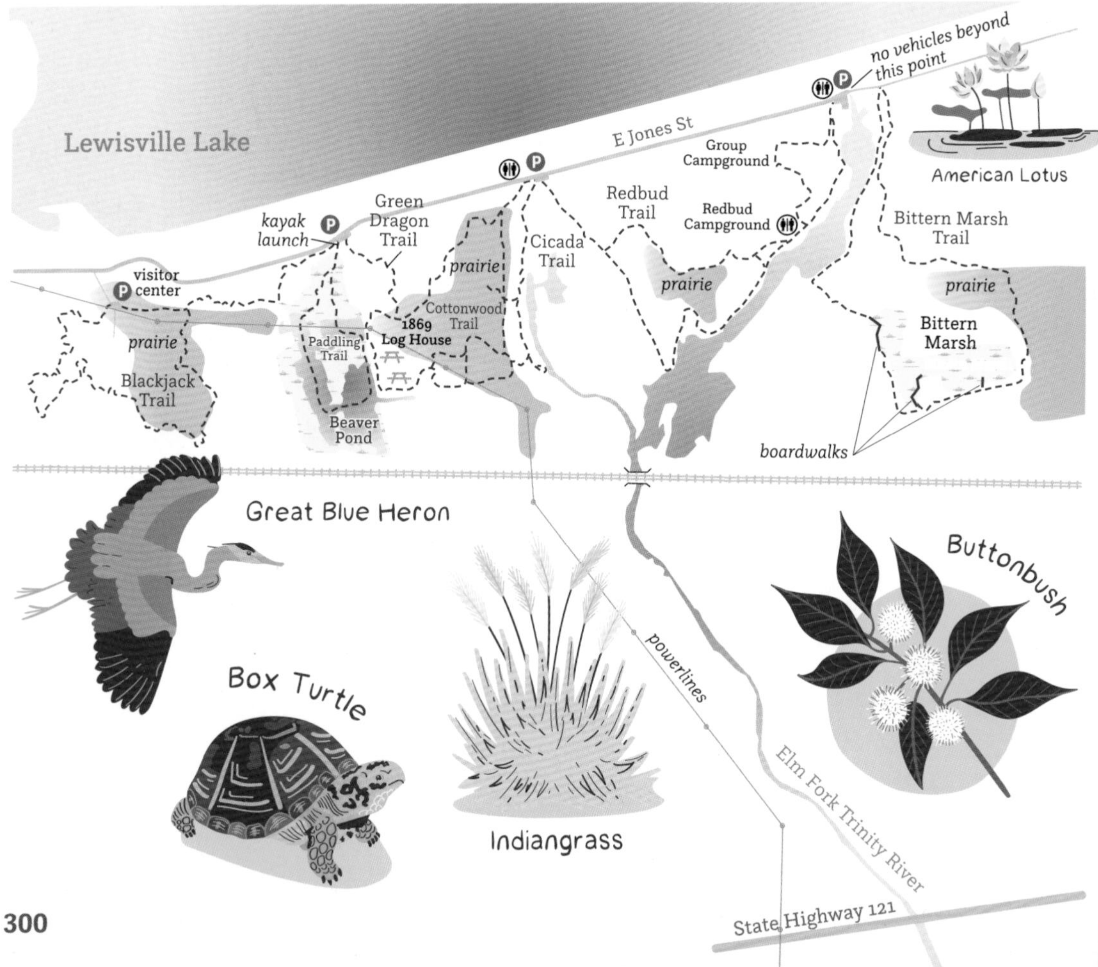

▲ Primeval and beautiful Bittern Marsh.

The 2600 acres of Lewisville Lake Environmental Learning Area (LLELA) spreads below the reservoir dam, where the Elm Fork exits, on US Army Crops of Engineer land from creation of the lake. Named for its association with nearby University of North Texas (UNT), it's referred to as "lee-lah." Eastern Cross Timbers ease into Blackland Prairie, creating upland forests dotted with prairie glades, marshes, bottomland woods, and multiple riparian corridors.

WHERE: 201 E Jones St., Lewisville, TX 75057. Lewisville, southeast Denton County.
PARKING: Gravel lots.
TRAILS: Dirt 7 miles. Detailed map and descriptions at llela.org.
DIFFICULTY: Easy to moderate.
FACILITIES: Visitor center (limited hours). Chemical toilets.
COST: $5 per vehicle.
DOGS: Not allowed except service animals.
NEARBY: Coppell Nature Park, Lewisville Lake's Elm Fork Trail and Pilot Knoll/ Old Alton Bridge Trail.

On a sunny spring morning with a perfect amount of chill, I embark on the Blackjack Trail with Scott Kiester, an Elm Fork Texas Master Naturalist who coordinates LLELA's more than 100 Master Naturalist volunteers from several North Texas chapters. Arthropod enthusiast Laura Kimberly joins. We startle a brown thrasher poking its long, curved beak in the leaf litter. It chastises us with a series of concise songs—brown thrashers have over 1000 songs, the largest repertoire of any bird.

Cross Timbers," says Scott. "It's never been farmed, never been cleared. This is what it looked like when people came west on wagons." Post oaks,

Studies on the delayed maturity coloration of male painted buntings and the overwintering and migration patterns of American kestrels are just two of the ongoing studies by UNT research teams at LLELA.

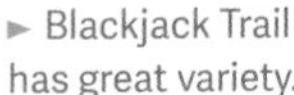

► Blackjack Trail has great variety.

which mark this ecoregion, reach a hearty three stories tall. Bur and Shumard oaks impress with massive trunks, joined by Buckley's oak on rocky outcroppings.

The trail dips and rises along the folds of a ravine, gracefully flanked by low coralberry shrubs about to bloom, and crosses a series of picturesque wooden bridges. Laura notices a tender young redbud with neat holes in the leaves, a sign of leafcutter bees. Cardinals vigorously peep from a roughleaf dogwood thicket.

Feather Edge

I've walked this trail before, but Scott presents it in a new light. We emerge from woods into the small, round Button Glade, its rusty stalks of little bluestem shining in the sunlight. "This little open glade only exists because there's a patch of clay soil here that trees haven't been able to penetrate," he shares. "This is the first hint that we're getting to the feather edge between Woodbine Sandstone and Eagle Ford Shale. The bedrock underneath forms the topsoil that creates slightly different plant communities. We saw little bluestem here one day and realized this had been prairie at some point." Volunteers began reclaiming the glade.

Reptile enthusiasts concerned about LLELA's box turtle population, volunteers from Friends of LLELA, Texas Master Naturalists, and University of North Texas (UNT) students set up telemetry to track box turtles and increase their population.

▲ A three-toed box turtle wears a UNT tracking device.

► A bobcat works the woods.

We progress along the trail, alternating shady forest and sunny glades as the soil changes. "This is Eve's Glade," says Scott, referring to a small copse of Eve's necklace trees draped in pink flower cascades evocative of wisteria.

Unnatural Nature

We leave the high glades behind for a creek winding through deep Cross Timbers. There's so much birdsong it's hard to hear conversation, so we fall quiet. A marker indicates a turtle is hibernating nearby.

Walking downward along a slope, trees start favoring green ash and cedar elm, two aggressive natives with wind-dispersed seed. Few coralberries or possumhaws adorn the understory, but smooth sumac and eastern poison ivy, which adapt to disturbed land, thrive.

▼ A resident bald eagle guards its nest.

▲ Each week brings a new wave of color to the prairie.

LLELA offers overnight camping in nine walk-in rudimentary sites near the Elm Fork. Large-group camping is available at the Redbud Campground.

"All this was a borrow pit to build the Lewisville Lake dam in the '40s and '50s," Scott says. It's choked with young trees due to regrowth not being managed, a phenomenon called go-back land." Yet Laura finds insects as plentiful as in old-growth timbers. A row of Chickasaw plums dripping with unripe fruit banks the trail; when ripe, it will be bird bacchanalia.

Blackjack Trail enters abruptly into a sloping utility corridor dominated by gigantic electric towers. Somewhere beyond the Elm Fork, which runs along the base of the slope, Scott notes, is where LLELA's nesting pair of bald eagles raise their young, already fledged this year.

Over the Prairie and Through the Woods

At present, only 600 of LLELA's acres are open to the public. But the long-term vision of UNT, Lewisville, and LLELA Restoration Manager Richard Freiheit is creating a national caliber nature preserve—one that educates new generations of nature professionals, provides needed respite from urban life, and improves water and air quality.

Richard and Scott's volunteers rehabilitate hundreds of acres on the slimmest of budgets through multiple workdays weekly. They forge access and survey plants to restore vast forests along Stewart Creek. Bringing back

◂ Great blue herons perch between fishing forays.

the Blackland Prairie entails chain sawing and processing untold masses of brush, which must then be seeded and planted with natives.

Those lucky enough to experience it as volunteers testify to the prairie's epic beauty and populations of rare grassland birds. Its riotous diversity supports an abundance of wildlife and provides ever-changing color.

"We put 10,000 plants in the ground one year," Richard says. To complement the extensive habitat restorations, they plan to create trails so that someday others may embrace these wonders and perhaps join in. "You know, restoration is never done," said Richard. "It's always doing."

Into the Marsh

The Elm Fork still runs through Lewisville Lake. It gushes out in churning turbulence down a mammoth rerouted channel. Great egrets and great blue herons lurk comically in black willows like gargantuan songbirds, catching stunned emerging fish.

North Texas Master Naturalist president Scott Hudson, photographer Daniel Koglin, and I connect with LLELA educator Erin Piper and Elm Fork Master Naturalist volunteers Denver Kramer and Rita Lokie. We head for Bittern Marsh Trail to revel in LLELA's only bottomland forest. The understory is refreshingly free of privet.

Beaver Pond Paddling Trail offers a mile-long kayak and canoe route through languid wetlands close to wildlife, especially wading birds and reptiles.

One arbor giant after another soars among much younger trees. We follow tiny deer prints in the trail for a while, dive through clouds of mosquitoes, and marvel at how moss on a fallen log replicates via tall filaments showering spores on female reproductive parts below.

Go-Back Land

"Where did the big trees go?" asks Daniel as we suddenly pass into a bright young forest. Erin explains, "It's just how different owners managed their land before the Army Corps got the land. Some cleared it completely, some liked it wooded, some left scattered trees," Now it's all go-back land, guided by LLELA's restoration crew.

Scattered trees in an old pasture form a bright, open savannah. In another, crowded young trees strive for dominance. In the bottomlands is a climax forest of mature trees, changing only when lightning or floods open new areas to sunlight.

"We want people to see these changes, to understand the successional forest, and imagine what it can look like," says Erin. "When you bring your kids or grandkids out here, this will be totally different."

Often found in old pastureland, fire ant mounds dot sunnier parts of the trail. Ants move eggs about the mound in response to temperature, causing it to collapse and expand. Erin explains that ants go ballistic when the nursery mound is touched.

Marsh in Flux

The young doe and fawn whose prints we've been following scamper off when we head to Bittern Marsh. Along the boardwalk, halberd leaf hibiscus thrusts bold, maroon stems with broad, ornate leaves. In a few weeks, they'll sport large, white blooms. Denver asks, "Do you hear the warblers? So many!" The songs are melodic and sweet.

After ambling to the second blind, a line of black willows fell victim to fluctuating water levels and died, but life adapts. Erin notes how a willow stump is growing plants and that rodents and woodpeckers are feasting on burrowing insects. The original Giving Tree, I comment.

▲ Bittern Marsh appears through the trees.

◄ The bottomland woods are dark and deep.

Though together only a couple of hours, we act like old friends, bonded by a love of nature. We share energy bars in the blind and Erin points to where the beaver dam used to be. Its abandonment and new dam construction is greatly changing the marsh.

River Walk

Clasping coneflowers by the hundreds fill the trail ahead until the boardwalk picks up and winds through the swamp. Trees along the swamp edge lean from the weight of great egrets. Their fuzzy white young perch in the bulrushes, swaying with the current. Carp splash noisily in the water. It's primal enough for alligators.

Denver deems it his favorite area for wildlife viewing because of occasional benches: "Sit still and you become invisible." At boardwalk's end, the trail disappears into the Elm Fork, well over its banks. Denver wears the tallest waders, so we nominate him to find an alternate path. We follow him through the swamp, leaping between raised stretches of mud while bullfrogs serenade enthusiastically.

Back at the lake outlet, even more wading birds have gathered, jousting with their long beaks for prime position in the willows. A group of dusky gray cormorants jiggle their heads cockily as they surf the waves downstream. Just having fun in nature, like us.

ADVENTURE 18 ELM FORK OF THE TRINITY RIVER

Ray Roberts Lake State Park

A wooded state park wraps around Lake Ray Roberts—a 29,000-acre Elm Fork reservoir—in several units, with many miles of biking, hiking, and equestrian trails.

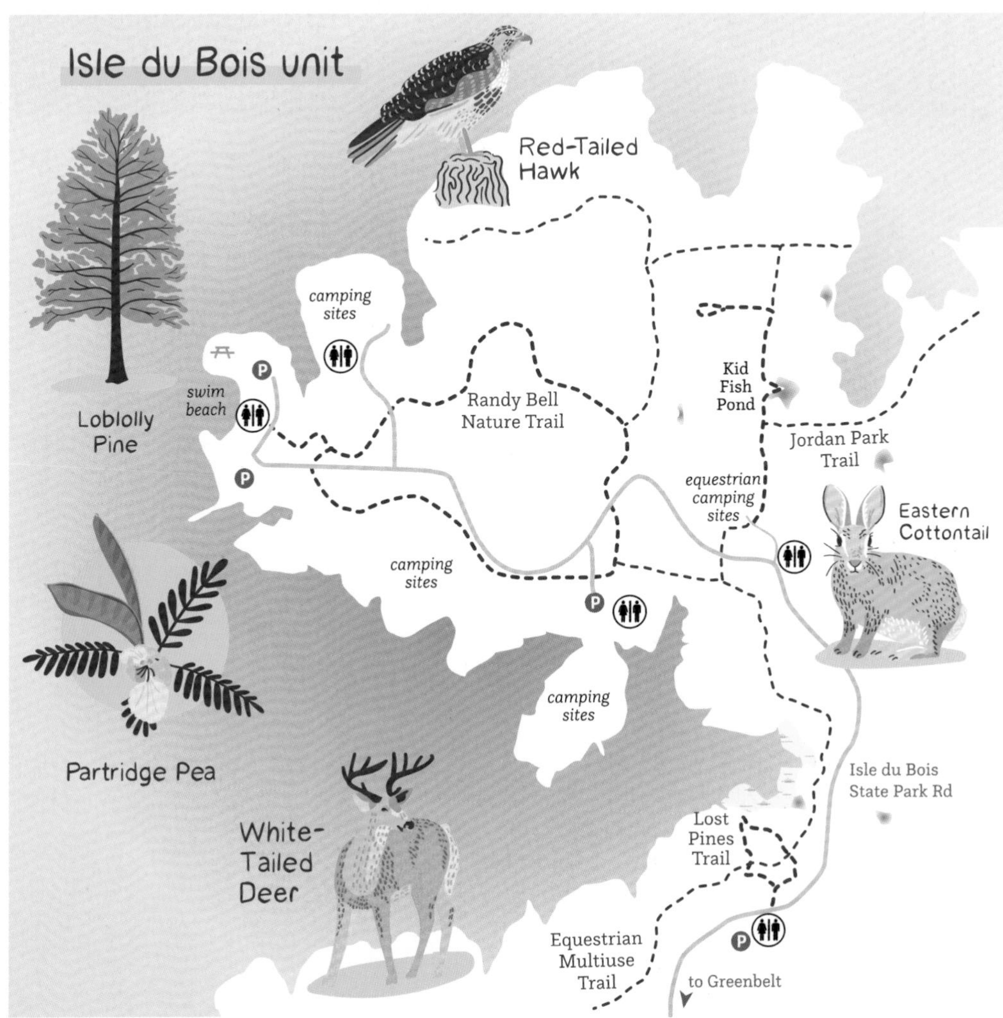

▲ The sun sets on a quiet cove at Lake Ray Roberts.

WHERE: 100 PW 4137, Pilot Point, TX 76258. Isle du Bois Unit, northeast Denton County.
PARKING: Paved lots.
TRAILS: Dirt/DORBA (off-road bike) 20+ miles, equestrian 20+ miles, paved 2 miles. Detailed map at website.
DIFFICULTY: Easy, moderate, and challenging options.
FACILITIES: Visitor center, nature center, restrooms.
COST: $7 per adult.
NEARBY: Ray Roberts Lake State Park Greenbelt Corridor, Ray Roberts Lake State Park: Johnson Branch.

Many swampy inlets and large swaths of prairie grace the rolling Eastern Cross Timbers terrain of Ray Roberts Lake State Park (RRSP), making it prime white-tailed deer habitat. Within seconds of stepping onto the Randy Bell Scenic Trail, a paved path that links most campgrounds in the Isle du Bois unit, a doe and fawn skitter away.

The more scenic northern section of the Randy Bell Trail meanders through a dense, relatively young forest of post oak, blackjack oak, cedar elm, and winged elm. With trees close together and limbs low to the ground, little understory can grow. It makes the small glades with Blackland Prairie remnants almost startling in their brightness. Partridge pea, avidly eaten by deer and requiring buzz pollination by native bees, is the reigning flower this early summer day.

Texas Parks and Wildlife is commendable for having a paved trail so parents with young children and the mobility-impaired can access wild nature. Randy Bell Trail intersects a loop crafted by Dallas Off-Road Bicycle Association (DORBA). I take the dirt path and soon I am one with the forest and utterly enchanted by a large patch of frostweed already four feet tall. Rare in this dry terrain, but a tiny swale holds just enough rain runoff.

◄ Partridge pea makes excellent seed.

The richness of game and edible plants has drawn humans here for over 11,000 years, as the nearby Aubrey Clovis site attests.

Returning to Randy Bell Trail, my ears perk up when the trail skirts a wet-weather draw flush from recent rains. It's a symphony of woodland birds: the peeps of northern cardinals and clear, dynamic tweets of Carolina chickadees, sundered by the raucous caws of blue jays and repeated cheeping chastisements of a downy woodpecker. Texas spiny lizards basking on hot pavement seem like a lure for roadrunners, but none appear.

Golden Prairie

Few know this part of RRLSP better than Denise Thompson and Susan Pohlen of the Elm Fork Texas Master Naturalists, both having been chapter project leaders for the park. We set out from the Bluestem Grove equestrian camping area, heading north on the Kid's Fish Pond Trail. Painted buntings perch in the taller trees along the way, singing their territories.

Once past a Mexican plum thicket, the big prairie of Isle du Bois's east side opens up in a breathtaking expanse rimmed by dark green wooded ridges. Acres of little bluestem's golden seedstalks rise from this year's new teal growth, interspersed with emerald patches of young lovegrasses. Their skinny blades shimmy in the slightest breeze. The field appears like a finely woven grass blanket.

"This air!" I exclaim, "It's so clean! As if you can smell the breeze itself." Denise concurs. "You don't get this kind of air anywhere but prairies. It is primo air." We scan the prairie and there's no sign of civilization, no pollution, like it's always looked this way. "It's great to come out in the winter and fall

To camp in the Isle du Bois unit without electrical noises and distractions, stay in the Hawthorn area located on a large lake peninsula. A short walk from parking and restrooms keeps the campsite scenery free of cars and buildings. Great base for a day at the park.

▲ Expansive prairies bring peace.

▲ Take the pond loop to experience both its public and private aspects.

when the heat's not so bad. You can walk many hours just wandering," says Denise.

We reach the Kid's Fish Pond, where large post oaks offer a shady respite. A maze of deer trails slip through the prairie grasses around the pond, a favored watering hole. A path around the pond passes through a verdant swale at its outflow to the lake, abundant with buttonbushes, a perfect area for amphibians and bivalves favored by smaller herons.

▲ The many layers of a prairie.

Johnson Unit on the lake's north shore is less crowded than the very popular Isle du Bois unit, especially the swimming beach. Paved and DORBA trails, plus an excellent long-distance dirt hiking trail, Dogwood Canyon, explore the park's quiet west side.

Quest for Equestrian

"There's a trail we can take out of here, not on the map, that leads to the equestrian trail," suggests Denise. Off we go, through a mosaic of woods and prairie dotted with star-shaped, hot-pink prairie gentian. Over twenty miles of bridle paths explore the lakeshore and Elm Fork of RRLSP. Hikers are welcome on the trail as long as they give horses a wide berth. The bridle path from Bluestem Grove south to the Greenbelt is particularly scenic for hikers.

The trail hops between cedar elm and persimmon copses, providing fortunate summer shade, often with white-tailed deer quietly resting in the shadows. We pass through a lush draw with pecan trees huddled around a small water catchment and a red-eared slider laying eggs. The aroma of purple passionflowers tumbling over saplings intoxicates. Susan searches the vines for fritillary butterfly caterpillars: "They've not been here yet; it's early."

We connect to the equestrian trail going west and emerge from some woods into bright sunlight. It's a bit too much on this hot day, even though it connects to a tantalizing dirt tangent of Randy Bell Trail leading to the lake. We could go east for five miles to Jordan Unit and another four more to Lost Lake. But the shady Lost Pines Trail calls to us.

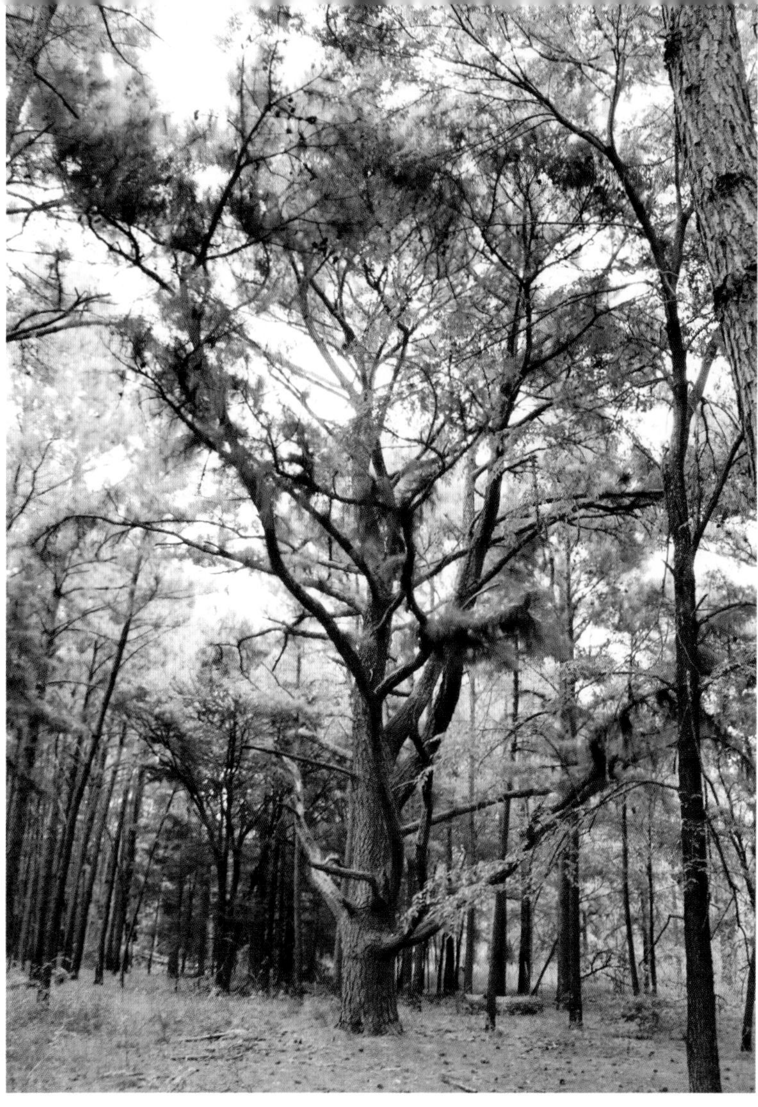

► Octopine!

Lost in the Pines

Towering loblolly pines are an incongruous sight in the short forest of Eastern Cross Timbers. How they got this far out of range is uncertain. A stand stretching across the Isle du Bois unit entrance gives the adjacent Lost Pines Trail its name. The sandy soil is evidently to their liking. "We call this one Octopine," says Denise, pointing to a pine off the trail whose swirl of limbs contorted around encroaching brush now cleared.

Elm Fork Master Naturalists are renowned for their skills in wildlife habitat rehabilitation of wild places. At Ray Roberts Lake State Park, they also offer guided hikes, present educational programs, and staff the nature center on weekends.

▲ Lake inlets are peaceful, with abundant wildlife.

As our trio ambles down the wide paths easy for the mobility impaired, we discuss the impact of a recent prescribed burn in the grove. Pockets unreached by flames are impenetrably thick with brush. The fire-rejuvenated beautyberry shrubs are now flush with blooms and equally restored blackberry vines are heavy with red and purple fruit. Pine cone nuts support the wily plains pocket gopher and sizable fox squirrel, which in turn attract owls.

We come to the crumbling brick hearth of an old homestead, surrounded by a rough-hewn fence where a very pregnant Texas spiny lizard rests in the shade. Susan suggests that we take a detour on the equestrian trail past some impressively large post oaks. A lakeside lagoon draped with briar vines and rimmed by graceful elderberry shrubs projects a mysterious air. But the resident beavers are not to be seen.

Another trail tangent leads us to a lakeshore marsh created by higher than usual water levels. The remains of crustacean shells, especially bivalves, are snared in the grass and reeds by receding water. Largemouth bass and freshwater drum congregate here for the invertebrates, as do fishing enthusiasts, both human and heron. A bench invites appreciation for the quiet inlet.

Wrapping up our hike, another twisted loblolly pine survivor exults over a bright clearing. Five-lined skinks invigorated by the heat zip about the leaves while other lizards lie prone on the sandy soil. A doe and two fawns wander through, grazing on inland sea oats and nibbling lichen off pine bark. On the forest edge, spotted beebalm dusted with gray and lavender pops in the shadows, complemented by giant coneflower's large silvery leaves and bold yellow blooms bending on six-foot stems, as if waving goodbye.

ADVENTURE 19 WHERE THE WEST BEGINS

Bob Jones Nature Center & Preserve and Walnut Grove Recreation Trail

Wide sandy trails wind through Eastern Cross Timbers in a nature preserve and along the Grapevine Lake shore in the tony suburb of Southlake.

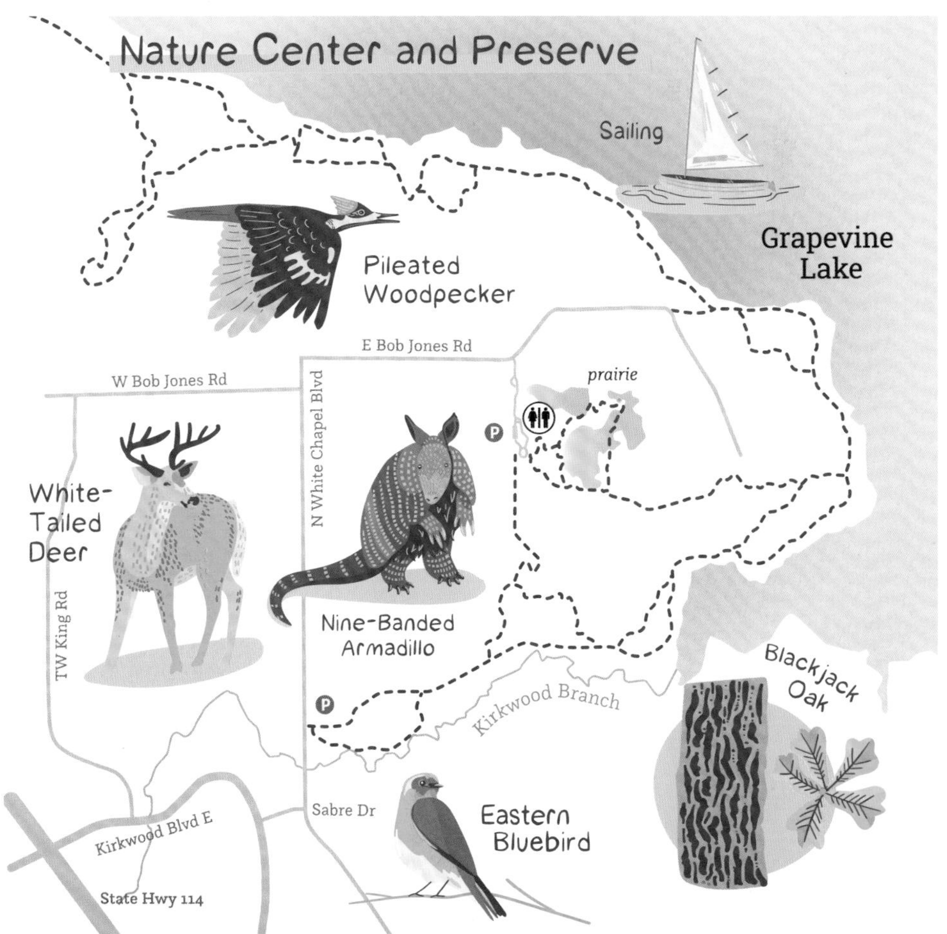

Bob Jones Nature Center and Preserve

▸ The nature center offers popular classes and summer camps for children, as well as impressive special events.

▴ Curious white-tailed deer peer at onlookers.

Tucked amid horse ranchettes and palatial homes with epic lawns in the affluent town of Southlake are the remains of a freed slave's late-1800s farm empire. In 2008, the 700-acre Bob Jones Nature Center and Preserve opened on the western shore of 7380-acre Grapevine Lake, a US Army Corps of Engineers impoundment of Denton Creek.

WHERE: 355 E Bob Jones Road, Southlake, TX 76092. Southlake, northeast corner of Tarrant County.
PARKING: Paved lot.
TRAILS: Dirt 3 miles. Detailed map at website.
DIFFICULTY: Easy.
FACILITIES: Education center (limited hours). Restrooms (chemical toilet).
DOGS: Not allowed except service animals.
NEARBY: Cross Timbers Trail, Rocky Point Trail.

The post oaks and blackjack oaks have long lost their leaves, exposing their branches that twist and contort, framed against a clear blue sky. Their sculptural shapes always make winter hiking in Eastern Cross Timbers a delight. The sandy soil, so different from the more common black gumbo clay found to the east, is a Cross Timbers hallmark. Fine as granulated sugar in some places, recent rain has compacted it nicely.

Nature photographer Daniel Koglin has been here since dawn, capturing images of bluebirds defending their box home from interlopers and white-tailed deer meandering through the woods. We stare at far-off dark shapes in an adjoining equestrian field, hoping to see resident wild turkeys, but they're Canadian geese. The former migrators now live full-time in North Texas, drawn by habitats like Grapevine Lake.

Wide, well-maintained trails emanate from the educational building and feature snazzy interpretive trail signs on plants, geology, and wildlife tracks

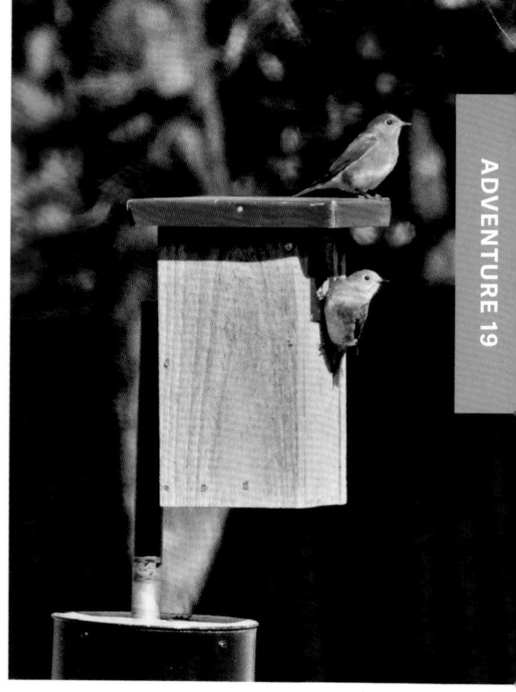

▲ An old red barn reminds visitors of Bob Jones's agricultural past.

◄ Bluebirds defend their home even before breeding begins.

in a spacious post oak and cedar elm savannah. Daniel's morning deer cross before us on the White-Tailed Deer Trail, bold since no hunters frequent here. Connecting to the Bluebird Trail, we note plentiful bluebirds. Truth in advertising.

Shoreline Forest

We turn onto the trail leading to the lakeshore and soon encounter the trailhead for Walnut Grove Recreation Trail. Our amble through the congested forest prompts a discussion of brushy overgrowth choking out unmanaged Cross Timbers across North Texas. Before agriculture, periodic wildfires swept through, and older blackjack and post oak trees with fire-resistant bark escaped damage. The result was an open understory of herbaceous plants that supported wildlife. Then cattle grazing kept forested areas open. Now both are gone, allowing overgrowth, especially by invasives, to proceed unchecked.

We reach Walnut Grove Recreation Trail, where lakeshore views from the shade of Eastern Cross Timbers offer an expansive feeling with crisp, clear air. The blazing bright sunlight showcases sculptural winter trees against a blue sky. Large sandstone boulders provide a fun scramble, but the shoreline stretches of rough cockleburs gone to spiky seed are horrifying, especially to owners of long-haired dogs.

A father amuses his toddler son on a tree swing in a shady shoreline motte while his daughter plays in the sand nearby. We debate continuing to the forested trails along the Marshall Creek inlet. The lakeside terrain is bracing and refreshingly free of the usual rowdy lake patrons, but lunch is calling.

WHERE: 3660 White Chapel Rd, Southlake, TX 76092. Southlake, northeast corner of Tarrant County.
PARKING: Paved lot.
TRAILS: Dirt 30 miles.
DIFFICULTY: Moderate.
FACILITIES: None.
NEARBY: Centuries-old sycamore tree, in the NW corner of Trophy Club Park along Denton Creek.

Walnut Grove National Recreation Trail

A reliable source of open space is public land around US Army Corps of Engineers reservoirs. While those on the rocky north shore of Grapevine Lake emphasize off-road bicycling, Walnut Grove National Recreation Trail on the gently inclined southern shore provides long saunters for horseback riders and hikers.

Equestrian trails are great for social hiking because they're wide enough to walk side by side. I'm here getting to know Barb Cutter of Texas Outdoors-Woman Network (TOWN), a Texas Parks and Wildlife Department program. She's been active in TOWN since it developed out of classes titled Becoming an Outdoors Woman. We share a commitment to getting more women into nature. Surrounded by a residential area with a very low crime rate, Walnut Grove is an exceptionally safe place for women to hike alone.

▼ Mature post oaks are an imposing sight on the savannah.

We head out on this early spring day from the Walnut Grove's Bluestem Equestrian Trailhead. Hiking, bicycling, kayaking, camping—Barb embraces it all. The nature emphasis of Girl Scouting seized her passion as a young girl, inspiring her to earn the Gold Award, given to fewer than 6 percent of Girl Scouts annually.

"All the different things that girls could do as they went through the program were just thrilling. I want to encourage young women to be able to have these kinds of experiences," says Barb, who has mentored many. She would eventually marry an Eagle Scout, of course. His sudden demise just before retirement helped her understand how much solace she received from nature.

Spring in the Cross Timbers

A broad trail and balmy southern spring temperatures make for a perfect hike. Post oaks and cedar elms

ADVENTURE 19

▲ Plum blossoms herald impending spring.

◀ The titmouse is a full-time resident at Grapevine Lake.

have not yet leafed out, so the fuchsia bloom clusters of eastern redbud and fluffy white clusters of Chickasaw plum blooms stand out in the bright understory. Low mounds of bitterweed with their tough needle-like leaves showcase hundreds of tiny yellow daisies. Smaller humps of trailing scarlet pea boast luscious coral flowers framed by small oval leaves.

We're in no hurry on this stretch of trail called Moonshine Highway by equestrians. We listen for birds and talk about being in the quiet bird interim after winter visitors depart, but spring migrators have not yet arrived. We startle a northern flicker pecking about the sand for ants, and it flashes a bit of red on its wings as it flies off.

As the Kirkwood Branch we've been following enters Grapevine Lake, white tridens' knotted rhizomes cling to the creekbanks, trying valiantly to keep them in place. Larval food for branded skippers and satyrs, it's one reason the area is a prime butterfly spot. Buttonbushes flourish in the inlet, promising thousands of spherical white blooms this summer—perfect for dragonfly and damselfly sighting.

> Equestrian trails at Grapevine Lake are closed to cyclists but open to hikers who must yield to horseback riders and never startle the horses.

Reservoir levels vary, leaving the trail distant from shore when waters recede and beneath waters when levels are high. It's been a dry winter and Normandy Beach, as equestrians call it, earns its name with a broad, white-sand expanse that stretches for a couple hundred yards. Lazy vines of Texas bindweed, a native morning glory that thrives in dry, shaded areas, have already begun to bud and in a few weeks will be covered in white blooms.

▲ Blue skies and clear air over the Grapevine Lake.

A Moment in Time

Our slog through the sand is tiring, and we rest at a gentle bay on the cape's point, shaded by sizable post oaks as we chat about our relationship with nature. "So beautiful, isn't it?" asks Barb. "Yes, and so unique," I reply. "No one else will sit here at this time of day with a breeze this direction and cumulus clouds starting to build, with a sailboat going lazily by and crows pecking on the beach. That's why nature never gets boring. You'll never get the same experience twice. Maybe that's why we are here, you know, to have these once in a lifetime moments."

"You have to make an effort to go see nature," says Barb. "You have to make plans. If you're going with a group, you have to get them organized. But I've never once regretted it. It's what makes life memorable. We are so lucky to have all this available to us." Yet too few will take that step, which is why groups like TOWN exist. "Women who don't know the skills want to learn the skills in a setting with other women, being shown, not told. Here's how I do it. Now make it your own," says Barb.

Taking in the brilliant spring day, we reflect on our childhoods, when wonder was a daily experience. We take in the kayaker zipping across the lake, the equestrian pair passing by on the trail, the woman walking her goofy golden dog, the barefoot runner sending sand flying as he makes his pace. Nature infuses us with the awareness that life is precarious and can change in a moment, as Barb knows so well—so seize it now and share generously.

ADVENTURE 20 **WHERE THE WEST BEGINS**

Sheri Capehart Nature Preserve

Impeccable example of Eastern Cross Timbers ecosystem features rocky outcrops, woodlands, and savannah grasslands populated by post oak and blackjack oak, with spring-fed ponds.

WHERE: 5201 Bowman Springs Road, Arlington, TX 76017. South-central Tarrant County, southwest corner of Arlington, just south of I-20.
PARKING: Paved lot.
TRAILS: Dirt 1.80 miles, paved 0.15 miles.
DIFFICULTY: Easy to moderate.
FACILITIES: None.
NEARBY: Oliver Nature Park, Blackland Prairie Park, Molly Hollar Wildscape, O. W. Fannin Natural Area, Thora Hart Park.

◄ A spiny lizard suns on a boulder.

Jim Frisinger and Annabelle Corby are passionate about Sheri Capehart Nature Preserve (SCNP). Jim has studied its Indigenous and pioneer history; Annabelle is a nature enthusiast and a wiz with iNaturalist in documenting the nature of SCNP. Together with others in Friends of Sheri Capehart Nature Preserve, they've helped transform it into a peaceful place that restores people and nurtures wildlife.

They join me in exploring the preserve. Between us, we have over 200 years of living and a lot of white hair. Like the former Environmental Protection Agency communications professional he was, Jim shows up with a folder of material on SCNP. Annabelle, a corporate retiree returning to her nature roots, grabs a bag for litter, and off we go.

The sixty acres of former ranchland preserves a fine example of Eastern Cross Timbers perched on an equally grand example of a cuesta, a geological formation created when hard sedimentary rock overlies a softer layer on an incline. The result is a sharp bluff on the western end and a long, slow slope to the remainder.

More than 1175 species of plants, animals, and bugs call SCNP home, and "just about every month we record a new one," says Jim, noting that "a couple of dragonflies are found here and nowhere else in town." Post and blackjack oak dominate the forest, with scattered spiky gum bumelia, Hercules club trees, and some impressive rusty blackhaw viburnum, whose ruddy buds promise umbels of tiny white flowers in spring.

With terrain from ridgetop to wetlands, the range of bird species is astounding. Skinks hide amid fallen leathery leaves that retain soil moisture. Warming up next to sunny rocks are rat snakes lying in wait for mice and voles. Occasional striped skunks and Virginia opossums pass through.

We amble first down a paved trail to a three-acre pond at the slope base. A boardwalk skirts it, ending in a dock where a young father and son enjoy catch-and-release fishing. Overlooking the pond is a small stone

amphitheater serving as an outdoor learning classroom. Jim notes that springs in the cuesta's layered sandstone keep the pond full.

A lush riparian corridor arises from the pond's outflow, where Friends of Sheri Capehart Nature Preserve is crafting an avian paradise with a grant from Fort Worth Audubon. Birds singing and flitting among feeders in a shady nook greet us. On our way, we pass through the Pollinator Meadow. A thoroughfare rerouting freed up a couple of acres, and the city prepared it for planting. A significant community effort is ongoing to install native plants and seeds.

Climbing the Cuesta

We head up the cuesta slope in a series of long switchbacks, with each curve a different view as we ascend. In this lofty place, thin sandstone soil and leafless winter trees impart a bracing aroma. Post oaks dominate with their dense, twisted trunks and contorted limbs. Their interlaced silhouettes trace a clear blue sky.

Jim notes how the trees shift to blackjack oak as we approach the cuesta top. Known locally as Kennedale Mountain, at 693 feet in elevation it dominates the surrounding land. At the top, the Iron Ore Knob's mineral-rich rocks sport a dazzling array of lichens and mosses.

Friends of Sheri Capehart Nature Preserve leads habitat restoration, creates trails, performs plant and wildlife censuses, and hosts regular walks, talks, and meetings.

▼ Casual fishing is popular here.

◄ The Pollinator Meadow rises from a former roadbed.

▼ Iron Ore Knob is rich with boulders covered in colorful lichen.

▲ Caddo Oak at its Texas Historic Tree Coalition induction ceremony.

A high bluff of angular edges and blocky rock forms the knob's western border. Visible to the west through tangled bare branches are spires of downtown Fort Worth. Jim shares the area's robust history of Native Americans and how they likely sent signals from this bluff.

At the Meadow Loop, we explore a slice of Fort Worth Prairie and contemplate how to control the rapacious thickets of Chickasaw plum and flameleaf sumac—great wildlife plants that can consume a prairie. After a captivating view of the northernmost pond from the bluff's end and a rest for Annabelle, whose litter sack is getting full, we continue to SCNP's star attractions.

Historic Oaks and Rare Yuccas

Jim was walking the Meadow Loop one day with master arborist Wes Culwell, who noticed a large post oak swallowed up by privet. Further evaluation revealed the tree to be at least 200 years old—a witness tree. Now freed from privet, its oak offspring grows in its shade along with a flowering Mexican plum.

Given the name Caddo Oak and placed in the Registry of Texas Historical Trees, the trunk is over fifty inches around. Its majestic canopy spans nearly ninety feet, yet it's barely forty feet tall, the flattened shape reflecting the shallow soil in which it grows. We stand awestruck in the adjacent prairie meadow and absorb its grandeur.

▲ A former center of ranch operations became beautiful Boulder Hill.

Farther down the trail, we turn into a prairie barrens patch that's like stepping into West Texas. Emerging from rusty-colored little bluestem is a multitude of Glen Rose yucca, an endemic species found in only seven North Texas counties. The long sharp blades sport fuzzy tendrils. This meadow is perfect for Comanche harvester ants that feed on the yucca seeds and only nest in deep sandy soils surrounded by oaks.

Preserve Partnerships

SCNP exists because of partnerships. Aware of the land's significance and pressure from developers, Trust for the Public Land purchased the property to give the city of Arlington time to arrange funding. Friends of SCNP works closely with the city's park department to provide support and educational outreach.

Boulder Path provides a good example. The city removed a concrete pad remaining from ranch operations and placed boulders along the quickly eroding old ranch road. Friends of SCNP stepped in with native plants and seeds, soil accumulated around the stones, and now the path is a beautiful meadow.

Annabelle and Jim are rightfully proud of SCNP and want me to see it all. Boulder Path takes us down to trails along the main pond, the water adorned with coots and mallards. The pond eases into wetlands where red-eared sliders adorn fallen logs, and long water snakes slither through reeds after frogs. A mass of cattails hosts a curious gathering of female red-wing blackbirds who scold us for interrupting their girl party.

◄ The spring-fed pond attracts water birds such as this great egret year round.

Friends of SCNP attract people who ply their passions, such as naturalists trained in plants (Jan Miller), reptiles (Michael Smith), and dragonflies (Brent Franklin). Jim Domke manages the trail cams, and Rudy Arnold and Derek Spiegener keep trails in shape and forge new ones. Bob Brennan documents its beauty with his photography.

We conclude our adventure back at the parking lot of permeable pavers, where Annabelle leaves her burgeoning litter sack next to the trashcan. It was a near-perfect afternoon with my feisty senior companions, proving that nature can keep you young.

ADVENTURE 21 WHERE THE WEST BEGINS

Tandy Hills Natural Area

Impressive wildflowers and epic views in a hilltop Fort Worth Prairie remnant, with wooded ravines and lush riparian corridor.

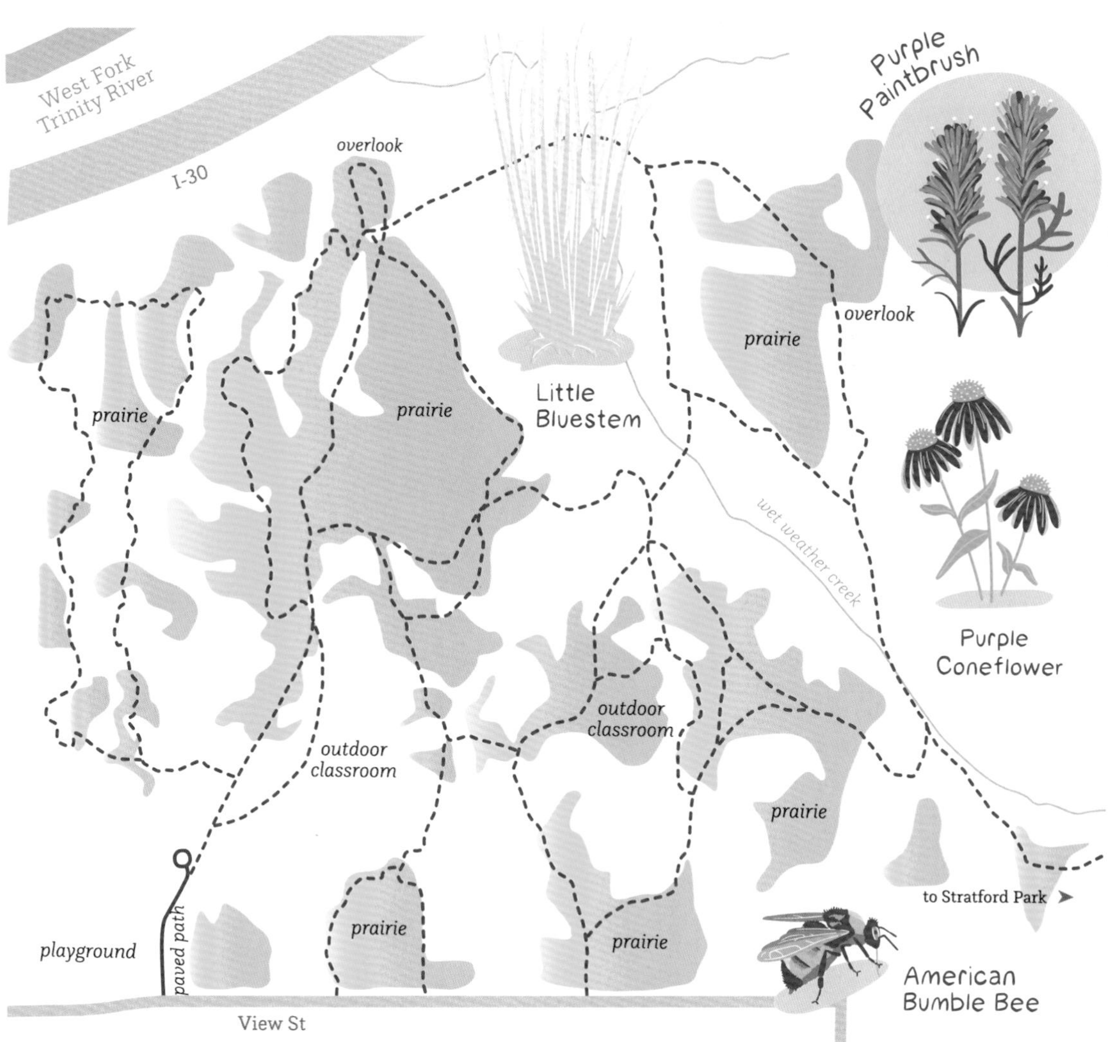

WHERE: 3325 View St, Fort Worth, TX 76103. East Fort Worth, near I-30 and Oakland Blvd.
PARKING: On street.
TRAILS: Dirt 4 miles. Detailed map at tandyhills.org.
DIFFICULTY: Moderate to challenging.
FACILITIES: None.
NEARBY: O. S. Gray Natural Area, Stella Rowan Prairie.

Don Young doesn't seem like a warrior: middle aged, long silver hair, wire-rim glasses, gimpy hip. But do something foolish at his beloved Tandy Hills Natural Area, like trample wildflowers for a photo shoot or set off confetti bombs for a gender-reveal party, and he'll have a strong talk with you about city regulations. Especially after party pyrotechnics twice set fire to the prairie.

"Mainly, I bore them into leaving by going on and on about what a treasure Tandy Hills is," Don says. Over past decades, he's defended the 200+ acres against illegal dumpers, off-road vehicles, and plans to frack on adjacent land. In his most recent success, Friends of Tandy Hills (FOTHNA), a group he cofounded, instigated Fort Worth's acquisition of fifty acres on adjacent Broadcast Hill, aided by the Trust for Public Land.

Joining us upfront at Tandy Hills is Carly Aulicky, North Texas Director of Outreach and Stewardship for Native Prairie Association of Texas, and Don's wife, artist Debora Young. Nearby, a mother kneels next to her small child and they look intently at a wildflower. She reads from a brochure and they look at the flower with renewed purpose. Debora gasps, "Look, they're using a Kids on the Prairie field guide," an educational booklet she illustrated.

Don's been visiting these hills interspersed by steeply folded rifts since he was eighteen. The neglected municipal land with epic views was perfect for teenage mischief but also communing with nature. Illegal dumpers, ATVs, and dirt bikers inflicted significant damage. Don bought a house across from the land with Debora. After long hours as a stained-glass artist, he found solace walking Tandy Hills' wooded ravines and prairie meadows.

Wild About Flowers

Our merry group heads into the Wildflower Loop trail through the front meadow into a sea of purple paintbrush that's shockingly fuchsia. Delicate lavender-blue Engelmann's sage, a Fort Worth Prairie endemic, somehow blends with it. A mound of green milkweed thrives in the midst, its large beige umbels standing out among the colors. A quick breeze skims the high limestone bluff on this warm spring afternoon. A Cooper's hawk rides it in pursuit of a songbird.

Another pastoral prairie spot thrives on a limestone bluff topped with a smear of soil. Don excitedly points out the petite, white prairie rose, the only native white rose in North America. With its long spiky leaves and five-foot stem of waxy ivory blooms, Arkansas yucca contrasts with the low gentle mounds of Engelmann's sage. The flanking ravine drops off sharply, allowing an expansive view to the west. How many others over thousands of years have stood here among the flowers?

▲ Visitors from Indigenous communities and pioneers to present-day hikers have watched the west unfurl from this spot at Tandy.

Prairies for Pollinators and People

Spittlebug nymphs are active, adorning nearly every plant before us in globules of white foam produced by sucking the juices from stems. A brawny inland ceanothus, also known as Jersey tea or prairie redroot, rises above the foam, thrusting round red clusters of unique triangular seedheads. The root aids coughs and respiratory ailments, and the frothy white blooms have enough saponins to be used as soap. A nine-banded armadillo appears to have rooted for grubs in the shady, moist soil beneath the shrubby plant.

Friends of Tandy Hills volunteers work with the city to implement long-term plans of habitat restoration and prairie preservation with monthly and seasonal workdays. Fun events include monthly star-watching parties, annual trout lily walks, a New Year's Day Manly Men Wild Women Hike, and (for ten years) Prairie Fest.

We scramble down a slope and cross a gentle prairie vale into a Carolina chickadee melee. Hundreds of tiny gray birds with natty black caps sing clear tones in simple, fast phrases, often in sets of three or four that syncopate. The vale is being encroached by young trees that will have to go. Maintaining a prairie habitat means constantly cutting back woody plants to slopes and ravines where wildfire historically would have contained them.

▲ The sun sets on a hilltop of prairie bishop and firewheels.

Emerging from the trees, we head to Barbara's Button Hill. So many of the delicate swirling white globes on tall leafless stalks grow here that "in a couple of weeks it's going to look like a starry night," says Debora. The hill will be redolent with an intoxicating floral vanilla aroma. Native bees treasure the blooms' profuse nectar. Orange tags in the trees indicate where S & S Trail Services will be rerouting the trail to reduce erosion and provide a better view of the hill, thanks to a Texas Parks and Wildlife grant.

The Low Woods

We connect to Hawk Trail, which makes a U around Tandy Hills' perimeter, cresting over prairie ridges (land of red-tailed hawks) and diving into riparian woods ridges (home to red-shouldered hawks). Trees shift from the tenacious, scrappy Buckley's and Texas live oaks to towering red and bur oaks nurtured by a seep-fed creek.

The damp shade instantly cools on this warm afternoon. Carly, our New Jersey import, is grateful. "Tandy Hills gets its reputation from the meadows, but this is an important part of it, too," says Don, "where most of our wildlife is." Damp soil features plenty of raccoon tracks with striking hand-like shapes and a few splayed-toe ones from opossums. It's easy to imagine bobcats snoozing on the big oak limbs and coyotes napping in the understory brush.

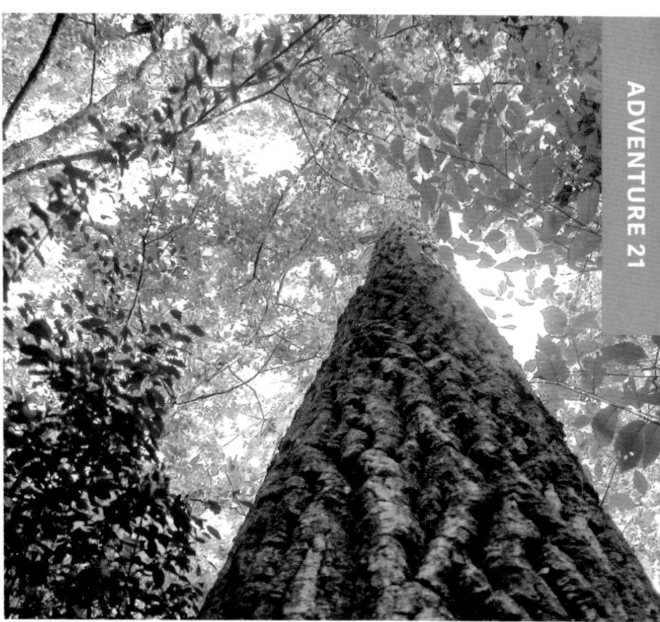

▲ Tandy's riparian areas rival its meadows.

◄ Some trees in the riparian corridor are over a century old.

The shaded limestone slopes produce thriving populations of trout lilies, attracting hundreds each year to celebrate the harbinger of spring. The layers of leaf litter provide excellent slithering opportunities for DeKay's brown snake and rough earth snake, along with plenty of little brown skinks.

Healing the Land

We emerge from the woods to topside prairie, its wildflowers in a spectrum of hues, and the view is enthralling. Fort Worth skyscrapers glint in the distant west. A broad and deep ravine spreads at our feet. "An old road led here and people had been dumping for fifty years. We hauled out hundreds of tires, big piles of glass and auto parts, tons of roofing shingles," says Don, referring to FOTHNA volunteers. "That's all we did for the first few years. Now we're shifting to habitat restoration."

Walking the Sunset Trail, on the ravine's western slope, robust trees belie its trashy past. Pocket prairies in slope undulations where soil gathers foster deep-rooted prairie grasses like big bluestem and Indiangrass and robust forbs like purple coneflowers. Autumn foliage views from this trail are considered delightful. S & S Trail Services will be rerouting this trail for reduced erosion and improved vistas.

Prairie Notes is a monthly photo journal from Tandy Hills of field reports, flora, and fauna sightings, woven with dry humor and dollops of philosophy created by Don Young.

◄ Wildflowers grow spectacularly thick at Tandy.

Preserving the Prairie

Back up topside on Hawk Trail again, we stop for one last western view, showcasing a grand panorama to Tandy Hills western forest with this season's mix of purple paintbrush, Englemann's sage, and various small yellow blooms. It's perfect—and thoroughly trashed with hundreds of tiny red pieces of metallic confetti. Closer inspection reveals swaths of crushed flowers that won't be creating seed for next year's blooms.

Skirting the front meadow, we pass through thirty square yards or so of shredded brush and trees. What looks like devastation is actually rebirth. "We were losing the meadow to brush encroachment. The parks department reduced it to mulch in one afternoon," says Don. After letting the debris decompose over the summer, volunteers will seed it with locally harvested native grass and wildflower seed come fall.

Homeward Bound

After a couple miles of exploration, my sore muscles remind me of how Tandy Hills earned its name and Don's hip is ready for a rest. New Jersey native Carly melted long ago. "The purpose of Tandy Hills is to make people happy," says Don. And also to make your legs strong.

The sun descends into the west, shadows grow long. The wildflowers for which Tandy Hills is famous attract pollinators and other flying insects which lure in a plethora of birds. An aerial ballet forms above our heads, the tubular chimney swifts powering through while the more aerodynamic barn swallows swoop around them.

A rare prairie remnant preserved with wildflowers that bring joy to generations. Woods that foster wildlife and provide a summer retreat. Open space available in the shadow of an interstate, countering tainted urban air. A place for children to learn the lessons of the earth. "Never doubt that a small group of thoughtful, committed citizens can change the world," said Margaret Mead. "Indeed, it's the only thing that ever has."

ADVENTURE 22

WEST AND CLEAR FORKS OF THE TRINITY

Fort Worth Nature Center & Refuge

A 3621-acre nature preserve flanking northern Lake Worth that captures a sense of the land in pioneer times with bison on prairies. Miles of water frontage and a wide variety of terrain.

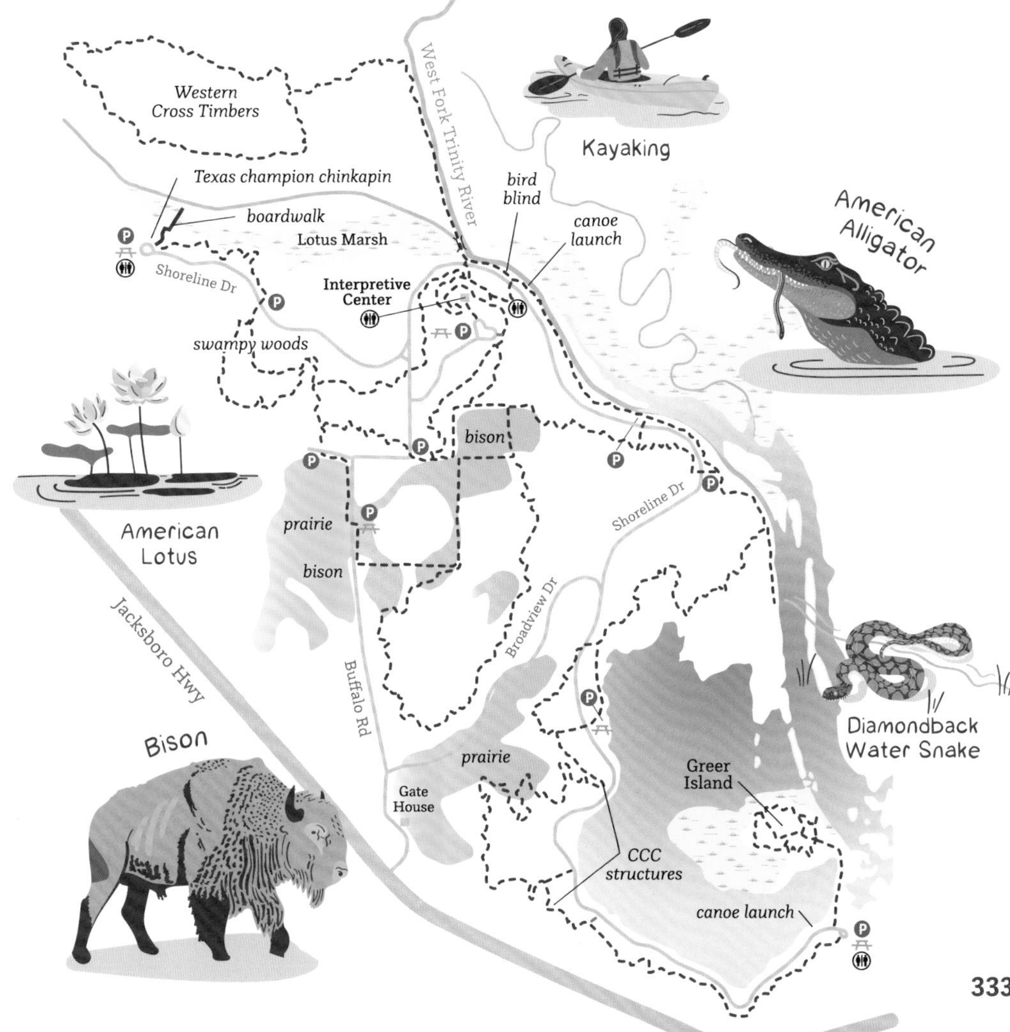

WHERE: 9601 Fossil Ridge Road Fort Worth, TX 76135. Northwest Fort Worth, south of Eagle Mountain Lake.
PARKING: Paved and gravel lots.
TRAILS: Dirt 20+ miles, paved or boardwalk 0.37 miles. Detailed map at fwnaturecenter.org.
DIFFICULTY: Easy to challenging.
FACILITIES: Restrooms at visitor center, composting and chemical toilets at Big River Canoe Launch, Marsh Boardwalk, and Greer Island parking lots.
COST: $6, discounts for children, seniors, military; $1 fee per dog.
NEARBY: Eagle Mountain Park, James K. Allen Nature Trail, Marion Sansom Park.

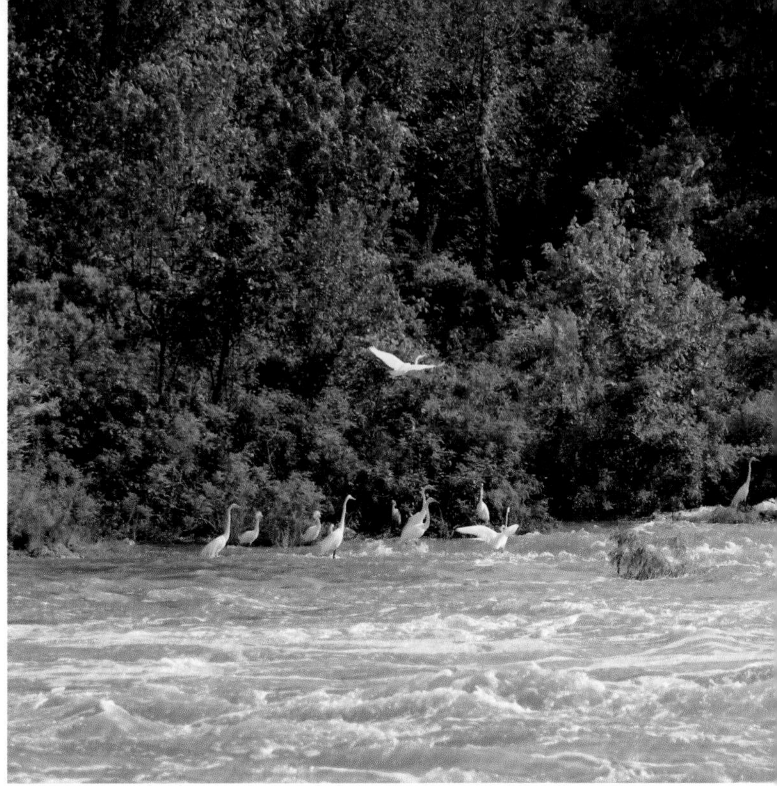

▲ Great egrets search for fish stunned by raging floodwaters.

In centuries past, herds of bison roamed the Fort Worth Prairie, causing roadrunners to scatter as they passed. Alligators swam the West Fork. Western Cross Timbers post oaks grew strong, reaching into the wide-open sky. Fort Worth Nature Center and Refuge (FWNCR) preserves all this and more. Oyster-like shellfish ninety to 120 million years old form limestone ridges. The US Department of the Interior designated FWNCR a National Natural Landmark.

Riverbottom Woods

Kate Morgan is working in a large greenhouse as I walk up. Raising native plants is her volunteer role in the Fort Worth Nature Center Natural Guard. Compared to her previous life as a high-energy physicist, it's relaxing work. Before we hike, she shows me a nearby post oak more than 250 years old. It soars, which few post oaks do, its massive trunk rising from the slope of

> "The refuge is 3600 acres and at flood times over 1200 acres is under several feet of water. You can't put a value on the refuge retaining that and letting it out slowly to keep Fort Worth, Arlington, and Dallas from flooding."
>
> —*FWNCR director Rob Denkhaus*

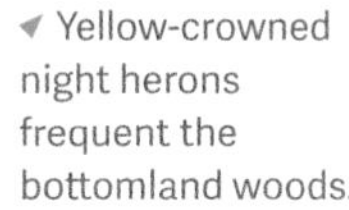

◀ Yellow-crowned night herons frequent the bottomland woods.

a draw. Leafless in late winter, it's pure sculptural majesty.

We start on the Wild Plum Trail and pass a pair of towering post oaks in the 200-year-old range that Kate calls The Sentinels, encountering another equally aged pair called The Sisters, plus an enormous escarpment live oak that schoolchildren liberated from privet.

Over 95 percent of known animal species are invertebrates which lack a spinal column, including insects, spiders, crustaceans, mollusks, and various aquatic creatures.

Reaching the Riverbottom Trail, things start to get wet. As Kate ferrets out a route, my imagination runs wild. At its spring peak, thousands of crawfish, crustaceans, and other water-loving invertebrates, along with amphibians, creep in the rich mire. Small herons—green, yellow-crowned night, black-crowned night, and more—stalk the water for a meal. Armadillos shuffle about for crustaceans. At night come the opossums, raccoons, and barred owls.

Water Wonderland

An expert hiker, Kate gets us back on track, past a huge bur oak with a basketball-sized squirrel nest and through a prairie parcel with tiny low wildflowers amid grasses starting to green. We cross Shoreline Road into drier forests. Rusty blackhaw viburnum is charming, their peppercorn-sized green flower buds ready to burst. The sweet, light aroma of Texas buckeyes in bloom wafts across the trail, entwining with Carolina wrens' whistling triplets.

Our path joins the brief paved Boardwalk Trail that starts from a lovely picnic area and parking lot, allowing the mobility impaired to enjoy the Lotus Marsh's beauty. We take a side trip to see its massive chinkapin oak listed on

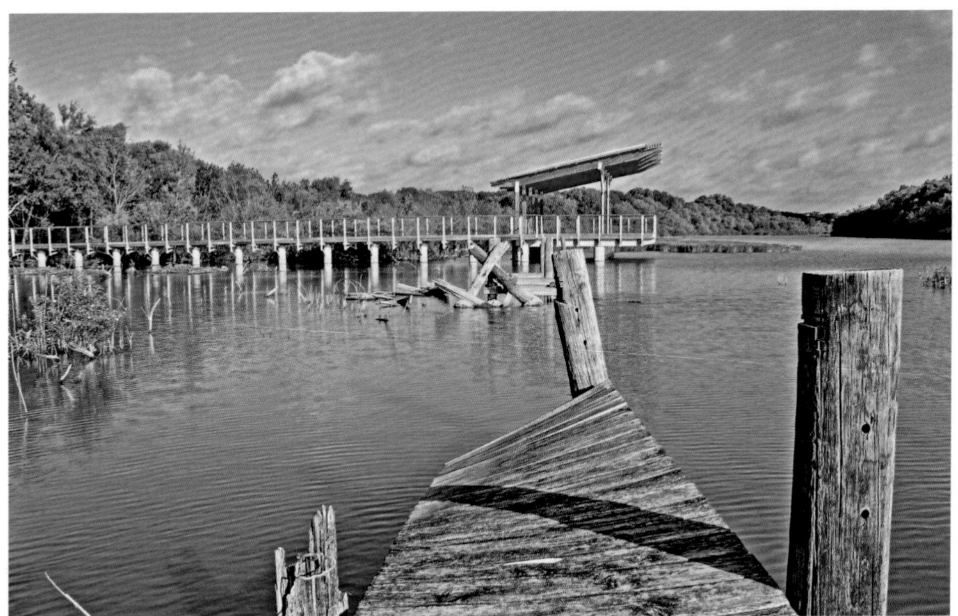

▲ A new boardwalk and shade structure rise beyond the ruins of the old.

> Twice weekly, Fort Worth Nature Center Natural Guard volunteers gather to help with trail maintenance, invasive species removal, greenhouse operations, brush management, construction projects, bison management, and more.

the state's historic tree registry, then amble down to the river's edge and on to the gleaming gray metal and wood Marsh Boardwalk.

We pass large chaotic buttonbushes, their seed balls still dangling, en route to the covered deck. Kate points out half-sunk remains of the prior boardwalk, destroyed in 2015 floods. Winter snow geese visitors have already departed north. In a month, migrators from the south will be passing through, creating what local bird legend Charley Amos calls "an insane amount of bird action."

By July, large, waxy, light-yellow blooms of American lotus will be everywhere. Various arrowheads—delta, grass-leaved, and broadleaf—blend with swamp smartweed's tangled floating leaves and spikes of teeny rose-pink blooms. Vast swaths of common reed hold the shore, sheltering northern cottonmouths, diamondback and plain-bellied water snakes. American alligators lurk in the water. Listen then for the unmistakable jazzy cackle of pileated woodpeckers, "one of the few places around where they are pretty reliable," maintains Amos.

▲ A pair of American alligators lurk in Lake Worth.

A Forest Beyond

Kate and I hoof it to the refuge's less frequented northern section. We pick our way along the wet, low dike separating Lotus Marsh from an engineered channel of the West Fork, where we hope to spy some of the refuge's American alligators. But there are only fishermen in boats today amid red sliders and river cooters perched on half-sunk logs. Wildflowers coating the sunny channel-side trail are putting on buds.

The impounding of Eagle Mountain Lake upriver in the early 1930s changed the West Fork's course. Outflow from the reservoir creates large sloughs that foster the wildness of the refuge's northern woods where ring-tailed cats and swamp rabbits live.

We turn onto the Crosstimbers Trail, a nearly four-mile loop through Western Cross Timbers. The twisting post and blackjack oak limbs cast lacey shadows on this bright, late-winter day. Far from roads, the open forest has an intense quiet, amazingly pure air, and several centuries-old trees.

Appreciating the trail takes subtlety. As we leave the channel behind and the trail rises, the bottomland dirt gives way to Cross Timbers' sandy soil and the flora adapts. The trail's south section swings close to Lotus Marsh and the soil changes again. Decomposing logs abound, covered in orange and gray lichen and brilliant green mosses.

Crosstimbers Trail passes through a large grove of possumhaw holly, leaves not yet emerging from slender gray branches, its small, red berries long ago stripped by birds. A common five-lined skink zips through fallen

▲ Pale yucca favors the Western Cross Timbers.

leaves. If threatened, it might drop a tail section that remains twitching to distract pursuers.

A bench beckons after a morning of brisk hiking. My feet are emphatic they're done for the day. Kate, who at 70 is more fit than most 30-year-olds, suggests that we return someday to explore sunny prairie openings up ahead with pale and Glen Rose yucca, where Rio Grande wild turkeys wander in search of grasshoppers. We'll look for plains pocket gophers flinging dirt in search of roots and see males get distracted in territorial fights while hidden bobcats carefully watch.

Spend a Day or More

At over 3600 acres, the refuge requires days to fully explore. Orient yourself first by driving slowly on the entry Buffalo Road, looking for the refuge's bison herd beyond tall fences, often resting in the shade. Then motor the four miles of Shoreline Drive from Marsh Boardwalk to Greer Island, noting Lake Worth on one side and a steep limestone ridge on the other.

"There are eight families of soils in Tarrant County and all are found on these acres, which is why we have such diversity."

—Rob Denkhaus, FWNCR director

Near the Hardwicke Interpretive Visitor Center, try the short but strenuous Caprock Trail along an adjacent fossil-shell outcrop with impressive views. Or go for the brief, paved Limestone Ledge Trail and its grand gum bumelias, whose bark was once processed by Native Americans for chewing gum.

▲ The West Fork at the refuge is serene.

◂ Rest with beautiful views on the Canyon Ridge Trail.

The Civilian Conservation Corps, the most popular of New Deal work-relief programs in the 1930s, employed three-million young men in construction projects during its decade-long existence.

In spring and fall, explore FWNCR's sweeping sunny grasslands on the Prairie Trail loop. Continue to the Oak Motte Trail through a fine example of Cross Timbers savannah for a three-mile course that promises to be abundant with wildflowers. Enjoy the aerial acrobatics of the scissor-tailed flycatcher, with its absurdly long forked tail and bold salmon belly, and western and eastern kingbirds that hunt like fighter pilots for flying insects.

Canyon Ridge Trail is a rocky six-and-a-half mile round-trip that rises to vista views, then dives into fierce gullies, dotted with the 1930s structures by the Civilian Conservation Corps. With little fear of humans, white-tailed deer are easy to see browsing on young saplings, doing their part to keep the forest from being overgrown.

Get up close to Lake Worth at Greer Island, where the refuge began and noted botanist Bob O'Kennon discovered a new beetle species. Connected to the shore by a buttonbush and black willow–lined dike, find a shore spot to watch kayakers and canoeists ply the quiet waters, winding through bobbing flotillas of waterfowl as flocks of white pelicans sail wind currents overhead.

ADVENTURE 23

WEST AND CLEAR FORKS OF THE TRINITY

Sid Richardson Tract Prairie

Step back in time to when Fort Worth was called "Queen of the Prairie" at a historic prairie remnant on the east side of Benbrook Lake.

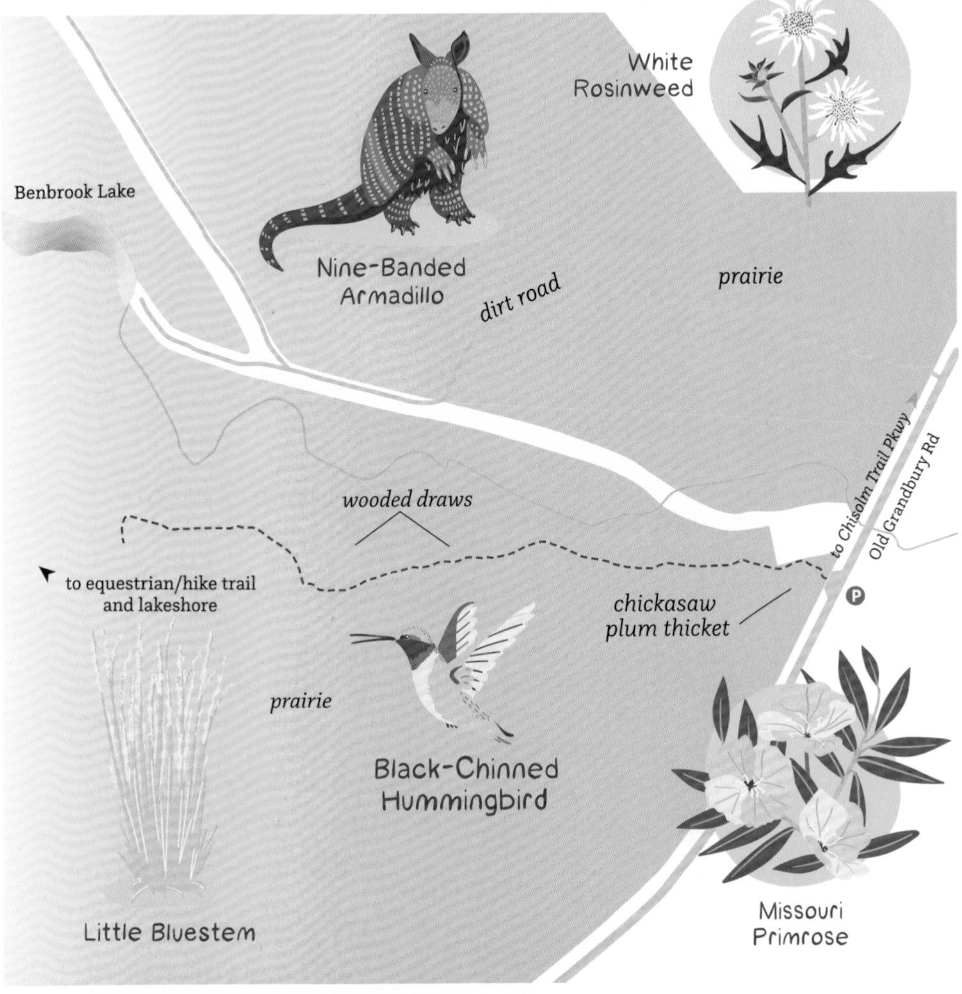

▲ In the prairie, the sky is half the landscape.

WHERE: 8032 Old Granbury Road, Crowley, TX 76036. Southwest Fort Worth, off Chisholm Trail Pkwy.
PARKING: Gravel lot.
TRAILS: Dirt 2 miles.
DIFFICULTY: Moderate.
FACILITIES: None.
NEARBY: Chisholm Trail Community Park, Oakmont Park, Rocky Creek Park.

When cattle by the thousands plodded past this spot along East Dutch Creek, known by Native Americans and settlers for its restorative seeps and shady vales, there were no reservoirs or railroads. Just the Wild West town of Fort Worth far away on the bluffs, where the Clear and West Forks meet, the Queen of the Prairie.

The rolling terrain before us is a rare slice of Fort Worth Prairie, what remains after most of the queen's prairie was plowed for progress. But these craggy hills were best situated for cattle accustomed to drought-hearty native fare. When the US Army Corps of Engineers (USACE) created Benbrook Lake in the '50s for flood control, large swaths of non-inundated virgin prairie ended up in their hands.

Prairie activists have long lobbied for maintaining the land as rare remnants. In the early 2020s, the Great Plains Restoration Council (GPRC) gained permission from USACE to manage the prairie by controlling invasives and pushing back brush encroachment. GPRC's vision is to engage adjoining landowners and expand the protected area to create Fort Worth Prairie Park.

Eternal Springtime Flowers

Suzanne Tuttle, former manager of the Fort Worth Nature Center and Refuge and board member of the Fort Worth chapter of Native Prairies Association

▲ A red admiral rests on old plainsmen.

Well-drained open areas like Fort Worth Prairie are prime for infestation by invasive South American fire ants, which can inflict scores of extremely painful bites. Always scan where you stand.

of Texas (NPAT), knows these 717 acres better than anyone. On this spring day, she's guiding me, fellow board member Jo Ann Thomas Collins, and Carly Aulicky, NPAT's North Texas Director of Outreach and Stewardship, in a prairie exploration on a glorious spring morning, sunny and cool beneath a cloudless sky.

The land slopes to a riparian corridor, and the trail rolls up and down gentle furrows carved by rain heading to the creek. Most soil in the Fort Worth Prairie is shallow and erosion-prone yet grows fantastic wildflowers, from the purple prairie verbena down low to the tall, white filigree flowers of roadside gaura and in between a plethora of native grasses in every shade of green.

Rather than waves of grass, little bluestem grows in discrete bunches. Between them thrive scattered wildflowers. The open spaces allow the modest rainfall to thoroughly soak and give young grassland birds and rodents areas to scamper. Snakes and armadillos like it, too. Being a bunchgrass, little bluestem withers under regular mowing, indicating this prairie's not been hayed or overgrazed.

Some tall showstoppers get our attention. A Texas thistle boasts a bold magenta flower beloved by bumblebees and painted lady butterflies. Unlike nonnative thistles, it doesn't dominate to the detriment of other plants. Prairie parsley radiates with large, succulent, deeply lobed leaves jutting from a celery-like stalk topped by a giant umbel of lemon flowers. A Drummond's

▲ Prairie verbena flourishes in challenging conditions.

◀ White rosinweed lives for decades and grows only in a small area of Texas.

skullcap finds a protected place at its base. Its purple trumpet flowers have spotted interiors to lure pollinators.

The dynamic Fort Worth chapter of Native Prairies Association of Texas advocates for prairie preservation through the Prairie Seekers training course, field trips, meetings, and more.

Lessons of the Land

Shadows race across the prairie. We look up at two pairs of black vultures flying low in search of food. Above them, a much smaller Mississippi kite works the updrafts, swiftly cutting steep arcs across the sky. Bursts of dynamically lilting birdsong with sections of buzzing emit from a small copse on the prairie. Carly, an ornithologist, identifies it as a white-eyed vireo expressing concern at our presence. Duly noted, we carry on briskly.

Suzanne notices lacey Barbara's buttons growing in one of the prairie's gentle folds, slightly lusher than other rain gullies. "If you find these there's probably a seep somewhere," Suzanne says. "See where that break in the hill is? Water's probably seeping from there. Yes, you can see the furrow it's created." A subtle parting of the plants a bit greener than the rest sprawls into a delta. Signs like this meant life or death to Native Americans and explorers in this arid land.

Within yards of this verdant swath lies a prairie barrens: a wisp of humus over well-drained limestone. Jo Ann exclaims, "When we get over here where the soil is the shallowest, we see the most species!" A carpet of low, intensely yellow four-nerve daisy is dotted by bold magenta standing

▼ Prairie diversity supports wildlife.

▲ Late spring brings abundant firewheels.

winecup, purple spires of Indian paintbrush, and soft pink evening primrose—perfectly complementing colors. Surely the color wheel maker used prairies for inspiration.

We move "at the speed of botany," as Suzanne terms it. Fifteen minutes spent on an area a few dozen yards square. She finds a huge, silvery dried leaf of last year's white rosinweed, then another and another. The abundance enthralls us. "It dies back to the ground completely every winter, comes up from roots which are fourteen feet deep," says Suzanne. "A very narrow range endemic, it only grows in a fifteen- to twenty-county area in Texas, indicating this is a very high-quality prairie."

A Prairie Beyond Time

There is holiness to this land being just as it was created. It's an intricate web of relationships between plants and wildlife and the soil that arises from slowly eroding limestone. The flora makes the most of the life it's been given, producing beauty and sustenance in return: pollen for bees, nectar for hummingbirds and butterflies, seeds for mammals and birds, and nourishment for insects and spiders that feed the birds.

The landscape invites close examination. "You could put a hula hoop out here and spend an hour just studying everything inside of it, so many species per square yard," says Suzanne. "And that hula hoop will change over the year, from cool season to warm. The palette will be different every week. Plants will tell you everything you need to know if you just look."

The farther we travel, the more it becomes a landscape unchanged for eons. Grasses move like water in the strong wind, setting the prairie in constant motion, like it's flowing. We crest a hill and notice how soil accumulates as we go down the slope, allowing big bluestem and Indiangrass to thrive, accentuated with the gray-green leaves and butterscotch blossoms of Englemann's daisy. Last year's thistle-like remains of eryngo gleam bronze in the sunlight.

The gully at the bottom is shady with cedar elms and bois d'arcs. A small stream flows through the base. It is chilly to touch, indicating it's from a seep

◂ Barbara's buttons thrive in a gentle seep.

rather than rainwater runoff. The vale is noticeably cool, a perfect place to camp. "Overgrazing by livestock ruined much of Fort Worth Prairie hydrology," says Suzanne. "This area used to be very rich with springs."

As we rise from the gully, the present world disappears. There's no sign of civilization, no poles, no lines, nothing but the barest wisp of a path. The prairie bursts into yellow Berlandier's sundrops, four-nerve daisies, and Engelmann's daisies, accented by Berlandier's flax with its large, waxy, burnt-orange flowers and fluted butterscotch tips.

Trail's End, Prairie Beginning

Carly scans for the painted buntings we can hear, but not see, somewhere in the scattered trees they favor. A nighthawk flies above us, beautiful curved, pointy wings with white stripes on the underside, searching for insects the prairie so bountifully provides. We move into a thicket of post oaks and mesquite, and the trail peters out. Rather than seek out the equestrian trail to Benbrook Lake, we return to the prairie.

It's always wistful to turn back after a rewarding hike, all good things coming to an end, but the trail provides new views approached from the opposite direction. Suzanne points out the fence line marking land owned by the Sid Richardson Foundation. A good neighbor, they are preserving their prairie through conservation ranching practices and regular prescribed burns.

Walking back in reflective quiet, we come over a rise. A sprawling housing development across from the prairie entrance dominates the horizon. The realization stops me in shock. It used to all be like what we just trod though, its flora and fauna, history and heritage, now gone forever. It makes this day on the prairie more precious than before, deepening my gratitude for those who embrace conservation.

Reaching the roadside parking lot, it delights us to encounter Jarid Manos, director of GPRC. He is preparing to take a couple of prairie newbies and potential benefactors on the trail, sharing the dream that the Queen of the Prairie might reign over her domain once again.

ADVENTURE 24

WEST AND CLEAR FORKS OF THE TRINITY

Trinity River Float Trip

Intimate exploration of the Trinity in kayaks and canoes includes a stop for play and exploration at a gravel bar.

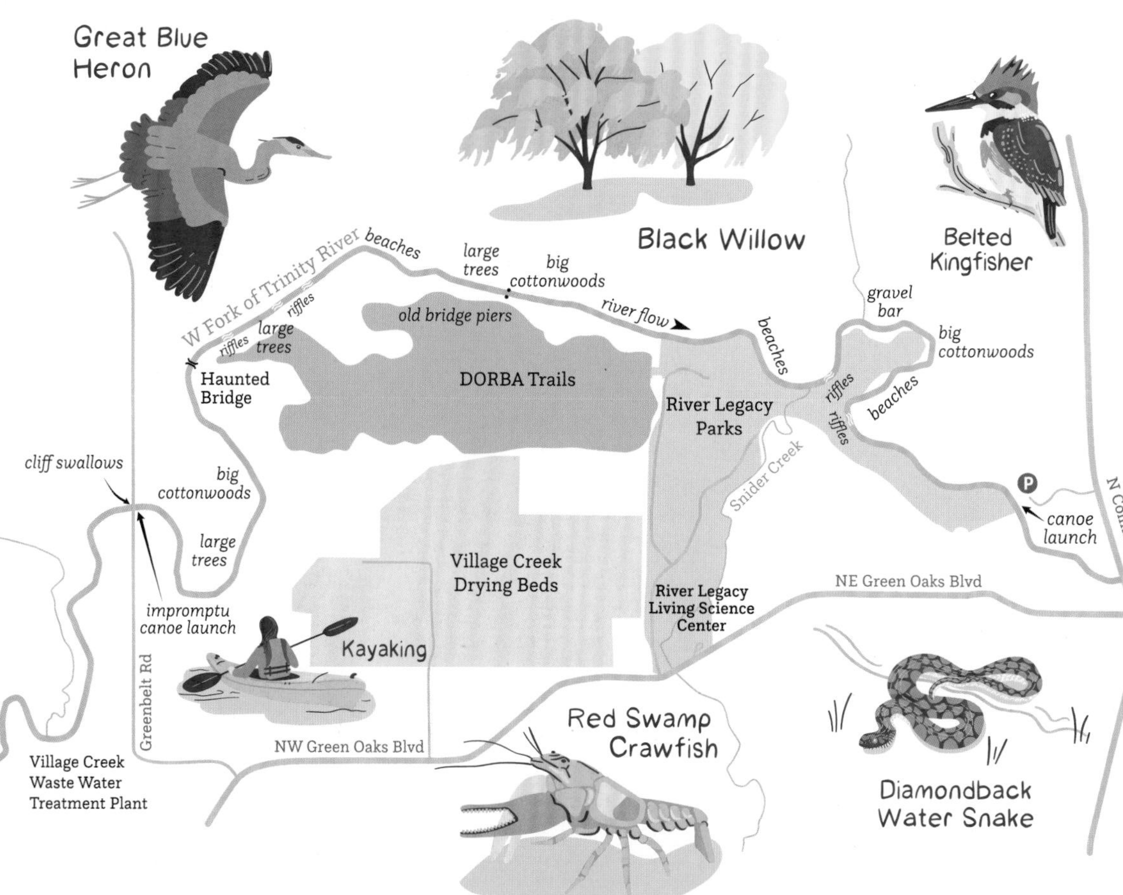

ADVENTURE 24

▲ Willow-shaded gravel bar on the West Fork, perfect for float breaks.

Rich Grayson of Texas Rivers Protection Association has been on the water since he was ten, floating down his childhood creek on a raft concocted by strapping together anything that would float: "It's a wonder I lived past twelve years old." He's gathered three longtime pals called the Strokers to scope out the river for a future trip.

WHERE: North Arlington, near River Legacy Parks.
PARKING: Paved lot.
DIFFICULTY: Challenging.
FACILITIES: None.
NEARBY: O. S. Gray Natural Area, Village Creek Natural Area.

I'm along for the float, confident of my company. The Strokers have over two hundred years of combined river experience. Rich, Ray Foster, and Carey Newton all learned to canoe around age twelve in Boy Scouts. Randy Stovall didn't start until his thirties. I've been floating for a year, which is why everyone but me packed a dry bag for securing valuables like phones.

Rivers can be challenging to paddle if inexperienced. Start out on paddle trails in contained water like Lake Worth at Fort Worth Nature Center and Refuge and the wetlands at Heard Natural Science Museum and Wildlife Sanctuary and Lewisville Lake Environmental Learning Area.

▲ A great blue heron follows the floaters.

We're floating an underrated section of the West Fork in Arlington with wonderfully wooded views and wide gravel banks perfect for lounging around. The river retains some of its original meanders, and broad shoals create chutes and gentle rapids called riffles that floaters find fun.

To avoid having to paddle back upstream, our cars are at the River Legacy East and Charles Allen of Trinity River Expeditions, a fellow Stroker, is shuttling us to the canoe put-in. Sporting a long white ponytail and laconic drawl, Charles is a river seer with fifty-eight years of float time, much of it on the Trinity. Everybody pitches in to load up.

For your first float trip on a river, try the Clear Fork, upper Elm leading to Denton Creek, or the lower Elm near Frasier Dam Recreation Area, which are all calm and easy. Trinity Coalition's website outlines load in and take out points, describes river segments, and features easy-to-read water gauges.

On the Water

We put in on public land underneath a thoroughfare bridge. Charles sets up a rope hoist for boats and humans to traverse a steep grassy slope. Rich and I slide in first and enjoy an aerial ballet by cliff swallows above us. Thousands of cars pass daily overhead and never know the swallows are there. Paddlers see the world from underneath.

Once all boats are on the water, we ready our paddles. Rich, who's guiding the canoe, zips to the front. "First boat effect," Rich says. "We'll see the best wildlife this way. Take it quiet." We look for beaver gnaws on riverside trees and slickened river otter slides on the banks, but find only signs of wild hogs digging on the shores, never a good thing.

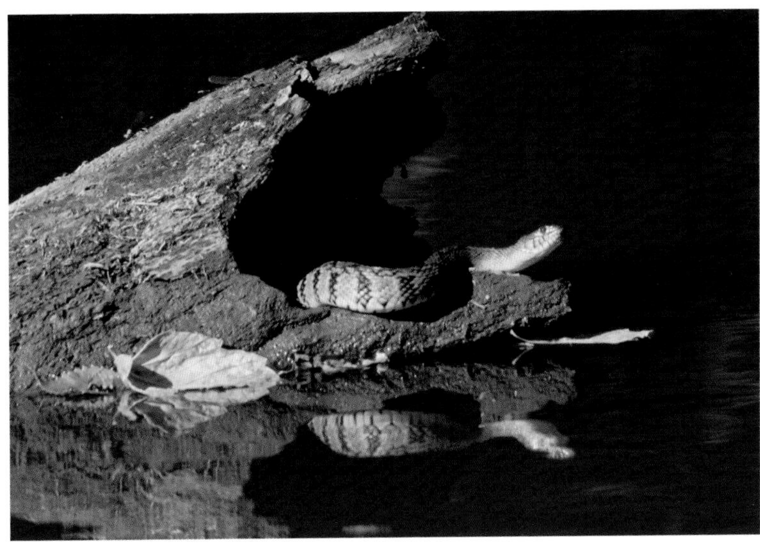

► A diamondback water snake watches as we paddle by.

Birds are a constant, though, and announce us with song. Songbirds thrive in riparian corridors with more abundant moisture and lusher plant life. A mallard pair rises with a noisy flapping, wheels around, and lands behind our boats, attracted by fish we stir up.

Rivers are conduits of geology and history. Carey signals us over to the side: "See these broken white lines here? That's a midden, where early Native Americans would toss old pottery." The midden was high up the bank on an inner curve, safe from flood waters. Farther down, a bare bank shows twisting striations where decades of roaring flood currents have scoured the bank.

Fun on the River

Spirits rise as the river runs. The Strokers' laughter, their recounting prior river adventures and floods, rebounds within the channel banks. Randy shares a favorite cartoon: "A reporter talking to a guy said, "You have eighteen kayaks. How did that happen?" Well, the guy said, "I sold three of them."

The water level in this stretch stays consistent due to over one hundred million gallons of treated effluent released per day from the Village Creek Municipal Wastewater Treatment. It meets Clean Water Act standards of 99 percent clean.

We pull our canoe over and Rich, a leader in the Texas Stream Team citizen monitoring group, tests for

Safe river floating takes an understanding of water hazards like underwater shoals and shallow rocky stretches as well as monitoring water levels and velocity. Always be aware of upstream weather conditions that can create flash floods.

▲ Huge bur oaks line the river.

E. coli bacteria from animal feces and other sources. Each time he will find the level acceptable for swimming.

Rich calls us to cease paddling, stop yakking, and experience the river. I feel the give and take of downstream currents beneath the boat pushing against prevailing winds in the opposite direction. We still drift forward, but it's a tango. My ballcap flies off. Everyone else's hats have cords. The things you learn.

A great blue heron hides in a fallen tree, curious about us and we're curious about it. A kingfisher emits its rasping rattle as it swoops across the river, hoping to spear a fish with its enormous beak. Occasional lines of bubbles from submerged turtles, catfish, and carp rise to the water surface.

To our right is one of the River Legacy Parks. To our left, an industrial district and municipal waste operations. Yet we hear nothing but birds and the fluid chatter of oars dipping in water.

Oneness with the Water

Rich found canoe pals in college: "Everybody else was partying in town. We were on the river." They'd stop on a sandbar and pile out with canned beer in coolers and tubs of food. Somebody always had a guitar. "Maybe it was the freedom of going someplace that was unrestricted, the feeling of freedom of moving on water," says Rich.

A flotilla of water striders atop skinny splayed legs floats by. Rich calls them "Jesus bugs." Box elders lean undulating limber branches out from the

▲ Box elders thrive on river and lake shores.

shore and their startlingly light green leaves shimmer on the water's surface. Hearty bois d'arcs arise among them, sending curved branches over the river. Massive pecans rising from the topside look like temples.

The kingfisher returns with a raucous display, moving with the speed and accuracy of a fighter pilot. Least sandpipers skim inches above the water with their strident peeps, landing in shoals with micro splashes. A great blue heron that's been playing tag with us meets up with a pal.

"If you are lucky and reverent, and hush for a moment the doubts in your head, sometimes God will whisper in your ear.... You notice. And noticing, you live."

—John Graves,
Goodbye to a River

Party at the Gravel Bar

In a deep river bend, the large gravel bar that Charles told us about comes into view. It just screams play. We pull ashore and scramble out, our inner kids awakened by this semisecret place of rocks and sand pushed to the riverside. A large black willow, pushed horizontal by flood currents, is covered in long fluffy, light-green catkins. We gather around it sharing tales and snacks.

I check out the gravel, a mix of river-polished stones, sandstone chunks, and limestone fossils, blended with odd clumps of asphalt, broken tiles, concrete lumps, bits of rebar, and various engine parts. The insides of bivalve shells glint alabaster in the sunlight. Rich picks up a slim, polished rock. With a gleam in his eye, he skips it four times across the water surface. "You only

▲ Our riverside cafe.

Knowing some basic strokes and float techniques before getting on the water can save a lot of energy and possibly prevent a dunking. Seek hands-on instruction from American Canoe Association certified teachers through outfitters or equipment retailers.

do that once," he says with a laugh. "Not gonna push my luck."

He finds the remains of a hellgrammite, the dark, spiny, fiercely jawed dobsonfly larvae: "It's an indicator of good water quality." Hellgrammites are top predators in shallow waters and look the part. Dobsonfly eggs hatch only at night. The infinitesimal hellgrammites grab air bubbles and float to rocky breeding areas.

We head to shallow pools in the gravel bar. Dragonflies hover above the surface and inject eggs into the water with a quick series of dips. Mud dauber wasps busily collect mud for nests. Carey wanders up: "Oh, my grandkid would love this."

The West Fork has it all, carved from earth, framed by sky, ever going by, always and never the same, bound for union with the Gulf of Mexico. Charles is waiting for us back at River Legacy and it's time to get back on the river and return to reality.

ADVENTURE 25

WEST AND CLEAR FORKS OF THE TRINITY

Village Creek Drying Beds and River Legacy Parks

A retired water-treatment facility serves as a haven for wetland birds and a variety of wildlife. An adjacent park provides wooded trails, river access, and a superb science center for children.

WHERE: 1439 NW Green Oaks Blvd, Arlington, TX 76006. North Arlington off the West Fork of the Trinity.
PARKING: Gravel lot.
TRAILS: Dirt 5 miles.
DIFFICULTY: Moderate.
FACILITIES: None.
NEARBY: Village Creek Historical Area, Crystal Canyon Natural Area, River Legacy East Park, Village Creek Historical Area.

Village Creek Drying Beds

Great Egret

Box Elder

P

Wood Duck

Black Willow

to N Collins St ➤

NW Green Oaks Blvd

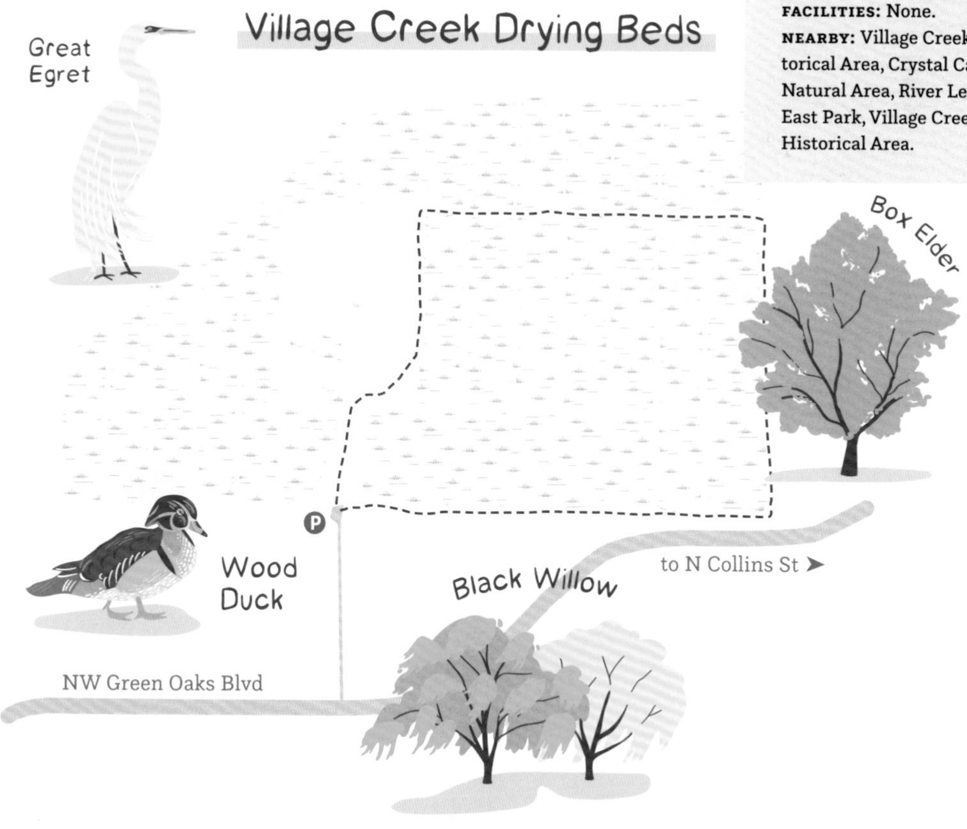

▲ Morning fog swaddles the Village Creek wetlands.

Village Creek Drying Beds

Walking through wetlands on a warm, sunny winter morning with Zach Chapman, an enthusiastic brainiac and iNaturalist ace, we head down the center road of Village Creek Drying Beds (VCDB). The rectangular cells now filled with rain were once used as settling ponds for wastewater. Scattered black willows dot the shores and occasional sandbar islands rise from the ponds.

Fort Worth Audubon Society, known for its forums and birding hotspot list, hosts informative meetings and birdwatching field trips.

A three-mile-long earthen dike surrounds the 240-acre complex, blocking urban sounds. Once inside, it's the domain of waterfowl and shorebirds, hundreds and hundreds of them, everywhere you look. It feels like I've stepped into a lost world. Charley Amos joins us, a legend in the Fort Worth Audubon Society.

As we walk the dikes, Charley dispenses bird wisdom while Zach ticks off avian identifications. Ducks divide into dabblers, who sit high on the water and scoop up aquatic plants, and divers, who sit low so they can launch quickly underwater in pursuit of fish and frogs. The cacophony of calls reminds us that waterfowl do a lot more than quack.

Charley notes the pied-billed grebe, one of VCDB's resident divers. A nondescript gray-brown, medium-necked bird with a large, sharp beak can trap or release air in its feathers, enabling it to sink or rise like a submarine. One thing unites their varied calls: they are loud.

▲ Village Creek Drying Beds are a lost world.

► A green heron surveys for prey.

The duo points out northern shovelers, American coots, and the ever-present mallards. There are northern pintails, "known as the duck El Greco painted, "Charley says. The black-bellied whistling duck with bold white eyeliner was "called a harlot; it wears too much makeup." The big-headed bufflehead gets its name from buffalo.

I am dazzled, yet Charley says: "This was once the number one spot in all of Texas. People came from all over the world. It was not hard at all to see over 100 species of birds here in a day. Now you have to fight for 50." When the site ceased operations for wastewater treatment, water levels became erratic. Bird numbers took a nosedive.

Each cell boasts a different configuration of birds. Divers favor the deeper ponds up front. Cells with extensive cattails attract red-winged blackbirds that erupt in dissonant, otherworldly sounds like modern classical music. Dike trees provide edge habitat for indigo and painted buntings. Killdeers circle low, making their eponymous calls.

A dike road going across the cells brings us closer to wildlife. A sprawling cell with wide edges and large islands boasts plentiful shorebirds. Zach adds greater and lesser yellowlegs to his life list, two sandpiper-ish migrators. Sharp-eyed Charley spots a natty striped Wilson's snipe, a brown shorebird with a ridiculously long beak.

VCDB is for more than birds. We spy a family of nutria, imported water rodents that eat grass roots and all, which denudes the dikes. Red-eared sliders occupy many islands and adorn floating logs. Nine-banded armadillos love the place. Charley describes being here in the dawn hours when coyotes and birds of prey drop by for breakfast. In the breeding season, skunks, raccoons, and opossums hunt for eggs.

Now midday, the mammals have gone home. Most birds settle in to nap until sunset feeding. Nestled waterfowl adorn the islands with heads drawn in or tucked under wings. Nutria gather in family groups to sleep. It's time to leave this world to its slumber.

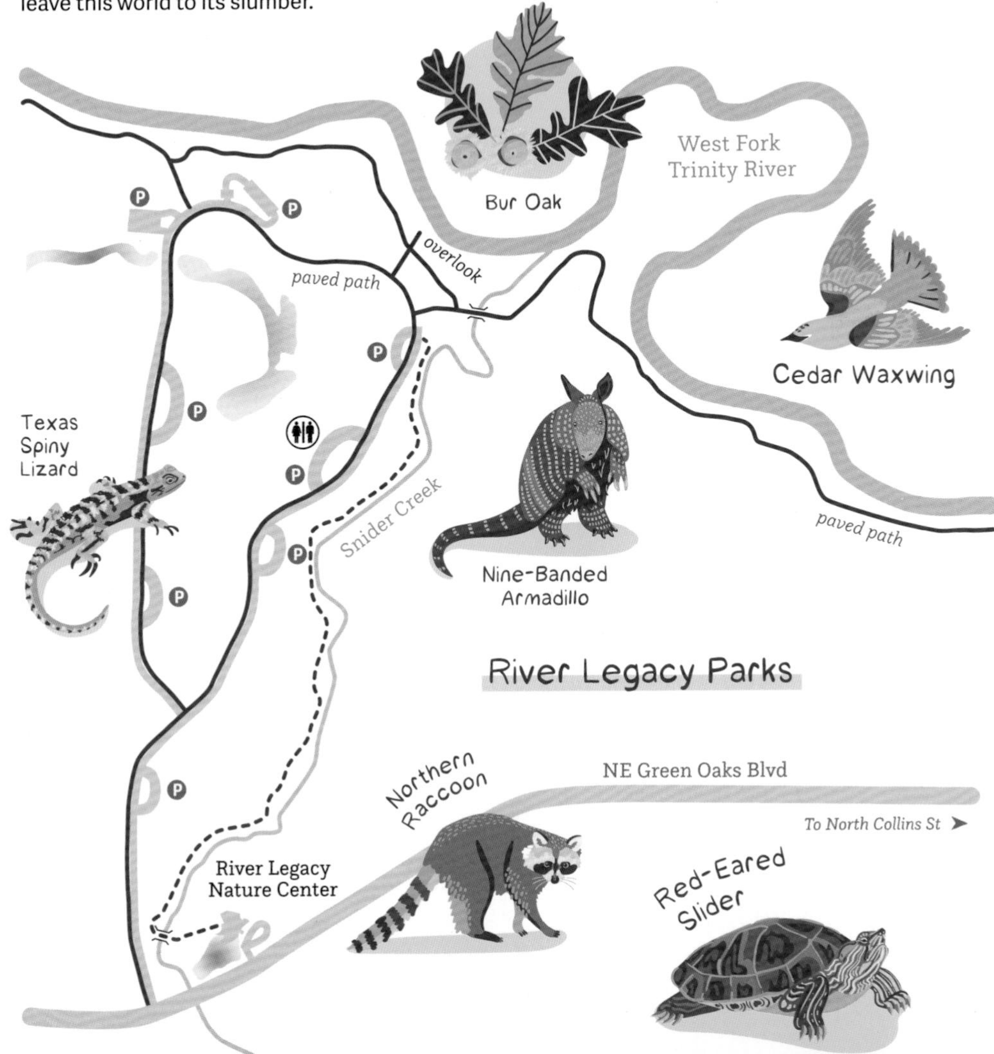

WHERE: 703 NW Green Oaks Blvd, Arlington, TX 76006. North Arlington, off the West Fork of the Trinity.
PARKING: Small paved lot.
TRAILS: Soft surface 0.25 miles, dirt 1 mile.
DIFFICULTY: Easy.
FACILITIES: Building with water and restrooms.
NEARBY: Colleyville Nature Center.

▲ River Legacy Nature Center melds into the terrain.

River Legacy Parks & Nature Center

Eager to see nature through Zach's wonder-filled eyes, I follow the 28-year-old to the River Legacy Nature Center, part of River Legacy Parks. He's been volunteering here since his Texas Master Naturalist training with the Cross Timbers chapter. His aunt and grandmother, both fascinated by geology and rocks, encouraged him. "When I was four years old, I was able to say the word 'paleontologist'."

The 12,000-square-foot modern nature center nestles into the groves of large cedar elm, pecan, and bur oak trees along Snider Creek. We stroll the wide paths neatly covered in decomposed granite or wood chips and suitable for even those in business clothes.

Zach and I break leaves from the Carolina laurelcherry, debate if the aroma is cherry or fruity vanilla, and delight in the ruddy midwinter buds of rusty blackhaw viburnum. We enjoy sandwiches while perched on log seats and watch hard-working Boy Scouts move organic material into the center's extensive compost demonstration area.

With his iNaturalist moniker Galactic Bugman, Zach happily chats about insects and their similarity to science fiction, another obsession, as we ramble. Just a week after a record-breaking freeze, the bugs are quiet. Within

The Cross Timbers chapter of Texas Master Naturalists trains nature stewards in Tarrant and Parker counties. Fort Worth Nature Center and Refuge, Shari Capehart Nature Preserve, O. S. Gray Natural Area, and Molly Hollar Wildscape are a few that benefit from their skilled efforts.

weeks, the forest floor will be flush with the purple blooms of marsh fleabane and common vetch that will have the bugs buzzing.

Beneath a sizable bois d'arc on a deck along a riparian corridor, Zach shares his story of how he uses naturalist studies to channel his autism. He found solace in the space and silence of nature when teased by kids in school and after the profound loss of the grandmother who raised him.

"Want to do the AISD trail?" he asks. And we're off, crossing the bridge connecting the center to River Legacy Parks and into the woods on the west side of Snider Creek, taking a dirt nature path used by Arlington Independent School District students. It's a gentle and woodsy half-mile path with an open understory and lovely creek views.

▼ Zach has a special love of dragonflies and damselflies.

▲ The AISD trail winds through the woods.

River Legacy Nature Center presents the nature of North Texas through interactive exhibits, aquariums and terrariums with native creatures. Even toddlers and preschoolers have clever eco things to do. An intriguing hands-on Discovery Room uses high-tech fun to get kids deep into nature. The center offers programs for after-school and homeschoolers, plus a top-rated summer camp.

We emerge into the central meadow and visit its pond, home to the park's forest-themed playground with an inexplicable *Tyrannosaurus* skeleton sculpture. Continue west to encounter the Dallas Off-Road Bicycle Association's ten-mile miasma of narrow dirt trails through the woods, not recommended for hikers due to fast bike traffic on tight curves.

Another choice is to go east on the West Fork trail and enjoy some river views with the backdrop of a capped landfill that towers like a rounded mountain. In about a mile, the trail crosses the Trinity on a snazzy steel bridge. A paddle launch beneath connects to the Trinity River Paddling Trail and adventures beyond.

Far-Flung Adventures

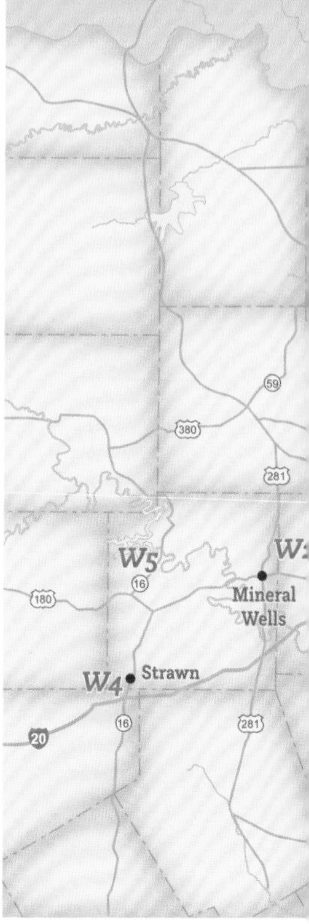

▲ Many beautiful places beckon within a two-hour drive of Dallas–Fort Worth.

► Get away from the city and see the stars.

North

N1: Cross Timbers Hiking Trail Epic trail along the upper reaches of Lake Texoma with many great vistas.

N2: Lennox Woods Preserve Nature Conservancy's old-growth forest and sanctuary with towering pine trees and rare plants.

N3: Northeast Texas Trail Once completed from Farmersville to Texarkana, it'll be the longest multiuse trail in Texas and fourth longest nationally.

East

E1: Lake Tawakoni State Park Serene 376-acre oak forest park with five miles of trails.

E2: Mineola Nature Preserve Nearly 3000 acres of pine forest and wetlands on the Sabine River.

E3: Tyler State Park Beautiful spring-fed lake, hundred-foot-tall pine trees, and impressive spring flowering dogwoods and redbuds.

West

W1: Cleburne State Park Quiet enclave with limestone bluffs around Cedar Lake and nearly ten miles of trails.

W2: Lake Mineral Wells State Park and Trailway Bluffs of 300-million-year-old Pennsylvanian era limestone around a 640-acre lake. Over twelve miles of park trails plus twenty miles on an abandoned railroad line.

W3: LBJ National Grasslands Over 20,000 acres of grasslands, forests, and lakes with seventy-five miles of hiking and equestrian trails.

W4: Palo Pinto Mountains State Park Texas' newest state park with over 4000 acres of Western Cross Timbers and more than twenty miles of trails.

W5: Possum Kingdom State Park Rugged canyon country of the Brazos River Valley surrounding a 20,000-acre lake with clear water.

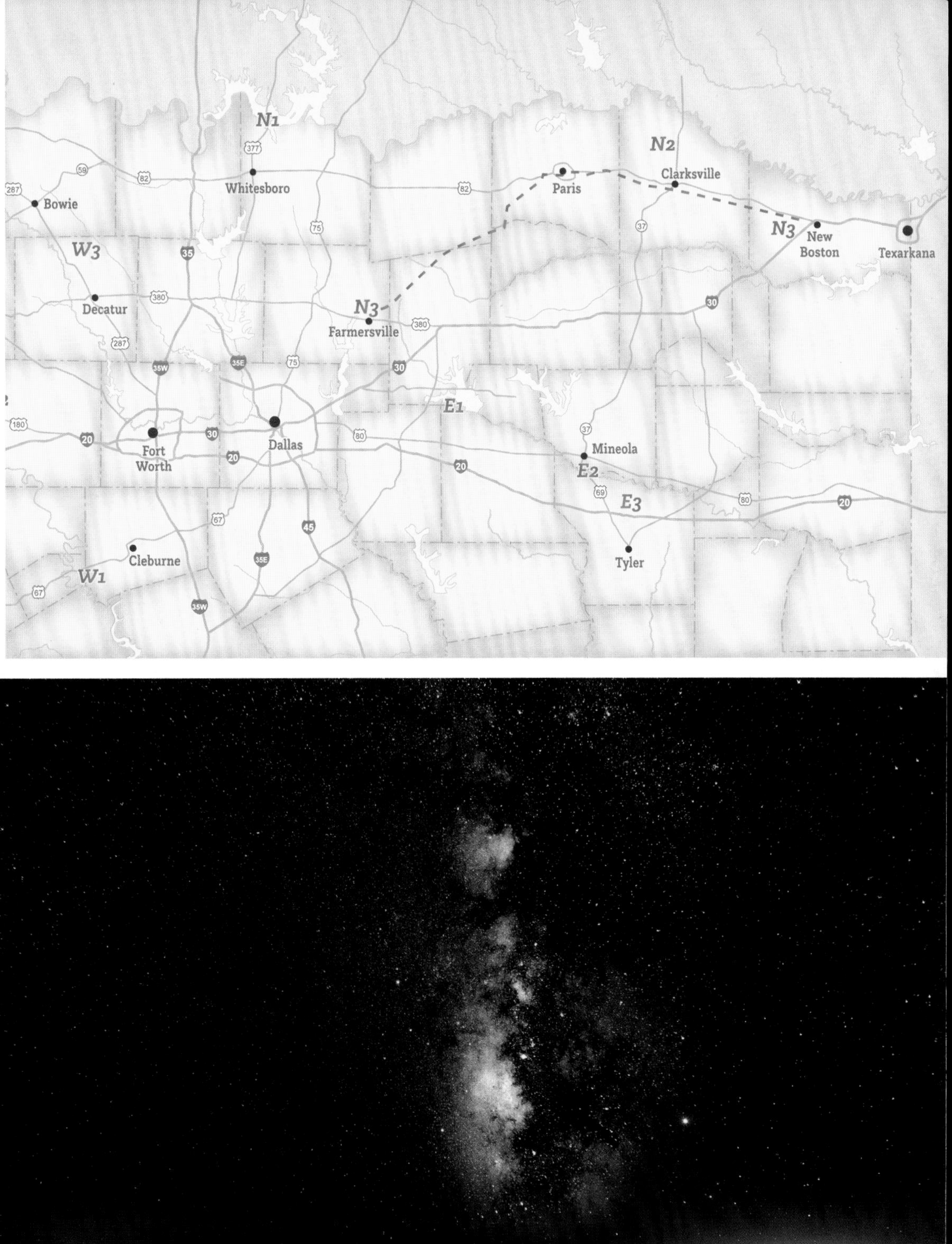
N1
N2
N3
W3
W1
E1
E2
E3
Bowie
Whitesboro
Paris
Clarksville
New Boston
Texarkana
Decatur
Farmersville
Fort Worth
Dallas
Mineola
Cleburne
Tyler

ACKNOWLEDGMENTS

Legions of North Texans and ecological professionals across the state helped this book come to fruition. For the full list of acknowledgments, please visit the book website, Wild-DFW.com.

These fine folks fielded countless emails and read many pages of text: Brandon Belcher, Dan Caudle, Carol Clark, Tom Dill, Carl J. Franklin, Scott Hudson, Sam Kieschnick, Jim Peterson, Rachel Richter, Michael Smith, Scooter Smith, and Suzanne Tuttle.

Research assistance and draft writing for the field guide provided by Denver Kramer (wildlife) and Bill Freiheit and Marylinda Jones (plants).

Hat tip to the professionals of Texas Parks and Wildlife, Texas A & M AgriLife Extension, The Nature Conservancy, and Botanical Research Institute of Texas. I am in awe of your impeccable knowledge.

These photographers happily accepted assignments and took just the right photos: Zachary Chapman, Adam Cochran, Grady Hinton, Justin Parker, Michael Puttonen, Denise Thompson, Diane Wetherbee, and especially Chris Emory, Stalin SM, and most of all Daniel Koglin. Gratitude for the photo archives of Bat World MidCities, Carol Clark, Nick DiGennaro, Sonnia Fajardo Hill, Carey Newton, Randall Patterson, Rajiv Roy, Karin Saucedo, and Don Young.

These naturalists were essential in rounding up last-minute photos: Julie Custer, Tracey Fandre, Kala King, and Denver Kramer.

Scooter Smith's maps were impeccable and essential.

Gratitude to these Texas Master Naturalist chapters whose tremendous volunteers were extremely helpful and inspiring: Blackland Prairie, Cross Timbers, Elm Fork, and my home chapter North Texas. And to the Collin County, Dallas, and North Central Texas chapters of Native Plant Society of Texas.

Many thanks to Carol Garrison for sending Timber Press my way.

PHOTOGRAPHY & ILLUSTRATION CREDITS

Species illustrations by Bologna Sandwich
Adventure maps by Scooter Smith and Sarah Crumb
Map on page 40 by Colorado Plateau Geosystems, via Wikimedia
All other maps and graphics by Scooter Smith

Photos
Adam Cochran, 12, 96, 121, 122, 131, 188, 252, 253, 255
Alan R. Lusk, 190 top
Andrew Brinker, 152
Annika Lindqvist, 120, 128, 129
Blackland Prairie Texas Master Naturalists, 102
Bob Brennan, 22, 145, 323, 324 left, 325, 326, 357, 358 right
Brent Franklin, 17 bottom, 190 bottom, 281
Bruce Stewart, 103
Carey Newton, 37 bottom, 58, 80, 347, 348, 349, 350, 351, 352
Carol Clark, 74, 159, 160, 161 left, 162, 167 bottom, 175 right, 249, 250 right
Cayambe, via Wikimedia, 68
Chris Emory, 8, 13, 15, 17 top, 24, 29, 31 top, 46, 49, 50, 101 161 right, 172, 258, 334, 339 left, 341, 342, 344, 345, 361
Cindy Kearney, 83
Clay Thurmond, 295
Daniel Koglin, 10, 27, 31 bottom, 35, 37 top, 47, 63, 76, 77, 99, 113 top, 126, 165, 180, 182–183, 187, 192, 193, 205 bottom, 211, 213, 215, 241 bottom, 243, 260, 262 right, 264, 265, 268, 269, 270, 272, 273, 274, 275, 276, 301, 305, 306, 307, 316, 317, 318, 319 right, 320, 336, 339 right, 354, 355
Denise Thompson, 167 top, 173 bottom, 309, 310, 311, 312, 313, 314
Denver Kramer, 116 left, 158, 215, 302, 303 bottom, 304 left
Diane Wetherbee, 84, 294, 296, 298, 299
Don Young, 42, 164, 329, 330, 331, 332, 343 right
Elaine White, 89, 124 bottom
Grady Hinton, 254, 255 left, 257
Greg Hume, via Wikimedia, 157
Hansell F. Cross, 123
Henry Aschner, 88 bottom
Jeffrey Gladden, 218, 221 bottom
Jennifer L. Weisensel, 263
Jim Bagley, 98, 324 right
Jim Wagner, 282
Julia Koch, 78
Julie Custer, 139, 156, 169, 217, 220, 226, 227 top, 228, 229, 287, 289 bottom
Justin Parker, 19, 20, 61, 109 bottom, 127, 166, 181, 219, 222, 304, 335
Kala King, 56, 108 left, 117, 118, 134, 147 left
Karin Saucedo, 54, 55, 64, 69, 88 top, 132, 135, 136, 239, 240, 241 top, 242, 250 left
Kate Rugroden, Bat World Sanctuary, 140
Kim Conrow, 81
Meghan Cassidy, 59, 146, 153, 154
Michael A. Smith, 322
Michael Puttonen, 280, 283, 284
National Oceanic and Atmospheric Administration, 48, 52
Nicholas Mirro, 144, 214
Nick DiGennaro, 4, 60, 67 left, 70, 72, 108 right, 110, 111 right, 112, 115, 116 right, 119, 197, 225, 292
Patrick Feller, via Wikimedia, 151
Rajiv Roy, 62, 114, 195, 196, 198 left, 199 right, 200
Randall Patterson, 71, 109 top, 124 top, 212, 221 top
Roger Sanderson, 143, 155
Ron Blakely, Colorado Plateau Geosystems, 40
Sam Droege, 65
Samantha Knight, 86
Sara van der Leek, 151 left, 303 top
Scooter Smith, 170 bottom, 174
Scott Carson Ausburn, 343 left
Sean Fitzgerald, 73, 93
Sonnia Fajardo Hill, 67 right, 163, 168, 170 top, 175 left, 176, 177, 319 left, 338
Stalin SM, 7, 91, 92, 94, 97, 148, 198–199, 202, 203, 205 top, 207, 224, 227 bottom, 230, 232, 233, 234, 236, 237, 245, 246, 247, 261, 262 left, 263 top, 286, 288, 289 top, 290, 291
Stephanie Jennings, 44
Steve Houser, 171, 173, 209
Teresa Patterson, 33, 53
Tom Streetman, 39
Tracey Fandre, 111 left, 113 bottom, 125, 130, 138, 142, 149
Vijay Tanwar, 278, 279
Zachary Chapman, 25, 147 right, 337, 358 left

INDEX

Stalin SM

Amy Martin, a lifelong Texan, has forged a varied career in journalism, laced with activism and leadership and infused with a deep spirituality and concern for the earth. A journalist and writer for over thirty-five years, she is the author of *Itchy Business: How to Treat the Poison Ivy and Poison Oak Rash, Prevent Exposure and Eradicate the Plant*, *Holy Smoke: Loose Herbs and Hot Embers for Intense Group Smudges and Smoke Prayers*, and *Ned Fritz Legacy*, a biography of Texas's most notable environmentalist. She is currently a senior features writer for *Green Source DFW* and has written for *Garbage* magazine, *Dallas Morning News*, *Dallas Observer*, *D* magazine, and *Dallas Times Herald*. Personal website: Moonlady.com. Book website: Wild-DFW.com.